A 'distant field of murder'

A 'distant

Jan Critchett

field of murder'

WESTERN DISTRICT FRONTIERS 1834–1848

MELBOURNE UNIVERSITY PRESS

First published 1990

First paperback edition 1992
Printed in Singapore by
Kim Hup Lee Co Pte Ltd, for
Melbourne University Press, Carlton, Victoria 3053
U.S.A. and Canada: International Specialized Book Services, Inc.,
5602 N.E. Hassalo Street, Portland, Oregon 97213-3640
United Kingdom and Europe: University College London Press,
Gower Street, London WC1E 6BT

The publishers acknowledge the
financial assistance received from the University of Melbourne's
Committee on Research and Graduate Studies

National Library of Australia Cataloguing-in-Publication entry

Critchett, Jan.
A distant field of murder

Bibliography.
Includes index.
ISBN 0 522 84527 4.

[1]. Aborigines, Australian—Victoria—Treatment—History. 2.
Western District (Vic.)—History. I. Title.

994.570049915

... surely it is time that England should interfere, and no longer permit those daily murders to be perpetrated with impunity ... I should indeed regret ... to make it a matter of Parliamentary inquiry but ... I owe it to the honour of England, whose colony this distant field of murder is ...

John Power to Lord John Russell, 30 Nov. 1840, Papers Relative to the Aborigines (Australian Colonies), *British Parliamentary Papers*, 1844, p. 123

For much of the time span covered in this book, the area now called the Western District of Victoria was an administrative unit, the Portland Bay District, formed for the purpose of controlling the expansion of pastoral settlement. In general the two terms refer to much the same part of Victoria. Readers should know that the Portland Bay District, when created in 1840, was defined as all that territory west of the Werribee River and a line north from it to the Murray River. In 1846 it was divided, the northern part becoming the Wimmera District.

Contents

Illustrations

Acknowledgements

THIS BOOK has grown out of my research over the last ten years and many people have helped to shape its form. For much of this time Greg Dening, Max Crawford Professor of History at Melbourne University, read my drafts, providing an extended conversation about my work that was invaluable. Others working on related themes, Marie Fels, Bain Attwood, Linda Wilkinson, Michael Cannon, Elizabeth Williams and Michael Godfrey, shared information and enlivened the research work. The influence of local Aboriginal people, while indirect, has been considerable, for they strengthened my sense of Aboriginal 'otherness' and stimulated my interest in cultures in contact.

The staff at libraries, archives, museums and the Victoria Archaeological Survey were always helpful: Tony Marshall and Margaret Murfett at the La Trobe Library, Ian MacFarlane at the Public Record Office of Victoria and Sandra Smith at the Victorian Aboriginal Cultural Heritage Unit, Museum of Victoria, were especially helpful.

Judith Scurfield (Map Librarian, La Trobe Library), Tom Robertson and Jim Wilson provided details which enabled me to establish the boundaries of Dawson's language groups on a map, while Mark Rashleigh drew the map. Gordon Sonnenberg prepared the map showing surviving Aboriginal place names.

Professor John Mulvaney kindly supported my approach to Melbourne University Press and my application for a Melbourne University grant to assist publication.

Rough drafts of the manuscript were read by Colleen Hosking and Josie Black. They offered helpful criticism as did others asked to read parts. Heather Martin-Trigg competently turned my handwritten drafts into the final printout and cheerfully endured the various revisions that preceded the final draft.

My colleagues at Warrnambool Institute of Advanced Education, especially Gordon Forth, provided a supportive environment while the Institute contributed materially with some financial assistance and by allowing a period of leave for research.

Introduction

KAAWIRN KUUNAWARN (Hissing Swan), 'Chief' of the Kirrae Wurrong tribe, later known as King David, was born in the area around Mt Shadwell in Victoria's Western District in 1822 or 1823. He witnessed the arrival of the first Europeans and was one of the lucky ones to survive the racial violence and the often fatal effects of European-introduced diseases. In the mid-1840s he commenced employment on Kangatong, the squatting property of James Dawson and Patrick Mitchell, where he worked till the mid-1860s when the Victorian Government required Aborigines to move to land set aside as Aboriginal stations for their use. Kaawirn Kuunawarn moved to the Framlingham station which opened in 1865 and lived there most of the time till his death in September 1890.

His was a long and eventful life like that of a number of Western District Aborigines born before European settlement. Their lifetimes spanned dispossession, the idealistic promises of the Port Phillip Protectorate, a period of adaption to the altered circumstances, the forced removal from the general community into the restricted life of an Aboriginal station, and finally, old age and death as the great depression cast its shadow over the whole community.

This book is concerned with the events that occurred as Kaawirn Kuunawarn changed from a youth into a mature adult: a period of catastrophe for the Aborigines of south-western Victoria. His generation faced circumstances as complex and threatening as those faced by men and women at any time in the past.

1

My interest in Aboriginal history and the details of the European settlement of this region grew out of friendship with the Clarke family of Framlingham. I began by studying the history of the two Western District Aboriginal stations established in the second half of the nineteenth century, Lake Condah and Framlingham. I did so against the background of the Framlingham community's fight for land rights—a fight which received national news coverage as I was completing my work. While the Aborigines went on to win their land rights, I found myself being drawn back to the time of European settlement: to first contact between the races, to Aborigines still living a traditional lifestyle, and to relations between Aborigines and Europeans living in close proximity to each other.

The more I learnt, the more I became dissatisfied with existing histories of the District. I looked in vain for Aboriginal names and for details of individual lives. Aborigines were to be found in a generalized sense only. They were not listed as individuals in indexes, even in an important work such as Margaret Kiddle's *Men of Yesterday*. There, as elsewhere, references were simply listed under the general heading 'Aborigines'. I was eager to pursue the themes being raised by contemporary historians such as Professor Geoffrey Blainey and Professor Henry Reynolds. Above all I wanted to examine the source material in such detail that I could establish a strong sense of two races living side by side for this was the impression I increasingly gained as I read the diaries, journals and letters of the pioneers.

The result is a history which examines the regional evidence concerning questions of national significance: the size of the Aboriginal population at settlement; the strength of Aboriginal opposition to European settlement; the nature of the Aboriginal response and changes in it over time, and the cost of Aboriginal resistance to both the pastoral pioneers and to the Government. It challenges ideas about the Aborigines strongly held in the general community—that they were nomadic at all times of the year, that their only shelters were frail mia-mias, that they had no attachment to a particular area of land, and that they were simple hunters and gatherers.

One warning is necessary. The modern reader, accustomed to the standardized spelling of European surnames and place names may become irritated by what appears to be a disregard for how words should be spelt. Wherever possible I have used the same spelling for a word but those I quote will most likely each have their own spelling. In the pioneering period many people simply spelt surnames and place names as they sounded them.

George Augustus Robinson, the Chief Protector of Aborigines, is the chief culprit but he had an additional problem. He wanted to collect as many Aboriginal words as he could. Without any linguistic training, he took the commonsense approach of writing down words as a series of sounds. As there was no system to his use of the sounds, the way a word was recorded often varied from day to day. Warrnambool, for example, was written at different times as Wornerbul, Wornabul, War.noobul, Warn.am.bul. The Aboriginal group, the Colijon, was often spelt Colijohn. When two Europeans recorded an Aboriginal word using this same approach, the differences in the way the sounds are indicated are often greater. James Dawson, the well known pioneer who wrote a book on the customs of the Aborigines of the Western District, used double consonants 'to express emphasis' and double vowels 'to express prolongation of the sound'. The Aboriginal word for hut written by Robinson as 'worn' became 'wuurn' in Dawson's book. The letters 'c' and 'k' are often used interchangeably for although the use of them make a word look very different (for example Corangamite as opposed to Korangamite), the sound is the same. The best thing to do if confused is to sound the word for it will be spelt not according to the dictionary or someone's idea of the correct spelling of it, but simply as the person involved thought the Aboriginal sounds could be best conveyed. In the long run (and this didn't take long) the European settlers dealt with this problem by calling Aborigines by European names and anglicizing the Aboriginal place names which were adopted throughout the District.

Over the years I have appreciated information and help given by Aborigines but this history is based largely on European sources—on official records, on letters, diaries and published accounts.

Two main sources have been used: first, the voluminous notes and reports of George Augustus Robinson who, because of his official position as Protector of Aborigines, was the main European involved with the Aborigines and, second, James Dawson's *Australian Aborigines: The Languages and Customs of Several Tribes of Aborigines in the Western District of Victoria*, first published in 1881. Dawson obtained his information from local Aborigines whom he had known for over thirty years and whose languages his daughter Isabella spoke. Kaawirn Kuunawarn was one of the most important of his informants but he also named Weeratt Kuyuut, 'Chief' of the Morpor tribe (Spring Creek, north of Warrnambool), the chief's daughter, Yarruun Parpur Tarneen, and her husband, Wombeet Tuulawarn.[1] In the late nineteenth century it became fashionable to gather information about the Aborigines and men such as Robert Brough Smyth and A. W. Howitt distributed questionnaires for Europeans in contact with Aborigines to complete. The difference with James Dawson is that he and his daughter personally discussed customs with named Aborigines whom they had known for a considerable length of time. Whenever Dawson is quoted, his source was one of these or other named Aborigines with whom he or his daughter had continued discussion till they were convinced they understood the Aboriginal answers.

I have been surprised by the wealth of information available and the extent to which it supports the claims of Aborigines about events of the past. I began my work in sympathy for the Aborigines but increasingly have realized the complexity of the settlement process for all those involved. This story is above all that of a great human drama, of two races brought face to face and forced to come to terms with each other, for neither could go away.

1

'and the shout was given that the black fellows were coming'

ACROSS THE Western District plains, along the sea coast and under the foothills of the Grampians, a strange series of meetings took place in 1841. They were between a lone European official, George Augustus Robinson, and group after group of the indigenous population. The Aborigines responded to the European initative, gathering in each locality to meet the representative of a power they were beginning to sense, to hear the message he had come to deliver and to extend to him their hospitality. These were grand moments, sometimes of awkwardness, but more often of ritual and ceremony, of gift-giving, of friendship around the camp-fire and corroborees which extended far into the night.

Robinson had made similar journeys through the rugged terrain and isolated areas of Van Diemen's Land, contacting the few surviving Aborigines and persuading them to surrender to European officials, after which they were transferred to an offshore island. But the situation in the Port Phillip District was different. Robinson's journey was not as in Van Diemen's Land a finale to dispossession: it was designed to prevent the bloodshed and injustice that occurred in the colony to the south. It took place near the beginning of European settlement and against a backdrop of heightened British concern about the treatment of indigenous people in British colonies. This had led to the establishment of the Port Phillip Protectorate, and the appointment of five men to 'do their utmost' to protect the Aborigines and take civilization to them.

Robinson, highly recommended by Governor Arthur for his service in Van Diemen's Land, had been successful in gaining the position of Chief Protector. He was the only one of the five men appointed to have colonial experience. The other four were selected in England and arrived in Sydney in August 1838. From there they travelled to Melbourne where they remained till 21 March 1839 when Robinson ordered his assistants to 'take the field forthwith'. The district had been divided into four regions with one assistant appointed to each. The man instructed to proceed westward was Charles Wightman Sievwright, whose district, the Geelong or Western District of the Port Phillip Protectorate, stretched from Indented Head westward to the South Australian border and from Mt Cole and Mt William south to the coast.

These men, as they set forth into what to them was a hostile environment for which they were ill prepared and ill equipped, were given instructions more suited to the anthropologist than to untrained and much harassed men appointed as go-betweens in the hostilities and confusion of a frontier settlement. They were to make a

> complete census . . . of the aboriginal population, distinguishing the number of each family, with the age, name and sex, as also the tribe to which they belong; the principal persons of each tribe, whether warrior, counsellor, elder, or otherwise; also the boundaries and aboriginal names of districts occupied by each tribe, the aboriginal names of mountains, lakes, rivers, and other localities; the difference of language, customs, and habits of each tribe, with their political relation, whether of amity or hostility . . .[1]

Each Protectorate region was to have an area of land reserved as a Protectorate station. With the site for the Western District not yet chosen, Sievwright established his base at Geelong. There on the eastern border of his district, hampered by lack of transport and occupied in investigating European complaints of Aboriginal attacks and claims of violence against Aborigines, Sievwright made no headway on taking a census.

Meanwhile Charles Joseph La Trobe, Superintendent of the Port Phillip District, faced an impossible situation. Harried by a constant stream of Western District settlers calling at his Melbourne office and powerless, through lack of resources, to answer their appeals for protection against Aboriginal attacks, he was without even the most basic information about the indigenous population.

The District was fast gaining a reputation for inter-racial violence even at 'Home'. So grave was the situation by late 1840 that Governor Gipps assured La Trobe that he would 'sanction any expenditure' necessary to reduce violence. Yet it was not simply a matter of money. The District was an extended one, sparsely settled, with Aborigines and Europeans in contact across the length and breadth of it. The appointment of a few police would make little difference.[2] Desperate for something or someone to ease the situation, La Trobe turned to the Protectorate which had been slow to begin its work to the west. He ordered Robinson out of his Melbourne office and into the field. He was to 'open a friendly communication (in person) with the aboriginal natives of the Western District and to obtain information on their number, location and disposition'.[3]

The task had not been sought but it was one Robinson viewed with satisfaction. Qualified for such work by experience over a number of years with the Van Diemen's Land Aborigines and by a natural ability easily to relate to Aboriginal people, he set out from Melbourne in March 1841. He was accompanied by two white servants, one a freeman, the other a convict, and a Tasmanian Aborigine. They had a spring cart and four horses.

Robinson's mission was a difficult one: for most people it would have been impossible. First, it was essential to contact the Aborigines: not just any Aborigines; it was important to meet the leaders of Aboriginal communities. Even if such people were located, there was no certainty that a meeting would take place. Such individuals had to be persuaded to come to a meeting, and if they came it was unlikely that they would speak English. So a method of communicating with the Aborigines had to be devised. Somehow the idea of friendliness, of concern, of interest in their welfare, had to be conveyed to Aborigines whose previous contacts with Europeans may have led to feelings of anger, suspicion and distrust.

Others might have been weighted down with the difficulties of the situation. Not Robinson. He appeared to have naturally evolved a successful pattern for meetings. Maybe he was simply following procedures that had emerged in the Tasmanian bush. His meetings were a strange blend of European and Aboriginal customs, but of customs only partially observed. It was almost as if it was acknowledged by the Aborigines that in the rapidly changing circumstances allowances needed to be made. But Robinson touched the right chords to evoke such a response. The incongruities, the fumblings, the misunderstandings of meetings in a cultural contact situation, are there for all to see. But more striking is the overwhelming success of meetings, the evidence of friendships begun and of ideas shared.

One feature of his approach was crucial to his success. This was his use of Aboriginal guides who belonged to the local area. They not only knew the local people and land; they could speak their language or dialect and so make communication possible. Their importance to Robinson became obvious at Lake Keilambete when it was time to proceed westward. Up to this stage of his journey Robinson had met Aborigines who were living in close contact with Europeans. Sievwright, the Assistant Protector, had his camp at Lake Keilambete. There some three hundred Aborigines gathered and met the Chief Protector. But from Keilambete westward the journey was more dangerous. Europeans were more sparsely settled and some of the Aborigines had little or no contact with them.

As Robinson was about to leave Sievwright's camp, he found that the Aborigines who had promised to accompany him had left. They had gone westward, he was told, and would watch out and wait for him. Conscious that such people were vital to his success, he wrote in his journal, 'But as I could not leave these things to chance I resolved to go back to Tarong [Lake Terang] and get two other natives'.[4] Two men of the Jarcoort tribe, Eurodap and Inergerook, volunteered their services. As they neared the Hopkins River, Manmate [strangers'] country, they became frightened and unwilling to proceed. Such hesitancy was to be expressed by Aboriginal guides many times on that journey. And the Aborigines were not worrying needlessly: those who travelled outside their territory without the proper formalities being observed were regarded as 'wild blacks' and likely to be killed. Eurodap travelled as far as the Winters' property on the Wannon but there he was killed by an Aborigine.

Luckily, on the western side of the Hopkins River, not long after the Jarcoort Aborigines had expressed their concern, Robinson's party came across a group of Aborigines some of whom were known to Eurodap and Inergerook. Four of their number agreed to accompany Robinson's party to Port Fairy. At each new place—Port Fairy, Mt Napier, Mt Clay, the Glenelg, Mt William—additional Aboriginal guides joined Robinson. Others left and returned to their own country. Robinson entreated, placated, and coaxed the Aborigines to stay. At Forlonge's dairy station Robinson was told that the natives were tired and intended returning eastward to Lake Terang. Determined that they should not leave him, he hurried the group on.[5] In contrast, at Mt Napier he was ready to leave ahead of the Aborigines who wanted to stay another day. This time, realizing that he could not force them to leave with him, he delayed his departure to suit the Aborigines.[6]

Robinson, in accepting the position of Chief Protector, had argued for the right to bring with him some Tasmanian Aborigines to help him communicate with the Port Phillip Aborigines. On this trip he was accompanied by 'Van Diemen Land Jack' (VDL Jack) whose country was between Mt Cameron and Cape Grim, on the north-west tip of Tasmania. There European settlement had preceded that of the Port Phillip District. VDL Jack remembered as a child crawling under the bushes to escape the attention of a party of sealers. As he watched, they shot two Aboriginal men and abducted many of the Aboriginal women.[7] Later he saw all his people removed from the island of Tasmania. He was a great favourite with the Victorian Aborigines, his woolly head attracting much interest. 'At his first introduction they offered him two widows.' He looked so different from them that they at first called him 'moke allumbe', somebody who had come back after dying.[8] He also impressed Captain Campbell at Port Fairy who offered to employ him at £30 per year but he was a disappointment as a messenger. At the head of the Hopkins River Robinson sent VDL Jack off with a messenger to contact the Aborigines of Lake Boloke. Jack rode ahead of the messenger who gave up and returned to Robinson. Meeting some Aborigines, VDL Jack called out to them in English and tried to offer them some damper but they still wouldn't return with him. In exasperation Robinson wrote in his journal, 'Had *Pevay* [VDL Jack], instead of riding on, frightening the natives, bawling in broken English (for he had not a word of Aboriginal) ... taken the messenger a communication would have been opened'.[9]

Robinson needed the local Aboriginal guides because they were able to convey to their people that he was an important person, a representative of the Government on an important mission. Without the Aborigines Robinson was nobody and in great danger. Near Mt William he sent back his only attendant, VDL Jack, to hurry the others but at nightfall they still had not arrived. Robinson was in a dilemma. There was a hoar frost, occasional gusts of wind, the howling of wild dogs, the noise of opossum and squirrel, none of which intimidated him. What terrified him was the chance of being found by the Aborigines of the area. He lit a fire but, frightened to stay by it, left a written message for his party. A day went by and it was 11.00 a.m. the next day before Robinson's party arrived at the cattle station where he waited for them. They had found where he had slept in the bush and had tracked his horse. 'Thought I had been killed by the natives', he wrote in his journal.[10] The local guides were so important that without them Robinson hid from the very people he was there to meet.

Aboriginal messengers played a crucial role in the successful organization of Robinson's meetings. These he despatched to each Aboriginal group as bearers of an official invitation. What they actually carried was a small printed card, similar to the visiting cards then used by fashionable ladies and gentlemen. Robinson travelled with a collection of such cards, some signed by himself, and others by Charles Joseph La Trobe, Superintendent of the District. He overestimated his needs, and some of those not used are still to be seen in the Mitchell Library.

For all the absurdity of the situation these cards worked: the Aborigines responded. They were after all familiar with the use of both messengers and message sticks. James Dawson, who interviewed local Aborigines about their customs in the second half of the century, wrote:

Messengers are attached to every tribe . . . They are employed to convey information from one tribe to another, such as the time and place of great meetings, korroboraes, marriages, and burials, and also of proposed battles . . . As the office of messenger is of very great importance, the persons filling it are considered sacred while on duty . . .

To distinguish them from spies or enemies, they generally travel two together, and they are painted in accordance with the nature of the information which they carry ... Thus the appearance of the messengers announces the nature of their news before they come to the camp.[11]

Outwardly confident, Robinson knew that on each occasion there was a chance that Aborigines might not respond. At Mt Clay, just east of Portland, he sent messengers to the local Aborigines inviting them to meet him. The Aborigines at his camp kept watching out for those who had been invited and pestered Robinson 'to look at letter [their word for his card] and tell them whether the Aborigines would come today'. He, of course, had no way of knowing. The cards did not include an invitation to a meeting and, even if they had, the Aborigines would have been unable to read them. The use of the word 'letter' indicated some knowledge of European ways, of how messages were sent by Europeans. Robinson parried the questions, giving no reply. He wrote in his journal, 'I was not willing to risk the reputation of my letters and postponed giving my opinion'. In this case 'Soon after dark the flittering of lights was seen at a considerable distance ... and the shout was given that the black fellows were coming'. Robinson must have heaved a sigh of relief. He wrote, 'My letter by this accidental circumstance acquired considerable reputation. Those who spoke a little broken English said ... Mr Robinson letter make black fellow come here'.[12]

The task was not simply difficult, it was dangerous. This must have been apparent many times but the potential for tragedy was brought home very clearly as Robinson camped at the Surrey River. There he received news of the 'horrible murder' of a settler and his man inland on the Glenelg River. From Robinson's point of view, the news came at a most inconvenient time. La Trobe was visiting Portland and Robinson had arranged for the Aborigines to meet him. James Blair, the Police Magistrate stationed at Portland, and the surveyor, Charles Tyers, were also to be introduced to the assembled Aborigines. But events did not develop as Robinson had planned and it was just as well. The Aborigines had corroboreed late and had not stirred when it was time for Robinson to leave to meet La Trobe. La Trobe had bad news: Mr Morton, an English gentleman, and his shepherd had been murdered by Aborigines. It was far from being a time for polite introductions and grand gestures of friendship. La Trobe warned Robinson not to bring the Aborigines any closer to Portland. Edward Henty, well known as the first permanent settler at Portland, and Blair rode out to give Robinson the news but were afraid to dismount. Tyers, who had previously asked Robinson to obtain an Aboriginal boy to work for him, now asked that such a boy be chosen from a distant tribe. Rumours were rife:

The blacks it was stated had stretched the man Larry out on his back and drove spears through the palms of his hands and, the report says, they had cut the flesh off his bone when alive and had eaten it and had eaten the flesh of Morton.[13]

'Mr Tyers had now the same horror of the blacks as Mr Blair and Henty', wrote Robinson.[14] Extermination was the theme of conversations:

> ... Henty said he had no doubt but the settlers were dropping them [the Aborigines]. Blair replied he hoped so. Blair said he was going up [the Glenelg] but he could not go without 12 police for he should have no power to restrain the settlers from shooting the women and children. Henty said if a black was to lift a spear or attempt anything at him he would, if he had a gun, drop him, if the rope was ready to be put round his neck the next minute.[15]

Against such a background Robinson continued with his work, for he had orders not only to meet the Aborigines but to obtain information. That his life was at risk did cross his mind: 'poor Morton's fate might ere long be mine'.[16] Yet he never wavered. While others hunted for the murderers of Mr Morton and Larry, Robinson bought more gifts and food for the Aborigines, collected details of clan boundaries and names of members of clans, and planned the next stage of his journey. Unharmed, he moved on, troubled only by an irritating skin problem, a 'pustulent irruption' transferred to him by the Aborigines of the Mt Clay area who had shown their friendship by embracing him and stroking him with their hands.[17]

Perhaps helped by his experience with the Tasmanian Aborigines, Robinson was skilful at handling the difficulties of his situation, and never courted danger. One night in the camp near the Surrey River he was woken by 'a loud rattling of spears' and the whispering of Aborigines outside his tent. Another man might have rushed outside fearing the worst, but Robinson's approach was a philosophical one:

> My conscience told me I had done nothing to cause an attack. At the same time ... I thought they might have taken offence without just cause, perhaps conceived an offence ... which is quite common among white people, much less savages. I ... resolved to wait the sun and all subsided.[18]

When an Aboriginal group arrived, they were armed with their spears, boomerangs, waddies and other fighting implements. They halted about 100 yards away from Robinson's camp and sat down: males in one group, females in another. Meanwhile, Robinson's native attendants, having ornamented themselves for the occasion by ochring their faces, putting reeds through the cartilage of their noses, and feathers in their hair, stayed in their worns (huts). Alternatively, they might sit down, looking at the ground and apparently not noticing the strangers. After a while an approach was made to the other group. At the great swamp near Mt Napier the approach occurred in the following way: 'Eurodap's female acquaintance soon went and took her seat beside him and Cor.rer.mur.-rer.min went soon after and sat beside a young man of my natives whom also he knew. Some minutes elapsed before they conversed'. Then the conversation began and 'all the particulars and purposes of my visit was talked over as well as my previous travels to other tribes'.[19]

Sometimes an Aboriginal guide acted as Master of Ceremonies, instructing the Aborigines in the intricacies of European meetings—of the direct approach, the need to stand and the shaking of the hand. The latter proved difficult to cope with—some Aborigines at first presenting an elbow, an arm, or even a head.

At one stage there occurred what Robinson called the ceremony of taking down names and conferring names. He wrote down the name of each Aborigine and then conferred a European name. Aborigines were fond of names and usually had several. They were eager to be given another, and this was the time and the manner in which many of the Aborigines of the District received their European names. Robinson found it very hard to find names for groups of fifty or more. Sometimes he looked up at the sky and gave the Aborigines the names of planets. Other times he remembered the names of the Tasmanian Aborigines and used them. Thus the names Truggernanna, Woorradedy, Eumareah, Wymurric, Tymermiddic, Mattille, and Wottenattelayea gained a new life. 'Mr Robinson' was conferred on a number of Aborigines. And the more common names such as John, Tommy, Charley, Ned, Cecilia, Judy, Maria and Daisy were used again and again. One Aborigine was given the name of the great explorer, Mungo Park, another the name of the sea god, Neptune.[20]

Viewing himself as an ambassador for Superintendent La Trobe and the Government, Robinson refused to carry guns. Instead, like the representative of a nation meeting one of another nation, he sent a formal invitation and carried with him gifts—trinkets, Victoria and Albert medals, knives, pipes and tobacco, hats, shirts, trousers, handkerchiefs and plenty of flour, potatoes and meat. Sometimes, from an elevated position, sitting on his horse, he leant down and patted Aborigines on the head as he was introduced to them. Otherwise he strode forth, extending his hand in greeting, startling the Aborigines who sat shyly, heads down as customary in their culture, waiting for an appropriate time to elapse before the introductions could begin. Where possible Robinson gave generously: 'I was willing to convince them by these substantial presents that the representative of the government was not deceiving them', he wrote.[21]

Gifts, he hoped, would ensure that the Aborigines listened to his message. He wanted to tell the leaders of the Aboriginal communities of the establishment of the Port Phillip Protectorate, of men appointed to look after their interests, and of land set aside for them as sanctuaries. But he was a realist at heart. As he travelled across the District and became more familiar with what was happening, the strongest message he delivered was not of Government plans for their future but how to

Distributing blankets: Robinson's sketch of the reaction of Aborigines to his gifts at a camp at Burrumbeep, 3 August 1841

save their lives. If he failed in this, he knew there would be no need for plans: the Aborigines would be extinct.

> I enjoined them to tell their friends to steal sheep no more, for if they did the white people would shoot them and then they would all be gone and then when I or any person belonging to me came again there would be no black fellow.[22]

Invitations, introductions, gifts and friendly talk spanned the gulf between the two very different cultures. The Aborigines, surprised at times and perhaps offended at others, certainly curious, perceived the good will and responded. They returned gifts with gifts. They established their fires and camps: one hundred fires marked the site of one of the largest meetings—at Burrumbeep. Boomerangs, spears, bags, mats, hat-cloaks and bands of emu feathers accumulated in Robinson's van as he proceeded on his journey. Ultimately some of these gifts came to reside in the Museum of Victoria where they can be seen today. Sometimes the good will was expressed in more than gifts and the sharing of food and entertainment; kinship ties were extended to the visitors by women being given in marriage to Robinson's guides. In the evenings the Aborigines provided entertainment for themselves and their visitor. Different clans provided corroborees and Robinson was invited to comment on how well the Aborigines danced. Often Robinson retired early to write down his notes or prepare for the next day. Sometimes quarrelling broke out between Aboriginal groups, the Aborigines using the European-initiated meeting in their own way to air grievances.

At other times, when the opportunity arose, Robinson had long conversations with the Aborigines, listening to their complaints about the Europeans. He did not acquaint them with the fact that the land had been claimed by the British Crown by right of discovery. Nor did he tell them that the implication of this was that they had no right to defend themselves or their right to land, or even to live by their own law, for the Crown's right was based on discovery, not conquest. There was no need for him to do so. The Aborigines had clearly been told by settlers to 'Be off', the same message as that implied in the stand of the British Government. The Aborigines complained to Robinson of the treatment they were receiving:

> Some White men, they said very good, but plenty very bad that these shoot too much black fellow, and take away their Lubra and picaninni and that by and by Black fellow all gone. They were poor men now White men had taken their good country, they said, no ask it but took it, Black men shew white men plenty grass and water and then White man say, be off come be off and drive them away and no let him stop.[23]

Robinson met large numbers of Aborigines—sometimes sixty to one hundred—but the meetings proceeded in an ordered fashion, despite the fact that many of these Aborigines had never seen a European on a horse or had their hand shaken before. Of his meeting with the Tappoc conedeet north-west of Port Fairy he wrote, 'I enjoyed the order and regularity of this day's proceedings'.[24]

Where there was less order it was largely due to Robinson who proceeded in a typical European fashion regardless of Aboriginal custom. He only observed Aboriginal custom to the extent he judged it necessary to achieve his objective. Meeting the Aborigines on the road to Port Fairy near Tower Hill, Robinson went forward. We Weet, one of the Aborigines accompanying Robinson, became master of ceremonies and asked them to stand. Robinson remained sitting on his horse while he received them. He leaned over, shook hands with each one and patted each individual on the head. Again north of Port Fairy, at Tarrone, Robinson went forward to shake the hands of the Aborigines. The Aborigines didn't know what to do. Two Aborigines familiar with Robinson's approach took charge, introducing each Aborigine to Robinson and telling him or her what to do. 'I shook hands with the men first', wrote Robinson, 'and patted them on the head. The ladies and their children were next introduced and the same ceremony gone through'. There is no doubt that the Aborigines, while co-operative, found the procedure frightening. Robinson wrote in his journal, 'The ladies looked abashed having their eyes fixed on the ground and the children, some of them cried and evinced fear. Indeed, not only did the ladies and children require encouragement but some of the men also'.[25] At times he was quite conscious that he appeared discourteous for he wrote of a meeting near Mt Napier, 'When the natives appear I break through all Aboriginal ceremony (which to observe would be a waste of time) and go forth and meet them'.[26]

By the time he reached the vicinity of Portland it was obvious that his approach was successful. Proudly he boasted in a letter to his wife,

> I have succeeded in opening communication with tribes with whom no previous intercourse had been established . . . until the present these natives were in total ignorance of the intentions of the Government towards them . . . The greater part of the country south of the Grampians I have visited and personally conferred with 800 natives among whom were the ferocious Tappoc—Mount Napier—Boloke—Mount Rouse—Port Fairy and Portland Bay Aborigines . . . I trust the Government and the public will do me Justice!![27]

Right across the District, following the route marked on the map, Robinson met group after group of Aborigines. He claimed that he had travelled 2500 miles, made a 'friendly communication' with all the tribes of the Western District and obtained 'the fullest information' about their number, customs, language, political and domestic relations.[28] Despite the great distance between the two cultures, signs of friendship were shown and accepted and an interchange of views occurred. It was an important step in relations between the two cultures living side by side throughout the District. Much has been written of the failure of the Protectorate, but in this one aspect, at least, it was dramatically successful. The tragedy is that little was to follow the promises so clearly and effectively conveyed.

Robinson, perhaps thinking of the fame he had achieved for his similar service to the European community in Van Diemen's Land, expected to be praised and honoured—but he was to be disappointed. He laboured over his report, not completing it till October 1842. La Trobe was not impressed. In transmitting Robinson's report to Governor Gipps, La Trobe confided to him that he had reproved the Chief Protector for his 'prodigal waste of the stationery furnished him'.[29] Governor Gipps wrote on the copy, 'Get somebody to read this report and make notes on its contents'. The summary was brief. Two hundred and sixty- four pages and six appendices were reduced to six pages of notes: 'there is not much information to be obtained by its perusal', the clerk commented. But as usual the odd gained attention. 'The case of cannibalism is I believe something new', he wrote, drawing attention to an incident witnessed by Assistant Protector Sievwright, the details of which were included as an Appendix.[30]

The disappointment of the administrators was perhaps inevitable. Robinson had done as he was asked, but more was required. Meeting and communicating was not enough. The remnant of the Van Diemen's Land Aborigines could be removed to an offshore island much to the

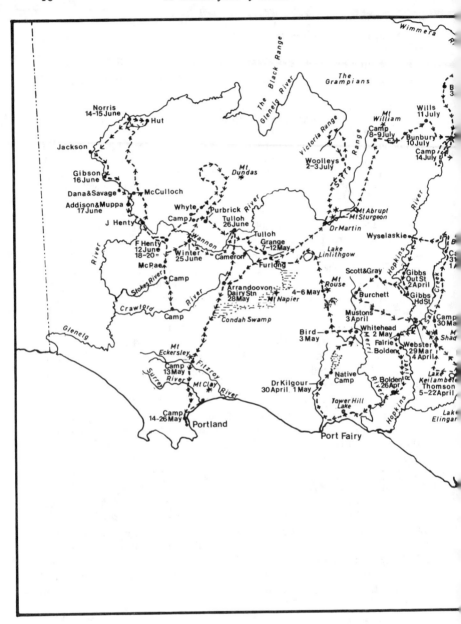

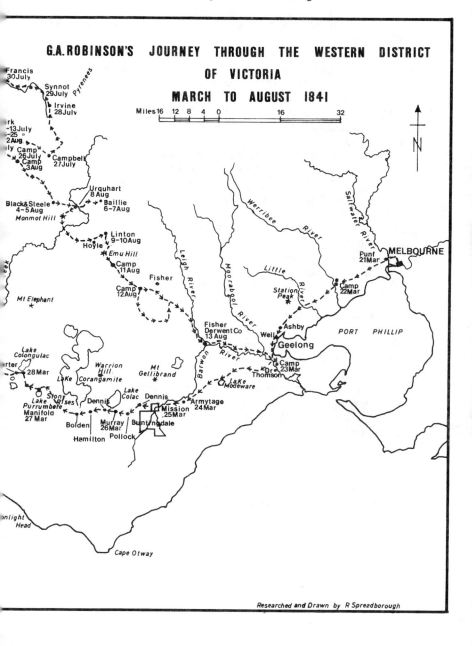

satisfaction of the settlers; but the Port Phillip District had been occupied later and the treatment of native peoples in British colonies had
attracted considerable attention in Britain. The Port Phillip Protectors
had been appointed as a means of avoiding the racial violence of the
other situation and there were expectations, especially in England, that
solutions could be found. Robinson's long report offered no solutions.
Moreover, by the time it was received, racial conflict had become much
more intense than it had been in 1841. The document was an outdated
one. There were now more urgent problems than those of collecting
information, of names of clans and tribes or even of numbers.

Officialdom bemoaned Robinson's long reports and frequent com-
munications. The Colonial Secretary of New South Wales, for example,
once considered forbidding him 'the use of pen and ink'.[31] His love of
writing was a characteristic that earned him little respect from his
superiors. Yet what was seen as his weakness makes him ideal from the
standpoint of an ethnohistorian who is often limited by the small
amount and poor quality of evidence available. As Isabel McBryde states,
'for some geographical areas and for some time periods sufficient
evidence may not be recorded'. In other cases evidence may not have
survived. If evidence has survived there are the problems arising from
'disparity in writers' capacity to observe and record, as well as in opportunities for observation and long term contact with Aboriginal groups'.[32]
In Robinson's case, however, there is no doubt: his journals are, to use the
words of McBryde, 'very rich and detailed documents'.[33] Even Vivienne
Rae-Ellis, author of a recent biography of Robinson, who regards the
accuracy of Robinson's official reports as 'suspect', believes that his
journals are another matter. While she categorizes them as a 'confusing
mixture of false and factual information', it is Robinson's statements on
personal motivation and achievement of which she warns the reader to
be wary.[34] After careful assessment she concludes, 'Robinson's true
achievement is the admirable record of Aboriginal life to be found in his
travel journals'.[35] The notes he made, some in pencil and some in ink,
some made in daylight, others by fire or candlelight, form the basic data
for this study of racial contact.

2

'the savage tribes are
. . . intermingled with us'

FIRST GLIMPSES of Europeans left Aborigines startled and uncomprehending. Later, around camp-fires, they laughed as they reflected on such experiences. At the time, however, their emotions were often disbelief or terror. The first white man seen in the vicinity of Port Fairy was thought to be a supernatural being. He was smoking a pipe and since smoke came out of his mouth, the Aborigines believed he was made of fire. 'Though they were very ready to attack a stranger, they took good care not to go near this man of fire . . .'. The first ship the Aborigines saw they believed to be a huge bird, or a tree growing in the sea. The unfortunate man who told others of what he had seen was declared 'insane' by the tribal chief who 'ordered him to be bled by the doctor'.[1]

The first encounter with a bullock shocked and terrified Aborigines fishing at a waterhole in Spring Creek near Woolsthorpe. Surprised, they fled as the stray bullock, which had a sheet of tin tied across its face to lessen its wandering, came down to drink at the waterhole. At night the great beast wandered into their encampment and disturbed their sleep with its bellowing. Trembling, the Aborigines 'covered themselves up with their rugs' and waited for sunrise. Daylight revealed what they believed to be a 'Muuruup [bad spirit], with two tomahawks in his head'. No one dared to move till the creature departed. Then

> . . . a council of war was held; and the brave men, accompanied by their wives and children—who could not, under such alarming circumstances, be left

19

behind—started in pursuit . . . The bullock was at length discovered grazing in an open part of the forest. The bravest of the warriors went to the front, and, with the whole tribe at their back, approached the animal. They asked if he was a whitefellow, and requested him to give them the tomahawks he carried on his head; whereupon the astonished bullock pawed the ground, bellowed, shook his head, and charged. This so terrified the 'braves' that they fled headlong, and in their precipitate retreat upset men, women, and children, and broke their spears. The natives afterwards told this story with great glee. It used to be narrated in a very humorous way by Gnaweeth . . . and afforded the women many a laugh at the expense of the men.[2]

Later, in 1841, near Mt Napier, Robinson noted the reaction of an Aborigine to his horse. 'His surprise was great when the saddle was taken off. Had it been part of the horse, his wonder could not have been greater. Probably, he thought it belonged to the beast', Robinson wrote.[3] Those who had the courage experimented, often with humorous results. Some Aborigines, given a pipe, at first put the bowl instead of the stem in their mouths.[4] At Port Fairy the Misses Campbell gave a woman a muslin frock. However, 'the husband had taken a fancy to it himself instead of his wife, and put the hind part in before'.[5]

The oddest aspect of the meeting of the two races in the District was the Aboriginal response to the question of who the newcomers were. The white man, the newcomer, was themselves in another form. It was a natural response for those who had had no contact with another race. William Buckley, the convict who escaped from Lieutenant Colonel David Collins's short-lived settlement at Sorrento on Port Phillip Bay in 1803 and lived with the Aborigines till 1835, believed he owed his life to this view. 'They have a belief', he said, 'that when they die, they go to some place or other, and are there made white men, and that they then return to this world again for another existence'.

It was a dangerous belief for both races for it must have clouded Aboriginal perception of the nature of European settlement and how to react to it and it is likely that some Europeans lost their lives as a result of it. Buckley stated, 'In cases where they have killed white men, it has generally been because they imagined them to have been originally enemies, or belonging to tribes with whom they were hostile'.[6] Robinson suspected this and made a note that the belief should be discouraged.[7] It was reinforced in the unlikeliest way for one very large group of Aborigines visiting the Kirkland hut. They were fascinated by the 'likenesses' of Katherine Kirkland's mother hanging on the wall, especially by those in the form of 'black profiles'. One can guess what they made of these: 'they said they were "black leubras"', Katherine wrote.[8]

In the best known cases the Aborigines acted on circumstantial evidence in recognizing a European as an Aborigine come back to life. Buckley stated, 'They called me Murrangurk . . . the name of a man formerly belonging to their tribe, who had been buried at the spot where

I had found the piece of spear I still carried with me'.[9] Robinson, at Koort Kirrup's camp at Emu Creek, recited the Aboriginal names of local individuals, clans and localities before he was recognized by Koort Kirrup's wife as Ben.nit.koy.yang who 'had died and come back a white man'.[10] With Charles Gray of Nareeb Nareeb the basis for identification is unclear. An 'old lubra' eyed him 'very intently', and then decided he was Tirrootmerrie, her husband come back to life.[11]

How widely or for how long Aborigines held the view that Europeans were Aborigines come back to life is not clear. In 1841 not all Europeans were believed to be Aborigines come back to life: even Robinson, with his knowledge of Aboriginal words and customs, was only twice taken to have been a blackfellow. The second occasion was on the way back to Geelong. At George Urquhart's station, just north of Skipton, Aborigines were impressed by what he knew. One man asked where he came from 'a long time ago when I was a black fellow'. But after a little discussion there was no more talk of him being a black fellow—he was simply 'like a black fellow for knowledge'.[12] For some Aborigines, however, the belief that they became Europeans after death lingered all their lives. George Lloyd in May 1853 talked to a group of Aboriginal women in Geelong. At that time there were only seventeen of the Barrabool Aborigines left—of more than three hundred known to Lloyd in 1837. When he commiserated with them over their declining numbers, their final comment in broken English was, 'Neber mind, Mitter Looyed, tir, by-'n'-by, all dem blackfella come back whitefella, like it you'.[13]

Contact between Aborigines and Europeans began before 1834, though the arrival of the Hentys to establish a permanent residence at Portland on 19 November of that year is regarded as the beginning of European settlement in what later became the State of Victoria. Sealers had been on the coast at least from November–December 1828 and they were soon joined by whalers. By the time of Edward Henty's landing at Portland in November 1834 there would have been at least a dozen white men working on the Victorian coast, on a seasonal basis but as part of a year-round cycle, estimates Ray Carroll, the historian of whaling in the south-west.[14]

Soon others followed the Hentys in their move across Bass Strait from Van Diemen's Land to the mainland shore to the north. Faced by the fact that the area was already being settled, the government in 1836 made an official decision to occupy the Port Phillip District with William Lonsdale being appointed the first Police Magistrate. In October 1839 Charles Joseph La Trobe arrived in Melbourne as the first Superintendent of the Port Phillip District of the Colony of New South Wales. By this time the distinctive nature of the frontier in the western part of his District was already established. Already Aborigines and settlers were living in close proximity right across the District, the result of an unusual pattern of European settlement superimposed on a pre-existing division of land between Aboriginal clans. It was this that made race relations in the District so volatile and the problem of keeping peace in the District insoluble, as La Trobe was soon to explain to Governor Gipps.[15]

European settlement was far from an orderly occupation of the Portland Bay District from east to west or from north to south. According to the historical geographer, J. M. Powell, pastoral settlement in the Portland Bay District is best thought of 'as the result of a growth of connections between ... three main nuclei', from Portland in the south-west, from around Port Phillip Bay to the south and thirdly from the north-east.[16] Expansion inland began from both the western and eastern limits of the District and the expansion across the District from north to south also began from both directions.

For a time there was indeed a boundary, a frontier, between the Europeans and the Aboriginal people as the Hentys and others clung to the coast and depended on the sea for their contact with the outside world. In the first two years the Hentys explored only some fifteen to twenty miles inland.[17] However, in August 1837 they opened up the Wannon country, having six runs established there by 1840 after which, according to Stephen Henty, other settlers joined them until all the country around them was occupied.[18] The Hentys in the Wannon were vulnerable as they had taken up land in the midst of Aboriginal people and with Aboriginal people not yet dispossessed of the land between their new settlement and the home base of Portland. At this time they admitted having 'very great difficulty in retaining the services of any men, owing to the hostile disposition of the natives ...'.[19]

At the same time settlement was expanding westward from the Melbourne-Geelong area. As news spread of the good prospects in the District, more and more settlers came across the strait from Van Diemen's Land. They were joined by pastoralists advancing south from New South Wales. In October 1835 Joseph Hawdon, John Gardiner and John Hepburn drove the first cattle herd down the central corridor to Port Phillip Bay. Others followed. In April 1837 when Thomas Learmonth established himself on the Barwon River about twenty miles north of Geelong, a line drawn a little more than twenty-five miles from the shores of Port Phillip Bay contained nearly all European settlement.[20] But settlers soon spread westward, the loss of Joseph Tice Gellibrand and G. B. L. Hesse in the country towards Colac and their probable murder by Aborigines causing only a temporary halt.

Far from being a steadily moving frontier of European occupation, the process of settlement has been described by J. M. Powell as occurring in three types of movement. There was, first, the slow expansion of the occupied area around the settled districts; second, the rush after the official opening up of Port Phillip with individuals moving ahead to take up new runs while others leap-frogged over them to establish a run; third, infilling—the occupation of areas not taken up in the first rush of settlement and the subdivision of the large runs.[21] William Learmonth, not arriving until 1844, counted himself lucky to be able to obtain a run: the only land left was at Darlot's Creek. It had been bypassed by others as the Aborigines were said 'to be very troublesome' there.[22]

During this process the Aborigines stayed where they had been. In one case, the Aborigines ordered Europeans to leave: 'It was their country, and the water belonged to them, and if it was taken away they could not go to another country, for they would be killed'.[23] Time after time Robinson met Aborigines who complained of being sent away from land taken up by a European squatter. In such cases they had usually gathered with others at a nearby station where they did not meet the same antagonism. In some cases they made agreements with squatters to stay on their own land. Rather than there being a complete taking over of land and a forcing back of Aboriginal people before the encroaching waves of settlers, the Europeans as they took up a run repeated the situation of the Hentys as they established themselves on the Wannon. Each settler occupied land which members of an Aboriginal clan considered belonged to them and from which they were reluctant to move far.

La Trobe summed up the dilemma of those who pioneered the District in his answer to a request from settlers of the Port Fairy District for protection against Aboriginal attacks in 1842:

... situated as you are, it is far easier to deplore your losses than to prevent them. The evils you complain of, are those which have everywhere accompanied the occupation of a new country inhabited by savage tribes. Even under circumstances far more favourable ... for instance, where a well-defined frontier or neutral ground could be interposed between the civilised and uncivilised—I need scarcely remind you, how little real security has been enjoyed. Here there is not even such a line; the savage tribes are not only upon our borders, but intermingled with us in every part of this wide district.[24]

The frontier was in fact a very local phenomenon, the disputed area being the very land each settler lived upon. The enemy was not on the other side of neutral ground. The frontier was represented by the woman who lived near by and was shared by her Aboriginal partner with a European or Europeans. It was the group living down beside the creek or river, it was the 'boy' used as guide for exploring parties or for doing jobs now and then. The 'other side of the frontier' was just down the yard or as close as the bed shared with an Aboriginal woman.

There has been a tendency to regard Robinson's 1841 journals as providing a glimpse of Aboriginal society as yet unchanged by European contact. This is true of some places in the District but closer study reveals that European settlement had impinged upon the Aborigines in an uneven way across the District. While some Aborigines impressed Robinson by the 'entire absence of all and everything connected with white people', for others the frontier had already passed, all that was left of their clan was a shattered remnant.[25] Some Aboriginal groups were already extinct, not only in the earliest settled areas west of Geelong but also in later settled areas, for example, north-east of Port Fairy.

In late 1841 it was possible to walk across the District to Portland and back to Melbourne, as James Ritchie did, and gain the impression that there were few European settlers. But if one took a different path as Robinson did, drawn by a desire to meet Aborigines, one met many more Europeans: so many that Robinson concluded that the District was already 'rapidly filling up'. At Burrumbeep he noted in his journal, 'All the country where there is water is occupied by stations, home or out: some have 2, 3 or 400 square miles of country'.[26] Recalling his journey west to the Glenelg in November 1841, Edward Bell gave a similar impression, commenting that Lake Boloke was 'the only vacant spot' he saw.[27] In September 1841 Robinson wrote to La Trobe naming four localities in different parts of the District suitable for Aboriginal reserves, but none was readily available as they were already occupied by Europeans.[28]

In fact European settlement was already well under way in late 1838. Under the dates 8 and 13 September 1838 Captain Foster Fyans, Police Magistrate at Geelong, sent to Sydney two lists 'which together named thirty-two men who from 1 August to 12 September had paid five pounds each for six month licences . . . in the "Western situation" of the "Geelong District"'.[29] In early 1838 David Fisher and an exploring party travelled across the District visiting the Grampians and the Pyrenees. It was at this time they established a station at Mount Shadwell (Mortlake).[30] One is reminded of Margaret Kiddle's statement in *Men of Yesterday*: 'By the end of 1838 the Western District was in tenuous occupation'.[31] Frederick Taylor was already at Mt Noorat in March 1839, and Matthew Gibson occupied land near Mt William during 1839.[32] By October 1839 the Colac country was comparatively crowded with stations, settlement having expanded westward from the more densely settled area north and north-west of Geelong.[33] There were already three or four runs between Lake Corangamite and the Hopkins River including those of the Manifold Brothers, of Frederick Taylor (for G. McKillop and J. Smith) and Henry Gibb on land that was to become the site of the township of Camperdown. By the summer of 1839–40 Charles Gray was established, the Burchetts had occupied the Gums station and John Muston had taken up land on Muston's Creek.[34]

In late 1839 Henry Fyshe Gisborne, the Crown Lands Commissioner for the District, travelling from Melbourne to Portland was able to make an overnight stay with Europeans every night except one. That night, the one before he reached Portland, need not have been an exception.

He wrote, 'it would have been possible to have reached one of Mr. Henty's sheep stations had I been aware of its locality'.[35] As early as 1839 Gisborne visited twenty-seven stations on which the number of European residents totalled two hundred and seventy-two. Some squatters had large establishments: Taylor (twenty-one residents on the station), Charles Wedge (thirty-six) and Thomas Anderson for the Derwent Company (twenty-four). These properties also had the largest flocks of sheep (7000, 5500 and 5700 respectively). There were already at least 70 226 sheep in the area west of Geelong.[36] Fyans's first tour of land-holders as Crown Lands Commissioner took place between 25 July and 4 October 1840, when he visited forty-one stations.[37] The number is small but the first station Fyans listed after leaving Geelong was John Thomson's at Keilambete, near Terang. Yet forty-four proprietors of stock from the area to the north and west of Geelong had appealed to the Governor of New South Wales in mid-1837 for protection against Aborigines. None is included in Fyans's 1840 list. If they are added, there were already eighty-five pastoral stations established before October 1840! On Fyans's second tour, during the time of Robinson's 1841 journey, he visited eighty-eight stations.[38]

The District was even busier in the early years of European settle-ent than these details reveal. Well before Robinson's 1841 journey people, sometimes with stock, passed across the District looking for land on which to settle or on their way into South Australia. Joseph Haw-on, for example, between 11 July and 12 August 1839 travelled from Port Phillip to Adelaide crossing the Glenelg. His stock, five thou-sand sheep and upwards of two hundred cattle, had travelled across the same route several months previously. Mr Bonney took three hundred head of cattle from the Glenelg to Adelaide between 18 March and 26 April 1839, accompanied by ten men and two native boys of the Bathurst district.[39]

In November 1838 Captain Hart with a party of men took cattle from the vicinity of Portland across to Adelaide via the Winters' station on the Wannon.[40] At that time, according to both Edward and John Henty, a number of runaways passed through Portland and the Wannon. About the same time, at Mt Emu on the eastern edge of the District, Robert Hamilton recalled seeing the Wedge Brothers passing with a large flock of sheep on their way to take up country at The Grange [Hamilton]: 'There was a very large party, several young men and Mr. Wedge himself, all were mounted and armed besides shepherds, bullock drivers and other working men'.[41]

Aborigines witnessed such events. Hamilton wrote, 'The natives were pretty numerous around the mount as the party passed and did not seem too pleased to see them'; Fyans claimed that Aborigines followed his party for miles when he made his first journey across the District in mid-1839; and James Blair stated that Aborigines 'tracked' the Whyte

Brothers 'on their route from Melbourne, and harassed them in every way . . .'.[42]

Joseph Hawdon and Alfred Mundy, in contrast, assumed that Aborigines who appeared in their track in mid-1839 did so wishing to make a friendly contact. Nevertheless they sped on in their tandem simply waving to the Aborigines, who ran after them, till the latter were left behind. At day-break at their camping place on the upper Wannon River they had been surprised to find a cow quietly grazing with the horses. Perhaps even stranger, Hawdon discovered it was one of his own left behind when his stock had been driven across the District some months earlier.[43]

It was in early 1838 that some fifty Aborigines of the interior saw their first 'shave'. David Fisher and Major Mercer had paused on their exploration of the interior and taken time to make themselves presentable:

> Major Mercer and myself being occupied in shaving, which operation being observed by some of the natives afforded them much amusement, and one of them signifying a desire to be trimmed, I undertook the task, which I accomplished amidst the yells, shouts, and laughter of some fifty savages with their lubras, who enjoyed the affair very much . . .[44]

A census of the European population taken in March 1841 revealed a population of 1260 of whom 1102 were males and 158 females. There were only 111 children. The census provides a lower figure for the size of the European population which was probably already larger than this. The *Melbourne Almanac and Port Phillip Directory* for 1841 gave a figure of 3000 for Geelong, Portland and the Portland Bay Commissioner's District. The population was largely of young men: males aged twenty-one to forty-five formed just over 65 per cent of the population according to the census, and males aged twenty-one to sixty formed over three-quarters. The imbalance of the sexes typical of the whole Port Phillip District was at its worst and persisted longest in the Portland Bay District.

At a time when Europeans found difficulty providing exact numbers for their own people, it is perhaps asking too much for exact figures on the size of the Aboriginal population, but estimates were made. Foster Fyans, the Lands Commissioner, provided a figure of 3000. James Dawson, collecting information from elderly Aborigines in the 1870s, made a rough and ready calculation. He multiplied the approximate number of individuals in what he called 'a tribe' by the number of 'tribes' present at the great meetings held at Mirraewuae, west of Caramut, to arrive at a figure of 2520 Aborigines. This figure excluded 'tribes' from the coast.[45]

What of Robinson's 1841 census? He collected all the details but for some reason never collated them. His evidence is very important because, like Fyans, his experience was first-hand and he travelled throughout the District. Compared with Fyans he had the advantage that his 1841 trip was made specifically to meet the Aborigines and to obtain details including numbers. One can doubt the accuracy of his recorded notes for a variety of reasons, but if one accepts them and adds the figures he collected, a total of 2949 Aborigines is obtained. This figure does not include the Barrabool of the Geelong area or the Aborigines of the Otway region. For 2844 of these people there are enough details to indicate the basic structure of the population: 759 were men, 1011 were women (including all wives some of whom may have been so young that they would normally be classified as children) and 1074 children. In contrast to the Europeans this was a population of families and related kin. As they became aware of the European intruders they must have been puzzled by the arrival of these people who lived mainly in small groups of men, whose main purpose appeared to be the minding of sheep.

Assistant Protector Sievwright who, like most of the squatters, moved into the District without a family, recorded the unexpected joy shown by the Aborigines when his wife and seven children joined him at his camp at Lake Keilambete. When, soon after, it became necessary to move the Protectorate encampment to Mt Rouse, a journey which lasted two days and two nights, 210 Aborigines accompanying the Assistant Protector, Sievwright's family was well provided for. At each night's stopping place 'their first care was to provide most abundantly for the comfort of my family, by erecting screens of branches to protect them from the weather and in furnishing firewood, water, etc'.[46]

Aborigines initially met few European families but one incident reveals their willingness to extend marriage ties and bonds of relationship and obligation to European families. Burguidenang, from the Terang area, was taken prisoner in June 1840 and escorted to Melbourne for trial. After five months of being heavily ironed awaiting trial in the Supreme Court, he was released without trial. Sievwright had visited him while he was in gaol and attended the Supreme Court. When Burguidenang met Sievwright near Lake Elingamite, his behaviour made it clear that he believed his release had been due to the influence of Sievwright. Sievwright described the meeting: the joy and gratitude of the Aborigine, his embrace, 'his head leaning on my shoulder, for upwards of a minute', his account to his friends of how the Assistant Protector had helped him, the gestures of the old men who then came up, placing their right hand upon his left shoulder and asking him to their huts where they gave him food and presented him with a necklace made of the teeth of a kangaroo. Two days later they returned to Sievwright's camp and in the evening they approached his tent with a gift to show their gratitude. Burguidenang bore in his arms 'his child, a young girl between two and three years of age and intimated that he brought her to give to my youngest son (11 years of age) and desired I would take the child in my arms and give her to him'. Sievwright, overwhelmed, through an interpreter tried to explain without offending that he was unable to do as asked. How much of the explanation the Aborigines understood is not clear but the newly established relationship and the obligation it carried is conveyed by Sievwright's statement, 'since which time his wife and child have remained near my tent, while he has gone on several expeditions to collect the surrounding tribes'.[47]

The interests, the outlook and the habits of the European men arriving in the District in the late 1830s and early 1840s can be gauged from the letters they wrote in response to La Trobe's request for them to reflect on their experience. Thomas Learmonth, for example, arrived at Geelong in 1837 with 2000 ewes. Purchasing another 1000 he travelled up the Barwon River about twenty miles from Geelong and took up land. At the time, he stated, settlers were afraid to venture far inland for the Aborigines were 'committing depredations within fifteen miles of Geelong' and there were suspicions they had been involved in the disappearance of Gellibrand and Hesse 'in the country ... towards Colac [to the west]'. Between Europeans 'there was a tacit understanding that no one was to take up a station nearer than three miles to another person', he explained, 'the intervening ground to be equally divided'. In the 'then lawless state of the infant colony', with no Crown Lands Commissioner to intervene, boundary disputes sometimes led to blows but in general he believed there was 'more good-feeling and consideration for the rights of others ... than might have been expected'.

The Aborigines, as Learmonth's letter indicates, were marginal in the new world being created. The words 'no one' in the statement 'no one was to take up a station nearer than three miles' referred to Europeans. Not included in the words used to encompass all people, they were outsiders not given a serious thought in the 'anxieties and labour [great and urgent] connected with the forming of ... sheep establishments'.[48]

To the European men, the concerns of making money, of buying stock, of taking up a run, of protecting the boundary against fellow settlers, were the important issues. The new world being created was a European one and the people with whom one communicated were Europeans. The Aborigines were a force to be reckoned with, if it proved necessary, but not to be negotiated with concerning the land. That one did with Europeans. There was a certainty, a confidence that the land was available to be taken up and that it was their destiny to do so that marked the attitude of the men. There was no rationalization of the taking of the land in Learmonth's account of events in 1837. The Aborigines were mentioned for their marginal influence—they were stealing property and they were holding up the progress of European settlement.

Unfortunately the Aborigines at times did prove a force to be reckoned with and in these circumstances the men took the stand of protecting what they believed was theirs. Niel Black wrote to his partner:

> I have no great apprehension of their ever troubling me much they have had enough of this place. A few days since I found a Grave into which about 20 must have been thrown. A Settler taking up a new country is obliged to act towards them in this manner or abandon it.[49]

John Robertson of Wando Vale, north of Casterton, confided, 'I have on four different occasions, when they committed murders, gone out with others in search of them, and *I now thank God* I never fell in with them, or there is no doubt I should be like many others . . .'.[50] Robinson wrote of Dr Kilgour of Tarrone, 'like all new arrivals, [he] is a declared enemy to the blacks . . . He thinks . . . the settlers will take the law into their own hands and punish the blacks'.[51]

Those who took such a stand against the Aborigines were not necessarily squatters. Often an overseer was in charge and responsible for protecting the property. A little further north on his journey, at Robert Whitehead's property, Robinson found an Aboriginal skull hanging up in the hut. The man in charge, Richard Sutton, had a large pack of dogs and a number of firearms. 'I believe the dogs are kept as much to hunt natives as kangaroos', Robinson wrote. Sutton impressed upon Robinson that 'the squatters must protect their property at all hazards'. When Robinson remonstrated and pointed out that if he broke the law he would be punished, 'he, like Dr Kilgour and other[s] said nobody would know about it'. Moreover it was easy to put the blame upon the Aborigines. As Robinson commented, all the European men had to do was 'Under pretense of being after sheep, ride furiously up to them, and in a threatening attitude, when the natives would be terrified into an offensive position, which would be the signal for an attack as they would be able to swear the natives made the first attack'.[52]

Some squatters' wives accompanied their husbands inland, bringing the comforts of home to the huts their menfolk erected. But their numbers were few in the early years. In the west there were the Henty women and Arbella Winter Cooke; in the east between Port Fairy and Colac there were by 1840 three squatters' wives, Mrs Alexander Dennis, Mrs Hugh Murray and Mrs Thomas Manifold.[53] In the north-east Katherine Kirkland was at Trawalla. There would also have been a number of wives in the more densely settled area north-west and west of Geelong. The isolation of these women is seen in the reaction of Katherine Kirkland's daughter to the visit of Mrs Gisborne. Katherine was delighted as it had been 'more than a year' since she had seen a 'lady'. But the effect on her daughter was totally unexpected:

> The sight of a 'white leubra', as she called her, seemed for a time to take away her speech; but she soon began to question her very closely as to where she was from, and whether there were any more like her in her country.[54]

One might have expected these women to be more sympathetic to the Aborigines than their menfolk. But this was a frontier society; the women, like the men, carried guns.[55] The case of Annie Maria Baxter (later Dawbin) is an interesting one. Not all squatters' wives would have behaved as Annie did but her story shows the courage needed, the near-ness of danger and what was true of them all—the attitude to the Abor-igines that they shared with their husbands.

Annie was the wife of Lieutenant Andrew Baxter who in 1843 took up Yambuck, a small squatting property, 18 kilometres west of Port Fairy. Lying between the Shaw and Eumeralla rivers it bordered the scene of the most violent and prolonged racial conflict in the Western District. The Baxters arrived after the Aboriginal attacks of 1842 but they witnessed and experienced the increased violence of the mid to late 1840s. Their home was on the western bank of the Shaw River and opposite it, within view of the Baxters, was an Aboriginal camping place.

More perhaps than other wives Annie experienced the danger of living in frontier circumstances. An outdoor woman, both lively and courageous, she placed herself in situations most women would have avoided. On one occasion while out riding accompanied only by a Euro-pean employee and an Aboriginal boy, she unexpectedly came across an Aboriginal hunting party of about twenty armed men. She persuaded them to lower their weapons and to talk to her before negotiating a safe retreat from them. Turning around as she left, however, she found four spears aimed at her back. She remonstrated and the Aborigines turned and went on their way. She wrote, 'I can readily fancy a person with weak nerves being intimidated by them! ... They are far from cowards when in their wild state ... and a fine set of men were there today ...'.[56]

On another occasion when Baxter was absent she sent for help and then with 'Dr Aplin, Tim, and Willie' searched for Aborigines who had harmed the stock. Annie, like the men, was well prepared: 'Even I looked a formidable person with my red shirt and black belt—in the latter was a pouch with balls, caps, cartridges etc.—and my constant companion—my pistol'. Tom carried 'a double-barreled gun', with pistols in a belt and 'a sword by his side'. The doctor had his pistols and 'a hand-some rifle'. Willie carried an unloaded gun and a pistol in his belt. At the camp of the unsuspecting Aborigines, Dr Aplin fired first. As the Abor-igines were very close, Annie knew he could not miss: 'I closed my eyes and said 'Poor creatures, may God forgive us!'. Aborigines yelled and began running. But this was a camp of women and children and the Europeans decided to fire only a couple more shots over the heads of the fleeing Aborigines. 'Then', wrote Annie, 'commenced the work of destruction; such burning "of mia-mias"—killing of puppies—breaking—spears and bottles; bags, rugs, everything pitched into the fire'. She saved some bags, two spears and some kangaroo skins which she 'bore off in triumph'.[57]

She did not always feel so brave. At a time when William Learmonth's sheep flock at nearby Ettrick was attacked and he had appealed to La Trobe for the help of the Black Police in whom the squatters put great store, and in response only 'our white Policeman' had been sent to the squatter's aid', she admitted, 'It really becomes serious when they are so near—and altho' far from nervous, I do not admire the idea of being eaten by savages!'[58]

She sided with Baxter over the need to whip an Aborigine for lying and watched the whipping: 'Nicky never flinched altho' his unfortunate back must have smarted . . . I witnessed the punishment and thought it very justly given'.[59]

She saw the end product of contact with Europeans for many Aboriginal women on this male-dominated frontier. The 'large camp across the river' of 1844 had by 1849 become the 'Camp Des Invalides'. 'Poor things!', she wrote of the sick women there, 'they really don't remind me scarcely of human beings'.[60] It was for the women suffering from venereal disease brought to the District by Europeans that she felt most sympathy. She tells the story of an attractive Aboriginal woman who became diseased as a result of sexual relations with shepherds from Ritchie's nearby station, Aringa. The disease took the hideous form of the woman losing her palate which Annie, perhaps mistakenly, gives as the reason for her being unable to speak above a whisper. Her former lovers at this stage put her into a 'tub of sublimate, used for sheep dressing, after which she fell into a rapid decline'. Annie was appalled at her appearance: 'I never could have imagined it possible to [for] anybody to exist in such a state. She made Baxter so sick . . .'.[61] When the woman died, Annie mused:

> What suffering that poor creature underwent! Neglected, unattended, almost starved at times—not a soul to care for her or mourn her! . . . Man (I mean white man) in this instance as in many more, has been only the means of making this poor woman's condition worse than it originally was; all she knew of him was to bring her to that fearful state in which she suffered and eventually died! . . . Which will God judge, the civilised, enlightened Christians or the unfortunate and despised Heathen?[62]

The largest group of Europeans outside the settled areas was that of the station hands. The 1841 census revealed that 'eighty-nine per cent of the classified population . . . were servants of various descriptions, and only eight per cent were landed proprietors, bankers, merchants, professional men and other employers'.[63] In contrast to the masters of whom Niel Black wrote that it was rare 'to meet a person in the Bush who is not a gentleman's son, or at all events had a good education', station hands were often convicts or ex-convicts.[64] 'Assigned servants came into the Western District with the Vandiemonians and overlanders . . . There were, too, old lags who had served their sentences before ever reaching the district'.[65] The 1841 census showed only 126 individuals to be assigned or emancipated though the number had risen to 686 (nearly 20 per cent of the population) by the 1846 census. But Kiddle reminds us that in 1843 it was reported that 'there is always a moving population in the Bush of perhaps 500 in each District more especially at the season for sheep shearing'. As shearers were usually of convict origin, it can be assumed that a large proportion of the moving population was of this class.[66] As only one of the 126 listed as assigned or emancipated was female, this group must be thought of as male.

Because of their larger numbers relative to their masters and because of their occupations as servants, shepherds and hutkeepers these were the males that Aborigines most encountered and who suffered most at the hands of the Aborigines, if death can be judged as the worst penalty. Of the forty Europeans officially listed as killed by Aborigines in the District of Port Phillip between 1836 and 1844 only seven were of the property-owning class while thirty-three were employees, mainly shepherds and hutkeepers.[67]

Robinson, who saw more the danger to Aborigines than to the Europeans, was appalled by the exposure of Aborigines to this labouring class. 'The past and the present state of the Aborigines is one of annihilation or destruction', he wrote. Convinced that most of the men were convicts or ex-convicts he judged their behaviour to be the worst he had seen in his sixteen years in the colonies.[68] Such men were usually armed and some of them took no pains to hide the fact that they considered the life of a native 'to be of no more value than that of a wild dog'.[69] At Dr Kilgour's, north of Port Fairy, three of the men were ex-convicts, a class Robinson described as 'a thousand times worse' than those who were still serving their sentence. Robinson told Kilgour that his men were 'as bad' as any he had met. He was disgusted by the swearing and the violence shown towards animals, the men thinking nothing of working and whipping till the bullock gave up and died. He prayed, 'God protect the natives against such inhuman scoundrels'.[70]

James Kirby also came into contact with such men while visiting a friend who had a public house on the Glenelg River. There the customers were 'nearly to a man, discharged convicts, or ticket-of-leave men, some hailing from the Sydney side, Port Arthur, Norfolk Island, and some from Van Dieman's Land'. Of them he wrote:

> Talk about the 'scum of the earth', it is nothing to what these wretches were when they got full of grog.
> I flattered myself I had done with savages, when I left the Murray, but the *black* savages there, although bad enough, were good men in comparison with these *white* ones.[71]

Much is written of the cruelty of this group. Some took Aboriginal women and kept them without their husbands' permission in their huts.

Others murdered Aborigines. Still others gave some of their master's sheep to the Aboriginal men in return for the use of Aboriginal women, blaming the missing sheep on Aboriginal raids. Others losing sheep through negligence averted blame by accusing Aborigines of stealing the missing sheep.[72]

Some individuals were notoriously brutal and violent. Protector Robinson, for example, was told by one of the Tulloh brothers who had settled on land at the Wannon falls and on the Grange Burn, of a man named George Robinson who had deliberately placed a child on a fire and kicked another to death. Perhaps one should be careful of information given by Tulloh: Robinson was warned in 1841 that the Tullohs were 'remarkable for lying'. James Blair, however, the Police Magistrate at Portland, did not have the same reputation and he told Robinson of a sawyer named Robinson, who had been guilty of crimes against Aborigines. He claimed the satisfaction of recently sending the man to Melbourne gaol for non-payment of a fine. Blair stated that 'the murder committed by this man upon the blacks was incredible and Mr Winter had told him he could prove a number which ... this man had committed ... He has been known to go up to a child and beat out its brains'.[73]

Yet, to be fair, there were others who found the stress of frontier too great and deserted their position. Squatters suffered as a result, complaining of the difficulty of retaining men especially in areas where Aborigines were hostile.[74]

Settlements such as Port Fairy and Portland were also places of contact, though Aborigines were wary of the streets of Portland in the early 1840s. According to Edward Henty in 1841 the Aborigines had not visited Portland for some years.[75] In contrast the Aborigines were not strangers to Port Fairy which by early 1844 was a settlement of about fifty dwellings of various kinds and sizes.[76] Some Aborigines joined the fun, laughter and drinking at the Merrijig. There is no indication of fear at Port Fairy but some felt disgust at the presence of Aborigines. Penelope Selby, visiting the Dawsons' Melting Down Establishment on the Lough at Port Fairy, wrote to her sister in England,

> The natives ... are a most disgusting set, we have plenty here carrying away the offal, and I am not surprised at the want of what we consider proper delicacy of feeling when all classes are constantly coming in contact with men and women in a state of complete nudity ... I have felt my own cheeks burn when I have seen ladies in company with gentlemen talking and laughing with savages in that state ...[77]

While the Europeans in 1841 were fewer in number than the Aborigines, they had little idea of the size of the Aboriginal population. Even Robinson was puzzled. At Mt Napier, a 'hot-bed for natives' according to settlers, he mused, 'and yet it is singular so few are met...'.[78] Henry

Fyshe Gisborne, the first Crown Lands Commissioner for the Port Phillip District, riding across the district to Portland Bay in late 1839 reported not seeing any Aborigines between Geelong and Portland.[79] Individual settlers reported to Robinson in early 1841 that they had not seen Aborigines in their area—at Claude Farie's and the Bolden Brothers' station, for example, on the Hopkins and a little later at Dr Kilgour's Tarrone station north of Port Fairy. Robinson, however, while at Kilgour's was able to collect the names of the local Aborigines upon whose land Kilgour had settled—the Yowen conedeet—forty-three of them.

Aborigines were more likely to be invisible than absent, as a story told by Samuel Winter demonstrates. Well known for his friendliness to local Aborigines, he was travelling south to Portland for supplies, accompanied by a native boy. At sundown they reached Emu Creek where Winter hoped to stay for the night, but not without gaining permission from local Aborigines. The native boy looked for obvious signs of Aborigines but saw none. He cooeed, 'native fashion'. There was no reply. Then Winter asked him to call out in his own language that it was Wenberrimin (Winter's Aboriginal name) and that he wished to camp by the creek. At that 'immediately a large number of natives came out of the scrub'.[80]

The adult male Aborigines were the enemy of the Europeans. It was they who speared the squatters and their men. It was they who harassed the stock and stole and maimed sheep. These Aborigines were not an unknown enemy. Whenever there were encounters or Aboriginal attacks, the Europeans were able to name the group and often the individual or individuals responsible. There was considerable associating of Aboriginal and European on the frontier, of men being offered temporary employment by individual squatters, or sometimes being offered both work and accommodation in return for the use of the Aborigine's wife, of lonely shepherds making friends with Aborigines and of many men offering alcohol, flour, a blanket or some clothing to Aboriginal men for the use of their wives. Many squatters prided themselves on 'domesticating' an Aborigine and then blamed fickleness when he turned on the European or returned to his people.

There was also the custom of having an Aboriginal 'boy'. Sometimes the term may have applied to an older man but Robinson mentions seven squatters who had 'a boy' and it is clear from the context that these were either youths or children.

According to Robinson's journal twenty-three squatters mainly from the western and northern part of the District had at least one Aborigine employed on their property in 1841. A number of these Aborigines carried guns.[81] They drove drays, took messages from one station to another, accompanied travellers between stations, drove bullocks, sheared sheep and acted as house 'boys'. There was considerable contact

Kuunawarn

Kaawirn Kuunawarn, 'Chief' of the Kirrae Wuurong tribe of the Mt Shadwell area; also known as King David, his name is usually stated to mean 'Hissing Swan'.

Davis, chief of the Hopkins tribe. 'Muddy Swamp'

A painting of an Aborigine of the Spring Creek area which shows how local Aborigines wore a piece of bone or wood inserted through a hole in the septum of the nose

Robinson's companion on his 1841 journey across the District: watercolour by Thomas Bock, 1837

Robinson with Van Diemen's Land Aborigines: The Conciliation *by Benjamin Duterrau, 1840*

MR. ROBINSON'S *Paper to the Aboriginal*

Natives of

Presented by

The Chief Protector

to   at

on this   *day of*   184

Robinson's card sent to group after group of Aborigines

Robinson's sketch of one Aborigine's solution to the question of what to do with a pipe (sketched in the Grampians, 19 June 1841)

Aboriginal hut, Portland Bay district, 1843, by T. W., an unknown artist

Aborigines of south-western Victoria, probably the Portland area, with bones through the nose, body markings and leaves around the ankles as worn for a corroboree: 1859 photograph by Thomas Hannay

between European and Aborigine though individual settlers had little idea of the Aboriginal population as a whole, or of the extent of the related kin of the Aborigine they referred to as their black or their boy.

Robinson was suspicious of such contact. Of a group of Aborigines consisting of one male, his wife and child plus two native women with one child living in two small huts near the shepherd's hut at Thomas Norris's outstation Robinson commented, 'no doubt encouraged there for prostitution'. Of two boys kept by Thomas Tulloh, one aged fourteen and the other aged nine, Robinson assumed, 'No doubt only kept to send after women'. At William Blow's station, Allanvale, where one native always remained with two families including two girls, he again assumed, 'no doubt kept at the station for prostitution'. At Mt Emu station, as if to confirm his suspicion of other places, he found that the Aborigines were allowed at the home station but not at the outstation. Glendenning, the manager, stated that the men there would take liberties with the women.[82]

No doubt Aborigines had their own reasons for living in close proximity to Europeans. A number of Europeans were killed by such men. Tom Browne of Squattlesea Mere (who as a novelist used the pseudonym Rolf Boldrewood) commented that the Aboriginal Tommy took part in a raid on his hut and then disappeared.[83] Whatever the purpose, a considerable number of Aboriginal men were in a position to learn some English and the habits of Europeans including driving drays, riding horses, caring for sheep and the use of guns. They were in an excellent position to deal with the European enemy if they so desired in those early days.

The Aboriginal women, including all wives some of whom would have been quite young, outnumbered the Aboriginal men. This was a society which practised polygamy and in such extravagance that Robinson felt unable to believe what he was told. When told that a man had eleven wives he noted it, but put down the more modest number of five. In another case where the natives said that Par.oo.rare.rer had eleven or twelve wives and many children, Robinson noted down eight wives and nine children. This, if anything, suggests that the number of women (wives) is a conservative estimate. In many cases the Aborigines had three or more wives.[84] A census of the Aboriginal population taken in 1877 revealed that males outnumbered females. But from all the evidence available in 1841 the reverse was true then. Maybe since the figure for wives included young wives one cannot make such a strong statement. But what can certainly be said is that no European at that time commented on fewer Aboriginal women than men as they did later in the evidence collected by the 1858–59 Select Committee.[85] Not only did females outnumber males, but in areas where frontier violence had not yet upset the population there were large numbers of children, and Robinson particularly commented on the presence of pregnant women.

As numerous references have already indicated, it was women who in large numbers also came to know the customs of the Europeans and for many of them venereal disease and an agonizing death was the penalty. In many cases they were treated as prostitutes. One squatter on the Glenelg ran a harem for himself and his men. In only one case reported by Robinson, a European had taken an Aboriginal woman as a *de facto* wife.[86] As well as the use of Aboriginal women as sexual partners by Europeans right across the District, some Aboriginal camping places were situated in places of easy access for European men travelling across the region. Of the Crawford River camp of Mimburn, Chief of the Tarerbung conedeet, Robinson wrote that it was commonly known in the area that 'his camp near the crossing place on the road to Portland (where the drays usually stop) is no other than a common Brothel . . .'. As for Koort Kirrup and his tribe at Emu Creek, their camp also 'was under a similar imputation with that of Mimburn'.[87]

Thus all across the District Aboriginal men, women and children came in contact with European men and a few women and children. What was unusual was the degree of close contact between the races, a contact that varied from friendliness to outright hostility from one pastoral station to the next. Relationships were complex, varying not only from one station to the next but rapidly changing over time as those who found themselves intermingled across the District attempted to come to terms with the presence of another race.

3

'that's my country belonging to me'

THOSE WHO CAME to the Portland Bay District, as the Western District was then known, judged it against a wider perspective, the drier plains of New South Wales, the greener pastures and gentler streams of the central part of Tasmania, the Swan River settlement, the farms they had grown up on in England or Scotland. These colonists moved against a wide canvas, a European world, and were conscious of their part in the extension of its power and influence. Some had farming enterprises in more than one colony, travelling from their headquarters to the other colonies when it was necessary.

Having travelled half-way round the world, Europeans found it difficult to understand the reluctance of most Aborigines to travel far. But theirs was a small world, intimately known. The Aborigines of the District, for example, were sufficiently isolated from the central area of the Port Phillip District that they were not influenced by the growth of Melbourne and the attraction it proved to Aborigines of the surrounding area. Those of the Protectorate's North-Western District, of Edward Stone Parker's station on the Loddon, however, strongly felt its influence. They received 'letters' from Aborigines to the south inviting them to visit Melbourne.[1] These were no more letters as we understand them than Robinson's visiting card: in one case Parker described the letter as simply 'a dirty scrap of a ship's log book'. But the purpose of the 'letter' was no doubt explained by the messengers who delivered the important fragment—just as was done by those who delivered Robinson's visiting cards. The 'letter' was a sign of European

influence and the arrival of the letters and the Aboriginal response to them
indicated relationship links between Aborigines of the North-Western
District and those around Melbourne.[2] The Aborigines demanded that
Parker arrange for La Trobe to meet them when they visited Melbourne.
They wanted to see the 'Governor'.

In contrast there is no mention of such letters arriving in the Western
District. Nor is there mention of any movement of Aborigines to see
what was occurring in Melbourne except for the Barrabool Aborigines of
the Geelong area—not very far from Melbourne. Some of the Colijon
and Wardy Yalloke Aborigines joined the Barrabool on one occasion
mentioned by Charles Wightman Sievwright, Assistant Protector for the
Western District.[3] Otherwise the pull of the growing European settlements of Melbourne and Geelong seem to have made little impact on
the Aborigines of the Western District. La Trobe visited Portland in
1841 while Robinson was camped near by with a large group of Mt Clay
Aborigines. There was no indication that they knew La Trobe was near
nor of any desire to meet him.[4]

The isolation of the region from the impact of a large European population was also reflected in the birth-rate and the late appearance of
European diseases. In the area around Melbourne where European
settlement was greatest William Thomas, Assistant Protector for the
Westernport District, reported that for the six months from 1 September
1841 to 1 March 1842 there were no births in his District. In the years
that followed he noticed that few children were born and these 'seldom
lived one month'. In June 1845 only one child remained of those born in
the preceding six years: 'one chief has acknowledged to me', he wrote,
'that he has no power to stop it [infanticide]; the blacks say, "no country,
no good have it pickanineys"'.[5] Parker also noted an early decline in
births in the North-Western District. In contrast Sievwright in early
1841 reported 'children numerous' and later requested a teacher
urgently. He had over one hundred children on the Aboriginal reserve at
Kolor (Mt Rouse).[6] The only evidence of a decline in births having taken
place by 1841 is that in areas settled for a relatively longer time the Aborigines were already extinct or almost so.

The late arrival of disease points to a similar conclusion. It was
1 December 1841 before there was much sickness amongst the Aborigines gathered at Lake Terang. And it was not till then that venereal
disease, which Sievwright had noted six months earlier as being
restricted to the Jarcourt tribe, had become general.[7]

According to Robinson, 151 groups of Aborigines were located across
the District. Though he called them 'tribes', they were clans—groups of
closely related kin which formed the most important social unit of the
Aborigines.[8] Clans were the landowning groups yet they were 'invisible'
to Europeans. Diane Barwick, writing of the Kulin, stated that what
most observers saw were actually bands:

... clans as such were apparently invisible to Europeans because all members did not live together permanently as an observable residential unit ... Clan lands were exploited by residential groups (now termed bands) whose membership changed over time ...[9]

From Robinson's description this seems to be true also of the Portland Bay District.

Membership of a clan was by descent and those who belonged were spiritually linked to a designated part of the land by ties that stretched back to the Dreamtime. Each clan territory had topographical features of significance because of their association with 'mythic beings, or deities, who in the Dreaming left part of themselves there'. Such sites provided access to an 'essential life-giving substance' for all members of a clan. Clan land was 'inalienable and non-transferable, held in trust for the mythic beings, and for human beings: for the dead as well as for the living, and for future generations'. The clan was thus based on 'a religious understanding', as the anthropologist Ronald Berndt has pointed out, and had 'religious responsibilities', including the carrying out of rituals to ensure 'the perpetuation of species associated with the particular mythic beings linked with that territory'.[10]

The name of each Aboriginal clan indicated their 'inherited responsibility for ... land'.[11] The Tappoc conedeet, for example, were the people of Tappoc (Mt Napier). The War.nam.bul conedeet were those whose country was at Mt Warrnambool.

Little is known of mythic beings in the Portland Bay District or of special sites associated with their travels. Almost the sole reference to such things in European sources is Dawson's account of how a bunyip carved a channel through Bukkar whuurong, a bank between Lakes Bullen Merri and Gnotuk.[12] Robinson claimed that during his 1841 journey he had made a friendly communication with all the tribes of the Western District and obtained the fullest information about them. Yet nowhere does he mention sacred sites. Such information was not shared with Europeans, even those who appeared sympathetic.

Whereas Europeans talked of 'land', the Aborigines referred to their 'country'. Each Aboriginal family had its 'own country'. The Aboriginal word for country 'Cha knaek' in Chaap Wuurong, 'Maeaering an' in Kuurn kopan noot and 'Maeaering' in Peek whurrong meant 'my country'.[13] Assistant Protector Parker wrote in 1854: 'to this day the older men can clearly point out the land which their fathers left them and which they once called their own'.[14] Robinson's evidence supports this. Eurodap, for example, the Jarcourt guide who accompanied Robinson across the District to the Wannon, belonged to the Kone.ne.gulluc section [clan], Tjarncoort nation [tribe]. But his 'country' was at Mittone, the hill at Manifold's outstation near the junction of the Portland Bay Road. Others were just as specific. Around Burrumbeep in

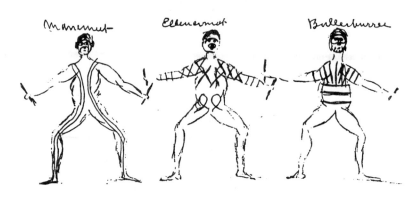

Members of a clan decorated their bodies and faces in a distinctive way. Robinson sketched the different patterns used by clans gathered at the Protectorate camp at Lake Keilambete in April 1841. The body markings of the Manemeet (Manmate), Ellengermot (from around Lake Elingamite) and the Bullerburer (from Lake Bolac) are shown.

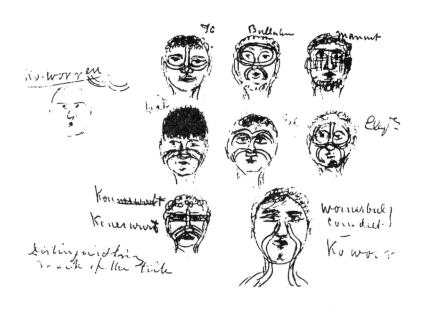

Robinson's sketches of the facial markings of the TC (Jarcourt), Bullerburer (Bolokeburer), Manmot (Manmate), Wdr (Waddowro), Col. (Colijon), Eleng. (Ellengermot), Konerwurt (Konewurer), Wornarbul (Warnabul).

the north Tung borroong told Robinson, 'that's my country belonging to me!!'[15] Dawson, who collected information some thirty years later than Robinson, stated: 'Each family has the exclusive right by inheritance to a part of the tribal lands, which is named after its owner; and his family and every child born on it must be named after something on the property'.[16]

Personal names 'were often taken from something in the neighbourhood, such as a swamp, rivulet, waterhole, hill or animal; or from some peculiarity in the child or in its parents'. Girls were sometimes named after flowers. The chief of the Kirrae wurrong, Kaawirn Kuunawarn's name meant 'Hissing Swan', after the noise swans made when he robbed their nests. The man often referred to as Camperdown George was named Wombeetch Puyuun which meant 'Decayed Kangaroo'.[17]

Aborigines felt strongly about their 'country'. Jacky White, forced by law to reside on the Lake Condah Aboriginal Station, expressed his feeling for his country in a letter begging Samuel Winter to come and take him back to the Wannon, only a few miles away:

> . . . if you will write to the government for us, and get us off here, I will do work for you and will never leave you . . . I always wish . . . to be in my country, where I was born . . . This country don't suit me I'm a stranger in this country I like to be in my country.[18]

This same aspect of Aboriginal culture was highlighted by Parker in a public lecture which he gave in 1854:

> Very few of the natives of the Upper Loddon . . . have seen the Murray; and only three or four natives of the Murray could ever be induced to visit the Loddon Aboriginal Establishment. In 1843, the . . . Lake Boloke tribe visited that establishment. But though the lake is not a hundred miles from the Loddon, the tribes had not previously met. It was with difficulty all parties could be kept in harmony. One of the most intelligent of the Worngarragerra, (whose country, by the way, was even nearer to them than the Loddon,) said to me indignantly, when remonstrated with for his unfriendliness, 'Maimmait talle, mainmait mirri-par-gar, mainmait nalderrun; yurrong,' that is, they are foreign in speech, they are foreign in countenance, they are foreign altogether—they are no good.[19]

It was not easy for Aborigines to move elsewhere when Europeans arrived. As far as they were concerned there was only one place they belonged, though they might have some rights in other places. Robinson in 1841 found Aborigines near to or on their own land despite the presence of European settlers. They were aware that the land had been taken but they had not moved away. One incident, in particular, makes this clear. Near Frank Henty's home station Robinson met a family group. When he asked them where the country was that they belonged to, 'they beat the ground and vociferated, Deen! deen! (here! here!) and then, in a dejected tone, bewailed the loss of their country'.[20]

The groups Robinson listed as tribes in 1841 were clans but at times he showed awareness of larger units to which a number of his tribes belonged. He suggested important boundaries when he detailed the reluctance of his Aboriginal guides to go any further and by his note on a change of language or by his puzzled comments on Aboriginal descriptive terms for 'others'.[21] Mistakenly, he gave the name Manmates to the Aborigines of the nation which he believed stretched from the Hopkins across to the Glenelg River. But the word was one the Aborigines used to designate strangers, wild blacks: it was a general term for strangers, not the specific name of a group.

Dawson, writing later, had the advantage that his daughter was able to talk to the Aborigines in their own language and that their Aboriginal informants had a better command of English. He described larger groups of Aborigines than Robinson's clan sections distinguished by their language. These language groups are what we call tribes.[22] It was clear even from the early contacts with the Aborigines that language was a barrier. Sievwright wrote, 'Language of the different tribes is quite distinct. Tribes not adjacent with difficulty understand each other'.[23] Dawson identified ten languages in the area from Dunmore in the west to Colac in the east but made no mention of any group west of Dunmore—an area with which it seems his Aboriginal informants were not familiar.[24]

The language situation was not in practice as fragmented as Dawson's account might suggest. The modern linguist, R. M. W. Dixon, points out that the word 'language' can be used in two quite distinct ways. 'First, in everyday discourse people identify themselves as speakers of a particular language, and make judgements as to whether their way of speaking is "the same language" or "a different language" from another's mode of speech.' Quite often the motivation for such a decision is largely political. From the linguist's point of view the Norwegians and Danes, for example, speak dialects of the same language yet will claim they speak a different language. This is the sense in which the District tribes claimed the separate languages listed by Dawson. 'The second sense is the technical usage of linguistics—two modes of speech are regarded as dialects of a single language if they are mutually intelligible.' The difference between the two uses of the word 'language' leads to very different perceptions of the situation. Dixon points out that in Australia each of the some 600 distinct tribes considered itself to have a different language from its neighbours. But from the linguist's point of view in many cases the speeches of neighbouring tribes are really dialects of a single language so that the 600 tribes, each with its own language, speak between them about 200 different languages. Dixon believes one language (in linguistic terms) was spoken between the Glenelg River in the west and the Gellibrand River of the Cape Otway region and inland to just south of Casterton, Hamilton, Mt Rouse and Hexham. Within the greater area of the old Portland Bay District his language map shows four languages being spoken. Dawson was aware of the fact that some languages were similar to others: he wrote that four languages which were very different from each other divided the people of the central plain. He believed that 'other tongues' spoken at the great annual meetings of the Aborigines might be termed 'dialects' of these four languages.[25]

Gunditjmara, the tribal name now familiar throughout the District for the Aborigines of the south-west, is not mentioned by Protector Robinson, James Dawson or R. Brough Smyth whose two volumed account of the Aborigines of Victoria was published in 1878, just before Dawson's book was published. It is first referred to by Lorimer Fison and A. W. Howitt who in *Kamilaroi and Kurnai* published in 1880 quote the Rev. Stähle, manager of the Lake Condah Aboriginal Station, as their informant. Stähle stated that Gournditch was the name for Lake Condah and mara meant man. He defined the territory of the Gournditch-mara as 'extending from the Glenelg River on the west to the Eumeralla River on the east, and from the sea coast as far north as Mount Napier and Hotspur'. Yet Howitt, in *The Native Tribes of South-east Australia* published in 1904, naming Stähle as his source, provided information which contradicted the statement of his informant. He stated that the territory of the Gournditch-mara extended 'from Mount Gambier to the Eumeralla Creek' but added 'and included the Kuurn-kopan noot and Peek-whuurong tribes described by Mr. Dawson' (both east of the Eumeralla River). That he was confused is made even clearer by his comment that 'The area occupied by the tribes described by Mr. Dawson may be roughly defined as lying between Portland, Colac, Ararat, and possibly Pitfield'! Howitt's map of tribal territories included in his book thus wrongly shows the territory of the Gournditch-mara extending eastward to the River Hopkins.

There are no contradictions in the information on tribal boundaries supplied by Aborigines to Dawson and to Stähle (for Howitt). These boundaries differ, though, from those provided by N. B. Tindale, the modern scholar whose map of tribal areas is the most commonly used reference on such matters. One cannot help but wonder whether he wasn't simply misled by Howitt's map which incorrectly showed the Gournditch-mara extending to the Hopkins. For whatever reason, Tindale shows the territory of the Gournditch-mara (referred to as the Gunditjmara) extending across to the Hopkins River. In doing so he is drawing a conclusion contrary to the information Aborigines gave to Stähle and Dawson.[26]

Nowadays there is doubt that Gournditch was a tribal name. When sounded it is suspiciously similar to Robinson's 'conedeet' and Dawson's 'kuurndit' meaning 'people belonging to a place'. Stähle may have asked for the word which meant 'the people belonging here' and been given

Boundaries of tribal groups according to James Dawson

'kuurndit': the word meant all those belonging to an area but he took it to mean the specific name of the people from the vicinity of Lake Condah. It is a similar misunderstanding to Robinson's when he thought the word for stranger 'manmate' was the name of a tribe to the west. Gunditjmara, once firmly established in European sources, became a tribal name.

The Portland Bay District consists largely of volcanic plains: covering 15 000 square kilometres these form one of the largest such plains in the world. Stretching from Melbourne across to Portland and from the Great Dividing Range in the north to the coastal plains and Otway Ranges in the south, the plains are almost horizontal with only a slight southward inclination. The Aborigines called the volcanic plain 'waark' and the tribal divisions reflected geographical divisions with the tribes of the volcanic plains keeping apart from those of the coastal plains. At the great midsummer meetings at Mirraewuae, a marsh to the west of Caramut, friendly tribes met for hunting, feasting and recreation. Those who attended were those of the plain and its northern boundary. They were from the Wannon area, Hamilton, Dunkeld, Mt William, Mt Rouse, Mt Napier, Lake Condah, Dunmore, Tarrone, Kangatong, Spring Creek, Framlingham, Lake Boloke, Skipton, Flat-topped Hill, Mt Shadwell, Darlington, Mt Noorat, Camperdown, Wardy Yalloke and Mt Elephant. None of the sea coast tribes attended, according to Dawson, 'as they were afraid of treachery and an attack on the part of the others'.[27]

There is additional evidence of contact across the width of the Western District Plains. Weeratt Kuyuut, 'chief' of the Spring Creek tribe and a messenger for his people, told Dawson that in his travels towards Geelong he had heard of Buckley 'as a chief who had "died and jumped up whitefellow" . . .'. Moreover, as messenger he had travelled unmolested over all the country between the Grampian ranges and the sea and between the rivers Leigh and Wannon.[28]

The contact for trading purposes seems to have been wider than that for social occasions. According to Dawson, Aborigines came together from distant places—the Wimmera, Geelong, Lake Boloke, Cape Otway and the coastal areas—to trade at Mt Noorat. He does not say that Aborigines from all these areas attended the meeting but the Geelong Aborigines certainly attended, bringing with them 'the best stones for making axes, and a kind of wattle gum celebrated for its adhesiveness'.[29]

Surveyor Tyers in the report of his survey of the District completed in early 1840 included a list of native names of hills, rivers and other features. His survey map on which some of the Aboriginal names are recorded reveals how, even as early as 1840, Europeans remade the District, replacing Aboriginal names with European ones. But it was official policy to use Aboriginal names and the result is that a large number of Aboriginal place names have survived and are still in current

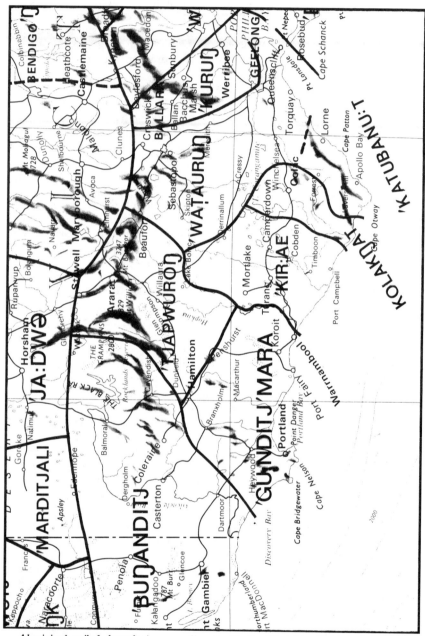

Aboriginal tribal boundaries according to N. B. Tindale's Aboriginal Tribes of Australia

use. Sometimes Europeans simply adopted the Aboriginal name for a locality, for example, Noorat, Keilambete, Terang, Urang Aranga. At other times an Aboriginal name was mistakenly accepted. Warrnambool, for example, was the Aboriginal name for Mt Warrnambool. At the time Robinson visited the District there was also an individual named War.nam.bul whose 'country' was near Mt Warrnambool. It seems likely that an early settler met a member of the Warrnambool conedeet near the mouth of the Hopkins or Merri and asked the name of the place. The Aborigine, knowing little English, may have thought he was being asked where he came from, where he belonged, or even his name. For whatever reason, the reply was War.nam.bul and this became the name of the new settlement. Later, local Aborigines gave their word for the locality that became Warrnambool to the manager of the Framlingham Aboriginal Station, William Goodall Jun. It was 'Wheringkernitch'.[30]

The area was not, as Major Mitchell described it, 'a fair blank sheet'.[31] All of it was intimately known and named: each marsh, waterhole, hill, mountain, lake and fall had a name. Each river which flowed all year round had a name which covered its whole length. For example, Taylor's River, also known as Mount Emu Creek, was called 'Tarnpirr'. But also 'every local reach' in these rivers had a distinguishing name. Even a clump of tea-tree scrub had its own name so that it could be precisely referred to.

European settlers were intent on establishing their own boundaries: the physical limits of their runs, their status in the new society being created, their relationship with local Aborigines. But over the years they were to be at times uncomfortably jolted into awareness of another set of boundaries, powerfully in place across the District. First to provide accounts of such experiences were those who hunted for evidence of what happened to Joseph Tice Gellibrand and George Brooks Legrew Hesse. These men went missing in the area west of Geelong in February 1837. After two unsuccessful attempts to find them, Joseph Beazley Naylor and Charles Octavius Parsons arrived from Van Diemen's Land to make a third attempt. The search party was joined by Aborigines to the west of Geelong and they accompanied the party to the margin of Lake Colac. On the other side of the lake they saw another group of Aborigines who appeared hostile. While the Europeans retreated from the lake, the Aborigines remained. An encounter took place and the Aborigines returned, claiming they had killed two Aborigines of the 'hostile' tribe. They brought with them proof of their success, a human leg, 'a trophy of the death of the two white men having been avenged'.[32] Hugh Murray, at whose tent on the Barwon River the Aborigines stayed on their return, discovered that the Barrabool Aborigines had killed an old man and a child of the 'Colac tribe'. They 'brought with them, on the end of their spears, portion of the man and child they had killed, which I saw them eat with great exultation during the evening'.[33]

KADNOOK

KOUT NARIN   KOOLOMURT
          MOOREE

KONONG
WOOTONG

*Koonong
Wootong
Ck*

Koroite R.

TAHARA

Arrandoovong Ck

Byaduk   PURDEET
                    KOLOR   NAREF
                                  NAREI

WEERANGOURT   CARAMUT

· Drik-drik   Caramut

EUMERALLA   KANGATONG   MINJAH

                                      QUAMBY

Tyrendarra ·   *Bullanbul C*

                                      Merri R.

YAMBUCK

          Yambuk   *Yangery Ck*

          URANG   *L. Koroit*
          ARANGA

                    L. Yambuk
                                      Warrnambool

·Adelaide

                    Albury

                              B A S S

MAP AREA   · Melbourne

Surviving Aboriginal place names based on late nineteenth-century sources

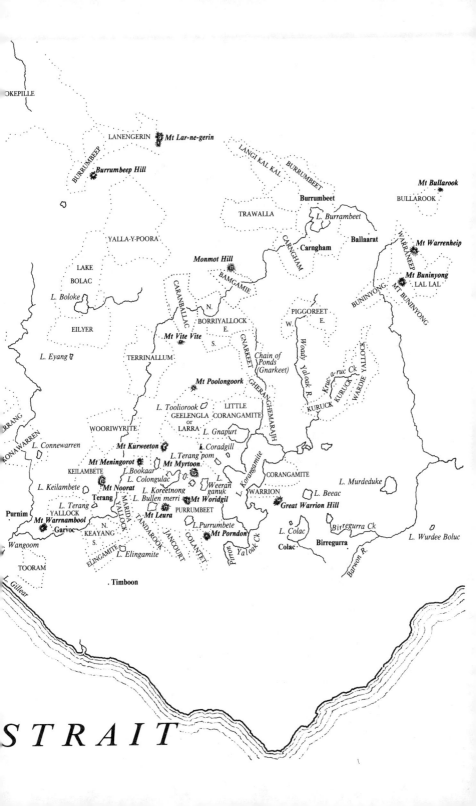

In July 1838 another party led by Alexander McGeary of Van Diemen's Land searched for Gellibrand and Hesse. Again Aborigines were involved. McGeary placed two Aborigines on watch with muskets and was lucky to survive.

> About the 13th of August at night I was watching the cart. The party were all asleep. A native rose from the fire, he walked towards me, he struck me with his leanguil on the jaw. It was a dreadful blow, knocked several of my teeth out. I had another blow under the temple. I fell dead, I made no noise, the party was not alarmed.
>
> I had two natives with me on the watch, they were armed with muskets. On my recovering, which I suppose must have been a considerable time, one of the natives told me in his own language that he had killed the native who was going to murder me. The other native also said he fired. They appeared quite overjoyed that my life was safe. The native who was shot was a stranger. The other natives cut him open, took the kidneys out and roasted them and ate them, rubbing themselves all over with the fat.[34]

The existence of the European mission station, the Protectorate camps and the later station, and the Chief Protector's use of Aboriginal guides on his 1841 journey were all forces attracting Aborigines and encouraging them to disregard their boundaries. But the boundaries were still there and acted upon even if there was greater danger than previously in keeping to custom. Eurodap, Robinson's Jarcourt guide who had accompanied him across the District from Camperdown to the Wannon, was killed while at George Winter's run by Pongnorer, a Wanedeet conedeet. The Jarcourt (Dantgurt) tribe whose country was around Camperdown bided its time and planned revenge on the distant enemy. In early 1844 they killed a Port Fairy Aboriginal boy as he returned home through their country. Some of the Jarcourt also visited the Wanedeet conedeet and remained with them till they discovered who the murderer was, and by some unknown means obtained a lock of his hair. This was wound around three small sticks about three inches long and carefully preserved, being placed as near to fire as possible whenever they stopped and made a fire. The idea was that as the hair became hot, the head of the murderer would also become hot and he would become ill. On returning to their country, they sent the hair on the sticks to their neighbours, the Colijon Aborigines, who took them to the 'Boonworong Tribe' of the Western Port District. There the Boonworong were to put the hair in a certain mud flat. As the hair in the mud rotted the murderer also would begin to rot and perish.[35]

In this case the Aboriginal guide travelled half-way across the District, yet those revenging his murder conveyed the hair from the murderer right across the District. This was proof not only of Aboriginal attitudes to strangers, and the strength of the custom of revenge killing, but of links of friendship or obligation that could be depended on over quite long distances.

Just as the physical nature of the land and its climate shaped the Aboriginal use of the environment and its possible use by Europeans, the social structure of Aboriginal society based upon an intimate relationship with a designated part of the land shaped the Aboriginal response to the new arrivals. It determined the small size of the Aboriginal groups which confronted European squatters and their men and ensured that Aborigines did not move away to some more distant area as Europeans occupied their 'country'.

It also influenced the way Aborigines reacted to those of their own race, for this great movement of people and animals, the second wave of human occupation of the District, was not simply the encroachment of one race on the territory of another. As Europeans with their horses, sheep and cattle passed by, Aborigines noted that people of their own race—strangers—accompanied the newcomers. Unlike the Europeans, they knew of their boundary infringements and the consequent penalties—as the Rev. Orton discovered. Aborigines whom he asked to accompany him westward from Geelong in search of a suitable site for a Methodist Mission to the Aborigines expressed their unease that they might be taken amongst 'wild blackfellows': 'One of them whom I had selected to attend upon myself beg^d me to protect him from them— saying if wild blackfellow come you say me very good black fellow you no let him kill me—you shoot him'. When Orton appeared to make light of this request and the fear behind it, the Aborigine 'vehemently exclaimed them very bad—plenty steal plenty kill'. As an explanation Orton noted in his journal, 'The tribes have very little connection with one another'.[36] Individuals of different 'tribes' were to do so, however, in the changed circumstances and the result was usually death for the intruder. This was the fate of another Port Fairy boy, one of two sent to Melbourne in 1847 for stealing at Squattlesea Mere. Jemmy, found guilty, was imprisoned for two weeks, while Tommy, found not guilty, was discharged. For a time they stayed with Assistant Protector Thomas and attended the Yarra Aboriginal Mission, Merri Creek. When one of them went missing, Thomas questioned local Aborigines. Eventually one told him, 'my blackfellows kill em [boy] sit down school no good long way black fellow that . . .'.[37]

4

'when the white people come the water goes away'

IN LATE 1841, just past Yambuk, James Ritchie paused on his journey to enjoy 'the soul satisfying view'. Stretching before him was a 'clear flowry country', a place of 'broad rivers' fanned by breezes from the sea. Even the dried lake beds were covered with an 'extraordinary luxuriance of fine grass'. The nearby river was alive with 'flocks of water fowls, swans, ducks'. Yet the scene caused a shiver of fear for he had no doubt that the 'natives' prized the land. 'Here is their cradle and their grave', he wrote, 'from the water and the land they could live a life of endless luxury'. Alone and on foot, he imagined that unseen, they were 'whetting their spears to drink his blood'.[1]

Major Mitchell saw the District in the spring of 1836. At that time, 'returning over flowering plains and green hills, fanned by the breezes of early spring', he named the region '"Australia Felix" to distinguish it from the parched deserts of the interior country . . .'.[2] First impressions were of a land of plenty, but even here in an environment favoured by Nature the effect of European settlement on the indigenous population was not cushioned by the abundance of nature.

Blessed by a temperate climate of cool winters and warm to hot summers, the region has a rainfall which varies from less than 600 mm on the central plains to over 1400 mm on the Otway Ranges to the south and the highlands to the north. The rainfall occurs mainly in the autumn and winter with the result that rivers often flood in winter and become a series of waterholes in summer. The region appears a well-watered one with a network of rivers, creeks, swamps and marshes dividing the plains, but water becomes scarce in summer and drought is a serious problem for those dependent on surface water.

'Plenty water for a long time, but when the white people come the water goes away.' 'The natives say it is the white people coming that drives away the water', wrote Katherine Kirkland. She noted in 1838 on her way inland to Trawalla from Corio Bay that Lake Burrumbeet, an immense salt lake, was drying up and that many lakes, both fresh and salt, had recently dried up.[3] For the three years that followed Lakes Burrumbeet and Learmonth were dry, the Moorabool River did not run and the Leigh and Barwon rivers ran only 'for a few weeks and then not more than a knee deep'.[4] Even the relatively well-watered coastline just west of Port Fairy was showing signs of drought as James Ritchie, who later took up the Blackwood run near Penshurst, discovered when he stayed overnight at John Ritchie's property, Urang Aranga. There he saw 'marshes of various dimensions from 10 acres to 300 acres', noting that the high, dry banks of the marshes indicated that they were drying up.[5]

In the north, Fiery Creek, so named because the bed of the creek smoked in the heat as if on fire, was dry for twenty miles. Thomas Chirnside, who established himself on a pastoral run at Mt William, noted a flock of sheep feeding in the middle of Lake Bolac. Lakes Repose and Linlithgow, named by Mitchell, had disappeared and the lower part of Mt Emu Creek was dry for many miles.[6]

On the northern plains between the upper reaches of the Hopkins River and Mt Elephant to the south-east, Aborigines told Europeans the same story. Ritchie, travelling through this area on his way back to Melbourne, was warned by settlers of hundreds of Aborigines who 'commonly frequented' two lakes that lay ahead in his path. The lakes, however, were nearly dry, something which had not occurred before 'in the remembrance of the oldest natives'. 'There are hundreds of dry lakes in this and almost every other part of the country', wrote Ritchie.[7]

Even two years earlier, in 1839, William Russell had decided that lack of water was the region's greatest drawback. After travelling with George Russell from the Clyde Company station on the Leigh River westward to Camperdown, north to Mt Buninyong and back to Geelong, he wrote, 'You hear of rivers at home, but there were only two that I saw in all my rounds . . . which deserved that name; the others are merely chains of waterpools, with not more water running into them than in an ordinary ditch at home'.[8]

Even during winter, conditions varied across the District as George Augustus Robinson noted in 1841 when the drought was well established. Travelling between March and August from Melbourne to Portland and back by a northern route, he commented on the lifestyle of Aborigines. At Tower Hill where the vegetation was an open forest of stunted banksia, gum and tea tree scrub running down to sandhills along the coast, he observed a native village. The men he met there were 'large, several above 6 feet and very stout . . . They were muscular and large men'. Food was readily available. There was a marsh which provided their 'chief support, roots etc.' while an abundance of 'cinerated shells' at their camping place was evidence of their exploitation of the shellfish from the nearby coast with its offshore reef.[9]

In a swamp area close to Mt Napier, Robinson saw evidence that Aborigines had hunted possum and caught grubs. He saw turkey, parrots, crows and other birds, all of which were eaten by Aborigines; and saw women and children collecting murnong—the root crop like a parsnip with a yellow buttercup flower—the plant most frequently mentioned in early documents as a staple Aboriginal food. Aborigines, according to Dawson, washed the tubers and put them into rush baskets made especially for the purpose, and then placed them in an earth oven to cook overnight. The women and children were also collecting grubs. 'The great swamp', wrote Robinson, abounded 'in rushes the roots of which are edible and afford the Aborigines an ample supply'. The rushes according to Beth Gott, an ethno-botanist, were Cumbungi (*Typha* species) which have underground rhizomes of a potato-like texture and flavour and are very rich in starch. There was also another root obtained from the swamp called tar.roke by the Aborigines. Around the swamp the land was lightly timbered and the Aborigines appeared healthy.[10]

Yet on the plains in the north, three miles south of Kirk's station, Robinson met Aborigines whose state 'was deplorable . . . a few branches of banksia was all they had to screen the wind and several *pundarerer*, bonnet or head covering of rushes, that lay on the banksia too plainly indicated the state of destitution to which these people are subject'. It was winter, mid-July, but this part of the Hopkins was dry except for large waterholes at Kirk's home station and an 'occasional water hole or 2 at long intervals'. Apart from a 'few stunted banksia' the plains were 'bare of timber'. Kangaroos and opossum were absent. The Aborigines, Robinson commented, had 'no animals to afford them covering'. Since there was little to shelter them in this area of 'few herbs and short grass thinly scattered', he thought their head coverings of rushes, which served as both cap and jacket, were an excellent 'invention'.[11]

The effect of approaching summer can be seen in the diary of James Ritchie who travelled across the District during November and December 1841, several months later than Robinson. Setting out from the Clyde Company establishment on the Leigh River to the north-west of Geelong, he travelled twenty miles on the first day's march across the 'arid plains' that stretched ahead to the west, coming across only one watering place. He had passed Mt Elephant before he commented that the country was 'much improved'. He was still further on at Whitehead's station, west of the Hopkins, before he noted, 'the feed was quite green, a striking contrast to the parched plains we have so recently crossed'. Yet

Robinson's sketch of an Aborigine wearing a head covering of rushes which served as both cap and jacket: a sign, he believed, of the 'complete destitution' of the Aborigines of the 'bleak plains' south of Mt Cole

he was passing through the middle of the District rather than the drier plain to the north. The Hopkins River, a series of waterholes when Robinson reached it in April 1841, was again a series of waterholes, 'the largest lakes I had seen . . .'. Summer, the dry season in this region, had not yet begun.[12]

Early settlers saw signs of the way the Aborigines lived in this environment and some can still be seen today—midden sites scattered along the coastline, the mounds found across the District and the extensive system of fish traps exposed on the bed of Lake Condah (now drained) and a further system recently discovered at Lake Gorrie. What they reveal is the extent to which the Aborigines were dependent on the rivers and marshes, particularly in the winter months.

Weirs across rivers and fish traps were common. Foster Fyans and his party on his first journey across the District enjoyed two meals of fish courtesy of the Aborigines when they discovered 'a native fishery'.[13] Thomas Learmonth and five others exploring the land west of Geelong in September 1837 reported finding 'a fishing weir of the natives'.[14] Charles Browning Hall, of La Rose and Mokepilly, discovered that fish weirs were 'numerous' in the Grampians. He wrote, 'we found many low sod banks extending across the shallow branches of the river, with apertures at intervals, in which were placed long, narrow, circular nets (like a large stocking) made of rush-work'.[15]

Robinson saw many such sites. Crossing a creek connected to the Hopkins, not far from the Woolshed (present-day Hexham), he observed a large weir at least 100 yards in length which the natives said was 'for catching eels when the big water came and was called by them Yere.roc'. A little further on at the fording place at Bolden's on the Merri River he saw the remains of an old stone weir which had been destroyed. At the falls on the Moyne River, about five miles from the store at Port Fairy, Robinson visited a lagoon. Round the bank he counted six places where the Aborigines had erected structures for fishing. He also saw a weir across the river for catching eels. At nearby Tarrone he saw a large weir for catching eels which measured '200 ft; 5 ft high. It was turned back at each end and two or three holes in the middle was [were] left for placing the eel pots as also one at each end'. The arrabine or eel pot was made of bark or plaited rushes with a 'willow round mouth' and had a small end to prevent the eels from easily getting away. The fishing, Robinson was told, was carried on in the rainy season.[16]

Most spectacular of all such structures was the extensive system of channels seen at the foot of Mt William. At the 'confluence of a creek with a marsh' Robinson discovered an 'immense piece of ground trenched and banked' for the purpose of catching eels. The system covered at least 15 acres. 'These trenches are hundreds of yards in length. I measured at one place in one continuous triple line for the distance of 500 yards. These courses led to other ramified and extensive trenches of a most torturous kind.' The result was impressive. Robinson said that the system resembled the work of civilized man while VDL Jack exclaimed in his own language 'Oh dear look at that. Black fellow never tired'. At intervals in the channels which at times wound round, at other times ran parallel and at still others went at angles, small apertures were left and in these were placed the eel pots. The gaps were supported by pieces of bark and sticks. 'In single measurement there must have been thousands of yards of this trenching and banking', wrote Robinson. 'The whole of the water from the mountain rivulet is made to pass through this trenching ere it reaches the marsh: it is hardly possible for a single fish to escape'.[17]

Another similar site not seen by Robinson has been discovered further west at Toolondo. The archaeologist, Harry Lourandos, has argued that

Robinson's sketch of the back of a yereroc or weir showing that the structure has been carefully erected to last: the holes in which eel pots were placed are to be seen across the base of the weir. The weir and eel pot below were sketched by Robinson at Tarrone, 30 April 1841.

The arrabine or eel pot was made of 'bark or plaited rushes . . . having a small end to prevent the eel from rapidly getting away'. Those fishing stood behind the weir and near the small end of the eel pot. As each eel was caught, it was bitten on the head and put on a stick with a knob on one end (lingeer).

both sites were more than 'devices for harvesting eels'. They 'operated as a form of swamp management, coping with excess water during floods and retaining water in times of drought'. In this way, by controlling the water supply, the Aborigines regulated and may even have increased the local eel population. They were, he concluded, if not 'eel "farms", at least managed eel habitats'.[18]

In size and impressiveness the Mt William site must equal the extensive system of channels and fish traps on the bed of Lake Condah studied by the Victoria Archaelogical Survey.[19] At Lake Condah basalt available in the area was used to contrive a complex system of traps, some having wing walls to direct fish into the channels. The channels were formed at various levels on the bottom of the lake so that as the water level in the lake rose some systems drowned and others became operational. When flood waters receded, large pools of water were left in which fish, particularly eels, were trapped.

Mounds are another distinctive feature of this District. Compared with eastern Victoria where no mounds are found and central Victoria, where only small mounds used primarly as ovens are found, the western region is distinguished by the number and size of its mounds. These areas of raised earth are sometimes found singly and at other times in clusters. From recent archaeological work in the Caramut area Elizabeth Williams found that large clusters of mounds (more than six) were restricted to those areas of high ground with good vantage, which were bounded by creeks on two sides and often by a swamp on the third. Many have been destroyed by ploughing but a large number have been recorded by the Victoria Archaeological Survey.[20]

There has been discussion about their function but according to Dawson these mounds 'were the sites of large, permanent habitations, which formed homes for many generations', the size of the mound growing over time through an accumulation of debris from 'the domestic hearth', decomposition of building materials and the destructive effects of frequent brush fires.[21] Varying from circular to oval, and from about 0.3 to 1.5 metres high, they are generally to be found on ground adjacent to rivers, swamps and other areas of wetlands.[22]

Aboriginal comment to Robinson supports Dawson's conclusion regarding the use of mounds. After crossing the River Hopkins near Hexham, Robinson and his party saw mounds, apparently for the first time:

> At two miles from the Woolshed . . . we saw a large mound of at least 4 feet high and 10 feet long and 5 wide. My native companions said it was a black man's house, a large one like white man's house. There were pieces of sticks among the earth, about 3 inches diameter, and it appeared that the whole had been burnt down. A short distance from this, about 200 yards, was the remains of another hut of similar description.[23]

Archaeologists believe that mounds were used for a variety of functions. They were used as ovens, as both ovens and camping areas, and as foundations for substantial huts. Robinson saw mounds which he had no hesitation in referring to as oven mounds. South of Mt William and associated with the large area (15 acres) of embankments and trenches for catching eels previously referred to, Robinson found at least 'a dozen' large ovens or mounds. 'They were the largest I have seen: the one I measured was 31 yards long, 2 yards high and 19 yards broad. They roast their food in these ovens.' Such large cooking places suggest that this was the place of great meetings in which large numbers of Aborigines took part.[24]

Peter Coutts and Harry Lourandos, both archaeologists, have argued that mounds were associated with wetland sites. To use Coutts's term, the mounds made 'house platforms', providing well-drained areas which could be occupied at any time of the year. Williams, however, on the basis of her recent archaeological work, has argued that mounds are more an adaptation to the circumstances of the District in general. She concluded that in this region all soils (whether on high or low ground), except for sandy deposits, become waterlogged for a number of months every year; a factor brought about by the 'high percentage of clay in the soils derived from the basalt'. Mounds thus made possible a 'more intensive settlement of the region' because 'settlements need no longer be restricted to the well-drained lunettes'.

Mounds so far have not been dated earlier than 2500 BP (before the present). They are therefore a comparatively recent phenomenon. Williams explains them as an adaptation to a changing climate which became wetter about 2000 years ago but points out that the change 'was not a simple function of environmental factors' as 'mounds did not appear at a time of even higher lake levels during the early Holocene'. The archaeological record shows a large increase in the number of occupied sites about the same time as mounds first appear. Both these changes are explained by the archaeologists as the result of social factors. They indicate a change in the social organization of the people of the District: from living as scattered hunter-gatherers to a semi-sedentary lifestyle characterized by more social interaction between groups and large, intergroup ceremonial meetings for celebration, discussion and exchange of goods. As part of the new social organization, labour was invested in the erection and maintenance of elaborate systems of fish traps and acres of earthworks, for only with increased production could the larger numbers coming together for a period of time be fed.[25]

First settlers also saw substantial housing with a number of huts sometimes grouped together. These huts appear larger than those found in the stone house sites discovered by the Victoria Archaeological Survey in the Lake Condah and surrounding area—though the most recently discovered sites at Lake Gorrie are of great interest, for their larger diameter suggests buildings more like those described in the historical records. There is considerable evidence of solidly constructed huts, including sketches by George French Angas, Mitchell, Robinson and a correspondent of William Thomas. Henry Fyshe Gisborne in his report of his journey across the District in late 1839 stated that 'the natives . . . build . . . much more substantial huts than those used by the Northern tribes'.[26] These huts were seen in the area from Terang west to the Wannon.

At the swamp near Mt Napier Robinson counted thirteen large huts built in the form of a cupola. Far from giving the makeshift appearance of a mia-mia, they looked from the distance like large mounds of earth. He wrote, 'They are built of large sticks closely packed together and covered with turf, grass side inwards. There are several variations. Those like a cupola are sometimes double and have two entrances; others again are like a niech'. In the same general area Robinson saw 'a fine large double hut, 10 feet diameter with two entrances and 4 ft high in centre'. Robinson walked through this hut. 'I went in at one door', he wrote, 'and came out of the second'.[27] In another description of the same site, he commented, 'one hut measured 10 feet diameter by five feet high, and sufficiently strong for a man on horseback to ride over'.[28]

E. R. Trangmar in *The Aborigines of Far Western Victoria*, published about 1960, quoted this passage but was far from correct in the conclusion he drew, 'It is the only instance ever recorded of a dwelling better than a mia-mia, wurley or gunyah, in the whole of this area'.[29]

Still in the great swamp area south of Mt Napier, the territory of the Tappoc conedeet, Robinson passed '20 well built worns or native huts. Some were placed near the river, others on aclivity of the hills and some on the top of an eminence'. He sketched one that had been erected on a mound of earth. At Mt Sturgeon Robinson saw and sketched a substantial hut. At the Protectorate camp at Lake Keilambete he noted in April 1841 that the Aborigines had covered their huts with turf to keep the rain out. A little later in the same month, he passed a deserted Elengermat camp of nine huts: 'each hut was large enough to contain seven or eight persons (adults)'. The huts 'were made in the form of a cupola with bark and sods over them with a doorway'.[30] During early 1842 he visited a camp site of the Nillan conedeet at a swamp near Mt Eeles—possibly the Lake Gorrie site discovered during 1989 by Robert Young and Andrew Carmichael. Robinson commented that 'they had a sort of village, and some of their habitations were of stone'.[31]

West of the Grampians and north of Harrow, Granville Chetwynd Stapylton, Major Mitchell's second-in-command, came across 'several Guneaks of very large dimensions'. One of these, 'capable of containing at least 40 persons' and 'of very superior construction', was so impressive that he believed that William Buckley must have been involved in their building.[32]

Charles Griffith also saw substantial huts and emphasized how different they were from the flimsy shelters built by Aborigines in the eastern part of the Port Phillip District. He entered one 'fully fifteen feet long, and high enough for a man to stand upright in'. Inside he found ten to twelve Aborigines squatting round a fire on the floor.[33]

James Dawson arrived in the District too late to see such huts but his Aboriginal informants told him that each family had a permanent dwelling or 'wuurn'

> ... made of strong limbs of trees stuck up in dome-shape, high enough to allow a tall man to stand upright underneath them. Small limbs fill up the intermediate spaces, and these are covered with sheets of bark, thatch, sods, and earth till the roof and sides are proof against wind and rain. The doorway is low and generally faces the morning sun or a sheltering rock. The family wuurn is sufficiently large to accommodate a dozen or more persons ...

These dwellings were large enough to be partitioned as the family grew up: one part was used by the parents and children, one by unmarried women and widows, and one by the bachelors and widowers.[34] Similar permanent housing was built in the Lake Condah area. Dawson confirmed this by corresponding with Job Francis at the Lake Condah Aboriginal Station. Francis reported that the Aborigines told him that they used to live in large mia-mias, sometimes thirty or even forty in one mia-mia. These were better built than those built in 1868: they kept out the rain.[35] While timber was the usual building material, in some areas where it was easier to obtain stone than wood and bark, the walls of wuurns were built of stones, the roof consisting of limbs and thatch.[36]

Thus sightings and enquiry corroborated each other. It was customary for Aborigines to build substantial permanent huts which were often to be found grouped together: the Aboriginal community was far more sedentary at one season of the year than has been commonly accepted. They were 'complex hunter-gatherers', a term used by archaeologists to describe hunter-gathering groups who 'live in sizeable settlements which are often termed 'villages'; construct large, durable structures; and manipulate the environment in ways that alter the availability or abundance of resources'.[37] But by the time of the sitting of the 1858-59 Select Committee of the Legislative Council on the Aborigines, those who provided written evidence on the nature of Aboriginal housing were almost unanimous that the Aborigines only built temporary shelters. The Aborigines lived in mia-mias: 'miserable mi-mis' according to one correspondent. 'Temporary, being primitive and scattered', another responded.[38]

Still later, before Dawson's book was published, R. B. Smyth collected information for *The Aborigines of Victoria* published in 1878. By this time the nomadism of the Aborigines was fully established. 'It is necessary for a tribe to move very frequently from place to place', he wrote. Their shelters were flimsy: 'Each little miam is built partly of bark and partly of boughs, or wholly of bark or wholly of boughs, according to the state of weather or the whim of the builder'. The only mention of substantial huts was in a footnote where he stated, first, that Assistant Protector Thomas believed that in some parts of the colony of Victoria, particularly the Western District, the Aborigines in the past had built substantial huts; and, second, that an unnamed squatter from the Wannon district had also reported that 'the natives had comfortable huts at the time he first occupied the country'.[39]

Far from being exceptional in building such huts, the Aborigines of this region were building structures similar to those found in many parts of Australia. Robinson, for example, found substantial huts in south-west Tasmania and particularly remarked on some which had been lined with the bark of the tea-tree making them exceptionally cosy. R. B. Smyth listed the places where explorers saw them, his list including: that the explorer George Grey found them on the Hutt River in Western Australia as well as on the road to Water Peak and on his way to Hanover

Bay; François Péron saw similar dwelling places at Cape Lesueur, Sharks Bay, Western Australia; Ernest Giles reported seeing substantial huts during his travels in central Australia; Sir Thomas Mitchell described some he saw while tracing the course of the Gwydir, and others were found within sight of the Nundawar Range and still others on the Lower Darling; Charles Sturt during his 1828–29 expedition found a group of seventy large huts on the banks of the Macquarie River.[40]

In this District permanent housing was built near water enabling easy access to a plentiful supply of fish including eel—a favourite food—and to roots such as those of the Cumbungi found in swampy areas. The substantial huts were basically winter residences providing protection against 'wind and rain'. They could be contrasted with temporary habitations which 'are also dome-shaped, and are made of limbs, bark of gum trees, and grass, scarcely rain-proof, and are smaller, opener, and more carelessly erected . . . They are only used in summer or for shelter while travelling, and have a large open side, with the fire in front'.[41]

Aborigines ceased to build substantial huts and assemble in villages shortly after the arrival of Europeans. Dawson gave no explanation for this but Smyth, whose two-volume account of *The Aborigines of Victoria* was published about the same time as Dawson's book, suggested that 'The inducements to plunder, their fear of the invaders, the depression caused by the appearance of a race possessing appliances so much superior . . . and the impossibility of preserving inviolate the lands which their people had held for ages, caused them to wander aimlessly from place to place . . .'.[42] The answer is much simpler. As the first settlers occupied the best-watered sites, the Aborigines were denied access to the places where such huts were built.

In taking up runs the Europeans were influenced by several things. First there was ease of access. In the early years the Hentys stayed close to the coast at Portland and the settlers who arrived at Corio Bay stayed within reasonable travelling distance of Geelong. In August 1837 an exploring party rejected the idea of occupying the area around Lake Burrumbeet on the grounds that the water of the lake was brackish and the area was too far distant. The link with the coast was important as stock came from Van Diemen's Land by sea as did supplies. The accounts of the Clyde Company provide ample evidence of the importance of the link.[43]

But next in importance was good pasture and ample water for sheep and cattle needed both. Land clear of vegetation was also favoured. Luckily for the squatters one of the advantages of the District for agricultural purposes was that many parts were immediately ready for stocking 'without an outlay for grubbing a tree'.[44]

James Ritchie, travelling across the District with a party of settlers and 200 to 300 head of cattle in 1841, appraised the places he saw for their suitability as a run. As this was early in the settlement of the District he was in fact visiting the sites that Europeans had decided were superior for their purposes which seemed to be mainly the running of sheep, though Ritchie noted that a number of stations also had a herd of cattle. The proportion of the two is indicated in the following: Clyde Company, 'about 10 000 sheep and a herd of cattle'; Mr Brown's station, 'about 8000 sheep and a herd of cattle'; Whitehead's station, 'about 8000 sheep and a herd of cattle'. Ritchie wrote, 'The Pentland Hills is mostly splendid sheep runs . . . the whole is almost quite clear and fine undulating fields admirably adapted for large flocks'. As he started to cross the open plains after leaving the Leigh River he noted that 'the greater part would be excellent sheep runs if water could be obtained'. On 26 November, proceeding westward from the Hopkins River, he came to Muston's sheep establishment. He had passed over 'a level country partly thinly covered with trees and partly clear; all excellent sheep land to a creek with abundance of good water'. The night of the 27th he spent at Whitehead's, on the west bank of a creek that contained many 'large water pools'. 'This', he wrote, 'is a very superior place in quantity and quality'.[45]

It was the drought combined with the European need for the best-watered sites that drew even the first European squatters to sites of great importance to local Aborigines. As they scattered across the District lured on by desire for a permanent source of water, each squatter established himself finally on a site without which it is likely local Aborigines could not survive without a fundamental change to their way of life. In some cases the effect was greater—the local Aboriginal group became extinct soon after the arrival of the Europeans.

The drama of this meeting can be re-created from surviving records. A fascinating study of contact and of water as a frontier occurs in the case of the Ome.gar.rer.er, a group of Aborigines already extinct when Robinson travelled across their land in 1841. Contact between the Ome.gar.rer.er and Europeans had certainly occurred before Europeans settled on their land. When Nicholas McCann first met them, probably in early 1840, one of the Aborigines mentioned Geelong, spoke some broken English and volunteered the information that a great number of men had travelled to Geelong with Bulganna and Wheelbarrow (Bullock Drays). McCann, however, entered their territory looking for a pastoral run for two Englishmen, Henry Loughnan and Lewis Lynch. McCann found a perfect site, 40 miles north-east of Port Fairy on Muston's Creek, five miles south of Robert Whitehead, but he soon realized that 'this rich spot was the abundant fishing and favourite ground' of Aborigines. 'We could . . . see by the great number of bridges along the large waterholes and the large number of woven fences erected across the shallow portions of the Creek, for the purpose of erecting their nets, that the natives were numerous.'

For about a month McCann and his small party (only four people) saw the smoke from Aboriginal fires but had no contact with Aborigines. Then one morning between fifty and one hundred Aborigines paid a visit. They asked for sugar but came with their own provisions: 'when the lubras turned out their baskets we found they had a fair supply of provisions with them—Possum, Kangaroos, Bandicoot and a number of Snakes'. The Aborigines collected stones, made fire places for cooking and prepared to stay for the night. They slept around their fires just outside the hut McCann had built, covering themselves with their 'possum or kangaroo skin rug'. After breakfast McCann asked them to leave, and from then on hostility was evident. On one occasion a spear landed near McCann who managed to frighten the Aborigines and retreat to his hut. At this stage the Aborigines attacked Whitehead's station 'where the overseer was speared through the throat and the bullock driver left for dead'. The Aboriginal tactics took effect. Loughnan temporarily decided to no longer live on the station and Lynch went down to Port Fairy. McCann believed there was no alternative to 'shooting the Blacks indiscriminately' so he resigned his position and took a wool clip to Geelong, arriving there on 4 May 1841. McCann's son said that after this Loughnan 'tried to carry on but finally had to give up, as the natives continually drove off his sheep'.[46]

In March 1841 Robinson began his journey across the District. In early May he arrived at Loughnan's station where he met a shepherd who gave the party directions on how to find Whitehead's. The local Aboriginal guides accompanying Robinson informed him that Loughnan's station 'was the country of the Ome.be.gare.rege Conedeet, now extinct'!

At Whitehead's, according to Robinson nine miles north of Loughnan's station, Whitehead was absent and Sutton was in charge. Sutton told the Chief Protector that they had only been troubled by Aborigines once, about a month previously, when they took two sheep and at the same time attempted to rob the hut. Guns had been fired and the Aborigines ran away. He said there were a large number of huts on the river when they first came and that Assistant Protector Sievwright had told them they were foolish to settle where the natives were numerous. Sutton volunteered the information that the Aborigines had not long since taken a gun and blankets from a watchbox belonging to Loughnan. McCann's account had included mention of the same incident; but Sutton made no mention of the Aborigines spearing Whitehead's overseer through the throat and the bullock driver being left for dead which McCann mentioned. With a Chief Protector in the vicinity it was probably wise to have had little trouble with the Aborigines.[47]

In December 1841 James Ritchie with a party of settlers and cattle arrived at Whitehead's, searching for a place to graze their cattle.[48] When he and his party enquired about the station to the south which they had heard had been lately deserted, they were told 'it was a dense scrub unfit for anything'. Instead it turned out to be 'one of the choicest runs in the country', 'abundantly watered', and having 'fine nutritious feed'. The party's search was over and there was no opposition to be encountered this time. The splendid site so attractive to the Aborigines, and for much the same reason attractive to the Europeans, was now firmly in European hands. The second occupants of the station site, in possession as early as December 1841, would have had no unwelcome visitors. Ritchie made no mention of seeing huts, or of signs of fishing in the creek. Years later Aborigines still remembered the fate of the people at Greenhill Station (Loughnan and Lynch's station). In the late 1870s William Goodall, the manager of the Framlingham Aboriginal Station, collecting Aboriginal names for local places asked Aborigines for their name for Greenhill home station. They simply said 'Gnegne' (no good).[49]

It was access to water which was important to both Aborigines and Europeans and, as in this case, the Aborigines might dispute the Europeans' presence, but even if one group of Europeans was forced to abandon the site, another would arrive. The struggle could go on with Aborigines losing some of their number, while each new party of Europeans arrived eager to take up the land.

[marginal handwritten note: Euro's need land to win.]

In the papers of Assistant Protector William Thomas there exists a very detailed description of a village site and its destruction. This may refer to the huts mentioned by Sutton or to a nearby site. It is the site Smyth referred to in a footnote. Thomas states that Muston was the first to settle in the area—in 1839. But it was Charles Smith who settled near the Aboriginal village about 1840 or 1841.[50] Thomas wrote:

> ... by Mustons and the Scrubby Creek to the Westward there was on the first settlers arriving in that locality a regular Aboriginal Settlement ... there was on the banks of the creek between 20 and 30 huts of the form of a Beehive or sugar loaf, some of them capable of holding a dozen people, these huts were about 6 feet high or [a] little more, about 10 feet in diameter, an opening about 3 feet 6 inches high for a door, which they closed at night if they required with a sheet of bark, an apeture at the top 8 or 9 inches to let out the smoke which in wet weather they cover'd with a sod. These buildings were all made of a circular form, closely worked and then covered with mud, they would bear the weight of a man on them without injury ... In 1840 a sheep station was formed on the opposite banks of the Creek to this Aboriginal Village or town. My informant who was a well educated man ... gave me a drawing he had taken of the Village ... [see Plate between pp. 66 and 67]
>
> These blacks ... were perfectly harmless and stationary in 1841 or the end of 1840 my informant stated that the grass got bare or scarce on the side of the creek where the sheep station was, and one day the Blacks were from their village up the Creek seeking their daily fare the white people set fire to and demolished the Aboriginal Settlement and it afterwards became the Sheep

Farmers . . . what became of the blacks he would not tell but at the close of 1841 when he went again shepherding in that locality he could not trace a single hut along the whole creek.[51]

The third European to provide evidence of Aborigines living in substantial huts close to water at the time of European settlement was Samuel Winter. Referring to Aborigines of the Wannon Valley he wrote, 'Previous to 1837 they had large well constructed winter huts, which were destroyed by cattle; they never rebuilt them, but lived under breakwinds of bark and boughs'.[52]

The destruction of permanent huts brought about substantial change in the way the Aborigines lived. Moreover, it changed the way of life so quickly that even pioneer settlers saw no evidence of permanent huts and village sites. The Aborigines now appeared nomadic building only temporary shelters. Winter took up Tahara in 1837 and the huts were destroyed that same year. What remained to puzzle those who followed were simply the mounds and for a while the weirs—the surviving evidence of village sites and of large concentrations of people coming together and cooking food which must have been abundant at certain sites at particular times of the year.

The Aborigines did not rebuild their huts because they had lost their land. While each Aboriginal group disputed to a greater or lesser degree the European taking of the land, it knew when the land was lost. There was no doubt in the mind of William Thomas's informant that after the destroying of the huts at the Muston's Creek site the land became the sheep farmer's. His unwillingness to tell 'what became of the blacks' is enough to suggest that the Aborigines had in frontier language 'been taught a lesson'. Further south at Tarrone two Yowen conedeet said, 'It was their country and white men steal it'.[53] Near to Forlonge's dairy station Robinson saw several native huts. And of the dairy station itself he wrote: 'Where the dairy station is there is a fine spring, the only water on the creek. The natives, therefore, are deprived of their water. A whole village . . . have been forced away from their ancient pool'.[54] At Campbell's farm at Port Fairy, Robinson heard that 'natives told the white men . . . that they steal black men's water and are no good, for when the blackfellow came they say, be off'.[55]

The failure to rebuild huts where it may have seemed practical to do so as at Winters' station where they had been destroyed by cattle, rather than men, may be a sign of Aboriginal acceptance that the old ways were no longer possible. Each group built permanent huts on its own land. The Aborigines at Winters' may not have been able to easily move to some other site on the creek, and no doubt they were already aware that any new position would also be temporary. The Europeans who destroyed huts tended to make this clear. Niel Black at Glenormiston, for example, reported coming across a hut of 'superior style' which he

Part of a fish trap system at Lake Condah: as the water rose, it was guided by a system of stone races into holding pools. Stone walls were built across the path and into these fish traps were placed. Note the winged walls in the foreground guiding the water and fish towards the place where there would be a fish trap.

Only the foundations remain to indicate the size and position of inner walls of the Aboriginal stone huts found at Lake Condah, Allambie and, more recently, Lake Gorrie.

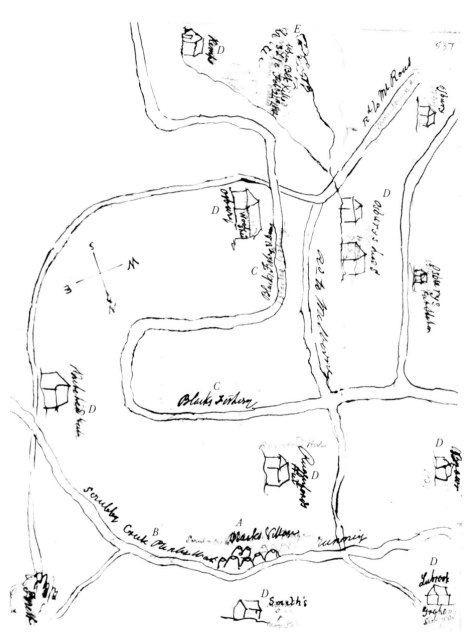

This sketch, from the William Thomas Papers, highlights the position of an Aboriginal 'village' on Scrubby Creek (A), shown as having plenty of running water (B), in relation to nearby weirs and dams used by the Aborigines (C). The attractiveness of the site to European settlers is obvious—Smith, Ruggerford, Whitehead, Osbury, Kemp, Brown, Lubrook (Loughnan?) (D). The site of the 1842 Muston Creek massacre is marked (E).

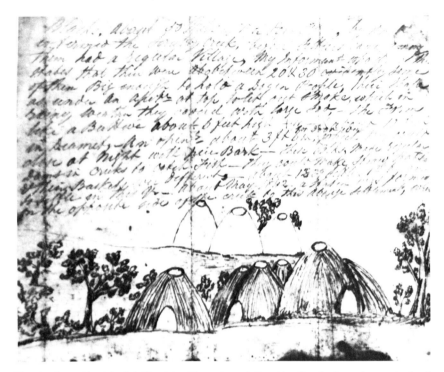

Sketch of an Aboriginal 'village' by Muston's and Scrubby Creek: from the notebook of William Thomas

Native huts, Portland Bay District, 1843, by T.W., who is known only by these initials

Woman and child at Port Fairy, 1843, by T.W. (artist unknown): the artist added the information that the woman and the rest of her tribe were in mourning for their chief who had died some weeks before. All of them had their faces 'wholly or partially bedaubed with a sort of white clay resembling chalk'.

The grave of George Watmore beside the Princes Highway, just west of Port Fairy—almost the sole reminder of the violence that accompanied European settlement

assumed to be the home of a native chief. The frame was completely covered with earth and it had 'a small hole in the south end of it to serve for both door and window'. Black ordered that the hut be destroyed and a sign was left to indicate to the Aborigines that the damage had been done by 'whites' and that 'we did not want them near us'.[56] Even at Winters' the Aborigines were aware that land had changed hands. They told newcomers to the area that they had given the land to Samuel Winter.[57]

The loss of permanent dwellings and the sites on which they were built brought rapid change to Aboriginal communities. The permanent huts were 'proof against all kinds of weather from excessive heat in summer to frost in winter'. During winter a small fire burning day and night in the centre of the floor kept the inhabitants warm. Charles Griffith found the hut he entered airtight and the fire quite efficient at heating the space. The loss of such huts must have contributed to lessening the ability of Aborigines to withstand diseases particularly as the drought eased. The winters of 1842–43 were damp and cold and Samuel Winter blamed the death of a great number of Aborigines through influenza during the colder months of 1843 on the fact that they had not rebuilt their 'large well constructed winter huts'. Whether there was such a strong link between the two is debatable but it is clear that Aborigines were far more exposed to the elements than previously and at a time of contact with a whole range of European diseases to which they had no immunity.[58]

The role of men and women was changing. According to Dawson the men shared the labour of making the permanent dwelling, but the women had to erect the temporary ones. It was the men's task to build and maintain the weirs and fish traps and to catch the eels. For both sexes the new way of living would have brought substantial adjustment.

Previously winter had been spent in the permanent camp by the rivers or marshes. Excluded from such sites, the Aborigines needed an alternative food source. They sought it at the settlers' stations, a move which brought new items of diet and access to alcohol as well as easier bargaining for the use of Aboriginal women. This process began at a different time for each Aboriginal group but it happened almost directly after a European settler occupied land in each locality for in choosing the site for a station the Europeans chose the place with a permanent water supply.

5

'and yet it is singular so few are met'

THE SIZE OF the Aboriginal population of the District was not something that troubled settlers. It was the ratio between their men and the men in the local Aboriginal group that mattered. La Trobe thought the issue important in 1841 but soon lost interest as he came to understand the situation of the settlers. Today the question is a significant one because scholars are endeavouring to establish the size of the Aboriginal population in Australia in 1788 and the relative importance of European-introduced diseases, as opposed to violence, in rapidly reducing the size of the Aboriginal population.

If the population were double or triple the size which has been generally accepted, there would be a far greater number of deaths to be accounted for. Such matters are far from being dry and abstract as the end result of the research is likely to force us to a reassessment of the colonizing process and the role of the pioneer. Answers are bound to threaten comfortable assumptions about the small Aboriginal population that was dispossessed and the amount of inter-racial violence, already claimed to be far greater than earlier historians have acknowledged. The Portland Bay District plays a central part in such discussion for it possesses the richest body of relevant primary evidence of any region of Australia (barring perhaps Van Diemen's Land).

No one knows how many Aborigines lived in Australia at the time of European settlement. Indeed it was not till 1971 that 'the first, full, official census of the Aboriginal population' was taken.[1] Before this all figures were estimates. The anthropologist, A. R. Radcliffe-Brown, arrived at the conventionally accepted figure of 300 000 (first published in the *Official Year Book* for 1930) by using estimates made by those who had pioneered the different areas of Australia, and used Foster Fyans's figure of 3000 for the Portland Bay District.

Estimates of the size of the Aboriginal population of the District at the time of European settlement have varied from 1800 to 25 000. George Augustus Robinson not only failed to collate the results of his 1841 census; he took his journals and notebooks with him when he returned to England in 1852, and there they remained until they were returned to Australia in 1948. James Dawson in the late 1870s calculated the size of the pre-contact population, using information supplied by elderly Aborigines. His novel approach was to establish a minimum size for tribes and then to find out how many tribes attended the great midsummer meetings at the large marsh, Mirraewuae, to the west of Caramut. He estimated 120 members to a tribe on the basis that when two tribes fought, each mustered thirty warriors, and for each warrior there would have been at least three members absent—the old men, women, children and invalids. Twenty-one tribes attended the mid-summer feasting at Mirraewuae: 120 multiplied by 21 gave a figure of 2520. This, he pointed out, did not include the tribes from the coast and was also thought to be too low by some of the earliest settlers.[2] The most widely accepted figure has been 3000, supplied by the Crown Lands Commissioner, Foster Fyans. But this was an estimate of the size of the population in 1845, eleven years after the first permanent European settlement.[3] By then the population had decreased from its 1839 size by 20 per cent, Robinson estimated.[4]

Comparatively recently Harry Lourandos, an archaeologist, studied Robinson's data to establish the size of the population. His estimate was a population of 8000 in 1841.[5] This was a significant figure, for it more than doubled the previously accepted figure of 3000. Lourandos claimed that 'Western district population densities', at least on the coast, equalled those 'on northern tropical coasts, traditionally assumed to constitute the most densely occupied zone'.[6]

The most recent and also the most challenging contribution to the debate on the size of the pre-1788 Aboriginal population has been Noel Butlin's *Our Original Aggression*, where he argued that the size of the population at the time of European settlement has been grossly under-rated, largely because of failure to take into account the impact of smallpox. Elsewhere in the world, he stressed, where Europeans introduced the disease into newly colonized areas with aboriginal populations the effect was a massive depopulation. Of all introduced diseases it was the 'biggest killer'; for example, a 75 per cent mortality is claimed by one authority for the Indian population of California. Combined with venereal disease, the effect was that aboriginal races virtually faded away, for 'in tandem' the diseases 'attacked the two ends of life'. 'The one killed at alarmingly high rates in exposed populations; the other . . . limited the opportunity to reproduce.' As these diseases to which Aborigines had no immunity would have spread ahead of settlement, Butlin argued that what Europeans saw was a greatly reduced population—even those who first moved inland. He suggested a population for New South Wales and Victoria of 250 000, a figure not far short of Radcliffe-Brown's estimate for the total Australian population.[7]

The work of Lourandos, Butlin and others has contributed to a review of the size of the pre-1788 population. In an important history, written to mark the bicentenary, John Mulvaney and Peter White more than doubled the commonly accepted figure for the Aboriginal population stating, 'It is . . . premature to give a definite figure for the Aboriginal population in 1788. But we consider that an estimate of about 750 000 people is a reasonable one'.[8] Already this figure is the one given in official sources.

'Frankly and explicitly speculative and hypothetical', *Our Original Aggression* deals 'not with history but with what might plausibly have been if reality was broadly consistent with a set of theoretical assumptions'. Butlin used the sophisticated techniques of population modelling, but historical information was important to his argument, being used 'to constrain the theoretical assumptions and to test the results'.[9] Butlin's argument includes detailed reference to the Portland Bay situation as he used Lourandos's research and Presland's published editions of Robinson's 1841 journals to aid his theoretical assumptions and to test his argument. Regional information thus played a significant role in his speculation about the size of the national population.

Against this background of a regional population of unknown size—but one whose estimated pre-1788 size had grown with time— from 3000 to 25 000 (Butlin's estimate), I re-examined the documentary evidence. The first priority was to establish the size of the 1841 population using Robinson's data: second, to closely examine Butlin's speculations since he postulated ideas about the size of the national population by drawing heavily on evidence from the Portland Bay District.

Certain limitations soon became apparent in Robinson's data. That he had difficulties is not suprising. Imagine his situation! He was unable to speak the Aboriginal languages spoken in the region—at least four, as well as dialects. Robinson's chief guide was VDL Jack, who also was ignorant of the languages. Robinson spent only a couple of days with each Aboriginal group he met. There was no time to learn the language, or learn from experience numbers, clan size and boundaries. Moreover, many Aborigines had a number of different names, so that names provided by informants could have been alternative names for the same people. He was given two different lists for the names of the Morper.er conedeet (the Spring Creek Aborigines). He wrote in his notebook:

> A second list of this section I took subsequent to the first and tho' most of the names are different they may notwithstanding be the same person as the natives have 2 and 3 names—it will be observed that the number of men was nearly the same.[10]

But at the end of the second list he felt it necessary to add, 'The total of women and children more than in the previous list'.[11] One is far from the certainty of the modern census!

Robinson was well aware of the difficulty of achieving his objective. He wrote, 'I am compelled to use, with all my experience, much caution and it is only by confronting several natives and repeating it [the information gained] that I can consider it correct. And notwithstanding this, I am liable to err . . .'.[12]

Despite such quibbles Robinson's achievement is important. The lists of names of members of group after group are impressive. However, lacking are the tabulated details such as provided by E. S. Parker for the North Western Protectorate District, or by William Thomas on the Aborigines of the Western Port region. There is little information on boundaries, compared with that which Robinson provided for the Tasmanian Aborigines. His information on his 'tribes' varies. Frequently he gathered from Aboriginal informants the names of all the males in a tribe, but only the numbers of wives and children. In other cases, however, he met groups of Aborigines who had gathered in response to the invitation to meet him: these Aborigines tended to be from a number of different tribes. He recorded their names, and tribal names, but there is no indication of how many absentees there might be in the same tribe.

Robinson made two lists of tribes (1842, 1845) and both were copied by clerks, perhaps many times. The original list may even have been prepared by a clerk working from Robinson's material. Whatever the explanation, the 1842 list of tribes contains seven cases where a tribe name has been repeated, one is repeated twice; there are six cases where different names are given for the same tribes. The result is that the 1842 list of 151 names is reduced to 137. Of these there are 53 for which there is no information on numbers, more than a third! Further, for some tribes only a passing reference is made to meeting with one or two of the group, rather than a listing of all members. I was unable to find information on location for nine of the tribes, with the location of another five known only in the most general terms. Localities, even when clearly stated, are vague statements, such as south-east of a place but there is no indication of how far south-east. It is important to be aware of these limitations, otherwise population figures may be accepted without giving them the necessary scrutiny. Elizabeth Williams, for example, drawing heavily from Lourandos, wrote:

> South-west Victoria is one region where we can obtain an estimate of population levels at contact. This is because Robinson, using Aboriginal inform-

ants, listed the territories of named bands, regardless of whether their members were still alive when he travelled through, or had died from disease before large-scale settlement had occurred. As well as listing bands and their territories, Robinson also counted people and noted their band affiliation.[13]

My quarrel is not with the suggestion that such estimates are possible, but with the implication that all the details are available for this to be easily done.

To state the limitations is not to deny the possibility of any conclusions. A large body of data does exist and Robinson more than anyone else—certainly more than Foster Fyans who made his estimate on the basis of twice-yearly journeys across the District—was in a position to estimate the Aboriginal population.

Robinson kept both a daily journal and books in which he kept language notes and lists of individuals in tribal groups. His meetings were an undoubted success, but the information he collected varied in detail and in his degree of certainty about its completeness. In his journal and language books there are numerous lists of names of individuals met and of the tribes to which they belonged. There are also tribal names for which no locality is given and for which he has no names of individual members. What of these and how to count them? The lack of names of individuals is not a sign that the tribe did not exist. The Colorer conedeet (Mt Rouse Aborigines), for example, are spoken of several times yet there is no list of individual names, nor even an estimate of the size of the tribe. The difficulty of frontier and its confusion, both for Robinson and the modern researcher, is apparent.

Unfortunately Robinson did not use his collected data to arrive at a population estimate. This may have been due to his finding the confusion in his records too great to deal with, or may simply have reflected his personality. He was always much keener on travelling and making notes than analysing and drawing conclusions. His resources were also stretched. He lacked enough secretarial help to handle the paperwork of the department efficiently and it was a difficult time for the Protectorate. Not long after his return from the journey through the Western District, some of the Tasmanian Aborigines whom he had brought with him to Port Phillip (including Truganini) were charged with shooting some settlers in the Western Port area. VDL Jack was one of those involved. As these were Aborigines Robinson had vouched for as civilized and Christianized, he must have felt personally under pressure. Two of the men, including VDL Jack, were hanged at Melbourne's first public execution. It was not a time conducive to calm research on field notes. Robinson was sent to the West again (March 1842) to investigate and report on an outbreak of hostilities in the area around Port Fairy, so that it was October 1842 before he forwarded the report on his 1841 journey to the Government. He included as Appendix F a list of 151

Western District Tribes. As for the population estimate, he wrote that it 'was not yet verified and some further time will be necessary to make the arrangement complete'.[14]

He never gained 'further time', or he gave up the task. The next time reference is made to numbers of Aborigines in the District is in the Annual Report for 1845. Surprisingly Robinson avoided using his own data and quoted Dr Watton, the medical officer in charge of the Mt Rouse Aboriginal station: 'The native population ... is stated by Dr. Watton ... at two thousand this is however in part conjecture'.[15] Appendix J of the 1845 Annual Report provided a second list of the Western District tribes. This time the list is shorter, 136 names compared with the 151 given earlier. These lists are the closest we have to what Robinson considered to be the tribes of the Western District of the Protectorate.

The limitations are apparent. Knowing them, can one say anything about the size of the Aboriginal population in 1841? The archaeologist, Harry Lourandos, already has. As part of his major archaeological study of the District in the late 1970s Lourandos, using Robinson's data, arrived at a figure of about 7900. My approach differs from his in the data used and the way the size of the population is calculated.

Lourandos stated that Robinson's papers in general were the source of his list of 172 District bands (Robinson's 'tribes').[16] In this chapter I have adopted Robinson's terminology for the groups he listed which he referred to as tribes. They are the same groups which Lourandos refers to as bands and which I have elsewhere referred to as clans. In contrast to Lourandos's approach, my starting point was Robinson's own lists of tribes made from the information he collected. Unfortunately, Robinson's lists were not accompanied by information on size of tribes. This information was gathered from Robinson's journals and vocabulary books (see Appendix 1).

Lourandos counted the number of local groups (his bands, Robinson's tribes) and then used various means to establish their average size. He concluded that there was an average of 40-60 individuals per band with an 'overall mean' of 43. Using N. B. Tindale's modern study of Aboriginal tribal boundaries, Lourandos then referred to the Gunditjmara tribal boundary and the area given by Tindale for its territory, 6993 square kilometres. Using the number of bands listed by Robinson which he believed belonged within Tindale's Gunditjmara tribal boundary, Lourandos multiplied the number of bands by their average size to gain a total population figure for the given area which allowed him to calculate the population density— 2.0-3.0 square kilometres per person. A similar approach was taken to an inland region and a mean arrived at for the coastal and inland figures—3.6 square kilometres per person. This figure divided into the area of the district, which he stated to be about 28 500 square kilometres, provided an approximate population size of 7900.[17]

My approach was simpler. Using Robinson's 1842 list of tribes, I recorded the number of Aborigines Robinson listed in each tribe and then totalled them (2949, see Appendix 1). It is important to realize that Robinson included Aborigines of the Grampians, the Pyrenees, Mt William and Mt Cole areas. These areas were technically in the Portland Bay District in 1841, but as far as the Protectorate was concerned much of this north-western area was in Assistant Protector Parker's district.[18] In fact, 111 of the Aborigines listed by Robinson belonged to groups included by Parker in his 1842 census of the Aborigines of his district. The Barrabool Aborigines of the Geelong area seem to have been omitted by Robinson, although they were in the Protectorate's Western District which technically stretched westward from Indented Head. For these there is a population estimate of 150 in late 1841.[19] If these are added to the previous figure it amounts to a total of 3099 (2949 + 150).

There is, however, a problem in accepting this figure. Of the amended list of 137 tribes, there are 53 for which there are no numbers at all, while some are simply mentioned in a passing reference. Such references may be the name of a place where a small group lived rather than the name of a tribe. For example, Griffiths Island at Port Fairy was called Mal.lone. Robinson noted down 'Mallone beer' in his 1842 journal, but it is unlikely that he counted it as a tribe name.[20] The island was only 77 acres in extent, just large enough to be walked around in less than half an hour![21] I therefore ignored most of these fleeting tribes except for nine concentrated in close proximity to Sievwright's Protectorate camp at Lake Keilambete, and later Lake Terang. Many of the individuals from these groups presumably made up the two to three hundred Aborigines Robinson recorded having met there.[22] But the Jarcourt and some Bolokeburer were also present (already counted), and an allowance needs to be made for this. If all 68 Jarcourt were there, and added to the 12 Bolokeburer mentioned by Robinson, 200 Aborigines could be regarded as belonging to the nine sections. The grand total for the District would thus become 3299 in 1841.

The area of the District must be established before population density is calculated. Lourandos stated it to cover 28 500 km².[23] Using a map and the northern boundary of the District as officially established in 1846 (before this the District was larger), I calculated the area as 42 881 km². The difference is surprising, but Lourandos provided no detail concerning his calculations. Including the Settled District around Geelong, because I have included the Barrabool Aborigines the area becomes 44 538 km² (17 293 sq. miles). This approaches the 22 000 sq. miles Robinson accepted as the District's area.[24]

It is important to note that the area by my calculation is smaller than Robinson's figure yet is much larger than that of Lourandos. I estimate approximately 3500 Aborigines in an area of 44 538 km² whereas Lourandos estimates 7900 for a much smaller area of 28 500 km².[25]

Such a difference in basics means the population density was much lower by my reckoning than calculated by Lourandos. My estimate of 12.5 km² per person is a much lower density than on the northern coast of Australia, where Lourandos quotes a density of 1.3 km² per person.

Cultural Group	Km² per	References
Gidjingali (north-east Arnhem Land) coastal	1.3	Hiatt, 1965:17
Aranda (Central Australia)	32.4	Spencer & Gillen, 1899
Walbiri (Central Australia)	90.6	Meggitt, 1962:32
Peek Whuurong (south-western Victoria) coastal—Port Fairy area	1.5–2.3	Lourandos, 1980
Northern Tjapwurong (south-western Victoria) inland	2.6–3.9	Lourandos, 1980
Western District	c.3.6	Lourandos, 1980
	12.5	Critchett, 1988
Gunditjmara (Manmeet)	2.0-3.0	Lourandos, 1980
	9.2	Critchett, 1988

Comparative population densities based on information from Lourandos's Table 5:5 and 5:6 in H. Lourandos, Forces of Change: Aboriginal Technology and Population in South Western Victoria, pp. 90, 95.

However, such figures are all unsatisfactory, because Aborigines in 1841 were not evenly spread across the District. In the area east of the Hopkins ten tribes were already extinct or near extinct (see Appendix 1). Meanwhile many large groups lived west of the Hopkins. If one calculates the density of population west of the Hopkins, given that a population of 2277 occupied an area of approximately 21 043 km², one obtains a figure of 9.2 km² per person.[26] This is much closer to densities argued by Lourandos, but it applies to only part of the District. This figure cannot be used to estimate the density of population across the District before European settlement, as it is obvious from many accounts that the plains were not as fertile nor as well watered as the land to the west, and would therefore have not supported such a large population as the more hospitable western part of the District.

Even though Lourandos claimed his figure to be for 1841, he made no allowance for Robinson's information that many groups were approaching extinction by 1841. Butlin also expressed his doubts about whether the estimate was intended as an 1841 or pre-contact one while Williams was positive that Lourandos's estimate was a *pre-contact* population density and thus takes into account death from diseases which may have preceded actual settlement'.[27] If this is the case, my population estimation is the only one for the size of the 1841 population. This allows some understanding of the size of the two populations in contact in the early years of settlement. Opposed to the European population of at least 1260 was a population of approximately 3500 Aborigines. Two thirds of the Aboriginal population were likely to have been women and children (see total in Appendix 1). On this basis, it is significant that there were approximately equal numbers of Aboriginal and European men in the District in 1841—1167 Aborigines, 1102, and probably more, Europeans.

In attempting to arrive at a pre-contact rather than an 1841 population the difficulties are even greater. But some things are far clearer than previous research has revealed. As Butlin and others have focused on the impact of smallpox, it is necessary to take up the debate on whether smallpox epidemics occurred in the years after European settlement and, if so, how widely they spread.

It is widely believed, though disputed by some, that there were two smallpox outbreaks between 1788 and 1850, the first in 1789 and the second about 1830. In marshalling the evidence for the geographical spread of the 1789 smallpox outbreak Butlin included a recorded 1803 sighting of typical smallpox marking at Westernport, Victoria. For the second epidemic Butlin stated that the tell-tale pockmarking was seen throughout New South Wales, the interior of Queensland, Victoria and the eastern third of South Australia. Amongst evidence of 'massive depopulation' in all these areas, he referred to western Victoria: 'Robinson found empty cells where formerly tribes and sub-tribes had lived; there were mass graves explained by surviving blacks as produced by some epidemic'.[28] In this way he established a case for two smallpox epidemics having being experienced in south-eastern Australia, except for Gippsland where no signs of smallpox were reported.

Butlin depended heavily on Robinson's evidence yet Robinson made no mention of smallpox on his journey in 1841. Judy Campbell, who has recently made a major study of the spread of smallpox in Aboriginal Australia, explained this omission by his recent arrival from Tasmania, where there is no evidence of the Aborigines having had smallpox.[29] Robinson, however, made points of contrast between the Victorian and Tasmanian Aborigines, so it is unusual that he failed to mention smallpox if signs of it were visible. Sievwright, the Assistant Protector for the Western District, in contrast, did so. In 1839, when his experience was limited to Melbourne and Geelong, he commented on the traces amongst the Aborigines of the 'ravages' of smallpox.[30]

Dawson, gathering information in the late 1870s, was certain that the Aborigines had suffered from epidemics, and the symptoms he described of one of them resembled those of smallpox. Because of its importance as the strongest evidence of smallpox his statement is quoted at length.

The first occasion which the natives remember was about the year 1830, and the last in 1847. The very small remnant of old aborigines now alive who escaped the first of these epidemics describe it as an irruptive fever resembling small-pox. They called it Meen warann—'chopped root'. They have still a very vivid recollection of its ravages, and of the great numbers cut off by it in the Western District. In remembrance of it they still chant a wail called Mallae mallaeae, which was composed in New South Wales, where the disease first broke out, and is known to all tribes between Sydney, Melbourne and Adelaide. The malady spread with rapidity from tribe to tribe . . . the infection being carried by the messengers who were sent forward to communicate the sad news of its ravages. It was considered to be so infectious and deadly, that when anyone sickened and refused food, and when pustules appeared on the body, the tribal doctor gave them up at once, and the friends deserted them . . . long afterwards . . . some of the relatives returned, and burned the wuurn and the remains . . . The aborigines say that the Meen waraan came from the west in form of a dense mist; and that the chief places of mortality were round the Moyne Lagoon, and on the sand hummocks to the east of Port Fairy.

At the last of these visitations, also, great numbers died near the sea coast, and were buried in the hummocks at Mill's Reef, two miles east of Port Fairy. The skeletons were exposed some years ago by the drifting of the sand, and were found to be buried in pairs. This proves that the deaths were not then considered to be caused by any contagious disease, else the relatives would have abandoned the bodies, and only returned to burn the bones.[31]

He mentioned a case in 1844 in which he saw an Aborigine 'as thoroughly marked with the small-pox as ever he saw a white man'.[32] As phrased, this seemed an exceptional instance. Elsewhere Dawson also made a note on 'plague among the Aborigines', listing a first attack among the Aborigines in the Port Fairy District in 1830 and a second in 1842.[33] Both outbreaks he 'supposed to be smallpox'. It is most unlikely, however, that the outbreak of disease in 1842 was smallpox. By early 1842 the Protectorate station was established at Mt Rouse in the heart of the District. Large numbers of Aborigines came and went providing Assistant Protector Sievwright, and later Dr Watton, with plenty of opportunity to note diseases. Nevertheless, there is no mention of smallpox in their three-monthly reports which include comments on Aboriginal health. Nor is smallpox referred to in any other report, letter, diary of that year. Dawson did not arrive in the District till 1844 so his note was not based on personal experience.

J. C. Hamilton in his recollections mentioned an epidemic in the far west, north of Edenhope, where 'large numbers of blacks' were discovered 'buried in pits near Ozenkadnook . . . They died of some epidemic before the white man came to that part of the country'.[34] The Aborigines told Hamilton, 'All about very sick, and tumble down dead like rotten sheep'. They had no remedy: 'poor fellow me', they said.[35] E. R. Trangmar, writing more recently, quoted Hamilton mentioning a large mass grave beyond Edenhope where between 60 and 70 skulls were discovered and reburied. Trangmar wrote, but his source is unknown, 'This was the result of an epidemic, assumed to be smallpox, judging by the pock-marked faces of the survivors'.[36]

To the north-east, also, settlers saw signs of smallpox. The historian, W. B. Withers, wrote of the Aborigines of the Ballarat area, 'several of the adults were strongly marked with smallpox at the time the locality was taken up for pastoral occupation'.[37]

Care must be taken before drawing conclusions from such discursive data. For example, Judy Campbell in an article, 'Smallpox in Aboriginal Australia', drew incorrect conclusions from comments made by Robinson. She wrote: 'Further west near Mt. Hesse in 1841 Robinson heard some tribes were extinct: only one youth, whom he saw, remained of the Teeringillum'.[38] The Teeringillum conedeet were the Aborigines of the Mt Elephant area. Of these Robinson commented 'killed by Europeans, Mr. Taylor and others'.[39] Near Mt Clay, north-east of Portland, Robinson met a 21-year-old Aborigine named Pul.ler.teer.rang and commented, 'his nose is rather pitted or scarred'. Robinson made no further comment. Campbell quoted this and followed it with more evidence seemingly of the effect of a smallpox epidemic:

> In another group, mostly young men, several said they were the only survivors of their tribes: an old man was the last of the Ureconedeet and two Killarerercondeet were 'all that are left of that tribe'.[40]

From various references in Robinson's notes it is clear that there had been large-scale depopulation in the vicinity of Portland. The Aborigines of Portland were the En.re.conedeet, also referred to as the Eurite. The only survivor was one man.[41] Of the Kilkarer conedeet, whose territory was the country between Portland and the Surrey River, there were six survivors.[42] There was another tribe in the area, the Borne. No information concerning the number in this group or its exact location have been found, but the implication is that it was also nearly extinct. Robinson wrote: 'The Borne, Kil.car.rer, Eurite sections combined with the Cart Conedeet [Mt Clay] when the first white men came to their country'.[43] A study of the context, however, makes it clear that Robinson blamed the great loss of life on the violent behaviour of the period of contact. In the official report of his journey he wrote of the 'severe conflict' which had taken place at the Convincing Ground during which a large number of Aborigines were slain.[44]

Campbell also referred to Robinson's meeting with a group of the Tappoc conedeet in a swampy area south of Mt Napier:

> Their food was abundant: there were different roots, including the mealy roots of rushes; the *worns* or huts were well-built. Robinson identified family groups, thought 'polygmy' more common than usual, and 'the women of this tribe are extremely prolific; most of them ancient'.[45]

The impression she gives is of a shortage of women with those present being old: obviously an unbalanced group suffering from the results of an epidemic such as smallpox. But the opposite is true of this group. Polygamy was common in the Western District, many Aborigines having three or more wives. In the Mane conedeet, for example, of twenty-one men listed, four had no wives, seven had one wife and ten had more than one wife.[46] Of ten men of the Yowen conedeet of 'Tarrone' north of Port Fairy, two had no wives, four had one wife, four had more than one wife. Robinson's comment was merely a relative one.

At the end of his formal meeting with the Tappoc conedeet Robinson stated, 'The women of this tribe are extremely prolific; most of them enceint'. It is the word 'enceint' meaning pregnant, which Gary Presland, as editor of Robinson's journals, has misread as 'ancient' that has led to Campbell's wrong conclusion. She has obviously referred to the published copy of Robinson's journals edited by Presland rather than to the original journals.[47] As a group the Tappoc conedeet consisted of 39 individuals: eight men, twelve women and nineteen children. It may be wrong to put undue store on the exact ages Robinson gave for these people but if the wives were 'ancient' this would be reflected in the ages given to them by Robinson. Four of the females were in the age range of 0–9, seven were aged 10–19, two were aged 20–29, one was aged between 30 and 39 and one was 40 years old. Of the three women for whom Robinson gave no age, two had infants and two were pregnant.[48]

Put in context, these seemingly strong pieces of evidence reveal no link with smallpox. Campbell also referred to Diane Barwick's work showing the disastrous effects of contact on the age and sex structure of Aboriginal groups.[49] Campbell presented the situation as if there were only one possible explanation for the structure of remnant groups; writing, 'Effects of smallpox on the age and sex structure were long-lived as Barwick's study of later Victorian populations suggests'. Campbell also equated the disproportionate numbers of men and women (lesser number of women) in remnant populations 'obvious by the mid-30s' as appearing to be 'a characteristic of post-epidemic populations'.[50] Yet in the Western District the 1841 details collected by Robinson clearly show that at this stage women (equated with wives) outnumbered men. Using Robinson's figures the population consisted of 780 males, 1050 women (wives), 1106 children. While this may be inaccurate, as numbers are lacking for some tribes and no details of age or sex are available for 105 people, it is at least a conclusion based on the available evidence.

It may be argued that the larger number of women is because Robinson did not list women, but wives, and wives were aged from the young (for example, ten years old) to the old. Unfortunately, there are few tribes for which details of age and sex are given. However, it is possible to count the number of males and females in a group Robinson met north of Dr Kilgour's.[51] He was then approximately twenty miles north of Port Fairy and the mouth of the Moyne River, stated by Dawson to have suffered the greatest number of deaths from the epidemic. Robinson obtained the names of thirty individuals. They were mainly Yowen conedeet, but there were also some who were Meen conedeet, How weet conedeet, Moporer conedeet and Art conedeet (nearby groups). Their ages ranged from twenty-nine down to two years; fifteen were male and fifteen females. According to Butlin, those most vulnerable in an epidemic were very young children and pregnant women. If Dawson is correct and the epidemic occurred about 1830, children born at this time would be eleven in 1841. Allowing some tolerance for Robinson's estimates by adding those aged eight or more, up to and including thirteen, the number is eight (8 out of 30). The largest group of Tappoc conedeet Robinson met was not so even in its sexual distribution but it lacked the unevenness portrayed in Barwick's post-contact population pyramids. In the group of twenty-six individuals there were thirteen males and ten females, with three infants whose sex is unknown.[52] The relatively even ratio of the sexes and the number of children born about 1830 do not suggest the ravages of a smallpox epidemic. Moreover, Robinson nowhere notes a shortage of women or of children, and his comments are more to the contrary.

Robinson does mention one group extinct through disease. This was a group on the Hopkins River somewhere to the north of Hexham. He is quite specific: 'They died about the time the first white man came. They were not killed by whites, but died from disease'.[53] He names the tribe the Bul.ler.bul.lecort. However, in another reference he provided numbers for this group.[54] He may have misunderstood the name of the tribe but his evidence is clear: one tribe extinct from disease. This quite specific but isolated reference reinforces the conclusion that there had not been a massive depopulation of the region caused by an epidemic.

Campbell also referred to William Buckley's experience. He was living with the Aborigines of the Barwon River area from 1803 to 1835. He therefore lived with Aborigines around 1830 when, according to Dawson, the first epidemic had occurred. Buckley's face was marked with the signs of smallpox. Campbell quoted Buckley's account of 'a complaint which spread through the country, occasioning the loss of many lives . . . It was a dreadful swelling of the feet, so that they were unable to move about, being also affected with ulcers of a very painful kind'. This was an afterthought; a comment made after Buckley had stated: 'I never observed any European contagious disease prevalent, in the least degree; and this I thought strange'. Buckley mentioned death from disease but he made no link between the symptoms and smallpox, with which he must have been previously familiar.[55] Deaths from smallpox cannot be ruled out but it is clear that most of the evidence marshalled by Campbell is not substantiated by a detailed study of the evidence concerning the Portland Bay District.

Butlin also makes significant use of Robinson's 1841 data, referring to 'empty cells where formerly tribes and sub-tribes had lived', and to 'age-structures of blacks in 1841, consistent with smallpox at about 1830'.[56] Leaving aside for the moment 'empty cells', Butlin bases his comments on 'age structures' on a population pyramid which he has constructed using information concerning age and sex of about 500 Aborigines taken from Robinson's published Journals (edited by Presland).

Using the pyramid Butlin pointed to 'the strong presence of both sexes aged 15–25' and the 'sudden drop in representation in the adjoining age groups'. He marshalled the possible reasons why this group had survived better than others and stressed their strong claim to be used as 'reference points for adjusting the population pyramid' to indicate the size of the Aboriginal population before European settlement (and smallpox).[57] Then, by means of a sophisticated population modelling approach, Butlin made adjustments to the size of this age group, taking into account problems they were 'subject to'—'white killing', for example. After consideration of various factors he arrived at the conclusion 'that the demographic evidence could point to an enhancement of Lourandos's estimate for 1841 by a little over 2.5 times—to the order of 20 000 ... in the Western District'. Shortly afterwards he suggested '25 000' in the Western District in '1788'.[58]

Before accepting Butlin's figures it is necessary to examine the reliability of his basic data. It is relevant that the groups used by Butlin were atypical, being collections of members of different tribes. There is no way of knowing the extent to which they were representative of the whole population, but it is unlikely that they were. One large group, similar to those used by Butlin but not included in the published journals, indicates how unusual such a group could be. This consisted of eighty-eight individuals met near Port Fairy. Sixty were males, twenty-five were females, with the sex of three unknown: thirty-one were aged thirteen and under, of whom sixteen were female and fifteen male.[59] Adult women were obviously poorly represented, yet every tribe for which Robinson collected details in the surrounding area either had more or about the same number of women (wives) as men.[60]

Moreover the groups used by Butlin were not evenly distributed across the district. Except perhaps for the group north of Port Fairy, they were in those areas earliest settled by Europeans and where there had been considerable inter-racial violence. They consisted of two groups from the Terang-Camperdown area, one from just north of Port Fairy, one from Mt Clay, and another just north of Mt Clay, a group at the Winters' station on the Wannon, and lastly, all those groups Robinson met in the Mt William area and east and south-east on his return trip to Geelong.

What Butlin's population data does not take into account is the large number of tribes from the Hopkins River westward to the Glenelg for which Robinson collected details from Aboriginal informants. These were not selected because Robinson's informants supplied the names of the men, the number of their wives and of their children, but he was not given details of age. Consequently the details were of no use to Butlin. The question remains, is it sound to speculate on the basis of such a sample?

Butlin mentioned the under-representation in his population pyramid of those aged 55–59—'particularly poorly represented', were the words he used. He took for granted that Robinson would be able easily and confidently to assign precise ages to individuals, differentiating so closely that he would be able to state an individual to be 50 as opposed to 55. There is also the question of what Robinson meant by the ages he provided, because they were largely intelligent guesses. What age did Robinson assign to one he thought 'old'? Is there any other evidence regarding the age structure of the population?

Considerable evidence exists that there were old people in the population. Buckley, for example, stated of the people with whom he had been living, 'The natives live to about the same age, generally, as civilised people—some of them, to be very grey-headed'.[61] Hamilton, arriving in the far west of the district north of Edenhope in May 1846, found that there were many Aborigines in the locality. They ranged from 'the infant on its mother's breast' to 'extremely aged men and women'. Some were very old: 'There were men and women of such great age when we came to the district first, so wrinkled, and with hair so white that they looked more like monkeys than of the human race'.[62]

Robinson, too, saw old people. At Black and Steele's station he met Mum.me.jur.nin, an 'old, old man', assigning him an age of fifty-five. He recorded an 'old' man as aged fifty; Jim Crow is noted as fifty, to Robinson he was 'an old man'; another man is described as sixty. These come from lists used by Butlin but more examples of old people occur if the narrative of the published Journals is consulted. Minbum is 'an old man, at least 60 years'. Robinson met an old woman, of the Dar.ko.gang conedeet in the area settled by Frank Henty. She is an 'old woman' aged between '60 and 70'. Robinson later gave her age as 70.[63] In Robinson's unpublished material there are more references to 'old' people. The Chief of the Elingamite, Too.mudger.long, was an 'old man'. The Chief of the Teer.rar conedeet was a 'Big Old Man', six others in this tribe were named as 'old', in the first list of the Morper er conedeet four men are noted as 'old' and in the Mane conedeet one is shown as 'old'.[64]

Even the complete tribe lists given by Aboriginal informants provide information which suggests the proportion of the aged. Eight tribes north of Port Fairy and in the area from the Hopkins River westward to Lake Condah, numbered 207 men, of whom twenty were indicated to be 'old'.[65]

At the other age extreme it is surprising that Butlin should expect infants to be amongst those who came sometimes from quite a distance to meet the strange white 'gentleman'. Yet these are the groups which Butlin studied. In the case where Robinson met Aborigines on their home territory undisturbed, he believed, by Europeans (the Tappoc conedeet already mentioned) the large number of infants and the obvious pregnancy of the women has already been noted. He also mentioned the large numbers of children at Sievwright's camp and among the Aborigines who came to meet him near Tower Hill.[66]

Taken altogether, both Campbell and Butlin have little reliable evidence on which to base firm conclusions. There seems to be more evidence of smallpox or some other epidemic around the edge of the District—north of Edenhope, Ballarat and around Melbourne. The strongest evidence for a smallpox epidemic in the District, and it cannot be discounted, is that provided by Dawson. He talked with Aborigines such as Weeratt Kuuyut (aged about 70 in 1871) who would have been a mature man at the time of the epidemic described as having occurred about 1830. That Weeratt Kuuyat appears not to have mentioned the 1789 epidemic, which occurred only twelve years before he was born and which would presumably have been talked about in his youth, is some evidence that it did not extend into the south-western part of Victoria. The puzzling factor is the lack of reported sightings of pockmarked faces. Was the population so vulnerable that almost every person who caught the disease died?

An examination of evidence from the neighbouring Protectorate region to the north-east provides some further information. Assistant Protector Parker noted that smallpox had 'made fearful havoc among the aboriginal population', but that was well in the past. In 1854 he stated, 'The few individuals who are to be met with, who are marked with the disease are not less than thirty years of age'.[67] James Kirby drawing on his own experience also commented on the age of those pockmarked seen near Swan Hill: 'We noticed that several of the blacks were pockmarked, but those who bore these marks were all old men'.[68] Parker believed that the Aborigines had experienced smallpox because they threatened to use sorcery to cause the outbreak and spread of a disease with symptoms similar to those of smallpox—dreadful sores, dysentery, blindness and death.[69] Such presumed evidence for smallpox therefore appears to support the 1789 epidemic rather than that around 1830.

Parker made what he regarded as a complete census of the population of his region during 1842.[70] At the end of the census he provided information on the age structure of the population. This is relevant to Butlin's pyramid for Parker's details were for the groups of which many were partly represented in the lists used by Butlin to compile his 1841 population pyramid. Parker acknowledged the 'impossibility' of obtaining precise information regarding the ages of the Aborigines, and recorded details concerning age under category headings.[71] These were Aged, Adult, Youths and Girls (those who appeared to be more than nine or ten years of age) and Children (those under that age). Of a total of 670 individuals, Parker listed sixty-two as aged (thirty-two males, thirty females). Exact age is unknown but it is clear that there was a considerable number of old people. Relevant to comments made both by Butlin and Campbell, that women suffered more than men during a smallpox epidemic, it is interesting to note that numbers of old males and females were almost even. Females are fewer in number than males in every age category but *closest in number* in the *aged category* (32 : 30). Of the under-representation of those over 50 in his Remnant Age Structure pyramid Butlin admitted that his suggestions as to cause were 'obviously speculative', but emphasized that 'the age-structures are not inconsistent with this disease experience [smallpox 1790 and 1830]'.[72] Parker's evidence throws doubt on such an opinion.

Diane Barwick, whose important study of 'Changes in the Aboriginal Population of Victoria 1863–1966' was earlier referred to, read Butlin's speculative study. She re-examined the evidence of twenty-six gentlemen who, in 1877, wrote about smallpox in Victoria. She concluded that it was part of a hysterical press campaign which followed a smallpox outbreak in Sydney. She found no evidence of smallpox in Victoria and reaffirmed her belief that the chief causes of depopulation were '"wanton slaughter", starvation, and the effect of European-introduced diseases, notably influenza, measles, tuberculosis and the venereal infections then labelled "syphilis" (the symptoms in fact suggest a combination of syphilis and gonorrhoea)'. She wrote:

> Analysis of the reported incidence of remembered pockmarking, together with the voluminous medical evidence on skin diseases among Victorian and other Aborigines, convinced me that all reports of Victorian epidemics resulted from medical and ethnographic ignorance. The rarity, seasonality and geographic peculiarities of reportage by these twenty-six observers suggest that they were reminiscing about outbreaks of *impetigo contagiosa* (the medical diagnosis, from the 1860's, of what laymen called 'native pock'), a streptococcal or staphyloccal infection; the staphylococcal form, if untreated, may cause the severe generalised disease *pemphigus acutus*, commonly known as 'butcher's fever'.[73]

The evidence about smallpox in the District is confusing but the large size of tribes and the large number of wives and children Robinson recorded in the area west of the Hopkins do not support Butlin's hypothesis that there was massive depopulation caused by smallpox prior to European settlement. Robinson does record 'empty cells' but in most of these cases an explanation is given—usually violence between the races. For details of these 'affrays', as they were often referred to, we are not dependent on Robinson alone as other evidence exists in official sources. Numbers were much lower in the eastern part of the District where European settlement had been greater for longer. Here racial conflict had been experienced over a longer period and there would have been greater exposure to European diseases and their effects especially venereal disease—with syphilis 'tending to reduce the ability of women to produce live children' and gonorrhoea, 'to reduce female fertility'.[74]

Using Robinson's data, the size of the population in 1841 has been estimated at approximately 3500, but there is no doubt that it had already declined since European settlement. Moreover, if one accepts Dawson's evidence of an 1830 epidemic, it had already been reduced before the arrival of European settlers. How far, it is difficult to estimate. I incline to something less than, or comparable to, Lourandos's figure of 8000, rather than Butlin's figure which I think extreme and not based on the evidence from the District.

To emphasize the high population density along the coastline Lourandos drew attention to the ease with which more than 400 Aborigines collected in a few hours to meet Robinson between Port Fairy and Warrnambool.[75] But two comments, hard to overlook, capture the tone of Robinson's general comments on the size of the 1841 population. On 1 May 1841 at Mt Napier which settlers had described as a 'hotbed for natives', Robinson commented, 'and yet it is singular so few are met: 700 miles had been travelled by one gentleman, and six natives only seen; and persons from Melbourne to Portland had not seen one'.[76] Further south near Portland, having visited 'the greater part of the country south of the Grampians', including the area Lourandos claimed to be one of the most densely populated parts of Aboriginal Australia, Robinson wrote to his wife.[77] Boastful and proud, with the end of his project in sight, he quantified his achievement. He had 'visited and personally conferred with 800 natives'!

6

'every gentleman's establishment ... has been molested by the natives'

IN THIS DISTRICT hundreds of people died at the hands of those of another race, but there is no mound to mark the fallen dead, as at Marathon, nor even a sign to indicate the mass grave where all the men of a clan lie. Only one simple monument comes to mind, a grave site marked by a wooden cross beside the Princes Highway, just west of Port Fairy. On it are the words, 'GEORGE WATMORE SPEARED BY BLACKS 1842', a reminder of the violence of the Aboriginal reaction to European settlement.*

Aboriginal attacks on European men, or their sheep, cattle or horses took place from the beginning of European settlement. 'Aggression' and 'depredation' were the words settlers used to describe such activities but another word, 'outrage', capturing more the settlers' sense of indignation at attacks on their property, became most favoured. It was used, perhaps for the first time in the District, by Captain Foster Fyans, the Police Magistrate at Geelong, who reported to Sydney in May 1838 that 'the natives' of the District were 'behaving in a most outrageous manner'.[1] They had been stealing sheep and attacking huts; a shepherd had been murdered and a horse speared.

Those who settled around Geelong were the first to complain of Aboriginal behaviour and to appeal for Government protection. The first request was made in mid-1837 by forty-four proprietors of stock

---

* Surprisingly no mention of the death of George Watmore was found in official records.

depasturing in the area around Geelong.[2] On 18 April 1840 a second request was made. This time thirty-eight 'Proprietors of Land and Stock' from the area around Geelong appealed for Government help, reporting that the Aborigines had committed 'outrages . . . on the persons and properties of the colonists'.[3] In September 1840 Foster Fyans returned from his first tour of the whole District reporting that 'every gentleman's establishment . . . has been molested by the natives'.[4]

The length of period for which 'outrages' lasted varied across the District. They lasted longest and inflicted the greatest harm in the area west of the Hopkins where there were strongholds to which Aborigines could retreat and where Europeans found it difficult to follow. Along the Glenelg River, at Mt Clay, in the stony area and swampy ground around Darlot's Creek, Lake Condah, Mt Eeles (later Eccles), and from Mt Napier stretching southward towards Port Fairy, the Aborigines had clan territory which provided a refuge from the initial effects of European settlement and a rallying place against those who had invaded the area. The retreats to which they could return protected them initially, as did the slightly later and slower settlement of the west compared with the eastern area of the District. After the move of the Protectorate camp from Lake Terang to Mt Rouse on 12 February 1842, Aboriginal outrages virtually ceased in the area east of the Hopkins River.[5]

There is no doubt that Aboriginal actions were at certain times so annoying and so persistent in some areas of the District that squatters were forced to move elsewhere. But were these actions, largely stealing sheep or cattle, or threatening shepherds, a part of a campaign by Aborigines to force Europeans to retreat? Were they a planned resistance to settlement or simply the actions of people confronted by easily available food or people driven by harsh drought conditions to take livestock because they were hungry? To what extent was there determination amongst Aborigines to remove Europeans? Is there evidence of a change over time—in weapons used, in tactics, in leadership?

These are difficult questions to answer, but a useful approach is to describe Aboriginal actions and examine the Aboriginal concepts of land ownership and the role of warfare in relationship to maintaining control of land. Aborigines, at least for some time after European settlement, must have viewed what was happening against their own cultural traditions.

The squatters took up land which Aborigines saw as their 'country'— land which had been given to their ancestors in the Dreamtime, as previously explained. Ownership of it was not something Aborigines fought about. The anthropologist, W. Lloyd Warner, after studying the Murngin of Arnhem Land over three years (1926–29), explained the situation in the following way:

> No land can be taken from a clan by an act of war. A clan does not possess its land by strength of arms but by immemorial tradition and as an integral part of the culture . . . In the thought of the Murngin, land and water, people and

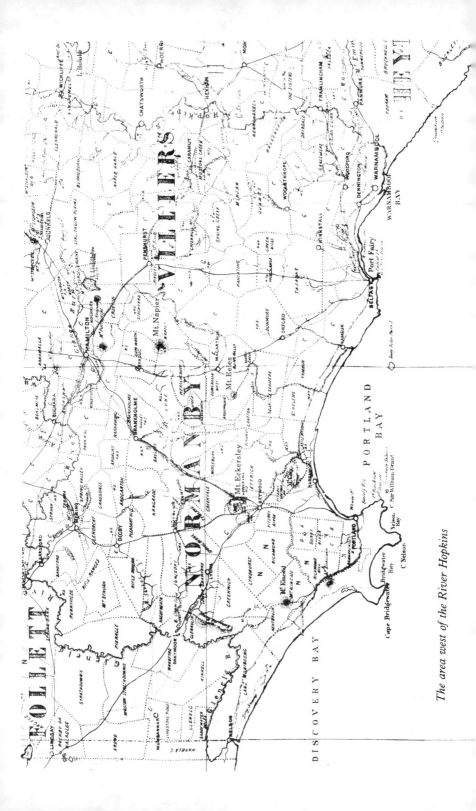

The area west of the River Hopkins

clan are an act of the creator totem and the mythological ancestors, who always announce in myth and ceremony that this is the country of such and such a clan; to expropriate this land as a conscious act would be impossible.[6]

Since the Aborigines did not fight over land, it is most unlikely that their initial reaction to settlement would be that of attempting to prevent their land being taken. The situation is further complicated by the function of warfare in Aboriginal society.

Aborigines used 'force of arms' but for different reasons from those of Europeans. Not only was ownership of land not disputed but according to the Berndts offences against property were also rare. Stone quarries and deposits of red ochre, for example, were 'traditionally inalienable'. But there were offences such as individuals seeing sacred sites without permission which had to be punished. Most offences were against 'the person'. These included the ignoring or killing of a child by a mother, running away with another's spouse and, especially important, murder, or suspected murder, for Aborigines believed most deaths were caused by sorcery. The most frequent example of punishment imposed by one group on a member, or members, of another group was the avenging party usually sent out to avenge the death of a fellow tribesman or clansman, or to punish an offender.[7] Dawson discussed this kind of activity in the Western District:

> A dying person, who believes that sorcery and incantations are the cause of his illness, intimates to his friends the number of persons in the suspected tribe whom they are to kill. Sometimes the individual who is believed to be the cause of his illness is named by the dying person . . .
>
> . . . when an individual is fixed upon as the cause of the death, he receives warning that his life will be taken . . . Immediately after the warning, a small party of the male friends and relatives of the deceased prepare themselves . . . When ready to start, they paint and disguise themselves, that they may not be recognised by the friends of the person whom they intend to kill. They proceed, well armed, by night to the vicinity of the residence occupied by their intended victim. It is difficult to surprise a camp, owing to the watchfulness and ferocity of the dogs belonging to it. The attacking party, therefore, form a wide circle, and gradually close round the wuurn, guiding each other by uttering cries in imitation of nocturnal animals. At the dawn of day, which is the time of the deepest sleep with the aborigines, and when it is sufficiently light to distinguish the person they wish to kill, they rush on their victim, drag him out of his bed, and spear him without the slightest resistance from himself or his friends, who, paralyzed with terror, lie perfectly still. After the departure of the attacking party, the friends cut up the body and burn it.

A man who fled from the avenging party was tracked for two moons—after this he was free—but if found, the man might be strangled or stunned and his kidney fat taken ensuring his death.[8]

Sometimes, according to Dawson, a man close to death incorrectly named his murderers. When these were killed in retaliation, a feud was begun which could extend over a long period. But there were customs for resolving conflict by carrying out an ordeal approved by both groups involved in the fighting. In this way an endless cycle of revenge killing could be stopped.

In European society war was and is declared against an invading force or by a military force determined to expand its control over a greater area of land and people or even between two large groups of people over a principle. In contrast warfare in Aboriginal society took place not between tribes but between small groups of people—between clans. The example of the Murngin will be used, as it was in Arnhem Land that there was the most highly organized warfare in Aboriginal Australia.[9] While it is unlikely that the Western District Aborigines behaved in exactly the same way as the Murngin it is likely that general Aboriginal customs concerning warfare would be similar. Indeed, specific examples similar to some of those described by the anthropologist W. Lloyd Warner can be given from the Western District.

Warner found the causes of warfare to be quite specific— 'the killing of a clansman by a member of another clan and interclan rivalry for women. The latter is the usual cause of killing. Blood vengeance forces further killing'. Behind the fighting, according to Warner, was one simple principle: 'reciprocity'. Where possible the 'same injury should be inflicted upon the enemy group that one's own group has suffered'. For a man killed, one man must be killed in return. If a woman is stolen, only the return of the woman and a ceremonial fight to allow the saving of face, or the stealing of another woman, will satisfy.

Warner identified six distinct varieties of warfare among the Murngin, each with a separate pattern of behaviour and an individual name. There was also another form in which only women participated:

> The names are nirimaoi yolno, a fight within the camp; narrup or djawarlt, a secret method of killing; maringo . . . a night attack in which the entire camp is surrounded; milwerangel, a general open fight between at least two groups; gaingar . . . a pitched battle; and makarata, a ceremonial peace-making fight which is partly an ordeal.

The first mentioned was the most common form of fighting and seldom resulted in killing. 'Gaingar', a pitched battle, more like the European battle, involving the Aborigines of a whole region, was a very rare occurrence. Even then the number killed was small. This kind of battle had occurred only twice in twenty years and only twenty-nine men had been killed altogether.[10]

Against a background where revenge killing and conflict over women accounted for most fighting, it is not surprising to discover that the Europeans killed in the Portland Bay District before 1842 were almost all guilty of violence against Aborigines or involved in disputes over Aboriginal women. Nowhere did a group of Europeans die as a direct result of a large-scale Aborigine-initiated encounter. It was one or at the most two Europeans at a time who died at the hands of the Aborigines. An analysis of the details surrounding the death of the Europeans killed by Aborigines suggests that it is likely that these individuals had been singled out for specific reasons. It is obvious they were not killed simply for intruding on clan land, as other Aborigines might have been. All Europeans were intruders, yet only sixteen white men were killed by Aborigines between settlement and the beginning of 1842.

The sixteen deaths are spread across the District; across some 350 miles and from the coast inland to the Pyrenees about 100 miles. No area suffered more than others. These men died in encounters with a small number of Aborigines. Moreover, the way the men were killed indicated that the Aborigines were close to the Europeans, as Peter Corris has pointed out in his earlier ethnohistorical study of the District.[11] In a number of cases death was caused by blows to the head by an implement such as a tomahawk. The wounds to the body of Patrick Codd killed by Aborigines near Mt Rouse indicate this closeness. There is a spear wound but only one:

> One wound in the left ear, penetrating the brain; one wound immediately under the left eye; one wound on the left cheek; one wound above the left eyebrow; one wound on chin; one wound across bridge of nose, severing the lower part, and cutting the upper lip; a wound along each side of nose; one wound into right eye; one wound with a ragged spear, entering the back of neck and penetrating through right breast; one wound on left knee; the whole of the back of skull beaten in, the bones protruding.[12]

In all but three of the sixteen cases reasons were given for the murders. The following examples indicate the detail available. William Heath was killed, Aborigines told an employee of John Henty, because 'he was in the habit of taking their women by night'.[13] In the case of Charles Franks and his man on the Werribee River there is the suggestion that he had been poisoning Aborigines.[14] Patrick Codd was murdered, Assistant Protector Sievwright assumed, because of violence he was involved in on Wedge's station at The Grange where he was overseer: he had been told by Codd that on one occasion about eighteen Aborigines had called at the head station and endeavoured to take possession of the hut and store. Armed conflict was the result, with the Europeans firing 'a small swivel gun, loaded with musket balls' at the Aborigines until they retreated. It was also suggested that Codd was 'infamous for his treatment of Aboriginal women'.[15]

Francis Morton and Larry were suspected of treating the Aborigines badly. J. G. Robertson, whose property was near by, implied that Morton was killed because of 'unpardonable conduct' towards an Aborigine named Long Yarra who worked for him and whose 'gin' Morton 'fancied'. Arthur Pilleau told the Chief Protector that a native woman told him that Morton had offended a native man, ordered him away and said he would kill him. Pilleau also stated, 'It is probable that Morton was killed through some mischief done to the natives by Larry'.[16]

Guns were not used to kill these men. In two cases the men were warned that they would be killed.[17] In all cases, except possibly two, the Europeans knew the Aborigines who murdered them, the closeness of contact between the races being indicated by the fact that local Europeans learnt some details concerning eleven of the murders from Aborigines.[18]

From 1842 onwards the pattern is largely the same. Despite the reputation of the District for violence during 1842 only ten Europeans were killed. From the beginning of 1842 to 1848 only nineteen Europeans were killed, making a total of thirty-five from settlement. Only in one case were two Europeans killed at the same time—Donald McKenzie and his hutkeeper, Frederick Edinge. Three cases are worth mentioning—those of McKenzie and Edinge, Christopher Bassett, and Abraham Ward's child. The latter case was the only recorded instance of the Aborigines killing a European child in the District.

On 8 August 1843 the three-year-old child of Abraham Ward of the Traveller's Rest at the A.ran.doo.vong crossing (now Branxholme) disappeared. It was assumed then confirmed that Aborigines had taken the child. It was killed, according to an Aboriginal woman, because it cried.[19] Earlier David Edgar reported that Aborigines had killed one of their children for crying for something to eat.[20] For those who lived largely in the open, a crying child could threaten the security of the whole camp and it is likely that Aborigines taught their children not to cry. Robinson was so impressed by the quietness of the Tasmanian Aborigines' dogs that he believed even they had been taught not to bark. In the surviving literature there is one further piece of evidence which suggests that the Aborigines taught their children not to cry. Katherine Kirkland of Trawalla noticed how easily an Aboriginal mother silenced her child by a simple nudge.[21] The child once killed was believed to have been eaten, a possibility that was likely judging by the reaction of some Aborigines near Lake Corangamite. One of their children had been taken away from them by Dr Clerke, some weeks earlier. Unfamiliar with European customs, they judged his possible fate by their own experience. They approached a European party, expressing their grief and asking whether the child had been eaten.[22]

Christopher Bassett was a squatter residing at the head of the Crawford River. According to reports he attended his sheep himself and usually did so unarmed. The Aborigines who murdered him 'stripped him of all his clothes drove pegs in his eyes and speared him through the heart'.[23] They also carried off more than 200 sheep. One wonders what Bassett saw or what he was guilty of that he should be treated in this unusual way.

The murder of McKenzie and the hutkeeper Edinge on the Glenelg River is unusual in that Koort Kirrup, the Aborigine alleged to have murdered them, was working on the property and was regarded as a trusted employee and a good workman. The circumstances were described by the shepherd, Joseph Wheatley. On 5 May 1842 McKenzie left the station, stating that he would be absent for eight days. Koort Kirrup's behaviour altered as soon as McKenzie left. On the fourth day Koort Kirrup told the others he would go kangarooing. He returned on 14 May only a quarter of an hour after McKenzie had returned. McKenzie had left his horse fastened by the bridle to a fence. Koort Kirrup, seeing the horse, asked whose it was. Wheatley told him that McKenzie had returned and, hoping to intimidate him, that 'he had brought plenty of "bong" a term used by white men when speaking to the natives of guns'. Koort Kirrup checked in the hut, appearing relieved when he saw no guns. McKenzie returned and Koort Kirrup helped him put sheep into the yard. All the clothes and blankets on the station had been washed that day and they were hung out to dry. Koort Kirrup examined the washing carefully and 'asked particularly to whom a new blanket of mine which was among them belonged'. On the following day while Wheatley was tending the sheep, Aborigines attacked McKenzie and Edinge, killing them. Wheatley fled to Daniel O'Neil's at Smoky River from where he obtained help and returned to McKenzie's. Edinge had been shot as well as speared. McKenzie's body was severely beaten about the head, there was a spear wound in the chest and he had been 'dreadfully beaten about the private parts which were frightfully swollen and almost shapeless'. A 'pilot coat' was on the body. The clothes were lying about six yards from the body. His shoes were in Koort Kirrup's hut. All the clothing, blankets and provisions had been taken from the station.[24]

Koort Kirrup's account, given to Assistant Protector William Thomas who was given the task of assisting Aborigines involved in court cases in Melbourne, is so different that only one conclusion can be drawn. Either Wheatley or Koort Kirrup was lying. Koort Kirrup stated that after McKenzie left the station, Wheatley was 'sulky'. He left with Parry and went to a waterhole called Ichekoopurt: they were staying near the stations of Cameron, Boutcher, Ward and Murcheson. He was told of the murder by Parry who also told him that two Aborigines, Polligenum and Koortbrun, had gone to McKenzie's and slept in his mia mia there, and that two others, Kartwonnun and Urtbonnum, were near by with some 'lubras': it was these four who had killed McKenzie.[25]

Some evidence exists of the bodies of the dead being used by Aborigines to gain special powers for use against the Europeans. At George Urquhart's Mt Emu station Robinson was given a charm or amulet consisting of fat taken from around the kidney or near the heart of a human being, tied up in a piece of skin or rag. It was especially prized for its power. The fat was procured from a victim of a hostile tribe and was believed to give Aborigines power over the enemy. 'This', wrote Robinson, 'accounts for the circumstance of the fat being taken from the white men whom they kill'.[26]

It is quite clear from various accounts and references that the Aborigines ate the flesh of some of their European victims. Thus Blair, Police Magistrate at Portland, in January 1842 reported to La Trobe that during the preceding eighteen months 'several white men have been murdered and eaten by the aborigines'. Morton and his man Larry, killed in 1841, were eaten. Fyans reported that the bodies lay nearly fifty yards apart with the remains of a fire between them: the flesh 'was cut in long slices from the bodies, and barely any left; the cheeks and ears also cut off'. Gibson's shepherd had his ear cut off. Ricketts's shepherd, Foreman, was cut into pieces and eaten. Those who came searching for him found only his boots left beside his dog. Ward's child was eaten. Odder perhaps, but again suggestive of some extra power being sought by the Aborigines, is the fact that when Bonsor, a Henty employee, died accidentally, the Aborigines requested his body to eat.[27]

In each of the murders so far described there is no mention of ceremonial dress or the arrival of an Aboriginal group obviously prepared for war. There is one such occasion on record when Aborigines painted for war began mustering on Winter's station after someone on a station on the Glenelg had poisoned 'fifteen natives' by giving them bread 'purposely made with arsenic'. Aborigines named Thomas Connell but he denied it on oath and Stephen Henty stated that he was to be believed. Samuel Winter wrote:

> I felt uneasy at seeing such a number of strangers, but my natives assured me it was only a very large corroboree. With much persuasion, I learned from my chief that they intended to kill every one on the station where the natives had been poisoned. I went with him to the camp, and I believe that had I not been with him they would have killed him for having told me. After much angry discussion, I induced them to give up their project. I assured them that the miscreant and his accomplices should be hung . . .[28]

Punishment in Aboriginal society varied according to the seriousness of the crime. For less serious crimes than murder, a beating could be a means of dealing with the situation. Robinson described one incident when a woman and a child were severely beaten. The woman's crime was that she 'had been away a fortnight with another man'.[29]

Beating was seen to be applicable not only to fellow Aboriginals: there are six cases of Europeans being beaten by Aborigines described in Robinson's 1841 journals. In a case involving the overseer of Captain Campbell's farm at Port Fairy, the beating was given because the treatment of Aborigines was not approved. The Aborigines had stolen four tons of potatoes. Campbell's overseer captured an Aborigine and intended to make him a prisoner. But the Aborigines reversed the situation and gave the overseer a beating. Robinson also found that Gibb's shepherd at an outstation near the Hopkins River had been beaten when he could easily have been killed. He was alone and saw three Aborigines before being hit on the back of the head. Robinson put this violence down to Aborigines seeking revenge against Gibb for his involvement in a party who went out and shot at a number of Aborigines. In another case, a man called Agnew, working on Baillie's station, had engaged the services of a black woman from her husband. The payment agreed on was two blankets. But the man 'kept her 2 days, beat and ill used her, and then turned her away without giving her anything'. The Aborigine watched and waited. It was three days later before Agnew went out without his gun. When he did so, the Aborigine gave him a beating with a waddy.[30]

There were other incidents where Aborigines demonstrated a measured sense of punishment. The evidence is clear that Aborigines did not kill whenever they had a chance. Hutkeepers and shepherds were vulnerable but even those who took little care were not necessarily in serious danger. There is, for example, amongst the stories of 'outrages' that of the very casual shepherd at Muston's station.

> It was hot weather and he was laying on his back with his hat over his eyes when he received a spear in his leg. He jumped up and saw a black going away with a sheep on his back . . . He will be more cautious in future where he sleeps. One sheep only was taken.[31]

Thomas Ricketts's overseer was thrown down by the Aborigines when they rushed into the outstation hut, but they left him unharmed, simply holding an axe over his head to prevent him rising while they took all the items they wanted.[32] Francis Henty and his men were annoyed rather than harmed. The events of 29 and 30 December 1837 were typical:

> December 29
> . . . Natives rushed Burns flock and succeeded in getting 3 sheep.
> December 30
> A large Tribe of Natives trying to rush the sheep again. One Native held Burns with a battle axe in his hand over him while the others stole the sheep. Burns succeeded in getting away by knocking the Native down who immediately took to his heels.[33]

The idea of reciprocity that Warner stated to have been the basis of Murngin fighting can be seen in the Western District in Aborigines' reaction to Europeans taking their women. One European reported that the natives told him 'by and by take white Miss, very good; white men take black gin and black men take white gin'.[34] A Welshman lost near Mt Rouse, found and taken to an Aboriginal camp for the night before being escorted to Mt Rouse, told of being offered an Aboriginal woman and of their reaction to his rejection of the offer: 'The natives said very good white man, black man have black gin, white man white gin'.[35] Robinson was also told that an Aboriginal had tried to have intercourse with Horatio Wills's wife and to take her away.[36] Unfortunately no further detail of the incident was given.

The District was a 'distant field of murder' in several ways. Aborigines killed Europeans. Europeans killed Aborigines. But Aborigines also turned on other Aborigines whose presence was due to European settlement. In Aboriginal culture death was the penalty for intrusion on the land of others but circumstances had altered as Europeans, oblivious of such boundaries, encouraged or forced Aborigines also to ignore them. Bradbury from New South Wales, for example, employed by James Hunter at Eumeralla, was killed by local Aborigines. Robinson at Port Fairy in 1841 mentioned that Captain Campbell's stock-keeper was a native of Adelaide. 'He says he was stolen by Johnny Griffiths [after whom Griffiths Island at Port Fairy was named] when he was a little boy and he has been with Griffiths ever since', wrote Robinson. A year later on a further visit he discovered that the 'Adelaide black' had been killed, speared by local Aborigines.[37] Europeans coming into contact with such incidents were appalled but had no perception that it was the European presence that was contributing to the greater frequency of such occurrences.

Two examples also indicate that Aborigines turned on those of their own culture after they had been harmed by Europeans. The brother of Tagara (Roger), in grief at the taking away of his brother by Fyans and the police, killed a local Aborigine. Illitbrin, a Wanedeet conedeet, shot in the mouth by Winter's shepherd, speared a boy from Mt Rouse. Robinson's explanation was that Illitbrin blamed the boy 'for making a noise and bringing the white ruffian' but Illitbrin may have seen the boy as responsible in a much more direct way.[38]

The murder of Europeans was not the outrage most complained about by Europeans. It was stealing—sometimes of cattle, calves and horses but usually of sheep. The number of sheep stolen varied from one stolen from the shepherd mentioned earlier taking a quiet nap at Muston's to hundreds of sheep. But how many were taken seemed not to affect the use of the word 'outrage' or the violence of the European reaction. The stealing of even one sheep was regarded as 'outrageous'.

This was a pioneer community in which sheep were regarded as precious. According to Thomas Learmonth, who in 1838 occupied land at Buninyong, Burrumbeet and Maiden Hills, the first settlers 'lived exclusively on salted provisions' as their original stock consisted 'entirely of breeding sheep'.[39] A shepherd killing a sheep was a serious matter leading to a court appearance. The value of the sheep and other stock can be seen in the prices they brought. In August 1839 good ewes were selling for from 30 to 40 shillings, wethers 25 to 30 shillings, working bullocks £35 to £45. For horses people paid very large amounts— £60, £70 and even £80. Costs of establishing oneself were high. It took three men (a hutkeeper and two shepherds) to look after every 1200 to 1500 sheep. These men had not only to be paid (shepherds, £30 to £40 a year) but also rationed at the rate of 12 lbs flour, 12 lbs meat, 2 oz tea and 2½ lbs sugar a week.[40] Thus men were naturally anxious about their investment.

It is difficult to be sure of the motive behind the stealing of sheep. An indication of contradictory evidence is given in Robertson's account of the 'wanton' killing of '610 fine ewes just about to lamb, for which 42s. a head had been paid the year before', yet his description of the scene indicated that Aborigines planned to use some of the sheep. Furthermore, they may have been forced to flee before more of the sheep had been cut up:

> There were 610 fine ewes . . . all dead; some skinned; others skinned and quartered; some cut open and the fat taken out and piled in skins, but most of them just knocked on the head with a stick; meat, fat, and all mixed with the fine sand of the stringy-bark forest.[41]

The clue to the situation is the word 'wanton'. Nearly every squatter who had sheep stolen complained of the wasteful maiming and abandonment of animals: of coming across sheep lying crippled with their hind-legs dislocated, their eyes reproachfully turned towards the newcomers as if imploring assistance. Was the aim to harass and annoy till the Europeans left?

There is some evidence that the aim of the Aborigines was to remove the newcomers from their country. At Niel Black's Glenormiston station, near the present Terang, where the massacre of Aborigines allegedly by Frederick Taylor was followed by attempts to keep away those who had survived, the 'remnants of the tribes' frequently came 'in a body of twenty and thirty at a time threatening to murder the sheph[ds] unless they left them the place'. Joseph, a shepherd employed by Thomas Learmonth at Buninyong, reported that the Aborigines repeatedly told him in their own language, which he understood, 'to go or they would kill me'. Acheson French of The Grange in September 1842 stated that the Aborigines had called at his station and 'desired the Hutkeeper to go away and leave them in possession of the hut'.[42]

Attacks were not only on isolated shepherds and hutkeepers and their huts. For example, Patrick Codd told Sievwright of an attack by about eighteen to twenty Aborigines on Wedge's home station at The Grange.[43] The swivel gun mounted there indicated that such an attack was not unexpected. The presence of a similar mounted swivel gun at the Winters' home station also provides evidence that Aborigines were envisaged as attacking home stations as well as outstations.[44]

Francis Henty, explaining the opposition encountered from local Aborigines when the Henty's inland stations were taken up, described Aborigines burning off close to the hut deliberately to annoy Europeans.[45] Geelong too, it seems, suffered from fires lit by Aborigines. P. L. Brown, editor of the Clyde Company papers, commented that at the close of 1840 'fires lit by the natives, devouring the yellowed grass, were into the township'.[46]

Aborigines, like Europeans, had a keen sense of outrage. They resented European actions, seeing individual Europeans as 'bad' people as an incident concerning Gibb Junior illustrates. Niel Black and Protector Robinson were out riding together when they came across a young man who had been shot by Gibb, probably the son of Henry Gibb of Hopkins Hill station. Robinson took the opportunity to show Black the evidence of shooting, 'the wounded parts in the young man's left shoulder and in the back'. Black suggested that the man had been stealing, but Robinson denied it:

> I said . . . he told me . . . he was quietly sitting in his mia mia, a long way from Mr. Gibbs when piccanniny Mr. Gibbs came to him and said, be off, and then shot him . . . The natives said, Mr. Gibbs no good. Mr. Black said, in reply, very good Mr. Gibbs. The natives said *Boroke* no, no good Mr. Gibbs.[47]

In the north of the District Aborigines complained to Robinson of European behaviour:

> The natives at Hall's were shot at Hall's hut; Hall was present. The natives showed me how they acted, said they told them to be off, pushed them out and then took up muskets and shot the two men as they were going away. They took all their things and put them in the fire.

At Woodland's, where John Francis was superintendent, Robinson talked to a young Aborigine who told him that on the occasion on which Francis shot Aborigines, 'the natives did not use or throw spears or any other weapons, that Francis, [and] Synnott with a party of men went to the camp down the river a short distance and made the attack on the natives and shot them'.[48]

Being driven from their land rankled. There was too much '"be off" all about', they said.[49] Robinson reported that the Aborigines wanted him to go round to all the settlers who drove them away and be 'plenty sulky and talk a big one'.

From the Aboriginal point of view much of the violence seemed to be without reason. Even a European bystander in the following incident was remembered by the Aborigines recounting the incident to have asked why the woman was killed:

> . . . a native woman had been killed at John Henty's out station . . . her name was Nar.rer.burnin . . . The man's name was Tom who shot her and the other man's name who interfered was George . . . She was at a water hole and the

man shot her and then kicked her and stabbed her with a bayonet several times and hit her with it. And then buried her in the ground. George said what for you kill this woman?[50]

An Aboriginal witness described an incident in which three Aborigines were shot by W. J. Purbrick's men at his Koroite Creek outstation: 'She said the men told them to come and they would give them damper. When they went, they shot them'.[51]

Exclusion from their 'country' was central to the Aboriginal sense of outrage. It is interesting in the light of this that Europeans who prided themselves on their good relations with the Aborigines saw themselves as sharing with Aborigines. Samuel Winter, for example, was told by settlers that Aborigines told them they had given Winter 'the Wannon country, no doubt partly with the idea that a good range of country would thereby be secured where they could live unmolested'. Charles Gray of Nareeb Nareeb welcomed local Aborigines handing out flour, tea and sugar and becoming a great favourite of the tribe. Thomas Chirnside at Mt William also adopted a friendly approach and claimed that relations with the Aborigines on his stations were peaceful. When he bought a station on the Wannon he took two Aborigines from Mt William to contact the local Aborigines and bring them to him. This they did and as at Mt William he 'gave them to understand that I wished to be friendly with them; that if they did not steal, they should be at liberty to roam about as usual'. Robinson in 1843 reported that a party of settlers looking for a station on the edge of the Grampians had been ordered by the natives to leave but had adopted a friendly approach and been allowed to stay. Captain Allen 'allowed them to stop, and at the time of my visit there were several families quietly located and usefully employed', wrote Robinson.[52]

There is no doubt that the Aborigines understood that their land had been taken. What seemed to upset them most was that their willingness to share had been followed by their being turned away, not wanted.[53] Was this what was behind the attacks on property and the stealing of sheep? If the European could take the land, the waterholes, and the food which had previously been there for the hunting and collecting, then the Aborigines may have argued that they should treat the Europeans in a similar manner. They should not ask, but take, as the Europeans had done. If, as Warner argued, 'the fundamental principle underlying all the causes of Murngin warfare' was 'reciprocity' then this is in fact likely.

The year of greatest inter-racial conflict was 1842. In August of that year the *Portland Mercury* reported, 'the country might as well be in a state of civil war, as few but the boldest of the settlers will move from their home stations'.[54] What distinguished Aboriginal actions of this time and later is that those who are named as leaders had considerable experience of European ways, sometimes having lived and worked as a trusted employee on a station. The names Koort Kirrup, Cold Morning, Jupiter, Cocknose, Charley and Mr Murray become well known. They feature in official reports and complaints and in the newspaper stories of the day.

Historians have tended to emphasize the racial violence in the Portland Bay District in 1842 by referring to two easily available items of evidence. These are the petition from the 'Settlers and Inhabitants of Port Fairy' and Boldrewood's *Old Melbourne Memories*, which vividly describes events summed up as 'The Eumeralla War'. A detailed study reveals that Aboriginal attacks were much more widespread. James Blair, Police Magistrate at Portland, wrote to La Trobe of a 'general move among the Aborigines'.[55] Virtually the whole district west of the Hopkins was caught up in a wave of Aboriginal attacks. These attacks could no longer be explained away as simply stealing of sheep, being destructive not only of sheep and cattle but of buildings and of equipment. Crops were deliberately destroyed. Many more lives were threatened than previously. This one might argue was an attempt by the Aborigines to remove the Europeans from their country. While there is no evidence of co-operation of Aboriginal groups across the whole District, the wave of attacks came at the same time across the District.

What triggered off the hostility is difficult to determine. The summer of 1842 was another year of drought. The District was rapidly filling up. Some Aborigines blamed the Europeans for the drought and they certainly contributed to the difficulties of the Aboriginal people in the circumstances. Sievwright commented in early 1842, 'There is not a pool of water, suited for the purpose of a station, of which they are not bereft'.[56] Was it this that caused the Aboriginal attacks? J. G. Robertson of Wando Vale wrote of 1841-42-43 as 'three bad years'. They were years of economic depression when at least twenty of the squatters in the Portland Bay District were sold off. Were Europeans in the difficult economic climate more ruthless in their attitude to Aborigines? Or was there a frustration concerning the Europeans? Did Aborigines perceive that they were undervalued, seen as unimportant, not taken into account even when they appeared to have been accepted as trusted employees?

While there is no evidence of a large-scale meeting of Aborigines, it is clear that there was considerable interaction between Aboriginal groups. Koort Kirrup, a Palapnue conedeet, for example, whose camp was situated at Emu Creek, was called to the camp of the Wanedeet conedeet at the Winters' station to help deal with the situation when in 1841 Aborigines in Robinson's party started taking local Aboriginal women. Koort Kirrup also had links to the territory at the mouth of the Glenelg River. When Robinson visited Hunter's station and the camp of the Nillan conedeet at Mt Eccles in 1842 he listed down among other names Yi.er.war.rer.min (Billy), a Yowen conedeet. There was a warrant out for the arrest of Jupiter, Jacky and Billy for 'outrages' at Hunter's nearby Eumeralla station. If the Billy mentioned by Robinson was the same

Billy for whom the warrant had been issued, this indicates close co-operation between the Yowen conedeet of 'Tarrone' station just north of Port Fairy and the Nillan Conedeet of the Mt Eccles area. Another Yowen conedeet, Mur.re.ying, was noted down by Robinson and some Tappoc conedeet, Aborigines of Mt Napier. Thus the Aborigines of Mt Napier, Mt Eeles and the country at 'Tarrone' were associating with one another. Additional evidence is that Robinson, travelling through the area in 1841, was given the name of an Aboriginal group called the Nillan conedeet by a Yowen conedeet Aboriginal who spoke of the Nillan conedeet 'very favourably'. Evidence of such co-operation may not indicate a new development; merely the existence of kinship links across the District.

Richard Broome in *Aboriginal Australians* mentions scattered evidence suggesting that the Aborigines were 'beginning to adapt their traditions to the needs of the military struggle with the Europeans before they were overwhelmed'. He specifically mentions Portland Bay Aborigines:

> A number of military leaders have been identified, significantly including people from outside the tribe. The Gunditjmara at Port Fairy were led by men with the European names of Jupiter, Cocknose and Bradbury, the last of whom was from New South Wales.[57]

Broome is incorrect in implying that leaders in the Western District came from outside the tribe. Jupiter and Cocknose, like most Western District Aborigines after 1841, had European names. But they were not European: they were Nillan conedeet, Aborigines of Mount Eeles. Jupiter was a name Robinson was likely to have given. He gave the name Jupiter to an Aborigine he met near Port Fairy on 27 or 28 April 1841. This may have been Jupiter of the Nillan conedeet.[58]

Bradbury, a Goulburn Plains Aborigine, was employed by Hunter as a stock-keeper but there is no evidence of his leading any attack on Europeans. He is mentioned as being involved in only one incident with Aborigines. In November 1842 the *Portland Mercury* described how a party travelling from Portland towards Port Fairy came across a group of Aborigines headed by Cold Morning. They disappeared after a shot had been fired by Bradbury. In this incident Bradbury was not leading Aborigines: he fired at the Aborigines. In fact no such incident occurred. A member of the party travelling to Port Fairy, Cecil Pybus Cooke, wrote to the newspaper to correct the story that had been printed. No Aborigines had been seen by the party. After crossing the Fitzroy River, Bradbury had commenced loading his pistol which unfortunately had gone off, shattering his hand. Cooke suggested that Bradbury had made up the story 'through fear of his master's displeasure'. Bradbury was far from being a leader of the local Aborigines. They murdered him in 1845, taking no pains to conceal the name of the murderer.[59]

One of the areas most troubled in early 1842 was the area to the north of Port Fairy. Dr Bernard, partner to Dr Kilgour of Tarrone, wrote to Fyans imploring help from either the police or the military forces to prevent a state of 'open war between the races'.[60] He detailed the attacks on Tarrone. There had been disturbances during the last six months of 1841. A spate of attacks had begun in the first week of January 1842 when a stock-keeper was threatened by armed Aborigines. On 16 January a party of about twenty Aborigines arrived at the stockyard at dawn but retreated when an alarm was sounded. On 24 January at 5.30 a.m. seven or eight Aborigines appeared at the stockyard at milking time. They divided into three parties, one coming round either end of the stockyard, the other through the middle of the stockyard and in the ensuing attack the overseer was speared. When the alarm was sounded and two armed men arrived to aid the overseer, the Aborigines fled. The next day the Aborigines stole a horse. During the same week two more horses tethered close to the huts were taken. On 1 February a man watching the cows was surprised, his arms pinioned behind his back, his musket seized and three horses taken. The Aborigines threatened to kill the man. One tried to use the musket but it did not discharge and the man eventually escaped. A party looking for the horses came across a recently abandoned Aboriginal camp in which horse flesh was roasting on the fire and the bones scattered about. Since then Aborigines had been about the property and spears had been thrown from a distance at Dr Kilgour. Bernard had also been challenged by Aborigines while travelling home from Port Fairy. The first time he pulled out his pistol and was allowed to continue, but two miles from Loughnan's, he was again threatened by ten or twelve Aborigines who endeavoured to surround him. He wrote, 'the whole property of the station is going to ruin. Five horses out of six being killed, the cattle cannot be watched, the calves are lost about the run, the Dairy ruined, and no man's life is safe'.

He blamed the Protectorate, as many squatters did. He claimed that Aborigines had been first brought to his station in 1841 by Chief Protector Robinson and that Sievwright, the Assistant Protector, promised Aborigines that Europeans who threatened or shot them would be punished, thus encouraging them to take a stand against Europeans and no longer to be intimidated.

Whatever crimes might be committed in the future by the Mt Rouse Aborigines, Bernard was not blaming them for the outrages he listed. His letter was dated 16 February. The Aborigines only arrived at Mt Rouse on 12 February. As for the charge that Robinson was responsible as he first brought the Aborigines to the station, Robinson's comment was blunt: 'fudge . . . who took them to Hunters and Brocks new station? I had not been to these or Richie [Ritchie]'.[61]

As Robinson's comment implies, the Aboriginal attacks were not confined to Tarrone. In his letter Bernard lists other stations in the vicinity attacked before 16 February— Ritchie's, Whitehead's, Burchett's, Loughnan's and Campbell's at Port Fairy.

Bernard's letter was followed by an undated petition to La Trobe from 'Settlers and Inhabitants of the Port Fairy District'. They complained of the Aborigines' 'numbers, ferocity, and their cunning' which 'render them peculiarly formidable'. They were being attacked both during the day and at night. The petitioners listed outrages suffered principally within the previous two months. They included those mentioned by Bernard:

Mr Ritchie—	Man killed, 100 sheep taken, and hut robbed of everything it contained, including a double-barrelled gun, with ammunition.
Mr Campbell—	300 sheep and 100 tons of potatoes.
Messrs Kilsom [Kilgour] and Bernard—	Five horses taken, and seven head of cattle killed; 56 calves; also 33 driven off; and two men wounded. The station has been attacked four times.
Mr Loughnan—	600 sheep taken, of which 130 were recovered; hut robbed, and two double-barrelled guns taken.
Messrs Bolden—	10 cows and 40 calves killed; hut attacked several times, and man severely wounded.
Mr Whitehead—	Three flocks attacked simultaneously, one of which was taken away, and the shepherd desperately wounded. The major part was eventually recovered; one man taken, but recovered.
Mr Muston—	200 sheep taken, and man speared.
Mr Burchett—	Shepherd fired at.
Mr Cox—	Two horses taken, station attacked, and flock of sheep carried off, and shepherd dreadfully wounded.
Mr Hunter—	Two horses killed, hut robbed, and men driven off station.
Messrs Hutcheson and Kidd—	Shepherd killed; found with a spear through his heart.
Messrs Carmichael and Jamison—	One horse taken.
Messrs Kemp—	30 sheep.
Mr Farie—	50 sheep.
Captain Webster—	250 sheep, and man wounded.
Mr Black—	50 sheep.
Mr Thompson—	260 sheep, and man killed.
Mr Gill [Gibb?]—	300 sheep.
Mr Cameron—	700 sheep taken, but mostly recovered.
Mr Bromfield—	180 sheep, station attacked and robbed, and hutkeeper severely wounded.
Mr Faloye [Forlonge?]—	A very valuable bull killed, and a number of calves.
Dr Martin—	Six cows, three bullocks, 20 calves.
Mr Woolley—	Man killed, and cattle driven off.
Mr Aylman—	200 ewes, and 150 lambs.
Mr Barnet—	450 ewes and lambs.[62]

Foster Fyans also listed all the squatters who had suffered from Aboriginal attacks between December 1841 and June 1842, confirming the large number of properties which had been attacked.[63]

Who were the Aborigines responsible for the 'outrages'? Bernard claimed that the Aborigines responsible for killing Ritchie's hutkeeper were also responsible for threatening his shepherd. He also stated that it was a party led by Murray, 'a tame Aborigine', that had threatened the shepherd and driven off the sheep at Loughnan's. Robinson in his report to La Trobe after investigating the situation in the Port Fairy area named Mr Murray (also known as Puntkum) responsible. He reported that when Kilgour's station had been first attacked, Murray had been at Carmichael's. He believed Murray was responsible for the attack at Loughnan's and that he was a leader in the sheep stealing. In a later letter he named Part.ke.un (Puntkum) as responsible for attacks in the neighbourhood of Tarrone. In his journal Robinson recorded the names of two men the Aborigines told him had killed Ritchie's man. They were Purt.ke.un and Til.lip.cor.re.way. These men had acted as guides to Robinson in 1841, travelling with him across to the Glenelg River. When Robinson first met Purt.ke.un he recorded that he was Yowen conedeet; that is, his country was at Tarrone. He also called him How.weet conedeet, of the country north of the Yowen conedeet. He met him again in 1842 and again noted that he was How.weet conedeet. Til.lip.cor.re.way was also known as Tarrone Charley. Thus both men were fighting in their 'country'.[64] In early May Blair reported the capturing of Puckninal (probably Part.ke.un) and the holding of him in custody.

Further to the west there was serious trouble at James Hunter's station on the Eumeralla River. On 8 January Hunter had appealed for help and Fyans had immediately sent two Border Police. They had not only failed to capture the Aboriginal leaders but one was seriously wounded in a struggle with the Aborigines. Two nights later the Aborigines had taken one of the Border Police horses valued at £80. As at Tarrone, the situation was reaching a crisis, with the place being

> robbed on many occasions, by the same gang of savages, constantly attacking and finally driving the people from the establishment leaving all to their mercy ... even the poultry killed and every article about the place destroyed ...[65]

Foster Fyans, sent to the Port Fairy area to deal with the perpetrators of the outrages, reported lack of success in capturing Tarrone Charley but he had more success in capturing those responsible for the attacks on Hunter's station. In April he captured Jupiter and Jackey and later Cocknose, Doctor and a boy. Two of the Aborigines died as a result of wounds but Jupiter and Cocknose (and Bumbletoe?), regarded as leaders in the attack on Hunter's station, were taken to Port Fairy and thence by ship to Melbourne for their trial. Attacks on Hunter's property ceased.

The two men captured and sent to Melbourne were Gar.rare.rer (or maybe Tar.rare.rer), alias Jupiter, and Ty.koo.he, alias Cocknose, both Nillan conedeet. The country of the Nillan conedeet was at Mount Eeles. Jupiter was about nineteen years of age while Cocknose was an old man. Robinson visited the camp of the Nillan conedeet while at Hunter's station on 20 and 21 March 1842. Again, as at Bernard's, Hunter's adversaries were local Aborigines, not those brought by Sievwright to Mt Rouse.

A third centre of Aboriginal attacks in early 1842 was Henty's station near Mt Eckersley, just north of Portland. Henty first reported an attack on 27 January. A large crop of oats had been 'burnt down' by the Aborigines. In mid-March there was a further attack. The Aborigines used large stones to knock down a building, they broke a plough, destroyed as much property as they could and drove the Henty employees off the property. Messrs Henty and Company turned to Blair for assistance to regain control of the property. Blair asked the officer in charge of the Military Detachment at Portland to send a party of three soldiers to form a 'Guard' at Mt Eckersley. This was done not so much for individual as for public protection, Blair explained to La Trobe. Mt Eckersley was one of the resting places for teams proceeding 'up and down the country'; travelling 'would become very unsafe if natives entertaining such hostile feelings were permitted to keep undisturbed possession of it'.[66]

While the guard was stationed at Mt Eckersley there was no further trouble. But a few days after it was withdrawn, in early May, the Aborigines seized and drove away a bullock team loaded with provisions proceeding up the country. There were two teams. One belonged to Tulloch, the other to the town carrier. When the Aborigines appeared out of the scrub they had thrown spears at the drivers. Tulloch's man fired several shots at them and they let him pass on, concentrating on the other team, the driver of which had been unable to fire his gun. Some of these Aborigines were known to Europeans and familiar with European customs as the following features of the incident reveal. The driver of the town carrier's team was called 'Tiger' by the Aborigines. This was the nickname by which he was known in Portland. One of the Aborigines, having taken Tiger's whip, called the bullocks by name and drove them off into the bush. Later two of the bullocks were found chained to a tree as a bullock driver would secure them.[67] Blair immediately despatched police to the scene of the crime but they returned to Portland without success in capturing the Aborigines. Shortly afterwards a number of Aborigines appeared at the Convincing Ground where a Henty Headsman, John Robson, recognized Cold Morning, said to be a leader in the attack, and with the help of fellow whalers captured Cold

Morning and another Aborigine. Cold Morning was taken to Portland and then sent to Melbourne for trial.

Cold Morning, according to Robinson, was Cart Conedeet belonging to the Mt Clay area. In the opinion of the *Portland Guardian* Cold Morning was of the tribe 'who ordinarily occupies the country between Portland and Port Fairy'. One of the other Aborigines involved was Jacky Jacky of Port Fairy.[68]

The Glenelg River was a fourth area experiencing Aboriginal attacks. On 23 May 1842 French, Police Magistrate at The Grange, informed La Trobe of the murder of Donald McKenzie, a settler on the Glenelg, and his hutkeeper, and the taking of 700 sheep from McKenzie's property. Koort Kirrup, who worked for McKenzie, was blamed but a large number of Aborigines were involved in the attack. Koort Kirrup and those involved were reported to have gone down to the mouth of the Glenelg after the murder, so that even though there was a warrant for Koort Kirrup's arrest, he was not captured till much later. Attacks continued on settlers in the Smoky River area, however, and the Smoky River tribe were blamed. According to Blair, Koort Kirrup and Peter were seen at some of the stations.[69]

In early July Thomas Ricketts's station on the Glenelg was attacked as were adjoining stations. This time the leader was stated to be an Aborigine named Bob, who had been 'domesticated' on Ricketts's station. The Aborigines had taken sheep and not only killed but eaten Foreman, the shepherd. Ricketts applied to both Blair and French for a trooper to be left at his station but neither could help him. French felt with such a small force and the 'hourly expectation of being called upon to render assistance to the surrounding settlers that he could not spare a man'. He had just returned from having reclaimed sheep taken by the Tappoc conedeet (Mt Napier Aborigines) from Thompson, a settler in the Hamilton area. The Aborigines had speared Thompson's shepherd, and then taking the flock from him, had driven them by a circuitous route of more than forty miles to the swamps and stony rises south-west of Mt Napier. The Aborigines fled into 'a large tea-tree scrub' at the arrival of French and his party and so escaped.[70]

By the end of July Blair was receiving notice of almost daily outrages. The Hentys and the Winters had suffered as well as 'Thomson' (maybe the Thompson mentioned above), Carey and McCrae. Trevor Winter, Butcher and a servant went out in an attempt to recover sheep taken by the Aborigines. When they came across the Aboriginal camp, they too found that the culprits were local Aborigines. They were 'principally Aborigines who had been residing on Trevor Winter's station and being fed by him for two years'. These Aborigines asked him why he was angry with them as they had not taken his sheep (they had taken those of his cousin):

What for you sulky? sheep no belong to you; come on, me no frighten; by, by, plenty we spear you, Blackfellow.

As the Aborigines prepared to surround the Europeans and an Aborigine was poised to use his spear, Winter shot an Aborigine. The Europeans retreated, pursued by the Aborigines. Three days later Winter with others went out to retake the rest of the sheep, and they came across many which had been mutilated and others eaten, before they reached the Aboriginal camp near where it had been previously. Again there was a hostile exchange. While the Aborigines with the remaining sheep were not more than twelve miles from the station, they had been driven at least thirty or forty miles to arrive there. They had been taken across many swamps so that the horses could not follow their track.[71]

To the north Europeans were being threatened. Horatio Wills wrote to La Trobe in March from Mt William, complaining not of local Aborigines but of 'the intrusions of the wild tribes of aborigines'. Attacks had been occurring for the previous two months. The cattle herd of his immediate neighbour had been reduced to half. In January Riley in the Grampians had reported to Blair that two hundred Aborigines had assembled on Barnett's station, and six armed Aborigines had come to his station. In late February or early March two horses belonging to James Brock had been taken to Mt Sturgeon. On 'Big' Clarke's Woodlands station in the Pyrenees, Aboriginal attacks which commenced when the land was occupied in 1841 continued through 1842. Not only were sheep taken, but Clarke's employees who attempted to recapture them were driven off. One man, Billy Billy, who was regarded as 'more notorious than the rest', took enough of Clarke's sheep to form a sheep station north of Clarke's station. The Aborigines 'made a bush yard and shepherded the sheep during the day and yarded them in the usual way at night'.[72]

The District was in turmoil by August 1842. Jupiter and Cocknose had been returned, and the attacks on Hunter's Eumeralla station recommenced. The *Portland Mercury* listed the attacks in the issue of 31 August 1842. To the attacks on Ricketts, Hunter and the Winters already mentioned it added descriptions of attacks on Cameron at the Crawford, Thompson at Yohoo Ponds, Corney of Wando Vale, Norris on the Glenelg, Henty on the Wannon, French at The Grange, on Desailly where a shepherd had been killed and sheep taken, Patterson on The Grange, Riley on the Wannon, Purbrick on the Wannon, Watson on the Wando, McCrae near Merino Downs, as well as attacks on stations at Port Fairy. The newspaper claimed that in the past four months 3500 sheep had been destroyed, four men killed and four men seriously wounded. There was a limit to how much settlers could be expected to tolerate without retaliation and according to the *Portland Mercury* it had been reached:

Can it be expected, we would ask, that the settlers of this district, that any man, any body of men, with the feelings universally planted in our nature, will sullenly fold their arms, and look passively on while their friends, their servants and themselves know not the hour nor the day when their hitherto peaceful homes may not be converted into houses of wailing, dismay and depair.[73]

Hunter appealed to La Trobe for help. Hand-to-hand fighting was occurring in which Aborigines stood their ground and attempted to repel the armed Europeans on horseback—but it is important to note that the fighting was over possession of sheep:

... on the 7th ultimo [August] a party of blacks, headed by Jupiter and Cocknose ... attacked my shepherd and drove off a flock of sheep ... my superintendent and several of the men ... went in pursuit of the marauders, and after a severe skirmish succeeded in recovering the property. On the 10th, the shepherds were again attacked by upwards of 150 blacks ... a part of the blacks took possession of the sheep and the remainder attacked the shepherds, who were in a position of great danger, but being well armed, they were ... able to keep their assailants at bay until assistance arrived, when the blacks made off, and the men obtained repossession of the sheep. On the 18th the blacks again attacked the shepherds ... and drove off 1,014 sheep ... a party went out to recover the sheep, and they described the road as strewed with dead carcases. About eight miles off the station they came up with the blacks, and it was not until they had overcome a vigorous resistance, during which three of the blacks were shot, and several others wounded, that they succeeded in recovering the remainder of the sheep, 511 having been killed or destroyed.[74]

The station had twenty-five employees, according to Hunter. Here there was some safety in numbers but Hunter claimed that the men refused to stay as the attacks continued. Warrants were again issued for the taking of Jupiter and Cocknose.

If a hundred and fifty Aborigines had attacked the station, as Hunter claimed, this was an example of a number of Aboriginal groups combining. According to Robinson the Nillan conedeet in 1841 consisted of only twenty-six men, twenty women and thirty-six children. However, one must be wary of figures provided by settlers. Three depositions concerning a 'collision' between Europeans and Aborigines in late 1840 show how estimates of numbers varied—the number of Aborigines they faced was estimated by the men as three hundred, more than one hundred and fifty, and about five hundred!

In the whole of the year the only period of peace occurred when Fyans and the Border Police plus the Native Police were in the area. Outrages had not been a feature of one season. They had begun in summer and continued through till the arrival of the Native Police and return of the Border Police in September.

At the end of November after the Native Police left the District 'outrages' began again. A party of 150 Aborigines attacked two men and a bullock dray loaded with provisions, tea, sugar, flour and rum. With the help of an Aborigine, the Chief Constable and two troopers from Portland found an Aboriginal camp. A captured Aboriginal woman informed the Aboriginal guide that two tribes had joined for the attack and that a tame black in the service of Messrs Whyte had driven off the bullocks and unyoked them. She mentioned the names of 'tame blacks' who were leaders in the attack.[75]

A local newspaper stated the size of the Aboriginal group to be much smaller, but it may still have consisted of members of two clan groups. The *Portland Mercury* named Harry (in the service of the Whyte Brothers for more than 18 months) as leader in the attack.[76] Blair issued warrants for the arrest of a number of Aborigines, amongst whom was Cold Morning. If he was involved, two Aboriginal groups had joined forces—the Cart conedeet and an inland group.

French suggested to La Trobe that some mounted police should be stationed permanently at the Fitzroy River, as the distance between it and the next station was some thirty miles 'through forest'. Drays could easily be plundered. If some such scheme was not instituted, he suggested, the Aborigines might turn to stealing from drays as it would be easier than stealing sheep and cattle.

Fyans in his report for the year 1842 suggested that settlers had exaggerated their losses and that newspapers had similarly exaggerated the situation, which was no worse in the west than it had been earlier in the eastern part of the District. He believed the Aboriginal attacks around Port Fairy had ceased, and that soon this would also happen on the Glenelg. The *Portland Mercury* concerned about the District's reputation, was eager to persuade readers that inter-racial conflict was not as intense as it might seem. The editor argued that the beginning of a local Press with detailed coverage of local outrages should not be taken as an indication of increasing hostility of the Aborigines but only of the desire of the Press to bring each case to the notice of the public and the authorities.[77]

'Outrages' continued, however, during 1843 and for years afterwards. Two drays belonging to Francis Henty were attacked five miles beyond the Fitzroy River. This time Koort Kirrup and Harry were blamed. Potatoes were taken from David Edgar's outstation at Mt Eckersley. In March Mr Meather, whose station was in the vicinity of those of Ricketts, Riley and Norris, had sheep taken. Mr Midden, a new settler on the Glenelg, lost sheep. Horses were taken from Mr McPherson and Messrs Murray and Addison on the Glenelg. In April the Winters' station was attacked and two Aborigines shot. The *Portland Guardian* complained on 29 July 1843 that the Aborigines were 'troublesome . . . in many parts of the district'.

In September 1845 Aborigines killed and ate a mare at Mr Scott's at the junction of the Crawford and Glenelg rivers, and killed William Brown who had taken up land in the 'New Country' on the South Australian side of the border.[78]

Just as it appeared that Aboriginal attacks might be petering out, violence of a level similar to that of 1842 erupted in the area around Mt Eeles. 'All of a sudden war broke out. The reasons . . . none could tell. The whites only wished to be let alone'—this was 'The Eumeralla War' made famous by Rolf Boldrewood, the pseudonym used by Tom Browne, at this time a squatter at Squattlesea Mere on the lower Eumeralla. The properties under attack covered a large part of the territory west and north-west of Port Fairy stretching towards Portland—Yambuck, St Kitts, Weerangourt, Dunmore, Eumeralla East, Eumeralla West, Squattlesea Mere, Castlemaddie and Ettrick. Maybe drought was a factor in causing the renewed violence: the summer of 1844 'was exceptionally dry'. From 'all sides at once came tales of wrong-doing and violence, of maimed and slaughtered stock, of homicide or murder', wrote Boldrewood. The 'guerrilla warfare' proved effective, forcing the squatters to 'the point when "something must be done". We could not permit our cattle to be harried, our servants to be killed, and ourselves to be hunted out of the good land we had occupied by a few savages'.[79]

According to the Dunmore Journals, Aboriginal attacks recommenced in the area in March 1845. From then on there was little relief for the European property owners until April 1847. The Dunmore Journals and the diaries of Annie Maria Baxter (later Dawbin), wife of Lieutenant Andrew Baxter of Yambuck, reveal a consistent response from the Aboriginal population. There is no seasonal pattern. In every month from April 1845 to May 1847 there is mention of being harassed by Aborigines except for November and December 1845; October (Native Police at Dunmore), November, December 1846 and January 1847 (Annie was in Van Diemen's Land during this period). There are twenty-one mentions of Aboriginal violence in the eighteen months for which there are diary entries in this period. Again, as in the Port Fairy settlers' 1842 petition to La Trobe, it is the number of incidents which stand out. These included spearing a man in the head, hanging around the house at night, spearing cattle, lighting a large fire on the run, and confronting individual settlers.

Station work could be interrupted any time as extracts from the Dunmore Journals make clear:

18 May 1845 —Crawfurd came and made out an affidavit regarding a skirmish with the natives . . .

9 June 1845 —Peter and James attacked by the Blacks and forced to fly—on the return with arms the Blacks had disappeared . . .

22 July 1845 — Blacks chased Mr Cunninghame, threw spears at him . . .

Aboriginal 'outrages' continued to the south-west of Mt Eeles on William Learmonth's station till at least the winter of 1846. By that time the presence of Border Police and Native Police was taken for granted. La Trobe, being notified of Learmonth's problems in early 1845, requested Fyans to place his police for the winter in such a way that Learmonth's property would be protected.

In March 1846 La Trobe asked Fyans to place a party of Border Police at Darlot's Creek. Fyans's comment in April makes it clear that the Aborigines were still a serious problem. The stationing of two policemen on Learmonth's run had had 'no effect'. 'In my opinion', he wrote, 'it would be wise for Mr Learmonth to withdraw from his property. I can suggest no other security'.[80] In July 1846 two squatters on the lower Glenelg were still complaining of their stock being 'completely at the mercy of a daring band of Aborigines'.[81]

'Big' Clarke also found continuing trouble on his Woodlands run in the Pyrenees. In 1845 John Hodgkinson refused to work at Woodlands after the Aborigines had driven off 1500 sheep, and a shepherd had been reported severely wounded and dying.[82]

The Europeans claimed that the Aborigines were devoid of gratitude. The *Portland Mercury* argued that since scarcely any attack on a station was made other than under the guidance of a 'tame black', the Aborigines were of an inferior nature:

> It would appear from this that the Australian savage does not occupy a sufficiently elevated position in the ascending scale of humanity to participate in the 'heaven born feeling' of gratitude but rather meets the bestowal of benefits by the detestable yearnings of insatiate cupidity.[83]

The squatters were simply stating fact when they claimed that it was those they knew who had turned on them. Those who appeared friendly in 1841 were those who led their people in attacks during 1842 and later. These men were on their own land, leading their own people and making life difficult for Europeans. The men known to be leaders were those who were the most familiar with European ways and were those most roundly condemned by the Europeans. Bob was described by the *Portland Guardian* as 'that base ingrate'. Foster Fyans described the Nillan conedeet as that 'gang of savages' and Cocknose and Jupiter, their leaders, as 'men of bad character'. H. E. P. Dana, Commandant of the Native Police, described Koort Kirrup as 'a man of bad and dangerous character'.[84]

This was a frontier on which the enemy was the known, someone from whom the station owner perhaps naively expected gratitude and loyalty. There was a blindfold at work: it was as if working for a European was assumed to mean an instant loyalty to the European. There was no perception that the desire to work on a station was perhaps seen by Aborigines as a means of learning new skills, of obtaining new goods, understanding the ways of the newcomers, of perhaps attempting to gain some status with them, perhaps even of increasing one's status amongst other Aborigines.

In the period after 1841 changes were noticeable in Aboriginal behaviour. Europeans perceived Aboriginal leaders, and blamed them for the increased number of attacks and for the seriousness of these attacks. There is some indication of Aboriginal groups combining for the purpose of attacking Europeans or their property.[85] Europeans had complained that Aborigines used guerrilla tactics: they attacked and disappeared. Now Aborigines as at Hunter's station 'closed with their antagonists'.[86] Of the long list of squatters who had suffered Aboriginal attacks in mid-1842 French stated that the Aborigines not only took sheep but 'attempted the lives of those in charge of their respective flocks'.[87] In an incident on one of the Hentys' stations Blair reported that the Aborigines 'had given battle to, and beaten off a party ... who endeavoured to recover some sheep which they had taken'.[88]

Aborigines demonstrated knowledge of guns[89] and experience of handling bullocks and sheep. In different parts of the District, Aborigines drove stolen sheep very long distances before taking them to their camp, showing their determination that the sheep should not be retaken.[90] Also, in different parts of the District, Aborigines erected yards for the sheep.[91] Thus they had begun to care for animals as the Europeans did—to confine and mind them till they were needed for slaughter.

Despite the taking of ammunition and guns, there is little evidence of their being used in attacks. Edinge, McKenzie's hutkeeper, was speared as well as shot. In the Port Fairy area a shepherd was fired at in the early months of 1842 and at Tarrone an Aborigine tried to use a musket: further north near Mt Rouse about the same time Aborigines fired at Charles Smith and a hutkeeper. But such references are few. It would seem that Aborigines instead developed the kind of weapons with which they were already familiar. In mid-1845 James Irvine of Dunmore and a stockman were threatened by Aborigines carrying iron spears. A few days later Aborigines threatened another Dunmore employee. An armed party seeking the Aborigines came across an Aboriginal camp. The Aborigines fled, leaving weapons behind: amongst them Europeans noted an iron tomahawk and, again, an iron spear which William Campbell described as 'a most efficient weapon for killing cattle'.[92]

The examination of Aboriginal customs and Aboriginal actions, as described by Europeans, leads one to the inescapable conclusion that the major violent aspect of the Aboriginal response to European settlement was the taking of property, largely livestock. An analysis of the return providing details of all Aborigines committed for trial between settlement and the end of 1849 leads to the same conclusion.[93] What most Europeans were concerned about was stealing. Of the twenty-six individuals from the western half of the Port Phillip District only eight were committed for murder (and three of these were for murder of Aborigines). Eighteen Aborigines were committed for trial on a charge of stealing, felony or threatening life. In the case of four of these individuals, the evidence of guilt was so slight that two were discharged without trial, one was acquitted and the other one sentenced to only seven weeks imprisonment (elsewhere the term is recorded as only two weeks). There is some evidence which indicates that the motive behind the stealing was to force Europeans to leave but the weight of the evidence suggests that Aborigines were insisting on gaining a share of what Europeans possessed.

7

'more than thirty are said to have been thus laid low'

ON THIS FRONTIER it was each settler and his men that faced local Aborigines. Solutions to any problems that arose between Europeans and Aborigines had to be resolved by the small group of people directly involved. In the beginning there was no official presence, no police or military forces that Europeans could turn to. Used to depending on government to provide protection, they naturally appealed for help to the first Police Magistrate, William Lonsdale, and later to the Superintendent of the Port Phillip District, Charles Joseph La Trobe. But they gained little satisfaction, particularly in the early years.

Even the Secretary of State for the Colonies in England heard in the most graphic terms of the plight of the settlers. It was an outraged resident of Dublin, John Power, who wrote to Lord John Russell, determined to make the Secretary of State fully aware of how 'the authorities' were 'constituted' in that 'distant portion of the British possessions', the Port Phillip District. Power, a friend to the family of Patrick Codd, murdered by Aborigines near Mt Rouse in May 1840, described the circumstances as expressed in a letter received from the District. Murder of settlers or their men was an everyday occurrence as Protectors of Aborigines, 'more properly called murderers', encouraged and supported the Aborigines. The only police, convict constables, were 'the most insolent wretches in existence rendered doubly so by the countenance and support they receive from the magistracy'. Police and military forces were so limited that those who called on the Governor seeking help to apprehend the murderers of Codd were told 'there was no force in the country that could be spared'. Appalled, Power argued that 'England should interfere, and no longer permit those daily murders to be perpetrated with impunity'. Shy of making a fuss he would have preferred not to have to force a Parliamentary inquiry 'but', he wrote, 'I owe it to my own feelings; I owe it to the honour of England, whose colony this distant field of murder is; but, above all, I owe it to humanity, not to let the matter rest, and I am determined that I shall not do so'.[1]

On this frontier La Trobe found himself almost powerless to provide protection for the settlers. It was a situation Governor Gipps found difficult to understand. In reply to the Governor's letter regretting the ineffectual state of the border police of the Geelong District, La Trobe insisted on his efficiency and pointed out the difficulties:

> . . . I feel called upon to undeceive his Excellency with regard to the powers of any limited number of police in an extended district circumstanced like that of Port Phillip.
> Of the very large number of stations now scattered over the face of the country . . . at a distance of from 50 to 200 miles and upwards from the towns of Melbourne and Geelong, a considerable majority may be considered open to attack . . . and these attacks . . . are seldom to be anticipated.

Moreover, the settlers were open to attack from 'one or other division of the tribes surrounding the district, or comprised within its limits'.[2]

To police the District La Trobe had a Crown Lands Commissioner without a full complement of border police, and they had other tasks to perform as well as to deal with 'collisions' between Europeans and Aborigines. Those distant from Geelong were virtually without protection. There was little even for those close to Geelong. William Russell, situated on the Leigh River within reasonable travelling distance of Geelong, complained as late as 5 March 1840 that 'there are only three Mounted Police and they are almost always in attendance on the Police Magistrate in the town of Geelong'.[3] The same concern was expressed by the *Port Phillip Gazette*. What, after all, could Captain Fyans and two policemen effect 'even with their best wishes and utmost exertion?' asked an editorial.[4]

In October 1840 La Trobe voiced his frustration with the situation. Taking into account the special circumstances already explained, he admitted not only that the existing police force was hopelessly inadequate to keep the peace, but it would not 'be easy to state what force would secure that end'. A month later he arrived at the conclusion that 'the peace of the district cannot be preserved by any police force which can be mustered or maintained in the present circumstances of the colony'.[5]

It was not a situation that extra money would easily remedy. La Trobe was forced again and again to face the problem. The Governor's insistence that lawless proceedings be stopped and his promise to sanction any expenditure necessary to achieve this made La Trobe's position worse. It revealed that the Governor still did not understand the problem. La Trobe reviewed his options. He could limit the area of settlement to an area that could be protected. The area would be impossibly small; and those who ignored the limits to settlement would feel encouraged to totally ignore the law, since they received no protection. Another alternative would be to reduce the proportion of assigned labour, the kind of labour often blamed for inter-racial violence. However, the amount of convict labour was relatively small.

La Trobe decided on two measures, neither of them likely to make a considerable difference in the circumstances he described. The first was that a friendly communication should be opened with the Aborigines, particularly those of the outlying regions. It was this that led to Chief Protector Robinson's journey across the District in 1841. Second, that the number of police magistrates be increased as the number of settlers grew. He mentioned the appointment of a Police Magistrate to The Grange.[6] There was already one at Geelong and another at Portland. The extra position would make three across a District that was 350 miles long and 150 miles wide.[7]

In early 1842 the problem of 'protection' for either race on the frontier was still proving intractable. Settlers from the Port Fairy area complained to La Trobe that as yet they had not received the 'slightest' protection: 'from Geelong to Portland Bay there is not a single station where even one [Border Policeman] is to be found, and unless in the retinue of the Commissioner when he makes his periodical rounds, they are scarcely ever seen in the district'.[8]

The protection asked for indicated the peculiar nature of the frontier, where violence occurred in the midst of settlement. Troops were not demanded for protection of an intervening area between settlers and hostile Aborigines: they were needed on the stations, for all through the District the two races were living in close proximity to each other.

Even as late as 1845 the Governor still failed to understand the unusual nature of the Western District frontier, as an interchange between the Governor, La Trobe and William Campbell J.P. of Dunmore Station revealed. In June Campbell reported collisions between Aborigines and Europeans in his area, and appealed for Government protection. Such was the tone of the appeals that the Governor assumed that the stations were so remote as to be beyond the reach of protection; and the area so densely occupied by the Aborigines that conflict and violence between the races was inevitable.[9] The Governor stated to La Trobe the inexpediency of depasturing licences being granted beyond the reach of protection. La Trobe forwarded the Governor's opinion to the Bench of Magistrates at Port Fairy.[10]

William Campbell was so surprised by the Governor's response that he wrote to him informing him that the Port Fairy district was in the centre rather than on the border of the Portland Bay District. The area had been partially occupied for more than seven years and there was no longer any unoccupied land available for newcomers. In the town of Belfast there was a Bench of Magistrates and at Mt Rouse, a distance of about thirty miles, a Protectorate establishment. No pastoral station was a greater distance than thirty miles from one or the other. The country was not very densely occupied by Aborigines. Nor was there a shortage of their traditional food. The squatters had been at Dunmore for three years, but had not previously been troubled by the Aborigines. They had always been allowed to pass across the land without 'the slightest molestation'.

Yet in these circumstances, those of a settled community, the Aborigines were still annoying Europeans and at times threatening life. Campbell implored the Government to send a force to protect the settlers arguing that it should be placed under the control of the magistrates or other gentlemen in the neighbourhood, to be ready to be called out when needed. At present the settler had 'a very difficult [path?] to sustain. He may be obliged to have recourse to bloodshed, in defence of his life and property'. He was concerned also for himself. As a Justice of the Peace called upon to lead parties of men to disperse Aborigines or to attempt to capture them, he wished to know if he had Government support and protection at such times.[11]

Forced back on their own resources, Europeans soon gained a reputation for violence in their treatment of the Aborigines. Rumours about the District led to attacks on the reputation of the squatters of the District by both Governor Gipps and Superintendent La Trobe. Several times settlers were forced to make carefully worded statements aimed at removing what they felt to be an unfair stain on their character. Attempting to defend the District's reputation, the *Portland Mercury* asked those who had experienced frontier life in other places to reflect on whether behaviour and violence in the District was any worse than elsewhere.[12]

One of Foster Fyans's first tasks as Police Magistrate at Geelong was to investigate charges made by Dr Collier that after the murder of a hutkeeper, Edward Henty had taken a party of fourteen men and exacted revenge upon the Aborigines. Fyans found no evidence to support the charge.[13] In December 1841 James Blair, the Police Magistrate at Portland, was asked by La Trobe to investigate an allegation by the Reverend Mr Hurst of 'the continued wanton destruction of the natives by the settlers in the western district'. Blair reported that the charge that men went out 'upon the sabbath, professedly to shoot kangaroo, but in reality to shoot natives in cold blood' was 'a clumsy fiction'.[14] But La Trobe's letter to Governor Gipps indicated his awareness of the inter-racial violence in the District:

That frequent and fatal collision took place in 1839 and at the commence-
ment of 1840 ... however difficult of legal proof, is too notorious to be
denied ...

It is clear from the depositions taken by Mr Blair, that whatever foundation
existed for the statements put forth by Mr Hurst, that it is to be found in the
occurrences of this period.

La Trobe assured the Governor that 'atrocities such as those mentioned
in Mr Hurst's statement, if they were even [ever?] practised, would never
be tolerated by the present class of settlers', and took comfort in the fact
that closer settlement meant that the 'chances of concealment' of violence were 'exceedingly diminished'.[15]

With Blair La Trobe was more blunt: 'there still is, and will be reason
for the utmost vigilance on the part of the local magistrates'. He warned
that occasional Aboriginal attacks on sheep and cattle were to be
expected and that the settlers could not always be depended upon to
behave as he would like them to:

The passions of men, circumstanced like the settlers in this colony, are easily
excited; and even with regard to the superior education and standing of many
of them, I need not remind you how very liable the mind of man is to be
moulded by the position in which he may find himself placed, and especially
in circumstances so materially affecting his interests.[16]

As Aboriginal attacks became frequent in early 1842, the settlers of
the Port Fairy area petitioned La Trobe for protection. They claimed
'enormous' losses at the hands of the Aborigines whose numbers, ferocity
and cunning 'render them peculiarly formidable'. They presented themselves as innocent sufferers with a rightful claim to protection against
unprovoked attacks on both life and property. But, as La Trobe received
the petition, he also heard news of the murder by Europeans of three
defenceless Aboriginal women and a child while they were sleeping.

The murders (known as the Muston's Creek massacre) had occurred
on the station of Smith and Osbrey at Caramut, north of Port Fairy. In
his reply to the settlers La Trobe expressed sympathy for them but
admitted that every other feeling had been overwhelmed by his abhor-
rence at the evidence of an act of 'savage retaliation or cruelty'
committed 'in the immediate vicinity of the station of two of the partners' signing the petition. He gave little comfort to those asking for
protection calling instead on the settlers to clear their names from the
suspicion of involvement in the crime:

Will not the commission of such crimes call down the wrath of God, and do
more to check the prosperity of your district, and to ruin your prospects, than
all the difficulties and losses under which you labour?

I call upon you as your first duty to yourselves, and to your adopted
country, to come forward in aid of the authorities, to clear up the obscurity

with which this deed is as yet involved; and purging yourselves, and your servants, from all knowledge of and participation in such a crime, never to repose until the murderers are declared, and your district relieved from the stain of harbouring them within its boundaries.[17]

When, instead of actively endeavouring to discover those guilty of the crime, prominent settlers concocted a story for which investigation revealed there was no supporting evidence, La Trobe was incensed. Anxious to clear their names, settlers had claimed that both Aboriginal men and women had been shot, the result possibly of an affray between settlers and Aborigines as settlers endeavoured to force Aborigines to give up their plunder.[18] Angry that the settlers tried to deceive him, La Trobe wrote to those who had put forward the story, stating that they must not consider themselves 'hardly dealt with' when he held them 'personally and individually' accountable for the contents of the letters to which they added their signature.[19]

The Governor saw the matter as a very grave one. He reported it to the Secretary of State for the Colonies and expressed to La Trobe his belief that publicity given to the incident in England would 'act most prejudicially upon the character not only of the District ... but of the whole colony'. If, despite the offers of reward for information, attempts to find the murderers were unsuccessful, the Governor believed he must consider extreme action—the abandonment of the whole District!

> I am directed by His Excellency to add that should all exertions to discover the Murderers fail, it will become His Duty to consider whether it may not be proper to cancel all Licenses in the District, (or at least to refuse to renew them) and to convert the whole into an aboriginal Reserve and that He will not shrink from the performance of such a Duty, if Justice and Humanity seem to require it at His hands.[20]

He ordered that a copy of his letter to La Trobe, partly quoted above, be sent to those settlers who had signed the letter of 23 April to La Trobe. Claude Farie and Niel Black, on behalf of those signing that letter, wrote an apologetic reply to La Trobe:

> ... we beg to remind your Honour that we did not state it as a fact, nor even as a rumour but merely as a probable supposition that the women killed were attached to a marauding party ... we can only regret now that your attention was ever called to it ...[21]

The *Portland Mercury* expressed the outraged feelings of the squatters. It declared that Governor Gipps's threat to cancel the licences in the Port Fairy District unless the murderers 'were given up to justice', was 'tantamount to declaring every settler in the Port Fairy district accessory to an atrocious murder'. The Governor's conduct was 'oppressive and unjust' and should be viewed with 'indignation'.[22]

Those who lived through the frontier experience recorded the violence. Official statements and depositions taken before magistrates show that many squatters were involved in violent affrays with the Aborigines, during which lives were lost. Those who ignore the books written about the pioneering period and the local oral history accounts of the settlement of each community may believe in the peaceful settlement of the District. But the tradition of violence is so much alive that anyone with any interest in the District's history knows that in this area the land was neither easily won, nor without a large cost in lives— largely Aboriginal lives.

Modern historians writing of this region have also discussed violence on the frontier. Perhaps the most well known study of the Western District, that of Margaret Kiddle published in 1961, accepted conflict between Aborigines and Europeans as a natural part of the pioneering experience. Peter Corris in *Aborigines and Europeans in Western Victoria* attempted an estimate of the number of Aborigines killed by Europeans before 1860, and arrived at the figure of 158 or 159. Only slightly later R. H. W. Reece referred to the years between 1837 and 1846 as the years the colony of New South Wales 'experienced the worst racial clashes of its history, the squatting districts of Portland Bay and Liverpool Plains being most severely affected'. More recently others such as Michael Christie and Richard Broome have written of the violence in the District.[23]

But Aborigines and Europeans met on the coastline before the spread of pastoral settlement. Little has been written of the struggle between whalers and Aborigines, yet there was a large whaling community at Portland in the years before and during the time the Hentys took up their inland stations. Fyans noted about sixty whaling boats working in the 1839 season.[24] Elsewhere, for example in the Bass Strait islands, sealing communities had exploited local Aboriginal people. Robinson noted in his Tasmanian journals and papers the details of the number of Aboriginal women kept by individual sealers, their forced removal from their families, the use of them as forced labour and the physical violence inflicted on them. Their position he equated with slavery, and commented that it was 'improper and disgraceful' that slavery should be allowed to exist in a British Colony when 'at home', 'millions' had been expended to end the slave trade.[25] Some of these sealers plied their trade as far afield as Kangaroo Island.

Brief references indicate that race relations on the Portland Bay coast were similar to those in other sealing and whaling communities. J. H. Wedge, reporting in 1836 the violent treatment of Aborigines at Westernport, lamented that 'the like outrages have been committed upon the Aborigines at Portland Bay'.[26] Blair, the Police Magistrate at Portland, certainly found the men unruly. He described the Portland population as composed of the 'very dregs of society'. 'The majority of the people here', he wrote in late 1840, 'are men who had absconded from whaling gangs and the lawless lives they have led ... render a much stronger force necessary to subdue them ...'[27]

In Edward Henty's Portland Journal there are only a small number of references to Aborigines, but these suggest that friendly relations were unlikely to have existed. In December 1834 Edward Henty, Henry Camfield, William Dutton, five men, and one Van Diemen's Land Aboriginal woman (belonging to Dutton) with 14 dogs explored the country east of Portland. They came upon an Aborigine and 'he the Men set the Dogs on'. The same kind of treatment was received by Aborigines who first ventured to approach the Hentys' huts and yards in January 1835. Their appearance was friendly but 'one of the dogs chased them and caught one by the buttocks which drove the other away. The dogs returned covered with blood'.[28]

Men also went bush to look for Aboriginal women. Henty's journal entry for 29 March 1835 read:

> Thos. Clerk—Brown—Jones and Page left the Fishery without permission on the 27th inst. at daybreak with a fortnight supply of Provisions for the supposed Purpose of getting Native women ...[29]

The journal records without comment the men's return only a few days later, leaving the reader 'wondering', as Bernard Barrett states, 'about the fate of the Aboriginal women and of any difficult Aboriginal husbands'.[30]

The strongest evidence of violence on the coast is the story of an incident at the Convincing Ground. Robinson was told the following story by Edward Henty:

> He said that some time ago, I suppose 2 or 3 years, a whale broke from her moorings and went on shore. And the boat went into get it off, when they were attacked by natives who drove them off ... the men were so enraged that they went to the head station for their firearms and then returned to the whale, when the natives again attacked them. And the whalers then let fly, to use his expression, right and left upon the natives. He said that natives did not go away but got behind trees and threw spears and stones. They, however, did not much molest them after that.[31]

The details of the story are vague. How serious was this clash? When did it occur? How many Aborigines were killed? Why was it never reported to the authorities? Why was it not mentioned in Henty's Portland Journal? Why was Fyans not given details when he travelled to Portland to investigate allegations by Dr Collier that the Hentys and their men had been involved in a massacre of Aborigines?

The incident occurred before 27 October 1835, much earlier than Robinson thought. On that date Edward Henty referred in his Journal to the stretch of beach as the Convincing Ground. The incident could have take place any time from 1832 onwards, as at that time the supply of fur seals in Bass Strait and Victoria was becoming depleted and the ship-owners began concentrating on whaling.[32] It is likely, however, that it occurred in 1833 or 1834. At Port Fairy in early 1842 Robinson met MacDonald, a Headsman, who told him the incident had happened eight or nine years previously. The cause he gave was quite different from that suggested by Henty: 'some whalers', he said, 'had got among or with the N-[Native] women'.[33] The incident, then, occurred in the earliest period of European settlement on the coast and no later than the 1835 whaling season—at least five years before Robinson visited the area.

The incident was a metaphor for the meeting of European and Aborigine in the District. In the first stand made by Aborigines to assert their rights, European arms won the day. From the European point of view the hostilities were seen as 'convincing' the Aborigines not to oppose Europeans and their actions, whether they were the taking of whales or or native women. But the response went much further than convincing the Aborigines involved. The Aborigines they sought to persuade, they killed. There was a pattern to the meeting that was to be repeated time and time again throughout the District: the need to convince the Aborigines not to steal European property; the use of guns; the killing of large numbers of Aborigines across the body of a whale or the bodies of sheep, cattle or even a horse. In some cases the total adult male population of an Aboriginal group was massacred in the one confrontation. And in many cases native women were the cause of conflict between the races.

The number who died on the Convincing Ground is unknown, as is the number who suffered at other times at the hands of the sealers and whalers. But the depopulation of the coast around Portland as discussed in an earlier chapter bears witness to the effect of the first sustained contacts between Europeans and Aborigines in Portland Bay.[34] In comparison the affrays that took place between the squatters and their men on the one hand and the Aborigines on the other are much better documented.

In September 1840 when Fyans, now Crown Lands Commissioner for the Portland Bay District, returned from his first tour of the whole District reporting that, 'every gentleman's establishment' had been 'molested by the natives' with many having 'suffered serious losses', he was concerned that the conduct of the Aborigines was growing worse. He blamed the Protectors for this as they gave Aborigines the idea that they would not be punished. Further, he pointed out that in two cases in which he had apprehended Aborigines believed guilty of murder, punishment had not followed. His suggestion was simple, 'to insist on the gentlemen in the country to protect their property, and to deal with such useless savages on the spot'.[35]

It was true that the Aborigines had little idea of the British law or the system of trial before a jury, or of state-inflicted punishment—of prison, of transportation, of hanging, or if judged innocent, of release. La Trobe stated in July 1840, 'In scarcely a single instance have the parties implicated in the acts of violence . . . been brought to trial; and in not a single instance has conviction taken place'.[36] But there was another kind of punishment and there was evidence of it everywhere—in fact of Fyans's suggestion being unofficially put into force: of gentlemen protecting their property and dealing with the Aborigines 'on the spot'.

While Europeans talked of the possibility of military protection, and many had perhaps seen military forces used against Aborigines in Van Diemen's Land or in the north of the colony, Aborigines in the Portland Bay District did not see a military force before 1842. The encounters were always of the same kind—with a station owner and his employees if Aborigines openly attacked Europeans, or by a small party of mounted and armed European settlers if Europeans were avenging a prior Aboriginal attack on European lives or property. It is usual to speak of the guerrilla tactics of the Aborigines, but in the years before 1842 the Aborigines saw only similar behaviour by the Europeans. They probably assumed that European fighting was of a similar nature to their own. There was nothing in the actions of the Europeans that would have led them to think that the enemy against which they fought was anything more than the local squatter and his employees strengthened in numbers, and at times by what appeared to be related kin on nearby stations. Even after 1842 when Border Police, Mounted Police and Native Police were used in the District, they were always in relatively small numbers.

Intermingled, both living on the same land, with easy access to the property of the 'other', and sometimes sharing the same women: these were integral features of the frontier as it existed in the Portland Bay District. It was a difficult and ironic situation. La Trobe could not envisage a police force large enough to keep the peace. Yet the settlers themselves in their small groups had the means of ensuring 'order' in their vicinity. Their horses and guns gave them a superiority which enabled them to achieve peace.

The fifteen men who provided sworn statements concerning the allegation that men went out on the Sabbath professedly to hunt kangaroos but in reality to shoot Aborigines insisted that this was not so. But the most direct method of dealing with Aboriginal outrages from first settlement through to at least 1847 was the organization of a hunting party. The statement of the proprietors of stock depasturing in the Western District around Geelong who appealed for protection in mid-1837 told the story. Their aim was 'to protect the colonists from native outrage, to prevent the utter extermination of the aboriginal race'.[37] It was obvious that without Government protection, the law was and would be taken into their own hands. Their belief was that this would lead to all Aborigines being killed. In some cases violence was only threatened but in many cases it occurred. Frederick Taylor's massacre was notorious. The Whyte brothers were among a party of nine men, five on horseback and four on foot when they attacked local Aborigines, killing all the men except one. John Robertson at Wando Vale admitted that he had 'on four different occasions, when they committed murders, gone out with others in search of them'. He was grateful that the Aborigines were not found on any of these occasions for he implied that if they had been he, like others, would have had blood on his hands.[38] Annie Maria Baxter mentions thirteen hunting parties organized by the men around Dunmore and Yambuck between June 1845 and April 1847.[39] William Campbell and John Cox, prominent squatters in the area, appealed for Government protection, warning La Trobe that if they did not receive it, settlers would 'be obliged in self defence to attempt the recovery of their property and there can be little doubt that the result would be unfortunate'.[40] Samuel Carter of North Brighton station admitted, 'The squatters often formed parties to shoot down the blacks, as it was a fight for life in many cases.'[41] Squatters could openly discuss the possible conclusion to such an outing and claim self-defence when Aborigines were killed in 'collisions', but some felt discomfort about their position. Tom Browne of Squattlesea Mere stated that the difficulty for those wanting to take direct action was that it was 'necessary to behave in a quasi-legal manner. Shooting blacks, except in manifest self-defence, had been always held to be murder in the Supreme Courts of the land, and occasionally punished as such'.[42]

Depositions provide the details of such encounters. Often they are brief; but three depositions concerning the same encounter taken on different days, with the individuals interviewed on different properties, allow a fuller picture to be sketched.[43] They concern a 'collision' in late June 1840 between Aylward, Knolles (Knowles) and Tulloh, and a group of Aborigines. The Aborigines had stolen sheep and the men looking for them came across a large party of Aborigines. The next day they approached the Aboriginal encampment where they saw plenty of signs of the stolen sheep. Aylward estimated the Aborigines to number nearly 300; Knolles rather more than 150; Tulloh about 500. Aware of the approaching Europeans, the Aborigines stood ready for attack. The young men were drawn up together in one line, and behind them, in another group, the women, old men and children. The Aborigines challenged the Europeans, using what Knolles described as 'very coarse language'. The Europeans on horseback fired upon them and then retreated a short distance. Seeing them retreat the Aborigines turned and pursued the Europeans. As soon as the Europeans had reloaded their guns, they charged again with the Aborigines fleeing before them. The 'engagement' lasted a quarter of an hour. Aylward stated that 'there must have been a great many wounded, and several killed . . . saw two or three dead bodies'. Knolles reported, 'Some of the Natives must have been wounded, but I saw none dead'. The Europeans then set fire to the camp, waiting for everything to burn before leaving the site.

Sometimes the hunting parties consisted simply of squatters and their men. Sometimes squatters joined parties led by the Police Magistrate at The Grange or Portland or a local J.P. such as William Campbell at Dunmore.[44] Sometimes Fyans called on local men to help him. In a case mentioned by Sievwright, Fyans led a large party of men which included Niel Black.[45] Black stated that eighteen settlers, some from fifty miles away, joined them. They searched for a week before finding the Aborigines. Two men were taken to Melbourne for trial. The others, Black believed, would not cause further trouble: '... 21 Horsemen Galloping full tilt after them is a sight they never saw ... before nor do I think they will ... take the risk of repetition of it'.[46] John Cox from near Mt Napier organized a hunting party which included Souwester, an Aborigine working for Cox at the time. James Bonwick, who visited the area about ten years later, claimed in the narrative of his tour of the District to have been told the details. The party, 'though few in number, mustered in rifles and pistols about fifty shots'. The unsuspecting Aborigines were interrupted at their breakfast. 'More than thirty are said to have been thus laid low.'[47] The Native Police were sometimes accompanied by others.[48] Dana wrote to the proprietors of stations on the Wando and the Glenelg in August 1843 giving them permission to lead the Native Police against Aborigines involved in 'outrages'.[49]

Hunting parties also dealt with Aborigines believed responsible for killing Europeans. In one of the early examples of such revenge, Aborigines murdered on behalf of the Europeans. The Aborigines accompanying a European party searching for signs of Gellibrand and Hesse killed two Colac Aborigines for the Europeans, returning to tell of their revenge. The Europeans were disconcerted. Captain William Lonsdale, Police Magistrate at Port Phillip, regretted the incident for he believed it would 'identify our customs with theirs of revenge and retaliation'.[50] He was correct in assessing their behaviour as being motivated by revenge, but less correct in his view of 'our customs'. Incidents across the District were soon to indicate that Europeans no less than Aborigines were motivated by a desire for 'revenge and retaliation'. In fact Aborigines understood the desire to kill in revenge but not the indiscriminate reaction of Europeans. Soon after the killing of Mr Morton, the settler on the Glenelg River, in 1841, Aborigines were reported to have said, 'What for white man plenty sulky all natives? Why not kill natives who killed Morton?'[51]

While the killing of Aborigines in retaliation for the murder of white men is not easily proved, scattered evidence makes it clear that this did happen. There were, for example, comments by settlers such as Arthur Pilleau, that for every white man killed twenty blacks were shot.[52] There were reports that after the killing of Mr Franks and his shepherd, ten

Aborigines were killed. Interestingly, the report to the Colonial Secretary was made from Van Diemen's Land. Those closest to the incident denied that any deaths had taken place, or denied any knowledge of the deaths while admitting they might have taken place.[53] Three or four Aborigines and maybe more were killed after the death of Patrick Codd.[54] Captain Campbell from Port Fairy stated that for Codd's life the lives of twenty Aborigines had been taken.[55] After Matthew Gibson's shepherd was killed on the Glenelg, a number of Aborigines were shot.[56] There are indications that the murderers of Morton were also killed.[57] Horatio Wills, Mr Rutter and William Kirk went to deal with the Aborigines who killed John Collicot, Wills's 'man'.[58] Sievwright accused Fyans and his party of an indiscriminate attack on Aborigines after the murder of John Thomson's shepherd. In this case no Aborigines were killed, but three were taken prisoner while others were shot and wounded, including the Chief of the Elingamite.[59] Koort Kirrup claimed that nine Aborigines (five males, four females) were killed by Europeans after the murder of Donald McKenzie.[60]

The threat to shoot was often present in meetings between the two races. G. F. Read Jnr recorded in his diary how after recovering some of the articles stolen by Aborigines from Thomas Ricketts, who has taken up land near the present Birregurra, a spokesman for the search party addressed the enemy who couldn't be seen:

> Rode down to the scrub this morning where we found the natives, who concealed themselves in it at our approach, and not wishing to enter the scrub from fear of having to slay all that made any resistance we told them that if ever they robbed another white man we would shoot every one of them.[61]

Similarly, Niel Black, who came across some Aborigines while out riding 'fired off two pistols and a gun to show them I had the power of injuring them severely if I chose to do it'.[62]

Early huts were built with the danger of attack in mind. At North Brighton Charles Carter erected a 'fortified hut' with port holes on all sides. Each port hole was covered by a sliding door which enabled the hole to be closed immediately a shot was fired, preventing the entry of a spear. When two Aboriginal boys called to notify Carter that the 'mob' intended to kill the family, he assembled all the guns for the boys to see and then demonstrated how he intended to kill anyone who attacked the hut 'by pointing the guns through the gun holes, and as quickly drawing them in and replacing the slides'. His son wrote, 'He made them understand he would shoot everyone that came to the place, but also told them he would not harm them provided they left us alone'.[63]

'We always kept a double-barrelled gun by our side, to be ready at a minutes notice if attacked', wrote Samuel Carter.[64] Almost every European was armed, including the women. The Clyde Company records reveal that there was 'a standard monthly issue of 1 lb. powder and 3 lb. shot to each hut'.[65] Guns were the one thing Black wished he had brought with him to the colony—'. . . a whole lot of double barreled guns at about £3 to £3/10/-'. When a friend sent him from Home a '"Richards" carabine, with patent Magazine primes for caps', he was appreciative. This would have been a percussion cap weapon and far more reliable than the old flint-lock weapon. He wrote to Gladstone, 'It is one of the best I have seen for a black hunt, an use to which I hope I may never have occasion to apply it'. He asked for twenty, or at least half that number, of carbines to be sent, adding that they were 'better than Fowling pieces'.[66] Of the weaponry carried by Europeans in the Glenelg River area in 1841, Robinson commented, 'The hostile array of the whites is terrific'.[67] When William Russell travelled across the country with George Russell in August 1839 each carried 'a brace of pistols'.[68] James Ritchie, walking across the District, carried a gun, powder and shot. Captain Hepburn always carried either 'a double-barrelled gun or rifle'.[69] Of the men at W. J. Purbrick's station Robinson wrote, 'the men were all armed, mostly double barrels and pistols'. In the Glenelg River area Robinson noted, 'All the shepherds I saw today have double barrel guns. The natives say "by and by no good"', while at Gibb's outstation he observed that the two shepherds each had a double-barrelled gun. Winter's home station, according to Robinson, was 'a complete armoury of small arms'.[70]

Doubts have been expressed about the effectiveness of the weapons at that time, but both Europeans and Aborigines found the weapons accurate enough. A single man with a gun could hold a large group of Aborigines at bay as Ritchie did in December 1841. As fifty Aborigines advanced towards him he turned 'to the first male and threatened to shoot him'. The threat worked: keeping them covered he walked away without interference.[71] Mostly there were a number of men and they were on horseback which gave them a distinct advantage.

Even more dramatic as an example of the effectiveness of the weapons used in the circumstances and manner of the time is the body count at the end of the Whyte brothers' massacre. The European party consisted of nine men, five on horseback and four on foot. Only one European was harmed, speared in the leg, but all the Aboriginal men except one were killed. Reports of the number shot vary: 41, 25, 51 men.[72] Robertson, who was a neighbour and moved into the area three days after the incident, stated that 51 Aborigines were killed. Fifty stolen sheep had been killed by the Aborigines, and after the massacre the bodies of the sheep and men lay all round, almost an equal number of each—'the bones of the men and the sheep lay mingled together bleaching in the sun at the Fighting Hills'.[73]

The Europeans had the means to defend their property and to recover it. Aborigines were killed either in the fighting as they endeavoured to steal, or by the European party which set out to recover the sheep or other goods. In either case the Aborigines were at close range. Many admitted in conversation that they had killed Aborigines. Knowles, working for Dr Martin at Mt Sturgeon, told Robinson that some time back La Trobe was going to put him in gaol for killing Aborigines while John Francis, superintendent for W. J. T. Clarke at Woodlands, told Robinson that he thought there would be no enquiry about his shooting the blacks.[74]

One of the Whyte brothers called in on Black on his way to Melbourne to report details of his 'affray' with the Aborigines. Niel Black was sure that there would be no trouble. The Whytes may be 'obliged to go to Sydney to stand trial for murder', he wrote, 'but it will be mere form. They must be acquitted'.[75] The Winters admitted killing Aborigines and one was killed by Bonsor, a Henty employee.[76] The Wedges had had trouble at The Grange. Charles Wedge, writing to his uncle in November 1839, listed the stock lost and stated, 'You may depend I do not allow these things to be done with impunity'. In another account Wedge wrote that the 'depredations' of the Aborigines did not cease till 'many lives were sacrificed, and . . . many thousand of sheep destroyed'.[77]

It was mainly men who were killed by these European hunting parties seeking to recover their property. In the case of the Whyte brothers' massacre Robertson mentions that the women fled up the Glenelg chased by the men, the children following. In this way many of them escaped. The terror of such chases is brought to life in the story of another of the well-known massacres of Aborigines. In the area around Glenormiston Frederick Taylor was established as overseer for G. McKillop and J. Smith by March 1839. He experienced problems with the Aborigines stealing sheep from the folds. Stories of his violent hand-ling of the situation were rife across the District. In early 1840 Robinson heard that Taylor 'had killed a whole tribe and the bodies were dragged together by the bullock trains and burnt'. In 1841 the Reverend Orton visited Protector Robinson and was allowed to peruse the official depo-sition. According to it, Taylor with a number of others set out to attack the native encampment:

> As they approached . . . they formed themselves into an extended line Taylor being in the centre. They found them asleep and immediately fired upon them and killed the whole party save one consisting of thirty-five persons men women and children. They afterwards threw the bodies into a neigh-bouring waterhole. The surviving native . . . assisted by some white persons . . . afterwards came to the spot, got the bodies out of the waterhole and laid them in rows four deep . . .[78]

Niel Black, who took up this station after Taylor (according to rumour) fled fearing a Government enquiry, wrote that in the opinion of Blacking, the former overseer, 'about thirty-five to forty natives have been dispatched on this establishment' and there were 'only two men left alive of the tribe'.[79] Years later Dawson was told how 'Bareetch Churneen', Queen Fanny, had swum across Lake Bullen Merri with a child on her back and thus escaped pursuing Europeans who had murdered nearly all her people.[80]

The Whyte brothers' massacre followed an Aboriginal attack on their sheep only days after their arrival. Taylor's alleged massacre (he was not tried as there was insufficient legal proof) followed almost as quickly after his arrival in the area. George Russell, from the Clyde Company station on the River Leigh, and Charles Gray, who had newly arrived in the area, rode to the creek called Taylor's River on a visit to Henry Gibb only weeks after Taylor's arrival in the area. Gray remarked that the signs of slaughter were still obvious.[81]

Taylor was notorious but many others also found it necessary to kill Aborigines in a more discreet manner. Niel Black on his first visit to the District in December 1839 noted distinctive behaviour and attitudes. He had gathered that the best way to do well was to take up a new run but to do so he believed it was necessary to 'slaughter natives right and left'. But he found it difficult to know for sure how many Aborigines were murdered, for:

> There is nothing but 'bouncing' [bragging] as it is called here and many persons bounce about their treatment of the natives. This they can only do by hints and slang phrases as the Protectors of the Aborigines are always on the lookout for information against the whites . . . I believe, however, numbers of the poor creatures have wantonly fallen victims to settlers scarcely less savage tho more enlightened than themselves, and that 2/3rds of them does not care a single straw about taking the life of a native provided they are not taken up by the Protectors.[82]

It was an environment in which even the most respectable colonists might find themselves in trouble, as Van Diemonians were well aware. Sometimes rumours spread quickly and without much foundation. In December 1839 George Russell's hut on the River Leigh had been attacked by Aborigines and the hut destroyed. In the affray two Aborigines were killed. It was, according to the enquiry, a clear case of self-defence but rumour spread to Bothwell in Van Diemen's Land. There Philip Russell wrote to George that he had been pleased recently to meet someone who was able to 'set at rest a report circulated here with considerable industry that you and Alex Anderson had been committed for shotting natives, and were shortly to be sent to Sydney for trial'.[83]

The Europeans defended their possessions—their huts, their men, their sheep, cattle and horses. With time, some came to employ Aborigines and to see them also as possessions. It was a dangerous position to be in as the case of John Stokel makes clear. He was the only European in the Port Phillip District to be found guilty of the shooting of an Abor-

igine between settlement and 1850.[84] Stokel was an overseer employed
on George Armytage's station, Murrandara, in the Wimmera. Stokel had
a number of 'black boys' and one of these, a shepherd, was murdered by
an Aborigine called Mr Mark in early October 1847. Stokel, suspecting
that Mr Mark would be at the Aboriginal camp on Robert Officer Jnr's
Mount Talbot station, went to the station and borrowed a loaded gun
from Officer. Having discovered his quarry, Stokel was forcing Mr Mark
to accompany him at gunpoint when the Aborigine suddenly began
running and refused to stop. Stokel fired and shot him in the head. He
decided to leave his injured prisoner overnight at Mount Talbot
station—with hands tied, fastened to a dray by a bullock chain and
padlock. The Aborigine escaped but died from his wounds and was then
buried by the Aborigines. What was unusual in this case was that there
was a European witness who was willing to admit seeing the Aborigine
shot and knowing the serious nature of the wounds. Moreover there was
a body, the proof of death having taken place. The body was exhumed
though by this time it was impossible to positively identify it as that of
Mr Mark. Stokel was committed at Horsham Police Court on 27
November for trial on a number of charges including murder and the
case was heard in the Supreme Court in February 1848.[85]

It is difficult to arrive at a realistic figure of the number of Aborigines
killed by Europeans. Peter Corris, who made a major study of race
relations in the District in the late 1960s, suggested that 158 or 159
Aborigines were killed by Europeans.[86] I have used the same approach as
Corris, using official records. Michael Christie has since criticized
Corris's work, arguing that the killing of Aborigines on the frontier was
rarely reported and thus his figure would be 'misleading'.[87] However, the
list of Aborigines killed (see Appendix 3), details of which were often
provided voluntarily by Europeans, shows that the killing of Aborigines
was often reported. In fact, once the Protectors were appointed there was
an incentive to report the death of Aborigines. Squatters were well aware
that it was excusable if deaths were the result of an Aboriginal attack.
There could be no other conclusion. The record shows that
approximately three hundred Aborigines were shot or poisoned before
1850, yet only five Europeans were charged with the shooting of
Aborigines.

As shown in Appendix 3, 257 Aborigines are known to have been
killed or to have died trying to escape capture. There was also the
unknown number killed at the Convincing Ground at Portland. As
Robinson found the Aboriginal clans of the area almost extinct or extinct
in 1841, it would seem likely that at least the equivalent of a large Aboriginal group was killed. In both Taylor's and the Whyte brothers' massacre approximately forty men were killed. If the whole group numbered
about sixty individuals, this would make a figure of 317 Aborigines
killed. In addition, in three cases, 'some Aborigines' were killed, and in

one case there was 'a fearful loss of life'. Thus a figure of 330 seems conservative. It does not include the unofficial information about Aborigines killed near Mt Eeles which Bonwick mentions. If twenty is added to make my figures consistent with those of Corris, the result would be 350 killed as opposed to his 158 or 159.

The District early developed a reputation for violence. It is impossible to know how many more Aborigines were killed and never reported. The bragging and boasting about killing Aborigines referred to by Black is one factor encouraging the view that large numbers of Aborigines were killed. The extremely common references by pioneers to the killing of Aborigines adds further weight to such a view. Boldrewood, for example, argues that it was just as well that the Aborigines' friend James Dawson lived at a reasonable distance from Mt Eeles and the violence of the 'Eumeralla War', otherwise there would have been trouble. The implication is that there was reason for Dawson to be troubled. Dawson, however, was not oblivious to what occurred, as a letter from Mrs Rutledge, wife of William Rutledge of Port Fairy, to her daughter makes clear. Her daughter had reported that a friend had been upset by a comment made by Dawson implying that the local squatters had been brutal in their treatment of the Aborigines. Eliza Rutledge confirmed the view of the situation given by Dawson. She wrote:

> I am returning you Mrs. McK's [McKellar] letter poor woman she ought to have known better than be annoyed by him but I believe he only told the truth, though not kindly. I should think Jimsey Irvine [James H. Irvine of Dunmore] could tell her a good many Blacks were killed about Dunmore at Waterloo and other Swamps.[88]

With no additional evidence to that of the historians closer to the events, one can only report their ideas as an indication, a guess-estimate of how many may have been killed by violence. E. M. Curr, for example, stated that between 15 and 25 per cent died by the rifle.[89] William Westgarth, after a visit to Dunmore and the surrounding Mt Eeles country in June 1844, concluded that the local population had declined by more than 50 per cent largely due to violence. He mentioned a 'native township' on the banks of the Eumeralla 'Lake or swamp ... said to contain five hundred' in 1842 but reduced to about two hundred in 1844. 'There could be no reasonable doubt', he concluded, 'that during these two years at least two hundred ... had been shot, or otherwise deprived of life in various encounters with the white settlers'.[90] Robinson suggested an upper limit and an extreme one based on one incident when he wrote of the situation in early 1841, '... the average of Homicides between blacks and whites West of the Grampians was ... forty blacks to one White man ... and if the statement of the Aborigines were admitted it would be trebled'.[91]

The impression one is left with is of great violence but it would be wrong to deduce that this was the greatest cause of the decrease of the population. Robinson did not think so. Asked in 1845 to reflect on the relative importance of the various factors, he wrote that the decline in numbers 'was attributable to collisions with Europeans, to intestine strife, to feuds, but principally to the effect of European disease . . .'[92] The impact of European settlement was disastrous: the Aboriginal population of the Western District was reduced to 645 by 1863.[93]

Of those Aborigines killed of whom we have records of age and sex, ten were children and twenty-seven women. In contrast, all of the thirty-five Europeans killed were men except for Abraham Ward's child. Five men from the Portland Bay District were tried for shooting Aborigines and of these, only one, John Stokel, was found guilty—and then not of murder, but of the lesser charge of inflicting grievous bodily harm. He was imprisoned for two months.[94]

8

'it's too bad to shoot the unfortunates like dogs'

INTERMINGLING brought fear and violence, attack and counter-attack, but it also made possible considerable interaction between the two races. There was close contact between the races from the beginning of European settlement. As early as June 1838 the Aborigines around Geelong were already 'in a deplorable state' with venereal disease brought to the District by Europeans. Foster Fyans, Police Magistrate at Geelong, feared that unless the 'intimacy' was checked in some way, it would lead to murders.[1] This use of the word 'intimacy' for inter-racial behaviour in a period of often violent conflict, highlights the complexity of inter-cultural relationships on this boundary. Aborigines knew the names of local squatters and their men. Europeans knew the names of local Aborigines. The Portland newspapers noted when individual Aborigines were in town, and kept readers informed of leaders and groups involved in 'outrages' on the surrounding stations.

To document this feature of frontier life is difficult, but at least two sources allow for some detailed study. The first is Chief Protector Robinson's journal. From this it is possible to gain an idea of where Aborigines were living in relation to Europeans. On many stations Aborigines, accompanied by their families, worked as employees. Robinson mentioned twenty-three squatters who had at least one Aborigine employed on their property in 1841—Campbell at Port Fairy, Thomson at Keilambete, Whyte, Purbrick, Winter, Norris, Tulloh, McCrae, Forlonge, the neighbour of Gibson, Thomson at Mt William, John

Henty, Martin, Urquhart, Baillie, Knowles, Bunbury, Kirk, Campbell south of Mt Cole, Synott, Blow, Linton and Gibbs. There were also other cases not recorded by Robinson.

Some of these Aborigines were given the same tasks as European workmen. Koort Kirrup, a leader of the Palapnue conedeet and one of the most influential Aboriginal men in the District, worked on Donald McKenzie's station on Emu Creek, a tributary of the Glenelg. He had the reputation of being a good workman. He made himself very useful on the station, put up a sheep yard and did 'as much as a white man'.[2] As payment he received rations for himself, his wife and his children. Koort Kirrup's son, Tom, was learning the skills of the bushman. He went out shepherding with Joseph Wheatley, employed by McKenzie.[3]

Colloquial English was part of the everyday language of such Aboriginal families. Robinson, visiting the camp of the Palapnue conedeet at Emu Creek, arrived ahead of his van. He met one of Koort Kirrup's wives and two of his sons. As he saw his van arriving, Robinson thought he should tell the Palapnue that there were Aboriginal members of his party with the van. Koort Kirrup's son, only seven years of age, was surprised: 'damn their eyes, bloody buggers', he said.[4]

At the Winters' station, where Robinson appears to have only met George Winter, the Aboriginal presence was seen as a way of reducing expenses. At a time when European workmen 'charged £1 per 100 [sheep] and grog and rations for working and shearing', Butcher at the Winters' 'got a few blacks and with their assistance . . . did it himself and saved the expense'. Pong.nor.rer, of the Wanedeet conedeet, also known as Joe, lived at the station. He drove bullocks, ploughed, and sheared the sheep. He 'does a variety of useful work, and is very industrious', wrote Robinson. 'Winter said he never knew him tell a lie.' Another useful man at the Winters' was George.[5]

Harry had been in the service of the Whyte brothers at Konongwootong for more than 18 months.[6] That is, he had been with the Whytes from not long after their arrival and their disastrous encounter with the Aborigines (March and April 1840). Bob, who lived on Thomas Ricketts's station, was regarded as 'domesticated'.[7] At Hunter's near Mt Eeles William Bradbury, a Goulburn Plains Aborigine, was employed as stock-keeper.[8] On his way back to Geelong Robinson met a capable young man who carried a reference as proof of his record as a worker. Robinson was so impressed he copied it into his journal:

Carngham, June 1841. This is to certify that William alias Puinguiwar is a steady, good and hard working Aborigine and will do a white man good if it lies in his power. To all whom it may concern, George Youille [Yuille].[9]

Others who were working were stated to be of good character.[10]

The historian, Henry Reynolds, has emphasized the extent to which settlers on the frontier were armed. He mentioned a visitor to the Swan

River settlement finding it 'laughable' to see shepherds carrying guns instead of crooks. The same could be seen in Port Phillip where 'shepherds all carried guns and had "the appearance of soldiers on duty"'.[11] Robinson noted the guns and also another distinctive feature of the life of many shepherds—close contact with Aboriginal women. To the image of the shepherd with a gun, instead of a crook, might be added the sight of the shepherd paying more attention to an Aboriginal woman than to the sheep he was paid to mind. Robinson commented at one station, 'the white shepherds . . . appeared to devote more of their time to the native women than to their sheep . . .'.[12]

The extent of intermingling of the two races at least in one area and at a particular time can be established using Robinson's journal. A study of the whereabouts of the Aborigines in the Glenelg and Wannon country can be made from Robinson's record of his journey through this area during June 1841. This shows the extensive friendly interaction of the races in the period before the violent Aboriginal attacks in this area during 1842 and later. At Duncan McRae's, Robinson was told that a man, his wife and child were at one of his outstations.[13] They had been there for eighteen months; that is, from the time of arrival of the Europeans. Nar.rer.burnin, the old woman killed at John Henty's station, a wife of the Palapnue leader, Koort Kirrup, had been living at McRae's. When she was shot at John Henty's outstation which was near by, Wor.ram, one of Mingburn's wives, was with her.[14] Mingburn, leader of the Kobut Kobut Burrer conedeet (or maybe the Tarer-bung—Robinson uses both names) had several children. Three of these, Two-penny, Piccaninny Bill and a female had been at Thomas Norris's station.[15]

Two women and a child were visiting W. J. Purbrick's.[16] A family was staying at Tulloh's station on the Wannon.[17] There was always a group of Aborigines at George Winter's.[18] There were two males at the Whytes' station.[19] Robinson also learnt that an Aboriginal named Tic.er.rite was living at Whytes'. It is impossible to know whether he was one of the two men already mentioned but Tic.er.rite was the son of Wone.bon.dul who claimed the area of the Whytes' station as his 'country'. Robinson, thinking of the Whyte brothers' massacre of the Aborigines, was impressed: 'a greater proof there cannot be of the love of the natives than their creeping into the service of the Whites to be on the spot that gave them their birth'.[20] There was a boy at Thomas Norris's. An Aboriginal family (man, wife and child) plus two women and a child were living in huts near the shepherd's hut at Norris's outstation.[21] At one of the Winter brothers' outstations a woman was with a shepherd. Another woman was out with a shepherd and a woman and girl were at the hut.[22] On 1 June 1841 two of Mr Tulloh's drays from the station on the Wannon River passed by Robinson's camp. There was an Aboriginal boy in each dray: one aged fourteen, the other nine. The boys' parents were at the Winters' station. Aborigines were also present at Henty's station.[23] According to

James Smead, a Henty employee, in June 1839 he had two Aborigines working with him. They had a hut built for them near his and 'generally' stayed with him and were fed by him. There was a large group of Aborigines close by for he stated that he was known to about two hundred Aborigines and often spent nights with them. Frequently he had twenty to thirty natives with him. He found them very useful in finding stray cattle.[24]

Some Aborigines carried guns: a sign that those who employed them believed the Aborigines were to be trusted. George with Winter's dray had a gun. 'Other blacks [were] permitted the same', recorded Robinson.[25]

But familiarity went hand in hand with violence. While Robinson was in the west three Aborigines, two women and a man, were shot at W. J. Purbrick's station in front of Aboriginal women who fled to tell others of the calamity.[26] Thomas Connell, a Henty employee, had poisoned a large number of Aborigines, according to them.[27] A native woman was killed at John Henty's outstation.[28] Francis Morton and his man were murdered by Aborigines. There was a fight between Aboriginal groups at Norris's, and Robinson's Aboriginal guide, Eurodap, was killed by Pongnorer at Winter's station.

Robinson claimed that nine-tenths of the 'mischief charged against the Aborigines' was the result of white man's interference with the native women.[29] Assistant Protector Parker agreed.[30] With the two races intermingled throughout the District, there were plenty of opportunities for the women to become the cause of trouble. Robinson saw only one case of a European man living with an Aboriginal woman and child as a family. That was George Yuille, overseer to James and Thomas Baillie at Carngham.[31] Relationships varied from a few minutes, to overnight, to months on end: from pleasant and friendly to brutal and violent. John Williams, for example, shot two Aborigines because they would not give him their women. The same man was seen at Captain Briggs's station 'in the very act of cohabiting with one of the women before the window of the hut and without the slightest concealment'.[32] Women sometimes offered themselves,[33] while some men used force to obtain women.[34] Others negotiated: 'I overheard Rutter [overseer for William Kirk] in treating for a black gin', Robinson wrote.[35] Such situations could lead to the murder of a European or some other retaliation classed by Europeans as an 'outrage'. Morton, a settler on the Glenelg, for example, had an Aborigine (Long Yarra) and his gin (Lewequeen) living with him. Morton's interest was in Lewequeen to whom he had taken 'a fancy'. When Morton was murdered by Aborigines, John Robertson, a neighbour, suspected Long Yarra and implied that Lewequeen was in some way the cause of the murder. Robertson wrote: 'There had been some unpardonable conduct on the part of Mr. Morton, who, I was of the opinion, was at times deranged'.[36] Near by, at Retreat, Thomas

McCulloch found Aboriginal attacks so 'outrageous' that he wrote to La Trobe asking for protection.[37] If Robertson's account is to be believed, McCulloch brought his problems on himself for he was the settler who kept a harem:

> Mr McCoulack, of Retreat . . . near me kept a harem for himself and his men . . . All the men and masters got fearfully diseased from these poor creatures; they, of course, quarrelled with the natives about their gins, and the natives, to be revenged for some of the insults, took away 48 ewes and lambs—they were followed by some of the neighbours and Mr McCoulack's own men. They rushed their camp, shot two of the natives, one of them a female, said to be Mr McCoulack's foremost black woman.[38]

Circumstances at the Winters' station perhaps convey best the actual situation. The Winters and their men encouraged the Aborigines to gather at the home station and there were usually Aborigines there. Yet there was a 'large swivel gun mounted at the home station which was intended 'to be used against the blacks if necessary'.[39] Friendliness and intimacy had an undercurrent of fear and violence even in a period of relatively peaceful interaction.

Conversely, even in a period of serious Aboriginal attacks such as those suffered by William Learmonth at Ettrick, there was intimacy between Europeans and Aboriginal women. In October 1845 Learmonth noted, 'Yesterday shepherd rode "Jack" into Portland to see the doctor, good proof that he had been encouraging the natives quite against my orders'.[40]

A similar impression of familiarity, but of distance, between the races is given in Annie Maria Baxter's diaries, a wonderful legacy for those interested in the past. An outdoor woman, Annie was also 'of outstanding personality with intellectual gifts and education well above the average'.[41] She used her diaries (consisting of 32 volumes) as the basis for *Memories of the Past by a Lady in Australia* which was published in 1873. Robinson's journal provided evidence of how Aborigines were living in a period of more-or-less peaceful co-operation before the violence of 1842. In contrast, Annie's diaries document interaction during a period when Europeans were suffering from Aboriginal 'outrages' in the area to the west and north-west of Port Fairy. This is the period referred to by Rolf Boldrewood as 'The Eumeralla War', and the Aboriginal attacks were suffered on a number of properties including Squattlesea Mere, St Kitts, St Helens, Dunmore, Weerangourt and the Baxter property, Yambuck, from early 1845 to about mid-1847. Learmonth's at Darlot's Creek, where outrages were still occurring in 1846, was on the western edge of this area and is sometimes mentioned.

What the diaries make abundantly clear is the closeness of the lives of black and white in the pioneering years, the inter-connectedness of their lives yet the very great distance between the two groups of people. Annie had Aborigines living close by, met Aborigines while out horse riding, hunted for Aborigines responsible for 'outrages', had a trusted Aboriginal in her home, cared for and buried a sick, abandoned Aboriginal woman. Once the Aboriginal attacks on stock ceased, a number of Aborigines were employed on the Baxter property. Aborigines were part of her day-to-day life.

The cause of Annie's personal unhappiness was her husband's spending a night at Glencoe with an Aboriginal woman before they moved to the Port Phillip District. He not only spent the night with the woman, but was so indiscreet as to haggle over the prearranged payment, a pair of trousers, at the breakfast table next morning. Mrs Geary, a friend who was present, later told Annie that when they were at breakfast 'in came a huge black fellow, and in *too* plain language expressed his purpose—which was to get his trousers and particularly specifying *how* he became entitled to them!' The ladies, perhaps partly embarrassed but certainly amused by the turn of events, left the table 'convulsed with laughter'. Poor Annie! There was more still to come. Mrs Geary said that she 'had never seen such a scene as was enacted between B [Baxter] and the black. The former disclaiming all knowledge of the other, and then his sable adversary entering into an explanation in very full terms'. Annie put on a brave front, appearing to find the incident very funny, but in her diary she recorded that she felt only *'pity* and *contempt* for the man who could lesson himself and me so tremendously'.[42] From that time on they no longer shared a bed. Years later as she was leaving Baxter to start a separate life, he protested his love for her and asked her to stay. Remembering the humiliation she had suffered she confided in her diary, 'I could scarcely refrain from downright laughter . . . A man who, eight years ago, I found making a Lubra his mistress! . . . Love indeed!'[43]

Aborigines were a familiar sight in the Port Fairy district. They took messages to nearby squatters and into Port Fairy. They took letters to be posted. They guided Europeans who had lost their way. In October 1844 Annie wrote, 'Yesterday a man was brought here by the Blacks, who found him by the next river, sitting crying . . . He remained until this morning and has returned to Belfast [Port Fairy] with a black boy as Guide'.[44] Old Man Jack, a trusted Aborigine, waited at the Rutledge 'Big House' to take Annie's horse and put it away for her when she visited Port Fairy. Annie met an Aboriginal hunting party while riding on the property. In February 1846 over one hundred Aborigines crossed the Yambuck and Aringa runs on their way into Port Fairy for a 'Corrobory'.

Details are recorded such as that it was the shepherds from Ritchie's Aringa run who were intimate with the poor lubra who died in the dreadful state described by Annie. Annie's servants warned her that one of the Yambuck men, Stevens, was 'partial' to the black women. One incident, the shooting of two Aboriginal children, highlights both aspects—the close contact yet the great gulf. Old Man Jack reported the death of one Aboriginal child and the wounding of the other. Annie visited the Aboriginal camp where the Aborigines named a well-known European, Arthur Cunningham residing at Dunmore Station at the time, as the man who fired the shots. Her reaction? 'It's too bad to shoot the unfortunates like dogs and I'll write to the man or speak to him of it.' But Annie's mischievous sense of humour took over. She travelled into Port Fairy and obtained a summons. Forging a signature, she delivered the summons to Cunningham:

> I told him if he liked, I would lose it etc—but he said 'No! I'll go thro' with it, it was quite a mistake my shooting the children, but my father said I should be hanged and now I'm for it!' I told him not to think too much of it, that perhaps he would only be tried for Manslaughter and transported! He said, 'I'll go anywhere, I'll do anything they wish, but it must be alone, without a Policeman and handcuffs—if it comes to that, I'll cut my throat'. I told him if he refused to go, that they would send him by water; that I should probably be in Melbourne about the time and would visit him in gaol, and if necessary attend to his last requests! He seemed to feel the attention and in a manner half promised me 'Jupiter' and his dog.[45]

The 'joke' continued for several weeks with Mr Cunningham worrying about his situation. At last he decided to 'go down to Belfast to answer the summons'. On his way he stayed overnight at Yambuck. He was much disturbed, and 'sat by the fire rocking himself to and fro in an agony'. Not till the morning when the man was ready to leave did Annie tell him the truth. It was a joke. Shocked, Cunningham threatened to report Annie, but as she pointed out he could hardly do that without harming himself. It was a good story; such a good one, that Rolf Boldrewood stole it and used it in *Old Melbourne Memories*, giving the credit for the joke to a fellow squatter. But as a story it also comments on the European attitude to the Aborigines. Annie believed it was wrong of Cunningham to shoot the Aboriginal children but her reaction reveals that it was not as wrong as killing European children. The crime remains unreported. Despite Annie's sympathy for the Aborigines, the 'other' remain 'the other'.

The same feeling of sympathy for, but carefully contrived distance between, the races is to be found in the period after the Aborigines were no longer committing 'outrages'. Marriage between a European and an Aborigine was so rare that when a Hopkins River stockman, Michael Sullivan, approached William Hamilton, a clergyman at Kilnoorat in mid-1847 to arrange to be married to an Aboriginal girl, the clergyman appeared unsure that this was allowable. He wrote to La Trobe, the Superintendent of the District, asking for advice. The girl was about sixteen years of age, spoke English 'pretty well', had worked in domestic service for some time and wanted to be married. Her suitor was 'upwards of forty years of age' and 'steadfast and earnest' in his desire to marry.

The clergyman gave no grounds for concern but seemed to be expressing it. La Trobe simply wrote on the letter, 'I do not see what business Gov't has with this matter'.[46]

By mid-1841 the Aboriginal groups of the area east of the Hopkins were almost extinct. Robinson's list of Aboriginal tribes makes it clear that few Aborigines had survived (see Appendix 1). Those who did had learnt the lesson. There would be no more stealing. Some managed to gain work on stations, and in return were given rations. Others moved from one place to another seeking the odd job and the payment that followed. William Adeney, who settled on the south-east side of Lake Colongulac, just north of Camperdown, travelled through the eastern part of the district in early 1843. He found, for example, that two Aborigines worked for Roadknight near Geelong. They were 'quite equal to any two white men if not superior for a job of this kind [travelling with cattle]'. They 'stop all day and make themselves useful for their food only'. At night they returned to the tribe and slept in mia mias. 'They are dressed as workmen and behave as respectably as any of them.'[47] He learnt that bushmen told 'newchums' that if they went up the country there was a fair chance of being killed and eaten. 'The real state of the case', he wrote, thinking of where he was as up the country, 'is that it is rare to meet with any blacks except near the stations of some of the settlers from whom they get dead sheep, flour, etc.'. In contrast, the Aborigines of the Portland Bay District, those to the west, were very troublesome; coming in a crowd of a hundred or more, stealing sheep, and even killing several men.[48] In February 1844 he wrote to his mother:

> The natives are not very troublesome not at all hostile but a little too prying and rather importunate beggars. While I write this I have a great black savage looking fellow who calls himself Mr Gibbs sitting on the same stool with me and his lubra is sitting on the floor in her opossum rug in the other room admiring my shepherd's white piccaniny they do not often trouble me and as I sleep alone at the hut at night I think it best to keep on good terms with them lest they should walk in some fine night and spear me but this they dare not do as they understand the system of reprisals.[49]

There was no longer a sense of fear or dread, but an underlying sense of the need for carefulness which William was still showing when his brother visited in 1855. Aborigines might call and do a small job for payment, but they were not allowed to be comfortable and stay the night.[50]

9

'the Governor would give them plenty flour, tea, sugar and Bulgarrer'

THE PORT PHILLIP Protectorate was established by the British Government after consideration of how best to protect the Aborigines and promote their civilization. It was an attempt to prevent the catastrophe that had occurred in Van Diemen's Land where, in Lieutenant-Governor Arthur's words, the Aborigines had been reduced 'almost to annihilation' partly by fighting amongst themselves but also by 'the warfare so long waged . . . between them and the white settlers, or rather . . . the bushrangers, and convict shepherds'. By 1835 he regretted that a treaty had not been signed with the Aborigines and 'compensation paid' for 'what they surrendered'. Instead 'animosity', excited by a sense of injustice, was 'exasperated into fury' by the injuries done to them by the convicts, with violent conflict being the result. Anxious to avoid a similar occurrence on the southern coast of Australia he advised the British Government that every effort should be made to come to an understanding with the Aborigines before settlement took place. Otherwise, he warned, 'it will be impossible to prevent a long continued warfare' in which 'the whites, as well as the Aborigines . . . as their mutual injuries accumulate, will destroy each other'.[1]

Those who conceived the Port Phillip Protectorate were well intentioned but the details on how the plan was to work were always vague. In the letter inviting George Augustus Robinson to accept the position of Chief Protector he was simply asked if he could help the Government by 'opening a friendly communication' with the Aborigines at Portland

Bay.[2] The four Assistant Protectors appointed in England, William Thomas, James Dredge, Edward Parker and Charles Sievwright, were given only the most general instruction:

> It will be your duty . . . to watch over the rights and interests of the natives and to endeavour to gain their respect and confidence. You will, as far as you are able by your personal exertions and influence, protect them from any encroachments on their property and from acts of cruelty, oppression or injustice.[3]

They were to report to Governor Gipps in Sydney where they would be given further instructions. But Gipps gave them little satisfaction, referring them on to Port Phillip where they were to report to the Police Magistrate. Not satisfied, the Assistant Protectors jointly wrote to Gipps requesting further information: they wanted to know about the supply of tents for temporary residences, by what conveyance they were to move themselves and their large families inland, how they were to organize for materials and labour once the sites of the various Protectorate stations were chosen, how they were to receive rations for themselves and supplies for the Aborigines. The Governor in reply pointed out that he did not envisage Protectorate stations at this stage; that they would be constantly moving with the 'different tribes'; for further instructions they should look to the Chief Protector. The Police Magistrate at Port Phillip was not to have authority over the Chief Protector but 'simply exercise a control in matters of expenditure'.[4]

The responsibility of providing sound guidance so that a vague scheme would work was one which George Augustus Robinson should never have accepted, but he did so without being told of all the position entailed. Years later the Superintendent of the Port Phillip District, Charles Joseph La Trobe, admitted, 'Mr Robinson was induced . . . to undertake a duty for which he was totally unsuited'. The problem was that he had been placed in a position—that of managing a Government department—for which he lacked both experience and aptitude. But beyond the limitations of the individuals involved there were problems in the scheme which most would have found difficult to overcome. La Trobe wrote that the failure of the Protectorate scheme must be 'mainly attributed to the impractical nature of the scheme itself, and the inapplicability of the details, by which it was proposed to pursue it, to the real circumstances of the Aboriginal Natives of the Colony'.[5]

By the beginning of 1841, even before Robinson's journey across the District, Gipps admitted to Lord John Russell, Secretary of State for the Colonies, that his hopes 'of any advantage being derived from the employment of the protectors' were 'every day diminishing'. They had shown themselves to be distressingly inactive; one had already resigned, another 'never quitted for more than a year the spot on which he seated himself . . . though there were no blacks there' while La Trobe had complained of 'the difficulty of getting another [Sievwright] to move from Geelong'. 'They are all encumbered ... with large families', he reported, 'and seem to have come to Australia with the expectation of establishing missionary stations, rather than of itinerating with and amongst the tribes'.[6]

Reluctantly Gipps agreed to the formation of a 'fixed station for each assistant Protector'. The advantage he saw was that these 'missions or stations' could become 'places of refuge to the natives, and of education for their children'. But there was a definite disadvantage. An Assistant Protector with duties on a station would not be free to check hostilities between the races across their whole district.

The Western District was slow to gain its 'fixed station'. On 21 March 1839 the Chief Protector, Robinson, had ordered the Assistant Protectors to 'take the field forthwith' and one month later he notified them of their districts. Charles Wightman Sievwright, Assistant Protector of the Western District, was to proceed 'in the direction of Geelong and the country to the westward'. As the site for his 'homestead and agricultural establishment' had not been decided upon, Sievwright proceeded only as far as Geelong which he made his base. It was not till 17 February 1841 that he moved to Lake Keilambete. Unfortunately the site chosen was already occupied by John Thomson who protested strongly. Less than two months later Robinson, on 6 April 1841, ordered Sievwright to move camp to nearby Lake Terang. Finally Mt Rouse was agreed on as the site of the Protectorate station, and Sievwright moved there on 12 February 1842.

The Aborigines showed interest in the provision of an official, some kind of base camp and the handing out of supplies. They wanted to see for themselves what was offered, even if it involved travelling further than was normal for them. Traditionally, each Aboriginal group had its boundaries, and it was not easy to move a hundred miles or so westward and relocate as Europeans might do. However, this was the expectation of Sievwright and Protectorate officials who insisted on seeing the bringing together of different Aboriginal tribes and clans as something that was good in itself: 'Nothing could be more desirable than the friendly intercourse which has been opened between them and those Strange Tribes of whom they stood so much in dread'.[7]

When Sievwright planned to move from Geelong to Lake Keilambete, he met the Aborigines he had come to know around Geelong to tell them of the move and express his hope that they would move with him. They 'used', he said, 'every argument to dissuade me from leaving them'. They collected the elders of the tribe together, and on the following day representatives came to his tent to explain that they needed to know more about where Sievwright was going and about the Aborigines of that area. They wished to send five 'of their warriors' with him, 'if he would answer for their safety', and allow them to sleep in his tent 'while in the enemy's country'.[8]

Reassured by Sievwright's promise of protection, an 'embassy' of the Barrable Aborigines accompanied him to Lake Keilambete. Once there, Aborigines soon gathered. When Robinson visited between 6 and 22 April 1841 he claimed to have met between two and three hundred Aborigines.[9] The Elingamite, the Jarcourt, the Manemeet, the Bullerburers (Bolokeburers), the Conewurt and the Wornerbul were all mentioned as being at the camp. Officially Sievwright recorded that the visit of the Geelong Aborigines had been a success and that the visitors had returned to bring back their people. Sievwright's son, however, told Robinson that the last Barrabool native had left just after Robinson's arrival because he was frightened.[10] There is no mention of these Aborigines returning.

With the move to Lake Terang came further visitors. A group of fifty-three Aborigines of the Colijohn and Wardy Yalloke 'tribes' from the east arrived in June. They explained to Sievwright that most of their kin had gone to join the Barrabool (Geelong) Aborigines and that they had come to stay for one moon. Their friends would come with the Barrabool Aborigines when a messenger was sent for them.

When Sievwright moved from Lake Terang to Mt Rouse he was accompanied by 210 Aborigines, some of whom may have been going back to their own country. For example, Sievwright's brother stated that Color, whose name was the Aboriginal name for Mt Rouse, joined the Protectorate camp at Lake Terang in November 1841. But the great majority were strangers moving to Mt Rouse.[11] When Robinson visited the Mt Rouse station in March 1842 he found 264 Aborigines there.

Robinson and Sievwright advised Aborigines to go to the reserve for protection and food. The station was an 'asylum . . . instituted to provide' for their wants,[12] as Robinson had told many of them during his 1841 journey across the District. When Sievwright visited the Winters' station in January 1842, about 150 Aborigines were gathered there to meet him. He told them of the reserve and invited them to join him. Next day the leaders stated that they would join him, provided that the chiefs who were with him at Mt Rouse would visit them first and perform necessary native ceremonies. Robinson suggested to the natives who had been troublesome at Hunter's station that they should go to Mt Rouse. In early 1842 he and Sievwright visited a camp of the Nillan conedeet and advised them to do this. Slightly later some of the Nillan conedeet were helped on their way towards Mt Rouse, first by Sievwright, and then by an Aborigine from the Mt Rouse station. When Robinson and Sievwright visited J. M. Allan's property, Tooram, east of Warrnambool, in early 1842, they invited the Aborigines to visit Mt Rouse. The answer given was that they were 'afraid of the other tribes they would meet there'. In each case the discussion had taken place with the aid of an interpreter. The Native Police also ordered Aborigines to go to Mt Rouse.

The Aboriginal reaction can be judged by the lists of those registered at the Mt Rouse station. Attendance was marked on a daily basis and these lists show that there was much coming and going. In November 1842 the figure varied from the largest number present, 263 in the middle of the month, to 116, the lowest figure near the end of the month. In December 1842 the figure varied from 136 on the first day of the month to only 18 for the last three days of the month.

The amount of coming and going is highlighted by the fact that the Native Police 'drove a party of between two and three hundred Aborigines from Lake Boloke and the River Hopkins' to the station in mid-October.[13] The Jarcourt Aborigines who had accompanied Sievwright to Mt Rouse from Terang had left in two groups, some in April and the rest in July 1842.[14] This possibly accounted for about fifty Aborigines. With them gone, there should still have been about two hundred Aborigines on the station; yet the largest figure for a daily enrolment after 1 October and before 12 November is in the middle of October—a figure of 263. Everyone on the station must have left before the arrival of the group with the Native Police! This is not likely but it does show the degree of movement on and off the station. Moreover, the figure of 263 had fallen to 148 near the end of the month. H. E. P. Dana, Commandant of the Native Police, had demonstrated the power of the Native Police: the Aborigines went to Mt Rouse as ordered but they didn't stay!

The evidence shows that a relatively small group of Aborigines stayed for a considerable length of time on the station. Of 360 names registered at Mt Rouse between October 1842 and the beginning of April 1843, 47 Aborigines were on the station for most of the month for at least two of the six months for which there are details. Most Aborigines came and went in groups, the number for the day jumping, for example, from 37 on one day to 46 on the next, dropping from 72 on one day to 44 the next, dropping from 130 one day to 30 for two days and back up to 76 on the following day. The average attendance figures provided by Protectorate officials hide this movement, providing an image of a stable population, whereas the opposite was the case.

Even those who came back over the months usually came for only a number of days each time. Woordi Yarburrh (also spelt Waddy Ar Barrh, Waddy Ubarrh and Waddy Artarrh) arrived on 7 October 1842 and stayed for six days. He arrived on 15 November and stayed for seven days. He spent some time on the station in January 1843, arriving on the 24th. In February he visited the station for several days in the middle of the month.

The Aborigines came from far and wide to the Mt Rouse station. Sievwright mentions the presence of the Bolokeburer of Lake Boloke, the Jarcourt of the Camperdown area and towards Colac, the Mopor from nearby Spring Creek and the Eterang conedeet, a group who, he stated, inhabited the Grampians towards Mt William.[15]

A number of men known to be influential in the Aboriginal world visited for the last three days of October 1842. Koort Kirrup (Palapnue conedeet), Karwutkoomowar (Kaawirn Kuunawarn-Hissing Swan), from the Mt Shadwell area and Warrandeon Kneon (Wane conedeet burn) were present. Others of whom I know no details arrived at the same time. They may have been important men also. They may have arrived simply because they were ordered to Mt Rouse by Dana and the Native Police. This at least would explain the arrival of Koort Kirrup. Dana sent a group of Aborigines from the Wannon to Mt Rouse at the end of October. But what of Kaawirn Kuunawarn arriving from the opposite direction of Mt Shadwell? The Native Police had been on the Hopkins in mid-October rather than late October. Did influential men have their own meeting at Mt Rouse? Did they come out of interest to see what was being provided at Mt Rouse?

The coming and going of the Aborigines was not a rejection of attempts to civilize and Christianize them. No religious services were held till after the move to Mt Rouse in February 1842, and these were abandoned when or before Sievwright handed over to Watton on 23 September 1842. Sievwright reported over two hundred Aborigines regularly attending divine service in the first few months of 1842. But little could have been gained from such a service since Sievwright was not able to speak an Aboriginal language, and differences in language were so great at the station that some Aborigines were not easily able to communicate with each other. At no time through the entire life of the station was any provision made for instructing children, though Sievwright asked for a teacher to be appointed, as there were more than a hundred children on the station.

As for civilizing in the general sense of learning the skills of caring for animals and planting crops, few were involved before the move to Mt Rouse, where Sievwright began agricultural operations immediately, although his approach was not one that was likely to be regarded as overbearing. He took into account the need for time for traditional tasks and recreation. His general programme was that the working day was from after breakfast till about three o'clock. Women after breakfast departed to obtain 'roots, opposum, etc.' while the men went to various tasks allocated to them. Some acted as stock-keepers, others ploughed, others drove the team, while others worked on widening the watercourse. At three o'clock rations were issued and the rest of the time was their own. Aboriginal skills were utilized: women and children with their digging sticks pulverized the newly ploughed land—much more effective than 'cross ploughing', according to Sievwright—while the men dragged 'the Harrows'. If it rained, the Aborigines were not expected to work.[16]

A possible reason for short stays was obvious even in the short period at Lake Keilambete and Lake Terang: the Protectorate and its employees were seen as niggardly and deliberately avoiding the distribution of food.

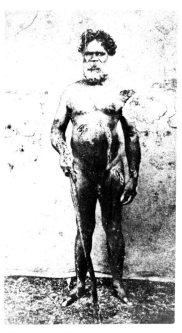

Wombeetch Puyuun, Camperdown George

A later photograph of Wombeetch Puyuun who died in 1883: he was the last of his tribe, as James Dawson proclaimed on the obelisk he raised over his grave in the Camperdown cemetery.

Aborigines at the Framlingham Aboriginal Reserve, 1867: King David is fifth from the left in the middle row while Camperdown George is third from the left in the same row.

Muulapuurn Yuurong Yaar, one of the Aborigines who provided information for James Dawson's book on the local Aborigines

Yarruun Parpur Tarneen, daughter of the 'Chief' of the Morpor (Spring Creek) tribe, Weeratt Kuyuut, and Dawson's chief informant on the customs of her people

Gnuurneecheean

Wombeet Tuulawarn, who assisted his wife Yarruun Parpur Tarneen in providing information about their people for Dawson's book

It was Government policy that food should be distributed only to those who worked, to the sick and to the young and the elderly so that the Protectorate camp and later the station could not be perceived as a place automatically to gain food. The distribution of food was the way Protectorate officials were to show the Aborigines the link between work and food. But it was a difficult lesson to teach when sometimes there was no food available for distribution and at other times food was refused as a punishment for behaviour that was not approved. For considerable periods of time while at Lake Terang, Sievwright and the Protectorate employees faced hostility from Aborigines over food. At Lake Terang Sievwright employed some Aborigines and in return gave them supplies until two murders and increasing tension between Aboriginal groups caused him to stop food supplies. The result was a seige with angry Aborigines attempting to take the provisions by force. Sievwright was threatened by spears and firebrands. When he left the camp for a short time the Protectorate employees were threatened as Aborigines attempted to take the supplies. As numbers grew at Lake Terang and with little work to be done due to uncertainty about how long they would be there, Sievwright's problems mounted. The small number who worked (eleven out of about approximately sixty-six in July 1841) and those supplied because they were young, old or sick shared their food with everyone else. The end result was that all were hungry. The Aborigines complained, stole food and augmented supplies by stealing sheep from local properties. By the end of August 259 Aborigines were at Lake Terang and they were hungry.[17]

Sievwright made no attempt to hide his inability to deal with the situation while Robinson, ignoring the problem, left on his journey to the west. Sievwright wrote, 'The neighbouring settlers state that they have suffered more by the depredations of the native of late than at any time previous to the arrival of this Establishment'. He begged that an early decision be made as to whether he was to stay where he was or move to Mt Rouse 'in order that no further odium may be incurred in the district from the effects of the protracted operations of this branch of the department'.[18]

The difficulty of providing food for the Aborigines was to remain a problem for the whole period of the Protectorate in the Western District; as was the non-arrival of provisions. In July 1842 Sievwright wrote to Robinson reminding him of his letters dated 31 March, 27 April and 17 May asking for blankets, clothing and medicines. He had received nothing. There was much sickness at the station and five Aborigines had recently died.[19]

On 23 September 1842 Sievwright handed over at Mt Rouse to Dr Watton. He had been ordered to do so, having been suspended not so much on grounds of incompetence as an employee, as on immorality in his personal life.[20] He was accused of having made advances to the wife of an Assistant Protector and of incest. Robinson was, as usual, quick to seize the chance to criticize and his report to La Trobe condemned Sievwright.[21]

Sievwright has in general been criticized by historians. Peter Corris, for example, wrote, 'A saint's job had been given to a sinner'.[22] In a sense there can be no questioning of such a comment but interest in Sievwright's private life has tended to overshadow research into his work as Assistant Protector. Too often Robinson's comments have been taken at face value. Yet Robinson was notorious for never having a good word to say for any of his colleagues and he had a particular reason to be critical of Sievwright for he had aspired to be Chief Protector. La Trobe in his evaluation of the Protectorate in late 1848 does not specially mention Sievwright. Instead he wrote of them all including Robinson, 'They one and all have had their failings. They each, under one impulse or another, undertook, and had pretensions to a task beyond their powers. They never at any time drew together, understood each other, or had mutual confidence . . .'.[23]

With Sievwright's removal the possibility of the station as a flourishing concern grew slighter. Earlier that year Robinson had been accused by the Governor of 'lack of regard to a proper economy in the expenditure of public money'. He had submitted a requisition for supplies for the Aborigines which was regarded as 'extravagant' and it was greatly reduced.[24] Thus Robinson by mid-1842 was looking for ways to reduce expenditure, one of which was to cut expenses in the west. Watton, appointed on a much smaller salary than Sievwright, was to be in charge, and Sievwright was not to be replaced. Eighteen pairs of trousers and thirteen blankets were issued during 1843; the following year only two pairs of trousers and no blankets were issued. The chances of gaining either items at Mt Rouse were slight, then non-existent.

Watton, like Sievwright, had trouble obtaining supplies. In mid-1843 he was 'at a loss' to know what to do respecting procuring supplies. He had 'again and again forwarded requisitions to Melbourne'. He had heard nothing from Robinson nor had any supplies arrived. Reluctantly, he borrowed from John Cox of Weerangourt who had been forced to move from Mt Rouse to make way for the Protectorate station and Acheson French of Monivae (local squatter and Police Magistrate at The Grange). He was lacking seven kinds of forms on which he was expected to provide official information. He reminded Robinson of his requisition for some tobacco which he had returned in February.[25]

With so few supplies to be distributed, the number of Aborigines at the station lessened dramatically. The average attendance in 1845 was 33 as it was again in 1846. There was no detailed report on Mt Rouse for the year 1846. Robinson stated that 'Dr. Watton feels he is not paid enough to supply one'.[26]

During 1846 the station was virtually abandoned by all Aborigines for a couple of months and in September 1847 there were no Aborigines there. By the time it was closed the station was of little importance to any Aborigines except as a place to obtain medical help.

Watton provided a number of reasons for the lack of Aboriginal interest. Deaths on the station were a cause of Aborigines leaving.[27] Sievwright gave this as the reason that a party of the Jarcourt left in July 1842: he said they did not want to be blamed for the sickness.[28] Watton also said that the Aborigines stated that they stayed away because of the difficulty of procuring wood for their fires and having to grind wheat to make flour.[29] Another reason, again to do with food, was that they refused to eat salt beef, the only meat available on the station.[30] At this time only the one or two Aborigines residing, and regularly employed, on the station were being given flour. Watton wrote in 1848 that the small sum allowed for supporting the Aborigines 'precludes the possibility of feeding more than a very limited number on semi-starvation principles'.[31]

At Lake Keilambete and Lake Terang hungry Aborigines stole the sheep of settlers in the vicinity of the Protectorate camp. They did not do this at Mt Rouse. Sievwright believed there was only one case when Aborigines on the station stole sheep, and then they brought the sheep to the station. The Aboriginal reaction was largely to by-pass the station. It offered little.

There was one service which had regular custom. Watton was a doctor and Aborigines sought his help till the station was closed and perhaps even afterwards. Between January and May 1843 he treated 88 cases of which 46 were of venereal disease.[32] During the first half of 1844 he treated 62 cases;[33] during 1845 he treated 142 cases;[34] and in 1848 he treated 227 cases.[35] The numbers seeking help thus increased over time; but in 1848 he noted for the first time that he was seeing cases of syphilis less frequently.

Protectorate officials were meant to provide protection for Aboriginal people against European violence. Sievwright while at Geelong investigated cases where Aborigines had been murdered and also where Europeans claimed they needed protection against Aborigines; but was generally slow to act. The distances were large and transport was difficult. He made the mistake of having 'people involved make depositions on oath' which meant the information he obtained could not be used. He found it a most frustrating aspect of his occupation, complaining to the Secretary of State that the 'Judicial System' failed to follow up the cases which he put before it.[36] Often, particularly in the latter part of the 1840s, Watton was asked to report on cases of *inter se* killing (killing of an Aborigine by an Aborigine). Only in the case of Alaverin did this lead to a trial and he was acquitted. Thus in practical terms neither Sievwright nor Watton successfully brought to justice men who

committed crimes against the Aborigines. Nor were they able to intervene or successfully prevent the Aboriginal customs of revenge killing or
killing a stranger.

Sievwright's difficulty in bringing Europeans to justice is well illus-
trated in the case of the Queen versus Sandford George Bolden for
manslaughter of an Aborigine named Tatkier on 27 October 1841. The
Bolden brothers (George and Samuel) had taken up a huge area of
country to the north of Warrnambool—embracing what was to become
'Merrang, Minjah, Muston's Creek, St. Mary's, Grassmere, Harton Hills,
the Lake, etc'.[37] On 27 October the Boldens and two stockmen out
riding on the property came across three Aborigines—a man (Tatkier), a
woman, and a boy. The stockmen accosted the Aborigines, asking what
they were doing on the run. When they replied that they were on their
way to Sievwright's camp they were told that they were not doing any
such thing, but looking for cattle. George Bolden and the stockmen then
proceeded to drive the Aborigines away by using whips to make them
move faster.

When a flat area was reached, Tatkier turned and threatened George,
who was riding just behind him, by swinging an implement. George
fired, shooting him in the stomach. Tatkier then fled to a waterhole.
While the stockmen stayed behind with orders not to let Tatkier escape,
Bolden returned to the home station for more firearms. In attempting to
escape Tatkier attacked one of the stockmen. Bolden, returning at this
time, fired and again shot the Aborigine, whose body fell into a
waterhole and sank, not to be seen again.

Meanwhile the Aboriginal woman had been run over by Peter Carney
on his horse. 'I afterwards saw her lying against a tree . . . she was not
dead but might have been hurt from the running over her', William
Kiernan, one of the two stockmen, wrote in his signed statement. The
boy had fled up a tree from which he had watched events before fleeing
to report them to Sievwright.[38]

After hearing the story Sievewright and some Aborigines went to the
site to recover the bodies. Sievwright left the Aborigines to do this while
he went to see the Boldens. George Bolden at first appeared to have no
knowledge of any 'collision' but then, since Sievwright seemed to know
the details of the incident, he asked whether the bodies had been found.
To this Sievwright replied, 'I believe so'. Then Bolden admitted, 'it was I
who shot the Native'. Since he appeared 'agitated', Sievwright told him
he would return the next day to take his statement.

The case appeared a straightforward one—an Aborigine had been
shot and had died as a result. There was an admission of guilt from the
person responsible and witnesses who described what had happened. In
court, however, events took an unexpected turn.[39] Judge Willis
emphasized that the body of the dead man had not been found and
without it there was no evidence of a crime being committed. The case

could not rest on the evidence of a death taken from a 'savage boy's statement'. Nor could the statement made by Bolden be used as evidence, as Sievwright had led him to believe a body had been found before he made the confession. In fact, Judge Willis stated that 'there was no evidence that Tatkier had even been shot at'—which corroborates the Reverend Joseph Orton's statement of the extent to which the evidence given in court differed substantially from that in the signed statements given to Sievwright. Regardless of protests from the Crown Prosecutor, James Croke, Judge Willis advised the jury that they must acquit the prisoner.

The Reverend Orton, who was present at the trial, commented that the Judge 'very many times interrupted the proceedings by remarks favourable to the prisoner'. He also made clear to the jury his wish that they should state that 'the prisoner left the dock with unstained character'. One juryman complied with the Judge's wish but Orton said that several jurors asserted the contrary.

The very presence, however, of the Chief Protector or Assistant Protector Sievwright was influential. It meant one had to take such a person into account when acting against the Aborigines. It was also the aspect of Sievwright's job most understood by the Aborigines. The Reverend Tuckfield complained to his colleague that in the beginning he could hardly speak to the Aborigines without their mentioning Sievwright and all he had done for them 'in furnishing some of them with firearms and promising them protection'.[40] Aborigines also emphasized to the settlers on the Crawford River the protection they were offered by Sievwright.[41] Tom Browne of Squattlesea Mere, who experienced the antagonism felt towards the Assistant Protector, clearly stated the squatters' point of view. His property was not far from that of John Cox who had to abandon 'the richest and best fattening run in a rich fattening district' to make way for 'the black Brother' at Mt Rouse:

> The pastoralists never approved of the protectorate system. They accused certain of the protectors ... of instructing the blacks if whites shot them it would be considered murder, and the offenders hanged, but that if they speared the cattle or the stockmen occasionally it was only ... an error of judgement, for which they would not suffer death.[42]

There was understandable animosity towards the Protectorate. Sievwright annoyed Thomson at Lake Keilambete by gathering together some two to three hundred Aborigines virtually on his doorstep. Niel Black was so incensed when the camp moved to Lake Terang he threatened Robinson he would write to England to complain.[43] John Cox was forced to move from Mt Rouse to make way for the final site of the Aboriginal station. The ill will caused by this can still be sensed in Tom Browne's account.

Strong feeling was evoked against the Assistant Protector largely, it seems, for doing his job, as he later claimed.[44] The strength of such feeling is best indicated by the reaction of one of the Portland newspapers to news of the murder of Aboriginal women and a child at Muston's Creek in early 1842. Settlers had hurried to let La Trobe know that they believed that the women and child were part of a larger party, including men, who had made an attack on a station and that the Aborigines had been killed in an affray which followed. The bodies of the men killed must have been removed. It was a suggestion investigated by La Trobe and found to have been entirely fabricated. Yet the *Portland Mercury* went much further in its claim, putting forward the suggestion that Sievwright had taken the bodies of the missing Aboriginal men. The Editor wrote of the general impression:

> ... that the women and children whose lifeless bodies were discovered had lost their lives in a nightly skirmish between the settlers and the blacks, and that, to raise an undue impression against the former, an aboriginal Protector, who shall be nameless, had induced the natives to remove the bodies of the men who had fallen in the affray, so that, to those not cognizant of the whole matter, it might appear an act of coldblooded and atrocious barbarity.[45]

The records of the Protectorate reveal the willingness of the Aborigines to investigate the facilities the Government claimed to be establishing in their interest, thus opening themselves to new influences. A small number attempted to live at Mt Rouse till driven away by either their own customs (moving away from sickness, need for wood for fires) or the inability of the station to provide food that was regarded as edible or indeed, at times, any food at all. For what they needed in the rapidly changing circumstances Aborigines would have had to turn to the squatters, as Robinson admitted in early 1848. It was 'undesirable' to encourage the Aborigines to congregate at Mount Rouse because of the absence of 'Religious and Scholastic Instruction'. It was preferable for Watton to visit the Aborigines in their camps and on the stations of the settlers. But this had not been done enough. Instead Robinson explained that he had endeavoured to interest settlers in the 'Work of their civilisation' as a means of saving the Goverment's money while allowing the work of civilizing to continue 'progressing'.[46]

The Protectorate station which had been envisaged as a place for civilizing and Christianizing the Aborigines had failed to show the Aborigines what it meant to be civilized. Clothes were not distributed, few Aborigines were employed in tilling the soil and there was so little food available that the link between work and the reward of food could only be shown to a select few. There were no classes in which Aborigines could be impressed by the European skills of reading and writing. There were no church services after the initial few months. Aborigines would have listened as they had in the first few months when Sievwright reported two hundred Aborigines regularly attending Sunday services. They listened without understanding the language but the rituals followed would have communicated the importance of such an event in the European way of life.

In 1841 Robinson explained to Aborigines that if they did not steal, 'the Governor would give them plenty flour, tea, sugar and Bulgarrer [animals]. But if they stole, the Governor would be plenty sulky and would not give them anything'.[47] On a later occasion he told the assembled Aborigines not to steal for if they did so 'the white people would shoot them'. He said little about what was to be offered on a Protectorate station but he must have mentioned that an Assistant Protector would be coming to settle amongst them, for in expressing his satisfaction with the outcome of the meeting he wrote, 'they appeared in high spirits and apparently thankful for what had been done and hoped I would send a good white man to live among them'.[48] What they received was literally that—a man and nothing more—Sievwright and then Watton. That so little was provided at Mt Rouse indicates how little importance the Government attached to the task of civilizing and Christianizing the Aborigines.[49]

The story of the functioning of the Protectorate in the Western District is a sad one but the records of the Protectorate provide a valuable resource for obtaining information on individual Aborigines. At Mt Rouse a register of names of Aborigines attending the station was kept and marked on a daily basis just as one would do today in a school. The long list of names, all Aboriginal, each name written as it was sounded, is an impressive document of acceptance of Aboriginality, of willingness to make the effort to write the Aboriginal names and associate Aborigines with the names.[50] Aboriginal names were also used in the list of Aborigines given medical treatment.[51] Sievwright's record of the names of Wardy Yalloke and Colijohn Aborigines who joined his camp at Lake Terang in June 1841 survive. Not all documents to do with the Mt Rouse Protectorate station have survived nor are lists complete but the register lists survive for late 1842 and early 1843. As this was the time when the greatest number of Aborigines were at the station, the names are a valuable surviving source.

However, the task of recognizing these individuals when they are mentioned elsewhere in other sources, such as Robinson's lists of clan members collected in 1841, is difficult. At times it appeared impossible. The crux of the problem for the researcher is that the European recording Aboriginal names, a collection of strange sounds often heard in difficult and trying circumstances, used the letters he felt most correctly indicated the right sound; but there are different ways one can indicate a similar sound. Sievwright, Robinson and Dr Watton all used their own way of spelling Aboriginal names. Each one was not necessarily consistent though this was likely. Dawson, writing of the same

Aborigines in his book published in 1881, further complicated the situation. He used his own way of indicating the way words were said. He explained in an introductory note that as he had found it 'almost impossible to represent the correct sounds' of Aboriginal languages 'by adhering to the rules of English orthography', the rules were 'laid aside, together with signs of accentuation'. Instead he used double consonants to express emphasis, and double vowels to express prolongation of the sound. He warned that the 'k and g which appear before consonants in the syllables of many aboriginal words represent sounds barely perceptible, yet indispensable to correct pronunciation'. There was a further odd sound, 'a nasal sound of "gn" or "ng"' which often occurred at the beginning of syllables in the Aboriginal languages.[52] So that Robinson's conedeet meaning, 'of the place', 'member of', became for Dawson kuurndit, and the Moporer conedeet, for example, became the Mopor Kuurndit.

Tackling individual Aboriginal names was confusing. It was easiest when the name was distinctive. For example, Koort Kirrup visited the station briefly. He was recorded as Karoop Koort. Even though the two words were in reverse order to that usually used by Europeans the sounds were distinctive. But luck was involved! Both words began with a 'k' so that when looking for Koort, I found Karoop which immediately was familiar. Other names were harder to find. A further difficulty is that each Aborigine had several names. There is no guarantee that a name given to Robinson in 1841 would be the same name given to Watton at Mt Rouse in late 1842 or early 1843. Robinson was often given names of Aborigines by an informant. The name the informant gave him might not be the name the individual would give. For many of the clan groups Robinson only recorded the names of the adult males.

Persevering with the list of odd sounding names, I found several that I was able to match with those in Robinson's lists or mentioned by Dawson.[53] Even more exciting was the linking of these names from the 1840s with well-known Aborigines who lived on the Government Aboriginal stations established after 1860.

By the time Government Aboriginal stations were established after the frontier had passed, Aborigines were mostly listed by European name only. This can be seen in the names on one of the earliest group photographs of the Aborigines gathered together on the Framlingham Aboriginal station after 1865 (shown in the Plate facing p. 146). The use of the European names, and the evidence of Europeanization—the shirts, the jackets and trousers, the trimmed hair, the neat beards, the use of both European first and surnames make Aboriginality appear a thing of the distant past. Only the breastplates around the neck of two of the Aborigines declaring them to be kings indicate a reference to the Aboriginal world. Yet this group photograph was taken only twenty-five years after Sievwright arrived at Mt Rouse. Aborigines who were twenty then would have been forty-five at the time of the photograph. Mature men of forty in 1842 would have been sixty-five. Except for the children, these people would have experienced the provisions of the Protectorate. Many probably visited the reserve, at least for a look. Which ones attended?

To make the link between the Mt Rouse lists of 1842 and the names at Framlingham or elsewhere in the 1860s it was necessary to find a reference to an Aborigine in which both an Aboriginal and a European name were used. Dawson was of tremendous help. He stated that Kaawirn Kuunawarn was Chief of the Kirrae Wuurong, the Mount Shadwell Tribe.[54] A surviving collection of photographs of Aborigines identified by name is in the possession of the Ritchie family of Port Fairy. These happened to be of Aborigines Dawson knew well. One is of Kuunawarn, the same individual known later as King David—one of the two men wearing a breastplate in the Framlingham photograph. In other places those wearing king plates may have been given them by Europeans without any reference to their status in the Aboriginal world. In this case, however, we have Dawson's word that King David was a man of great influence. Listed as Karwutkoomowar, he visited Mt Rouse for the last three days of October 1842. Dawson's most valued informant for his book on the Aboriginal customs of the Western District was the 'Chiefess' of the Morpor Tribe, Yarruun Parpur Tarneen, daughter of the Chief, Weeratt Kuyuut. Her husband Wombeet Tullawarn also contributed. Photographs of both the 'Chiefess' and her husband are in the Ritchie collection. Yarruun Parpur Tarneen is also identified as Louise, wife of Castella.[55] Wombeet Tuulawarn has the European name Castella. In the list of names of Aborigines required to reside on Framlingham Aboriginal Station in 1876 are King Davie, Castella and Mrs Castella. These are not Aborigines far removed from an Aboriginal background: they are the Aborigines from whom Dawson collected a wealth of detail about Aboriginal culture and both men visited the Protectorate station at Mt Rouse. The husband of the 'Chiefess' of the Morpor tribe visited the station in February 1843 for seven days. He was recorded as Wane Tuulavarn. Another Aborigine named in the Ritchie collection is Muulapuurn Yuurong Yaar. Listed as Mullapoernin, she was at the station for most of November and December 1842. One other famous Western District Aborigine well known to Dawson was Camperdown George, whose Aboriginal name was Wombeetch Puyuun. He was the last surviving Aborigine of the Camperdown area. After he died Dawson erected a magnificent obelisk which still stands in the Camperdown cemetery in memory of the passing of the Aborigines. Wombeetch Puyuun is also listed as attending Mt Rouse. He may be Woombitean who visited in late December 1842. He is certainly the Oombete Pooyan who attended for five days in January 1843 and seven days in February 1843. Earlier, in July 1841, Robinson had been given his name. Robinson was at Mt Sturgeon at the time but the names he was given appear to be those of the Jarcourt.[56]

It is therefore possible to link Robinson's clan lists of 1841, the Protectorate station attendance lists, and the Aborigines later drawn on to Aboriginal stations as part of a policy of protection and restriction adopted by the Victorian Government after 1860. The links are important, providing a firmer sense of the life of individual Aborigines and of the background experiences which they brought with them to the later Aboriginal stations.

10

'making them feel that they shall not murder and plunder with impunity'

THE POWER OF the state may appear a rather abstract concept but to those who have experience of it, it has reality embodied in the local police, the local courts of justice and beyond them the more prestigious courts which deal with serious crimes. Beyond the police and the law courts is a body of law which can be appealed to either to condemn or protect the individual citizen. The law has its cases of precedence handed down from generation to generation. It has its representatives who protect the individual, those that put the case against him or her, and the Judge who has to guide the jury of citizens who in serious cases decide the verdict. All the actors have a role to play, a role established over hundreds of years.

The first settlers in the Portland Bay District arrived ahead of law enforcement officers and courts of justice. These were distant but not totally powerless, for the settlers knew of the law and the power of the state; but what of the Aborigines? They had no knowledge of such things. How were they to be shown the power of the state? How were they to see what the law defined as acceptable behaviour? This chapter focuses on the way in which the power of the state was demonstrated to the Aborigines.

In the years up to 1842 Europeans confronted local Aboriginal groups, attempting to convince them of the wisdom of not troubling Europeans in any way. Their call for the protection of police or military forces, and the intervention of the judicial system to assist their interests, went largely unheeded. But from 1842 onwards the Aborigines could not but be aware of the power of some external body intervening in the situation. Aborigines were captured by Border Police or Native Police and marched across hundreds of miles to Melbourne. Alternatively, they experienced their first sea voyage, some of them travelling via Launceston to Melbourne. In both cases the trip involved much that was unknown. Arrival meant gaol, often a terrifying episode. As Aborigines from different areas spoke in different languages, the Aboriginal prisoner was likely to have no one with whom he could speak fluently. It would have been an experience similar to that of prisoners of war taken captive by men of another culture. There was physical pain caused by the irons attached to their legs, and mental anguish. There was the different food, the isolation from those of their race, the imprisonment and the threat, made clear to them by fellow prisoners, of the possibility of their end being that of death by hanging.

It was easy, as Europeans of the day did, to make light of the situation and claim that Aborigines cunningly evaded trial and therefore the penalty of the law by claiming their English was too poor for them to understand the working of the judicial system. But William Thomas, Assistant Protector with responsibility for the Aborigines around Melbourne who spent time with each prisoner instructing him in English and the system of trial by jury, while not denying the intelligence of the Aborigines and their knowledge of conversational English, believed that the British concept of a trial was too difficult for them to understand. Language was the key to communication. If their knowledge of English had been much better they could have been taught to understand; or if he had been able to talk fluently to them in their own language, again he could have instructed them. But neither was possible.[1] Yet if the purpose of the system of inflicting penalties through a judicial system was a demonstration of power, and the taking of life by hanging a demonstration of the ultimate power, then Aborigines were recipients of effective demonstrations of such power. Fluency in English was not necessary. Hanging could be seen and was seen by Aborigines and described to others. Capture meant loss of freedom, an effective demonstration of power.

It was the forces of the state marshalled against the recalcitrant clans that brought Aboriginal resistance to an end. Faced by a virtual 'civil war' in mid-1842, La Trobe admitted to the Colonial Secretary, 'I am inclined to fear at times that this state of things is beyond all remedy under present circumstances'.[2] Yet peace was established. It was the careful placing of small numbers of Native Police and/or Border Police in the area of hostile Aborigines, and their actions backed by the operation of the British judicial system, that won the day. In the end the Aborigines were dealt with on their own terms. It was not necessary to have a large military force. The enemy was really a series of enemies, each being a relatively small group of people. They could be dealt with one by one or even simultaneously by a small number of individuals, providing they could follow the Aborigines to their camping places normally inaccessible to the Europeans. Once a Native Police force was established the end of Aboriginal resistance was a possibility. Not that it appeared so at the time. Settlers were scathing, describing the idea of the Native Police force 'as one of the absurdest of the absurd farces that had been played upon them these past few years, under the plausible term of protection'.[3]

As Aboriginal attacks increased in 1842 so did the number of police in the District. In early 1842 with the outbreak of general hostilities, La Trobe ordered Foster Fyans, the Crown Lands Commissioner, and the Border Police (twelve men) into the Port Fairy district. They were ordered to stay till the outrages ceased. Fyans was told to make his permanent headquarters to the east of the Lakes (Colac) while the trouble continued. La Trobe also ordered five of the Mounted Police to go to the District, two were to be stationed at the Grange and three at Portland. 'More', it was quite out of his power to do, he informed the Governor. There were only thirteen mounted police and a non-commissioned officer in the Port Phillip District and five had been sent to the west.[4]

Fyans attempted to capture those responsible for attacks in the vicinity of Port Fairy in early 1842, but he was unsuccessful. The description of the attempt by Fyans and his Aboriginal assistant, Bon Jon, to capture Charley, makes clear the difficulties of Europeans, and the effectiveness of Aboriginal knowledge of the land and of their weapons in such circumstances. The setting was an area of 'very broken ground' and 'heavy underwood'. The two men were on horseback and Fyans had discovered that his pistols had become wet in the rain and were useless:

We were fast coming up with the supposed murderer, who knowing the ground used it to his advantage, passing into the ravine where the fallen trees told much for him, throwing us out considerably, many of the trees laying from one rising ground to another, where it would be impossible for a horse to go over or under. In such strongholds for natives to act in, it was no easy matter to manage with this noble savage . . . From time to time he delivered three spears, to no effect . . . Bonjon was close on him in a very rugged ravine. The native making for a fallen tree, dipping his head, under he went. Bonjon, dashing his horse at it, bounded over it first rate, lighting on the shoulders of his opponent. Horse and men all came to the ground in a crash. Up jumps the savage. Snatching up his shield and leanguil, away he went. I was soon along-side of him, cutting at him with my sabre to no effect. Protecting himself with his shield in a running fight some fifty or sixty yards, he was making for a gum tree, which he gained. Rounding it, he darted out, making a wicked blow at the legs of the horse, with his eyes rivetted on mine, his shield ready to receive and ward off any sabre cuts. Again he rounded the tree, receiving the point of the sabre in the shoulder. This appeared to infuriate the savage.

Coheying shrill and loud, he again rushed from the tree, striking the horse on the head with the shield, making a blow with the leanguil which I met with the sabre. The weapon being several pounds weight, and used with such strength of arm, it is a most formidable instrument. Repeating the blow, he gained his object, struck the horse above the nose with the sharp point of the leanguil, entering on the right, and out of the opposite side. The animal immediately fell ... I was at the mercy of the savage, and only for my trusty boy Bonjon ... I really felt that I should not be spared by the savage, who was a powerful man. On seeing Bonjon he left us, coheeing often and loud.[5]

Fyans had more success in capturing Aborigines responsible for the attacks on James Hunter's Eumeralla station. In April he captured Jupiter and Jackey and later Cocknose, Doctor and a boy. Two of the Aborigines died as a result of wounds but Jupiter and Cocknose and Bumbletoe (sometimes called Bumblefoot) were taken to Port Fairy. From there they were sent by ship to Melbourne for their trial. Attacks on Hunter's property ceased. Fyans saw their capture and sending to Melbourne to trial as a means of lessening the militancy of the Nillan conedeet. Informing La Trobe of the apprehension of Cocknose and Doctor and the death of the Doctor from gunshot wounds, Fyans stated that 'the tribe on Mr Hunter's Grounds are of the wildest and most savage nature ... and I have great hopes that the examples made will be the means of bringing them to a good order'.[6] On 22 April Fyans captured Tagara (or Al.ke.per.rete) generally known as Roger, accused of the murder of Patrick Codd near Mt Rouse.

To the west James Blair, the Police Magistrate at Portland, had found it necessary to ask the officer in charge of the Military Detachment at Portland to act as a guard at Mt Eckersley, to protect settlers as they passed by it on the way inland.[7] Cold Morning, accused of being leader of an Aboriginal attack on a dray in early May, after the guard was withdrawn, was captured by a Henty headsman and sent from Portland to Melbourne for trial.

In May 1842 Chief Protector Robinson visited four Western District Aborigines in the Melbourne gaol. They were Tagara (Roger), Jarcourt, charged with the murder of Codd; Part.Po.ar.rer.min (Cold Morning) Cart Conedeet, charged with robbing drays; Tare.rare.rer (Jupiter) and Ty.koo.he (Cocknose), both Nillan Conedeet charged with robbery at Hunter's station. Robinson commented, 'they showed me their irons and complained of the hardship they suffered'.[8]

By August Jupiter, Cocknose and Bumbletoe had been returned to the District, having been released without trial. In October Cold Morning also returned home without trial. Roger was not so lucky. He was found guilty of killing Codd and sentenced to death by hanging.

British justice as the Aborigines encountered it in the District reflected the cultural circumstances out of which it evolved. Though technically the Aborigines were equal British subjects, they were not allowed to give evidence in court. The Crown Prosecutor stated the legal position:

> ... an infidel who has no notion of a future state of rewards or punishment is not an admissible witness ... no power short of the legislative council (with the sanction of the Privy Council at home) can remedy the evil ...[9]

But the bias in the judicial system began well before the court case. The police intervened in any situation at the request of the settler. It was the settler's description of events that was officially received and to which police responded. In the case of murder, there was at least some tangible evidence—a dead body and signs of Aboriginal involvement, spear wounds and bruising caused by waddies. But what of lesser crimes? Here Fyans and the police were dependent on the word of the settler or his men—not only for what happened but also for the explanation of the motives behind Aboriginal behaviour. Evidence suggests that the life of a shepherd was not highly prized. The death of such men was often recorded as simply that of Morton's man, or Wills's shepherd. And there is much evidence of the poor character of many employees. Yet the words of a shepherd, for example Wheatley, in the trial of Koort Kirrup for murder, were taken down in detail. Surviving intact, reproduced in various sets of official documents, such depositions gain status. They come to seem expressions of the truth—at least till one stumbles unexpectedly on Assistant Protector Thomas's carefully recorded exchanges in halting Aboriginal words as he endeavoured before trial to obtain an Aboriginal view of the events. Such notes were not copied and recopied. They were not sent to La Trobe, from La Trobe to the Colonial Secretary, nor from the Governor to the Secretary for State. They remain single documents easy to overlook, but signs of an inbuilt sense of fairness in the judicial sense—a sense of fairness that was difficult to implement in colonial circumstances.

The legal system had its own procedures for ensuring protection for those accused. James Croke, the Crown Prosecutor, was aware that Aborigines were being arrested without knowing why. He tried to ensure that settlers accusing the Aborigines of crimes did so officially with the accused Aborigines present.[10] This was difficult to enforce. The law also provided that the Aborigines, like Europeans, could not be tried if there was no evidence of crime or if witnesses were unavailable. The law had a developed sense of what behaviour constituted each category of crime and how one should proceed to prove guilt.

The European's sense of outrage ensured the issue of a warrant, followed by the arrest of the Aborigine who was taken to Melbourne, but it at times far outweighed the seriousness of the Aboriginal actions viewed in legal terms. The case of Jupiter, Cocknose and Bumbletoe illustrates the point. There were two possibilities, according to Croke. They could be tried for robbery or assault. Two European participants provided signed statements concerning the events which had led to the arrest of the Aborigines, but each witness had made two signed statements on different days. In each case information given in the second statement contradicted that in the first. Moreover, Croke's careful reading of the signed statements for evidence of a crime being committed led to his conclusion that there had been no crime![11]

Notes of his reaction to the depositions survive. In these he emphasized the failure of the witnesses to provide evidence of crime. In his notes Croke underlined significant words used by those who made the statements. One of the Europeans attacked by Aborigines on Hunter's Eumeralla station was Jemima Purnell, Hunter's housekeeper. According to her statement, Aborigines—Jacky, Billy, Jupiter, Bumbletoe and Cocknose—had come to the hut demanding flour and shirts. She gave them some damper and they departed. They returned the next day, attempting to take one of the horses while keeping her and her husband confined to the hut. When her husband asked them to leave, she said the Aborigines made *'motions'* of resistance and defiance. Her husband *'gave'* a little flour and they went away. On the third day they returned demanding shirts and trousers. The Aborigines, having *'endeavoured'* to intimidate the hutkeeper and his wife, were given some flour and a shirt by the Europeans and they departed. 'Forced to give' constituted the crime of robbery in Croke's view and he could find no evidence of this having occurred. McCurdy, the second European to make a statement concerning these events, claimed that Jupiter had thrown spears at him but that he had left the station because 'he was alarmed by the threats and noise of the natives'. Croke commented in the margin, 'a curious reason for departing'. He found McCurdy's statement about Jupiter too vague to be satisfactory:

> McCurdy was never asked nor does he . . . state how near Jupiter was to him when the spears were thrown [.] if he was not within spears throw of Jupiter there could be no assault . . .[12]

The men were released without trial and returned to the District.

The incident raises questions about other similar reports. Were they, too, cases where Aborigines were forcibly taken from the District on such slight evidence? There are disturbing ramifications. How violent were Aboriginal reactions to Europeans in 1842? It is odd, to say the least, that Fyans's 'gang of savages' described as 'driving the people from the establishment [Hunter's] . . . even the poultry killed and every article about the place destroyed'[13] turn out to be a small group of Aborigines who asked for flour and shirts!

Jupiter, Cocknose and Bumbletoe were returned to the District but Roger, found guilty of the murder of Codd, was sentenced to death by hanging. Again, details surrounding the arrest and trial are disturbing. Codd was murdered by Aborigines on 19 May 1840. James Brock, who

had been with Codd at the time of the attack had stated that he would
have no trouble identifying the murderer. Roger was well known in the
vicinity of Mt Rouse where Codd was murdered, yet it was not suggested
that he was the murderer until March 1842. When Roger was arrested
and taken into custody, both Assistant Protector Sievwright and John
Sievwright wrote to Robinson protesting that Tagara (they used his
Aboriginal name) was not guilty.[14] Assistant Protector Sievwright
explained that in early March 1842, nearly two years after the murder,
when Brock had visited the Mt Rouse Protectorate station, he had sent
for Tagara who was residing at the station as he thought he might have
information concerning the murder, since the surrounding country
belonged to him and his family. Brock stated that he was not one of the
Aborigines involved in the murder. About eight days later, however,
Brock called on Sievwright saying that he now believed Roger (as he
knew Tagara) was the murderer. Sievwright was convinced that Brock
had 'argued himself into his present position'. John Sievwright also wrote
to Robinson. He had been at the Protectorate camp at Keilambete in
January 1841 and knew the accused man well. He believed that the
murderer was probably Tagara's brother—a man who 'resembled him so
much both in stature and general appearance that we could hardly
distinguish one from the other'. He stated that he had been told in
Brock's hut at Mt Rouse that the native who killed Codd was a tall man
with grey hair. Tagara did not have grey hair.

On 16 July 1842 a preliminary hearing of Roger's capacity to stand
trial took place. Sievwright, who had been asked to supply an interpreter
for him, stated that there was no one who knew his language.[15] John
Sievwright did his best but admitted that he was not familiar with
Roger's language. A number of witnesses including Robinson and the
Reverend Benjamin Hurst from the Buntingdale Aboriginal Mission
stated that they believed Roger could not understand what was
happening. The jury had difficulty in arriving at a decision but gave
their verdict: he 'was of sufficient mental capacity to enable him to take
his trial'.[16]

When the trial began Brock agreed that he had described the
murderer as a fine, tall man but denied saying he had grey hair. He
admitted that he had not identified him at the first meeting in early 1842
but had done so shortly afterwards when he saw him naked and 'recog-
nised him immediately'.[17] He said that he knew Roger's brother but he
identified Roger as the murderer of Codd. Patrick Rooney, the other
survivor of the Aboriginal attack the day Codd was murdered, was also
called to give evidence. He had not seen the murder but expressed his
belief that Roger was the murderer.

The jury returned after only five minutes deliberation with a verdict of
'guilty'. In those few minutes the Reverend Hurst had managed to
explain to Roger the purpose of the proceedings. Before the verdict was

announced, as part of the normal court procedure, Roger was asked whether he had anything to say before the judgment of the court was pronounced. For the first time the court heard his version of events explained by John Sievwright. He had been working at Webster's Mt Shadwell station. He named men with whom he had been working including European men who could have provided him with an alibi, and stated that it was his brother who had been involved in the killing of Codd.

Judge Willis was not to be diverted in any way. He pronounced the sentence of death by hanging after pointing out that Roger had had the 'best professional assistance available', and 'a fair and impartial trial':

> You would not, had you killed a man of your own description, long have escaped with life; neither will the laws by which you have been tried for killing a white man suffer you for any length of time to remain alive.[18]

The Judge saw the situation not only as proving the power of the legal system but as a way of providing an example. He wrote to La Trobe, '. . . I think if the sentence is to be carried out the example would have a better effect if the execution took place at Mt Rouse rather than at Melbourne'.[19]

Roger protested his innocence, his 'tribe' named others as the murderers, and those Europeans who knew Roger well believed he was innocent.[20] But sentence had been passed. La Trobe in a private communication with Governor Gipps stated that he hoped to avoid Roger's execution despite 'judge and jury'. He believed that the death of Codd who had previously worked as overseer for Wedge at the Grange was not unprovoked:

> If my information was really to be relied on Mr. Codd's conduct towards the natives had been criminal in the highest possible degree and I fear that by his death the sly murder of many of that race was avenged . . .[21]

On 10 August the Executive Council of New South Wales met concerning Roger's position. La Trobe's letter was reported by Governor Gipps but the Council decided that 'the sentence was according to Law' and authorized the execution to proceed.[22]

Roger met his death without terror. Those in the watching crowd saw him sit patiently on the steps of the scaffold for a quarter of an hour while some unknown problem was solved. Then with a firm step he mounted the scaffold.

From England, Lord Stanley wrote to Gipps to express his doubts as 'to the Wisdom of the course' taken. He was concerned that La Trobe's plea had not been taken into account:

> If so material a plea in the Prisoner's favour was really overlooked or unheeded, it would be very difficult to justify the execution of the Capital Sentence. If it was not overlooked, some Record ought to have been preserved and transmitted of the reasons for which it was overruled.[23]

Cold Morning, in gaol at the time Roger was hanged, learnt what happened from prisoners who also managed to convey to him that he too was to be hanged. Thomas arrived one morning to find Cold Morning in great distress, noting that when he arrived Cold Morning was trembling and then he cried. When at last he spoke it was to ask, 'why you hang me up I no kill white man'.[24]

Sometimes the brush with the judicial system had the effect Fyans had hoped for: at other times it did not. As soon as Jupiter and Cocknose returned to the District in August, attacks on Hunter's station were resumed. Thomas, however, felt confident that Cold Morning 'would no more trouble our courts of Justice'. He had been told by a gentleman who resided at Portland that not only was Cold Morning after his return to the District 'an altered character, but his tribe was altogether different and no longer [an] annoyance'. The *Portland Mercury* also believed that Cold Morning had learnt a lesson. He had entertained people with stories relating to his time in Melbourne, particularly of 'no good white fellow with long hair, name him George [Judge]'. He had helped a settler recover stray cattle and on being asked by the gentleman whether the Aborigines would steal more sheep he replied, 'Ba'al tak em sheep now, white fellow hang. No good. Glet plenty kangaroo—plenty possum'.[25]

The three Aboriginal leaders returned to the District with additional information about Europeans and what might happen to them in the future. But their removal had consequences that Europeans could not have foreseen. Cold Morning told Thomas that his two wives would have cried and torn their faces every night he was absent and his brother would have been 'sulky'. Roger's brother, like his other relatives was very upset at Roger being taken away. He killed an Aboriginal boy, admitting to Sievwright that he had done so 'because the white men had taken away his brother'.[26]

Fyans and the Border Police were in the District from March to late June 1842 and were ordered to return to the District in August. Fyans was ordered to take all the Border Police with him, and the police magistrates at The Grange and Portland were directed that all police were to be under Fyans's orders. The taking of Aborigines guilty of 'outrages' was to be considered 'paramount to every other duty'.[27]

Fyans found it impossible to capture the Aborigines attacking Hunter's property. He wrote, 'we are unable to do any service in this part of the country: we find the horses almost useless and are obliged to lead them for miles'. On 12 September 1842, however, the Native Police arrived at The Grange. Fyans ordered them close to Mt Eeles. 'I really believe that is the only means of our ever being able to take Jupiter and Cocknose again, or to restore peace to this place', he wrote to La Trobe.[28]

Fyans and the Border Police remained in the District from September until 17 December. The Native Police arrived on 12 September and returned to Melbourne on 12 November. Although H. E. P. Dana,

Commandant of the Native Police, had nine troopers with him, he was short of horses and was therefore only able to take four troopers with him 'in pursuit of natives or patrolling the District'.[29] The other five were left to help the Police Magistrate at The Grange. Dana and his men captured four Aborigines on suspicion of murder in the Glenelg River area. They also attempted to track Aborigines guilty of attacking Ricketts's station: a search which was abandoned after tracking the Aborigines for three days and a distance of sixty miles, by which time the men had exhausted their supplies. At the Winter brothers' station Dana met some Aborigines, warning them that 'if they stole sheep they would certainly be taken and sent to gaol'.[30] On his return to Melbourne Dana reported that the District had been quiet since their arrival. He expected good results from 'the fear with which the wild blacks regard the men and their knowing that now they can be followed to any place they go to'.[31]

Dana's claim was far from an idle one. In the winter of 1842 the Native Police travelled very long distances not only across but around the District. They were seen by many Aborigines and made demonstrations of power which were understood by those whom they met. They left Melbourne on 25 August escorting Dr Watton to take up his position at the Mt Rouse Protectorate station where he was replacing Sievwright. On the 31st they camped near some Barrabool Aborigines but the Native Police were ordered not to go near the 'Barrable blacks'. At daylight Dana paraded the Native Police 'to the astonishment' of the watching Aborigines. Their progress across the District attracted attention as one might expect. On the night of 9 September, about two miles east of the Hopkins River, the Native Police could hear the Aborigines around the camp all night. The carbines were loaded with ball in case of attack. At the Hopkins River the Police unexpectedly came across 'a large tribe'. Dana marched his men through the middle of them, forbidding any communication with the local Aborigines. Their camp was again surrounded on the night of 11 September as they moved closer to Mt Rouse. The Native Police, alarmed, wanted to use their guns but Dana held them in check. They left for Mt Rouse followed by a party of Aborigines. At the Mt Rouse station they were again kept separate from the local Aborigines.

On 12 October Acheson French, Police Magistrate at The Grange, ordered Dana to proceed to the Hopkins and Lake Boloke [Bolac] and to 'drive' the Aborigines to Mt Rouse. At Wyselaski's station on the Hopkins about thirty Aborigines were encountered and ordered to go to Mt Rouse. Dana and his men waited till they saw them on their way. Further on they found that Aborigines had been warned and had fled. But they came across them in a thick forest between the Hopkins and Salt Water Creek. Dana told them that they must go to Mt Rouse or he would shoot them. From the Hopkins the Police turned northwards, crossing to the

Grampians. On their way they found some Aborigines hiding from them behind logs. As the Native Police came up they ran off 'in a great fright', Dana wrote in his journal. From the Grampians the Police proceeded down the Glenelg. On their way to Thomas Norris's station they came across some Aborigines who attempted to flee. The Native Police 'got them together' and 'drove' them to Norris's station. There they camped with other Aborigines waiting his direction to go to Mt Rouse. On 30 October he met more Aborigines. These he ordered to camp at the Wando River and wait for him. On 1 November he ordered them to go to Mt Rouse and they obeyed him, for he noted in his journal that on his way across to The Grange he met the Aborigines crossing to Mt Rouse.[32] Power had been sensed and seen.

The worst year of inter-racial conflict in the west was 1842 but the worst period for 'collisions', the word used in official reports, between the Native Police and local Aborigines was the winter of 1843. The Native Police—thirteen men including the Sergeant, all mounted—were back in the District on 4 July 1843. By this time the Police Barracks at Mt Eckersley were completed and they had a base in the District. Windridge and five of the native policemen were stationed there for the winter while Dana and four police patrolled the District.[33] A number of the Border Police were also posted for the whole of the winter of 1843 in the neighbourhood of the Glenelg River. Fyans had listed Ricketts, Forlonge, De Soillys, Mathers and Bell as stations which had especially suffered from Aboriginal attacks during the winter of 1842. He suggested to La Trobe that during the winter of 1843 he should quarter two men on each of the stations.[34]

It was at the end of that winter that the native troopers on their return to the home barracks told such lurid stories of their activities to a horrified Assistant Protector Thomas that he protested to La Trobe, an action which brought about an inquiry by La Trobe into the behaviour of the police when in the west. Marie Fels, in her recent study of the native police, *Good Men and True: The Aboriginal Police of the Port Phillip District 1837–1853*, wrote:

> This was the winter on which most contemporary judgements about the police are based, the year they arrived back at Merri Creek scandalizing Thomas with the figure of seventeen people killed, causing the inquiry by La Trobe, alienating Thomas, provoking Dana to his intemperate threat to horsewhip Thomas all the way to Melbourne—incidents reverberating still in the present.[35]

The first clash between Dana's men and Aborigines occurred when the former went to track Aborigines who had stolen one hundred and eleven sheep from Henry Dwyer's Victoria Valley station. Once Dana's men found the tracks of the Aborigines, they 'followed them for four days, up and over the Victoria Range, across the heads of the Glenelg River, through swamps and scrub, finding the sheep in the end, in a well-constructed sheep yard within dense forest . . . about fifteen miles from Mt Zero'.[36] In the ensuing encounter four Aborigines were killed and one wounded, Dana reported to La Trobe. He admitted that more could have been wounded but he did not see more. The *Port Phillip Gazette* claimed as many as twenty were killed. The *Portland Guardian* reported the successful encounter, expressing confidence that the occasion would leave an 'indelible impression upon the native mind . . . that aggressions upon the settlers are not henceforth to be ordinarily done with impunity'.[37]

On Dana's return from the north he took up the search for Abraham Ward's three-year-old daughter, believed to have been taken by Aborigines. Out searching with Mr Edgar, Dana and his men encountered Aborigines with stolen sheep. The Aborigines fled into a swampy area with Dana and his men following. In the middle of the swamp they came across an island on which there was an Aboriginal camp and many dead and mutilated sheep. Exploring the neighbourhood, the police discovered the body of Christopher Bassett and it was assumed the sheep had been taken from him. Dana and his men waited until near morning and then crossed the swamp to encounter the Aborigines who had stayed near by. Eight or nine Aborigines were shot before they retreated. In his report of this incident Dana stated that punishment was necessary:

> The same tribe of natives killed McKenzie and his man, Ward's child, and now Bassett, and the country they fly to . . . is such that but few white men could follow them . . . I trust that Your Honour will not consider that I have exceeded my duty . . . making them feel that they shall not murder and plunder with impunity.[38]

In October a group of Aborigines stole goods from George Lockhart's dray which had broken down and been left on the side of the road not far from Mt Eckersley. Notified of the problem, Sergeant Windridge and five men went to the site and followed the tracks of the Aborigines. When they came across the Aborigines two were killed and one wounded. A native trooper received spear wounds and Windridge was bruised but all the stores taken from the dray were recovered.[39]

While in the district the Native Police had intervened at the Winter brothers' station where a large number of Aborigines had gathered, and some were killing calves and stealing sheep at night. Winter had asked Dana to remove the Aborigines. Two boys were caught stealing and on their father's advice Dana gave them a beating, four lashes each with a small whip in front of the whole tribe. Later the boys came up and said they would never steal sheep again.[40]

In five cases Aborigines guilty of 'outrages' had been dealt with and Dana patrolling constantly had covered 2500 miles in four months. From the settlers' point of view the way things were developing was very satisfactory. At the end of September the *Portland Guardian* was warm in its praise of Dana and the Native Police. It stated its hope that a meeting at The Grange in honour of Dana would be well attended and in November 'very much regretted' the departure of the Native Police on account of the 'effective service' they had rendered.[41]

Back at their barracks, however, Thomas was distressed by what he heard. They appeared to have killed seventeen Aborigines in their first encounter for the season—the one with those who had taken Dwyer's sheep—and to have been very violent in their approach to their work. There had been floggings of Aborigines till 'blood spurted over the by-standers' and Dana had sent a letter to the settlers on the Wando and Glenelg 'tantamount to giving them permission in the event of any affray with the blacks to go out' [and deal with them]. He was perturbed by the vulnerability of the Aboriginal population to such a force: if Native police were being encouraged to behave in their customary way towards strangers 'their feeling no remorse at taking away the life of another black, rather delight . . . especially if the tribe be far off, will render the native police Core [Corps] one of the greatest scourges to the sable race', he wrote to La Trobe.[42]

Dana defended himself and his men against the charges to La Trobe's satisfaction. To Thomas's charge of seventeen killed in the first incident he answered that this would have been impossible. He had not been armed, the corporal had only his sword, and among the men there were only ten rounds of ammunition. He insisted that his men were at all times 'good men and true', well-disciplined, never taking up their arms unless ordered to do so. The only floggings had been the punishment of the boys at the Winters' station, carried out with the permission of the Aborigines. In his letter to settlers he had included the instruction that native troopers were not to be ordered by settlers to fire upon Aborigines unless resistance was made or in defence of their lives.

Fels, who reviewed all the evidence, concluded that the seventeen deaths were the total from all the 'collisions' during the winter and that to describe them as 'atrocity, slaughter or extermination is to misuse language'. The Native Police, she argued,

> contributed to the pacification of the Western District not by a reign of terror . . . but by being perceived by local Aboriginal groups who killed or captured stock animals, to be efficient and effective to such a degree that it was difficult to avoid detection and capture (sometimes with loss of life).[43]

In 1844 the Native Police returned to the District as they did every year up to and including 1849. They were stationed at well-chosen sites—six were at the Glenelg River, four near Mt Eeles on the edge of the great swamp, four at the barracks at Mt Eckersley and two at The Grange. It was a relatively quiet year. Dana reported that 'the settlers appeared to have suffered comparatively nothing this Winter from the natives'. The demonstration of power in 1843 had perhaps made an impression. Dana suggests another factor which may explain the decline in attacks. He mentioned the 'frightful disease and mortality of the natives' and commented that 'a few seasons as fatal to them as this had been and they would cease to exist in the country'.[44]

During this season Dana's police managed to capture Koort Kirrup who had eluded capture since May 1842, when a warrant for his arrest for the murder of Donald McKenzie and Frederick Edinge had been issued. Local policemen, despite the use of disguises, had failed to capture him, but a white sergeant with four of the Native Police in disguise succeeded in capturing Koort Kirrup at 2.00 a.m. on 8 August 1844. Perhaps the most influential of the Aboriginal leaders in the Glenelg-Wannon area had been taken prisoner.

Dana justified the use of the Native Police for the capture of Koort Kirrup, describing him as of

> bad and dangerous character and supposed to be concerned in several murders amongst which was Mr Morton and his servant and has also been recognised on various occasions as principal leader in the attacks on the sheep station of the Messrs. Henty and other settlers in that part of the country.

He stressed that he had been requested by many settlers 'on the Glenelg, Wannon and Emu Creek to use every endeavour to have him taken as they were expecting an attack upon their stations'. Dana had also been given information that Koort Kirrup, after the murder of McKenzie, had taken refuge in the country at the mouth of the Glenelg River where he had gathered Aborigines together with the aim of using them for an attack on the stations at the junction of the Wannon.[45]

La Trobe in July 1846 prepared a long paper for the Governor in which he reviewed cases involving Aborigines over the preceding five years.[46] He hoped this would enable the problems of bringing natives 'to justice' to be more forcefully brought to the attention of the 'Home Government'. He discussed all 'the cases of note' but singled out that of Koort Kirrup as the one 'which in all its bearings places the various difficulties in the way in the clearest point of view'.

Before dealing with each case La Trobe outlined the enormity of the problem. He admitted that the acts of violence which he was about to enumerate were 'but a very small number of those committed by Aborigines'. Aborigines had murdered with impunity not only Aborigines but Europeans:

> ... not only have the constant murders and acts of violence, *among themselves*, with very few exceptions been allowed of necessity to pass, so to say, unregarded; but, that many of the most startling instances of murder which the aboriginal natives may from time to time have perpetrated upon Europeans have been perpetrated with the most perfect impunity.

He pointed out the 'inapplicability' of British law or, as he put it more precisely, 'the inapplicability of the forms by which it is beset'. He stated that this had been 'tacitly acknowledged in dealing with the natives committing ... minor offences' and demonstrated 'again and again' in more serious cases. His review left him, he reported, with 'a very strong impression of the uncertain and varying mode in which the law or forms of laws ... have been brought to bear upon the class of cases under consideration'.

The case of Koort Kirrup highlighted the difficulties of gaining a satisfactory conclusion from the processes of the judicial system. Koort Kirrup had a reputation for intelligence and a reasonable knowledge of English. He had been a trusted employee of Donald McKenzie and had lived on his station for several years. It was therefore assumed by those who knew him that he had understood that in killing McKenzie he was guilty of a crime and that he would understand what a trial was. At the First Session of the Court (January session 1845) the majority of the necessary witnesses were present as was an interpeter. But with time as Koort Kirrup's case was remanded session after session, the witnesses from the Glenelg District refused to attend any longer:

> ... they obeyed their subpoena, month after month, going and returning, to the utter neglect of their private affairs, and to their personal and pecuniary loss; until each, having travelled 1,500 or 2,000 miles in vain refused further attendance.

Finally, after sixteen months in gaol, Koort Kirrup was released. No one could be found who understood his language or who could explain to him the functioning of the court system. It was a troubling result even if one assumed that he was guilty, as La Trobe did. He wrote, 'if there had been the slightest belief of the man's innocence [it] would have been as grievously unjust, as it was perhaps illegal ...'. Moreover, La Trobe believed Koort Kirrup was more capable of understanding the court procedure than Tagara (Roger) hanged for the murder of Codd, or another two Aborigines who were transported for life, one for murder and another for sheep stealing. There was also the problem of what to do with him once released. To give him free passage back to Emu Creek hardly seemed appropriate. He was released into the care of Assistant Protector Thomas. Koort Kirrup stayed with him for three months and then he left returning to his tribe on Emu Creek, a tributary of the Glenelg, by walking overland across the District through the intervening tribal territories.

In 1845 William Learmonth on Darlot's Creek experienced 'outrages', and the stations around Mt Eeles also began to suffer attacks again. In response to appeals, the Native Police were sent to the area. Four men were despatched to Port Fairy and Dana proceeded there via the Wimmera.[47] The Native Police were in the area again in 1846, and two Port Fairy Aborigines recruited to the Native Police in December 1845 were sent to stations near Mt Eeles in early 1847.

According to Annie Maria Baxter, Cocknose, the Nillan conedeet leader, was captured in April 1847. She wrote in her diary, 18 April 1847, '"Cocknose" the ringleader of the Wild Blacks is happily in the watch-house in Belfast, and the settlers around here are determined to hang him if they can'. Again it appears that the Native Police, in this case in the form of two Port Fairy Aborigines, the first two local recruits to the Native Police Corps, had brought outrages to an end. Souwester and Port Fairy Jack, the two Native Police, had arrived at Eumeralla on 10 April 1847. Dana was not with them, nor was a sergeant. They reported to local gentlemen—to Charles Hamilton McKnight at Dunmore, to John Cox at Weerangourt and to William Rutledge, the Magistrate at Port Fairy.[48] Port Fairy Jack had worked for McKnight and Souwester had worked for Cox.[49] The squatters, it seemed, had gained what they had asked for from the time of the 1837 appeal for Government protection. It was what William Campbell asked for in 1845.[50] The squatters (or local magistrates) had armed officers at their disposal. The two men were effective as Rutledge acknowledged when he wrote to Dana stating that they had carried out 'important service' by capturing two Aborigines at Browne's station. Samuel McGregor agreed. They had 'certainly been a great check on the Natives in this Neighbourhood', he wrote to Dana. 'I am sorry and so is (I may say) every settler in the neighbourhood that they had to leave so soon . . '.[51]

Two Aborigines were certainly captured by Native Police in April–May 1847 and lodged in the Port Fairy Watch House.[52] It seems likely after Annie's comment that one of these was Cocknose. Yet there is no further mention of Cocknose in offical records nor of his trial. The only link between Aborigines being tried and Port Fairy in this period is that two young Port Fairy boys were brought to Melbourne in early 1847 for trial. They were Picanniny Tommy (Figur) and Jemmy.

The two young Aborigines were charged with having broken into Browne's hut in January 1846 and taken clothing, firearms and other articles and with having thrown a spear or spears at the wife of Thomas Pye. Jemmy (Peevittunning) was 15 years old and Tommy (Figur) 11 years old. They were tried on 28 July 1847. Tommy was acquitted and Jemmy imprisoned for two weeks. William Thomas was interpreter. This case makes odd reading, like the earlier one concerning Aborigines of the same area, Jupiter and Cocknose, also arrested for robbery and assault.[53] Thomas Pye, an employee at Browne's, in his deposition stated that early one morning Aborigines came out of the dairy and then the front of the house. One boy was carrying 'a double barrell'd gun and pistol', another a 'single barrell'd gun' and Jemmy a bundle of clothes which Pye later discovered contained two pairs of trousers, three shirts, a small flannel petticoat and a box of caps. The Aborigines rushed at Pye and his wife and Johnny threw spears at his wife. He offered to give Aborigines flour if they would give back the guns (the only ones on the station) and clothing. The exchange took place and the Aborigines left. Mary Pye's deposition began with an outline of the events a day earlier—4 January. On that day five Aborigines had come to the hut acting in a threatening manner and using abusive language. Her husband threatened to fire at them and they then went away. Her account of the events on 5 January agreed with that of her husband except that she stated that they seemed to be angry with her and not her husband. They said 'Bora Tom only bugger Lubra'.

Croke, if he had been present, might have pointed out that nothing had been taken. Again there is the odd feature that the Aborigines intended to take a bundle of clothing. Thomas's notes of his attempts to discuss their 'crime' with the two boys survive. To his question as to whether they threw spears, he received the reply 'No. No. Another one Blackfellow Little Blacks never carry sp. [spear?]'.[54] Yet one of the boys never returned home. Local Aborigines killed him, taking his kidney fat, weighted his body and threw it into the Yarra.[55]

Returning to the events of early 1847, if Jemmy and Tommy were the Aborigines in the Watch House, what happened to Cocknose? Tom Browne, owner of the station where the alleged felony took place, published his recollections in *Old Melbourne Memories*. According to him both Jupiter and Cocknose were killed in the same encounter between Mt Eeles Aborigines and the Native Police. This encounter probably occurred in the winter of 1845 as he stated the police arrived after 'half a ream of foolscap had been covered with representations to the Governor', and reports of outrages and encounters and appeals for Government protection in early 1845 survive in the official records.

Eight troopers of the Native Police were present. Among them were Buckup, Yapton (Yupton) and Tallboy. White troopers were also present but not Browne: 'I took it for granted that blood might be shed, and I did not wish to be an eye-witness or participator'. From his viewpoint the situation was critical. This was three years later than the events of 1842 but frontier conflict was obviously present and serious:

> The matter at issue was now grave and imminent. Whether should we crush the unprovoked émeute [Fr: popular rising], or remove the remnant of our stock, abandon our homesteads, and yield up the good land of which we had taken possession?

Patiently day by day the Native Police searched for the Aborigines. When at last they found the main body of the tribe, 'the wild men had little chance with their better armed countrymen'. The Native Police despite the terrain were mounted on horses. At the end of the encounter 'all the known leaders of the tribe are down': 'Jupiter and his associate with the unclassical profile were never seen alive again'.[56]

These events may have occurred a year later, in the winter of 1846, for Annie Marie Baxter stated that in September 1846 the Native Police

were at Yambuck looking for Cocknose's camp and that they had
captured three Aboriginal women in the hope that they would lead them
to Cocknose's camp.[57] Also in 1846 Campbell wrote to La Trobe, asking
him to convey the thanks of the residents of the Port Fairy District to
Dana for the protection and security which had been afforded them by
the Native Police.[58] If Boldrewood's account is accepted, Port Fairy Jack
and Souwester were involved in a mopping-up operation in 1847. This
would seem likely as Rutledge stated that they captured two Aborigines
'who had committed some depredations last year'.[59]

Further, if Boldrewood's account is correct then there was another
clash, not in the official records, between Native Police and Aborigines
in which lives were lost. That would not be surprising. The details of
some of the other incidents only came to light in answer to questions
asked of Dana by La Trobe.

Port Fairy Jack and Souwester were among the first Portland Bay
District Aborigines to join the Native Police. Eight men joined in 1845,
twelve more in 1846 with a further two recruits in 1847.[60]

Trouble was still being experienced in the Grampians in 1845, and in
1847 at Darlot's Creek where two police were stationed but without
effect. As late as the winter of 1848 the *Portland Gazette* noted with
approval that Dana was back in the District again, as the blacks were
usually troublesome about this time—but the truth was there was little
need of them; their work had been done.

A number of Aborigines were removed from the District through
penalties inflicted by the law. One was executed. Three were transported: one for life, one for ten years, one for seven years. One was
imprisoned for seven weeks. Others of course were held in gaol for
months on end awaiting trial before being eventually discharged without
trial. Two Western District Aborigines, Wenaburn and Konghomarnee,
became seriously ill while waiting trial. They were discharged by Proc-
lamation but had already been removed to the hospital because of ill
health. They died there shortly afterwards.

In February 1848 when Philip Chauncy visited the Wannon country,
there was no longer any need for settlers to protect themselves or their
property. He noted that the Aborigines were 'inert', almost 'more inert
than in West Australia . . . some of them [appear] to be almost dying with
hunger'. And the settlers, once armed whenever they left their building,
'lived in as great security as in any country in the world—never locking
the doors at night or indeed in many instances possessing locks'.[61] It was
a result that had been achieved perhaps partly by the passing of time, the
spread of disease and the actions of individual settlers, but to the extent
Aboriginal resistance centred around leaders, it had been achieved
largely by the use of the Native and Border Police and the demonstration
of power that was embodied in the judicial system.

11

'if ever anything is done with the natives, it will be by their good example'

THOSE MOST concerned about the Aborigines longed to see them gain the benefits of being brought within the British Empire—civilization and Christianity. Though there was debate whether Christianity was the 'shortest cut to civilization' or whether 'somehow or other, the two might be brought together, or even that civilization might lead to Christianity', there was strong official support for the work of bringing Christianity to the Aborigines.[1] The Superintendent, Charles Joseph La Trobe, for example, wrote,

> The primary object of our exertions, and of all our schemes with regard to the Aboriginal Natives of the country, which under God's providence has become the theatre of European colonisation, is . . . to Christianize them.[2]

The British Wesleyan Methodists were one of the most active denominations involved in missionary work in newly colonized areas of the world and it is therefore not surprising that they extended their operations to the Australian colonies. The Reverend Joseph Orton, appointed minister in charge of the Wesleyan Mission in the colonies of New South Wales and Van Diemen's Land, arrived in 1831, proceeding to Van Diemen's Land which became his base. His first priority became a mission to the Aborigines of New South Wales but for a time the obstacles in the way of establishing a successful mission seemed insuperable.

In 1836, however, came news of 'a favourable opening at a new settlement . . . named Port Phillip—opposite to Launceston [in northern

Van Diemen's Land] and only a few hours sail from thence'. Orton hastened to explore the situation, acquainting the Wesleyan Missionary Society with the fact that the site when chosen would be 'in the territory of New South Wales—though upwards of 500 miles from the seat of Government—and quite adjacent to Van Diemen's Land. There is a probability of its being under distinct local Government very soon'.[3]

Arriving in Melbourne in April 1836, Orton was the first person to preach a sermon in Melbourne. He talked with William Buckley, the escaped convict who had lived with Aborigines for thirty-two years, ('He may have been preserved for a gracious purpose . . .') and used him as an interpreter to have discussions with local Aborigines. He gained support from local Methodists for the idea of a mission and advised the Aborigines of his intention to 'send missionaries to instruct them'—news which he believed they received with pleasure and expressions of willingness to co-operate. Moved by the attendance of Aborigines at a sermon he preached in Melbourne he confided in his journal,

> My soul truly went out after their best interests. I felt as though I could have sacrificed every personal comfort for their welfare. I longed to be able to communicate . . . I c^d but anticipate the happy time when these poor creatures, degraded below the brute, will come to a knowledge of the truth, and . . . participate in the blessings of the Light of the Glorious Gospel.[4]

Convinced that a mission should be established without delay, Orton reported his success to the Wesleyan Missionary Society in London and wrote to Governor Bourke seeking a grant of land and some financial assistance. In March 1838 missionaries arrived from England—the Reverend and Mrs Tuckfield and the Reverend and Mrs Hurst. In early June Orton, who had been to Sydney to discuss the missionary activities with the new Governor (Gipps), returned home well pleased with developments. The Governor had given permission for an area of land to be selected and had pledged financial assistance. In mid-June the Tuckfields sailed for Port Phillip.

Three years after his earlier visit to Melbourne, Orton, in early 1839, set sail from Van Diemen's Land for the purpose of selecting a site and overseeing the establishment of the mission. Faced by the need for sacrifice—months of absence from his family and the hardships of bush travel—he was forced to remind himself of his Christian duty, 'I view the undertaking as a very arduous one and sometimes almost sink in the anticipation', he wrote in his journal.[5]

Compared with the Protectorate officials, Sievwright and Robinson, the missionaries showed themselves inexperienced in the bush. Before Orton's arrival Hurst and Tuckfield had 'almost perished' on an exploratory journey. Two of their horses had died from sheer exhaustion and though the men reached home they were 'almost starved and naked'. As they travelled across the District by the 'Lakes' and towards the Hopkins River, Tuckfield reflected on the wretchedness of his circumstances:

> I now return to rest in a miserable hovel consisting of a cloth thrown over a few sticks in which I have already spent two almost restless nights. I feel my health in danger—I pray that the Lord will enable my poor bodily frame to sustain the endurance without injury.[6]

Although they were anxious to meet Aborigines, the missionaries found it virtually impossible. Those they sought hid from them: a fact Orton explained as due to their being unable to distinguish between 'our intentions and the settlers and their hostile designs'. 'They are', he wrote, 'so hunted by the settlers that they are quite afraid to show themselves'.[7]

It was with dismay that Orton realized that even in the new settlement the chances of a successful mission were slight. The greatest difficulty was not the 'migrating habits' of the Aborigines but the rapid occupation of Aboriginal land without adequate provision for the Aborigines. Even at this stage of settlement he could see that if proper provision was not made for the Aborigines, they would become 'pilfering—starving—obtrusive mendicants, and after enduring incalculable deprivations, abuses and miseries will gradually . . . become extinct'. The question of regulating 'over-extending colonisation' and making proper provision for the Aborigines must become, like the issue of slavery, a 'great national question'. Philanthropists and Christians should join together to force the 'Imperial Parliament' to adopt more just measures.[8]

Orton admired 'the design of the scheme' of the Protectorate but in practice, he said, 'it is cramped in its operations for want of a well digested, liberal and extensive plan'. More financial support was necessary: 'one tithe of the revenue from the sale of lands would accomplish the object'.[9]

Somewhat discouraged, the missionaries chose a site on the south side of the Barwon River near Birregurra about thirty miles west of Geelong. Before leaving the others to begin their work, Orton set out a number of important points to guide their actions. Their main objective was to be 'the religious instruction and salvation of those who may be by the gracious providence of God placed under your care. All other matters are to be viewed as secondary and subordinate'. The Aborigines were to be encouraged to settle at the Mission establishment and to begin cultivating the land to help provide food for themselves. Only those who worked should be fed as an 'incentive to habits of industry'. At first the cultivation of land was to be under the control of the missionaries but in time it was hoped that areas of land could be allocated to Aboriginal families. The acquiring of the Aboriginal language was to be seen as of 'vast importance' as a means of teaching the gospel. Schools were to be established both for adults and children. The missionaries were to take it in turn to travel as much as possible with the Aborigines and throughout all the undertakings, 'attention to system, order and regularity' was to be observed. 'I can scarcely conceive that you can spend too much time or patience in the observance of order among so undisciplined a race of our fellow creatures', he wrote.[10]

Though Gipps approved in principle an allocation of land for the use of the mission, he became cautious when faced with Orton's request for a square of land measuring two miles from the centre to be reserved. On Orton's letter he noted that how much could be set aside depended on the site chosen: 'If they fix on valuable land, or such as is in demand by the settlers, it will be quite out of my power to give them the quantity they have asked for'. The application was opposed by the Surveyor-General who pointed out that valuable land could be unavailable for other use for five years if reserved for the use of the mission. The reservation when granted was of one section—640 acres—one-sixteenth of the area asked for.[11]

Even Foster Fyans, the Crown Lands Commissioner, protested on behalf of the missionaries. Though he had not one good word for the Protectors, he wrote of the missionaries: 'They are plain, good and worthy men, and if ever anything is done with the natives, it will be by their good example . . '. He could see the need for a large area of land to be reserved:

> The mission requires a large tract, some for cultivation, and the other parts to be kept free from Europeans . . .
> Were they squatters they could keep the ground for a few pounds yearly—and surely their object . . . ought to be worthy of notice.[12]

The Government refused to increase the area reserved but gave the mission some protection from European influences by announcing that grazing stations would not be permitted within five miles.[13]

At the Buntingdale Mission, if nowhere else, a genuine attempt was made to civilize and Christianize. The missionary in charge, the Reverend Tuckfield, had been trained in language work and had considerable success in learning the language of local Aborigines. On 18 June 1839 the missionaries arrived at the site previously selected and began their work. In the same month Assistant Protector Sievwright arrived at Geelong: thus the work of the Protectorate in the Western District and the Methodist Mission were to proceed contemporaneously.

As a source for information about the Aborigines the mission records are disappointing. Names of individuals were not kept. With two exceptions, named Aborigines are either perpetrators of revenge murders or their victims. The exceptions were Karn Karn, an Aborigine who for a time appeared to be interested in settling on the station, and Wer.e.rup, an Aboriginal doctor. The Reverend Tuckfield and his colleague the

King Tom (Mount Elephant Tribe, about 1878) who was persuaded to wear European clothes, but never shoes, only in the last years of his life

King Billy, Ballarat Tribe, and his two wives about 1878: one of the wives, Queen Mary, later became the wife of King David.

Weeratt Kuyuut—'Chief' of the Morpor (Spring Creek) tribe whose language was Kii wuurong—a great warrior and messenger who was known to Aborigines throughout the District. About seventy at the time of the photograph, he was looking for a suitable young woman to be his wife.

Dawson's twenty-feet-high memorial obelisk to the Aborigines erected in the Camperdown cemetery: the first date, 1840, marks 'the beginning of the extinction' of local Aborigines and the second, 1883, the death of the last local Aborigine.

Reverend Hurst showed no interest in individuals as individuals or customs for their own sake. Interesting customs were observed and commented on but only because they hindered the work of the missionaries. The special language skills of Tuckfield were put to work as soon as possible not to explore Aboriginal custom in depth as he had the chance to, but to translate parts of the Bible into the Aboriginal language and to teach the children to read so that they might read the scriptures. Thus language was seen as the medium for transferring knowledge of Christianity rather than of extending what was known of the Aboriginal way of life.

By late 1839 Tuckfield was able to converse fluently with the Colijohn Aborigines in their own language on topics of general interest.[14] He was probably the only person in the District to have this skill before Isabella Dawson, who as a child learnt Aboriginal languages from Aborigines working on her father's station. But from Tuckfield's point of view it was all to no avail. As he confided to a fellow missionary involved in similar work in South Australia, 'for the want of abstract terms and terms which relate especially to the ordinance of the Christian religion and unknown to them previous to our coming to them, it is extremely difficult to impart spiritual instruction to the mind'.[15]

E. S. Parker, Assistant Protector of the North-western District of the Protectorate and a local preacher of the Wesleyan faith, facing the same difficulties, wrote:

> What can be done with a people whose language knows no such terms as holiness, justice, righteousness, sin, guilt, repentance, redemption, pardon, peace—and to whose minds the ideas conveyed by such words are utterly foreign and inexplicable?[16]

Such statements are not to be regarded as implying that Aborigines lacked a complex language or intelligence. Though the missionaries described the Aborigines as 'degraded human beings', a reference particularly to their religious state, they all stressed the capabilities of the Aborigines. Orton commented that their 'intellectual capabilities are unquestionable'. While Tuckfield, impressed by their manner as the work of teaching began, commented: 'They are attentive and manifest powers of mind capable of receiving instructions of any kind'. Hurst wrote that 'the indications of intelligence and natural capacity which we frequently witness, convinces us that the prerogatives of human nature are as much the inheritance of the blacks as of the whites'. For Orton they were 'brothers'. Arguing that Christians should clamour for proper provision to be made for the dispossessed Aborigines, he stated that this was the only way 'to avert the wrath of that righteous God who most assuredly heareth the voice of our brothers' blood'.[17]

What the records make clear is that the number of Aborigines was rapidly declining. In early May 1840 the missionaries noted that the size of the Aboriginal tribes who most frequented the station had declined during the previous year by at least 10 per cent. And they were not aware of more than two children under twelve months of age in the three closest tribes. Children had been born but they were half-castes and had been killed. The main reason suggested for the decrease was venereal disease: the chief handicap that they believed they faced in their work was the 'depraved conduct of the hut-keepers and shepherds, who . . . induce the natives, particularly the females to leave the Mission station'.[18]

There was much coming and going on the mission station as on the Protectorate station at Mt Rouse. There Watton explained the small numbers after 1843 as due to lack of provisions. They were better off elsewhere! But the missionaries were generous with food: to win souls, they needed the Aborigines to be near by. After January 1840, when Hurst took up residence at the station, they even took it in turns for one man to stay on the station while the other accompanied Aborigines who left the station—in an attempt to learn their language and gain their confidence. But, despite the missionaries' generosity, the Aborigines came and went. In sharing his experience with the Reverend Tiechelmann, Tuckfield explained that the Aborigines could not be persuaded to settle on the station, even after £600 a year had been spent on food and clothing for them:

> Our plan had been to feed those natives regularly who stay about the station and make themselves useful; and all the children who attend school have their food three times a day but after all that we can do and notwithstanding the supply of food and clothes which have been afforded them we have the utmost difficulty to keep them on the station any length of time.[19]

The site was in the country of the Colijohn but had been chosen because it was on the boundary of four tribes of Aborigines. In this way the missionaries had hoped to attract Aborigines from a number of 'tribes'. In the beginning they attracted little attention. For the first four months the average number of Aborigines on the station was 25. However, by December 1839, after the arrival of a group of Dantgurt (elsewhere referred to as Targurt or Jarcourt) there were 100 Aborigines on the station. The Dantgurt said they had heard of the station and had 'come to see it'. On 15 December there were between 50 and 60 children in the school. By 22 December all had left and the missionaries were alone for Christmas 1839.[20]

There could be 150 on the station at one time, as happened once before May 1840 and again in May 1841.[21] Early May 1841 was a period of joy for the missionaries. The Aborigines on the station gave Tuckfield and a colleague, Mr Skevington, two of their children to care for. Karn Karn was building a house and other Aborigines were showing interest in his progress. When the house was completed Tuckfield proposed to try Karn Karn and his wife 'with regular rations to see what effect it will have'.[22] By 23 May some members of four tribes were on the station. They were joined on the 24th by fifty 'Bullokbur' (Bolokeburer), Aborigines whom Tuckfield had not seen on the station before. Management problems arose. Sunday morning prayers had to be held in the open because the school rooms normally used were not large enough. The Sunday service and the breakfast which always followed were controlled by drawing on the ground a very large circle with a sharp pointed stick. The Aborigines were then asked to stand side by side with their toes touching the circle. The person conducting the service stood in the centre of the circle. Afterwards the Aborigines stayed in their appointed place while breakfast was distributed. More than a hundredweight (50 kg) of bread was needed for breakfast. The station was 'a bustling village' with Aborigines at work in the gardens, bringing the water, cutting wood, felling trees, scrubbing.[23] It was a time of optimism and hope.

By 14 June 1841 all the Aborigines had left except the six boys the missionaries had taken into their own homes. In September 1841 the six boys left and in May 1842 Tuckfield confided to a colleague, 'we have not a single black on the station ... I fear our present Mission is a complete failure'.[24]

By early 1843 the decision had been made to restrict the group entitled to be on the station to the Colijohn and those of the Dantgurt 'related to them through marriage'. Tuckfield gave as his reasons for the change that he had learnt that each tribe was 'perfectly distinct', that each tribe had 'well defined limits' and that having clear-cut ideas of who were friends and enemies and long histories of causes for grievance (some still unsolved) against other groups, the Aborigines were 'little disposed to confide in those who profess equal concern for the welfare of every tribe'. Having notified the Colijohn Aborigines of his decision, he had opened a subscription list for the purpose of purchasing a flock of ewes for them so that they might learn to handle the stock and learn the concept of property. As the Aborigines complained of not being properly protected on the mission station Tuckfield wrote to La Trobe asking for permission to call a policeman if 'strange' Aborigines came to the station with hostile intent.[25]

But the mission was not successful even when confined to one Aboriginal group. In his report for 1846 Tuckfield admitted that he seldom had any Aborigines on the station as the surrounding tribes continued to frighten away any who showed interest in attending. In the same year he wrote to La Trobe notifying him of the Society's decision to abandon the Buntingdale Mission. In this he accepted the lack of success as God's will: 'that more good has not been realised is amongst the immutable dispensations of a wise and gracious providence, for reasons that we cannot comprehend'.[26]

Civilization and Christianity were offered but in a form that made no allowances for Aboriginal custom. Food was plentiful but distributed along lines that seemed fairest to Tuckfield the children first—men and women equal quantity and at the same time—latecomers to wait their turn. James Dawson wrote of the local Aborigines, 'There are strict rules regulating the distribution of food'.[27] Tuckfield showed no awareness of such rules. An Aborigine was killed by another Aborigine in mid-1839. The reason given was that he was believed to have influenced Protectorate officials not to hand out food to strangers who had arrived the day before. Whereas the reality was that it was mission policy to feed only those who had worked. On another occasion all the Aborigines on the station resorted to their arms. Some Waddowro Aborigines had arrived while the young of both sexes were being given their food. The newcomers asked for food. Williamson, the overseer, said they would be given food with the other old men after the children who had been at school finished. One Aborigine who argued that he should be fed ran, seized his spears and confronted Tuckfield and Williamson:

> All the blacks dispersed to their respective houses and took up their spears. Mr Williamson retreated also . . . I put the pistol in my pocket, not loaded. Mr W. took the gun. I went to the man who took up the spear and asked him what he took up the spear for, look hard in his face. He said he was angry but this anger was then all gone. I bid him throw his ammunition on the ground and go to his knees. He looked and trembled as if death had seized him and said he would never do it again.[28]

On another occasion he recorded that he was kept busy seeing that the Aborigines obtained their food 'in a proper manner':

> They are very suspicious and jelous of each other. I am obliged to divide it for them myself and see that one does not get more than the other. Yesterday one of the men threw the murreone [? weapon] to the head of his wife because she would not give him some of her dinner . . .[29]

Tuckfield attempted to keep the Sabbath holy with people whom his colleague Hurst described as having not yet been 'made acquainted' with the 'gospel'. Thus a people encouraged to be busy all the rest of the week found themselves unexpectedly castigated on a Sunday for simply doing a normal chore of daily life such as making a basket. The Reverend Orton recorded in his journal that:

> On one occasion Mr Tuckfield observed a woman making a basket on the Sabbath on which account he expostulated with her on the impropriety of such conduct—endeavouring to convince her that people would go to the bad place—when she immediately with much confusion threw her work behind her.

In January 1840 Tuckfield complained that despite the fact that he had given the Aborigines 'extra quantity of food' and had spent most of the day with them he had not been able to prevent them 'from breaking the Sabbath'.[30]

The site itself caused problems and interfered with custom. Waddowro Aborigines had helped select the site but it was in Colijohn country. As a result the two tribes were antagonistic, 'warring for supremacy' at the mission station, to use Tuckfield's phrase.[31] The station, while on the boundary of several tribes, was seen by the missionaries as outside Aboriginal boundaries. By pledging themselves to treat equally all who arrived, the missionaries created a situation where Aborigines who were strangers or enemies could come on to the land of the Colijohn without the customary procedures being followed.

There was no compromise. Change was to be all or nothing. Karn Karn completed the building of a house and other Aborigines showed great interest. However, there was a problem: those with a number of wives wanted a larger house, something Tuckfield would not allow.

> Two of the persons who appear anxious to build said that as they have 3 wives each they should require a much larger house . . . I told them that they might have as large a house as they were disposed to build but if they intended to imitate the white man in one thing they should in another viz. in the disposal of 2 of their wives out of the three. To this however they would not consent.

No more houses were built. When the other Aborigines left shortly afterwards, so did Karn Karn.[32]

The missionaries found themselves in circumstances at times so difficult that they were forced to drive away the Aborigines they had encouraged to collect. In mid-January 1840 with several different groups of Aborigines on the station and hostility always on the point of bursting forth into violence, Tuckfield admitted he took comfort in having a gun with him. He commented, 'it is scarcely safe to manifest our displeasure at their conduct except we have a gun with us'. Shortly afterwards, with the Aboriginal camp so noisy at night that sleep was impossible, Tuckfield ordered the overseer, Williamson, to stop the noise. He did so, firing a gun into the air twice. The Aborigines were quiet after that. The next day Tuckfield was intentionally cold in his manner towards them and made sure their houses were moved a considerable distance from his house.[33] Another time he decided the best way to proceed was no longer to issue food. This caused the Aborigines to leave.[34]

The missionaries describe Aboriginal customs observed on the station—revenge killing, arrangement of marriages, a token fight to put at rest an old grievance, a meeting to arrange an emu hunt—and also make it clear that customs were changing. A group of Aborigines came on to the station carrying guns.[35] The Colijohn Aborigines appealed to Tuckfield for help, voicing their fear that the Barrabool Aborigines would come 'and shoot them while asleep'. Guns, not often used in encounters with Europeans, were being used against 'strangers' of their own race.

Aborigines visited the station from a considerable distance. The

Bolokeburer arrived from Lake Boloke. The Colijohn and Jarcourt, whose country stretched from the mission station across to Camperdown, were frequent visitors. The Waddowro (Barrabool?) Aborigines from the area around Geelong visited, as did the Yarra Yarra Aborigines. On 12 December 1840 Tuckfield noted that one of the Dantgurt (Jarcourt) Aborigines was murdered by natives of the Waddowro and Melbourne tribes.[36]

The Mission, like the Protectorate, was an acknowledged failure. In 1846 La Trobe referred to it as 'a total failure'.[37] Tuckfield, in the same year, reported that as far as 'the moral and spiritual condition' of the Aborigines was concerned, 'little, if any apparent good has been effected'.[38] Not one Aborigine had become a Christian.

Ironically the finances of the mission thrived. A flock of sheep obtained with the aim of encouraging the Aborigines to take an interest in the 'acquirement of property' had flourished and proved a good source of revenue. The mission was not only able to pay its way; it could look forward to expanding. By mid-1846 it owned 2000 sheep and 120 head of cattle. It also made money by allowing nearby settlers to graze stock on the reserve.[39]

Orton's worst fears had been realized. Visiting the mission station in late November–early December 1840 he had found 'the great object of the Mission' 'forgotten' or 'kept remotely in view'. There were three missionaries, an overseer/bullock driver and occasionally a pair of sawyers, 'all very busy doing *little or nothing:* at least so with reference to the great object of the Mission':

> The principal accomplishment . . . is the formation of a comfortable Homestead with all the desirable conveniences and luxuries of cows pigs poultry and a Horse for each person not excluding the ladies to take an evenings ride over the Estate . . .

The plan had been to take turns 'travelling among the natives to induce them to come to the station'. This has not taken place. Nor had there been training of the Aborigines to do the various tasks about the place; instead European servants were employed. He saw a discouraging 'destitution of arrangement and order' which he feared would cause the mission to be 'a failure or a comparatively useless burden to the society'.[40]

Returning early in 1841 Orton noted some improvements in the management of the mission and was impressed by progress both in the school and in the work of religious instruction. Tuckfield, he admitted, was quite suited to mission work for he showed 'superior tact in managing the natives', but there was in him a 'want of order'. He needed to be 'under judicious direction'. Again he concluded that there was 'a sad deficiency of system in the entire management of the station'.[41]

A year later things had not improved. On his last visit to the mission before returning to England, Orton's evaluatory comments make it clear that from his point of view part of the blame for the failure of the mission must be taken by the missionaries. The organization of the mission was 'extravagantly expensive and inefficient'. The missionaries were involved in a disagreement which he described as 'a serious evil' demanding 'immediate attention'. 'Mr. Hurst', he wrote, 'is not interested in the Mission nor has he ever been'.[42]

There were few Europeans who could speak an Aboriginal language but Tuckfield could do so. He also was possibly the only one to confront the Aborigines about their customs and make a direct attempt to change them. It was an approach which evoked an Aboriginal response of special interest because of the rarity of such statements. Tuckfield wrote:

> I have at times endeavoured to take advantage of some of their superstitions and incantations to convey the more correct and important truths of the Gospel to their minds. When I have taken their own notions as a medium to convey instructions, some have appeared to receive what had been said with credit, while others have expressed their surprise at my attempting to correct their errors and destroy the notions which they had received by traditions from their fathers, having such an imperfect knowledge of their language and being so short a time among them.[43]

12

'instances of violent collision . . . are now rarely heard of'

THERE IS NO DOUBT about the resistance of Aborigines to European settlement in the Portland Bay District—there never has been. But those looking for the equivalent of the Maori Wars, for strong chiefs linked in a supra-tribal entity, for strategy and tactics, for resistance groups and collaborators, for pa (Maori fortress), for trading in guns, will not find them. Nor will they find a Pemulwuy, the great warrior and leader of the Eora people on whose land the first European settlement in Australia was built—for Eric Willmot, the noted Aboriginal educationist, engineer and authority on the life of Pemulwuy, has argued that he led 'a twelve year campaign' of 'persistent attacks on crops and towns'.[1]

There were no great wars or battles but there was certainly 'war' in the sense of men of one race being forced to take up arms against those of the other. To Europeans who would have preferred an unoccupied country, the Aborigines were 'a nuisance', 'troublesome', a cause of anxiety which at times seems to have become so strong that to take up the weapons of war seemed the only solution.

Governor Gipps's threat to close the District to European settlement and make it an Aboriginal reserve was in reaction to European violence towards Aborigines which was provoked by the strength and persistence of Aboriginal attacks. These were not on a grand scale, nor experienced across the District at the same time, but were still of significance and where there were refuges, they lasted for a considerable length of time. Those who went out armed to deal with the Aborigines were not only brutalized convicts and ex-convicts but our most respected pioneers—men who would not have done so without good cause. Among them were men such as William Learmonth of Ettrick who, ashamed at breaking the Sabbath by delivering five cows to Cameron of Portland, admitted, 'I find it a difficult matter here to make people pay the least regard to the Holy Day, and indeed from living away from the means of grace I find it even difficult to respect it as I ought'.[2]

Aboriginal attacks added not only to the anxiety of those who pioneered the District, but also to the cost of pioneering both to individuals and the state. Relatively few Europeans lost their lives, but many suffered great financial loss through the taking of sheep, cattle or horses. Some squatters had thousands of sheep stolen.[3] Aboriginal actions also impeded the settlement of the District. The Darlot's Creek area was left unoccupied till 1843 because of the presence of the Aborigines. The area of land to become the Tandarook station was not taken up till 1840 for the same reason.

In many cases Aborigines annoyed Europeans and forced them to abandon certain areas at least for a short time. Taking a long view, such activity was not very significant but, to the individual European settlers forced to move elsewhere, the experience was a costly exercise. Thomas Ricketts abandoned his station on the Barwon, the furthest outstation from Geelong at the time, when it was plundered by the Aborigines in August 1837. George Russell's hut on the River Leigh was attacked by Aborigines in early December 1837 and after this the site was vacated for some months. Alfred Taddy Thomson who had taken up land under Mt William was driven out of the area during 1841 'by foot-rot and blacks'. Loughnan and Linch's station south of Whitehead's on Spring Creek was temporarily abandoned. Land taken up near Mt Emu was abandoned for a time. The Hentys gave up the outstation where Bonsor was attacked in June 1838, moving a few miles further away. Henry Gibb moved his sheep after his shepherd was attacked. Niel Black abandoned an outstation in 1840 and John Ritchie was forced to do the same with all the outstations at Urang Aranga in early 1842. After the murder of Donald McKenzie by Aborigines, his station at Emu Creek was abandoned for a time, while in 1844 the Hentys were forced to abandon their Mt Gambier run.[4]

Sometimes a series of owners were forced to abandon land. Matthew Gibson, for example, abandoned his station on the Wannon. It was taken up by Thomas Norris who suffered so severely from Aboriginal depredations that he also departed. The Aborigines were still troublesome when James Riley took over the station.[5] In November 1841 Edward Bell took up Englefield, previously occupied by Norton who had been forced to abandon it because of Aboriginal attacks. At this time there was no settler higher up the Glenelg. Bell was forced to vacate the station also but later reoccupied it.[6]

For some squatters, Aboriginal attacks led to ruin. Mr Cameron was forced off his property on the Crawford River in the middle of 1842, and had to offer his stock for sale at half price.[7] Ricketts suffered so severely from Aboriginal attacks that he became insolvent in 1844, his station being purchased by James Blair, the Police Magistrate at Portland.[8] Simeon Lord and Sir John Owen, owners of Fulham, a Glenelg River run which was attacked repeatedly during 1843 and early 1844, were forced into receivership by their losses of sheep and mounting debt.[9]

Throughout the District station owners had to pay for the extra labour made necessary by Aboriginal attacks. 'Big' Clarke at Woodlands in the Pyrenees found that shepherds refused to take out their flocks alone. Consequently he was 'obliged at great cost, to send two shepherds with one flock. Nor was it safe to leave one man as hut-keeper'.[10] The cost of labour which was scarce and expensive thus was doubled. When Aborigines warned Daniel O'Neil, who was minding the sheep of the murdered McKenzie, that they were going to take the flock, Messrs Henty, 'executors to the estate', sent additional men to O'Neil's to guard the sheep.[11] Augustine Barton left his property near Mt Rouse, having decided to return to England 'as sheep did not pay'. He warned friends to have 'nothing to do with sheep' at Portland Bay 'where . . . you require 2 shepherds for each flock as the men are afraid to go out alone on account of the natives'. He had needed '14 men to manage a station with nothing on it but 2000 sheep—when 4 or at most 5 ought to have done everything'. Shortly afterwards he received a letter from a man 'with whom he had left his sheep on terms' notifying him that three hundred of them had been killed by the Aborigines.[12] Alfred Taddy Thomson at Mt William was forced to put 'two shepherds with double-barrelled guns to each flock to no purpose, and at last was forced to leave'.[13]

As the 1850s approached, the Government took stock of its Aboriginal policies and evaluated their success. La Trobe's verdict was that all the measures and policies had been 'total failures' except for the Native Police, which had been partially successful in that it achieved one of its aims, the Europeanization of the Aborigines involved. Even here he doubted the permanence of the change: if the Police Corps was abandoned, he predicted that the Aborigines would return to 'savage life'. The Protectorate had 'totally failed to effect any of the higher and more important objectives aimed at in its formation'. The Wesleyan mission had failed to civilize or Christianize even 'a single individual'. In examining the evidence of civilized behaviour among Aborigines he listed the use for a time of European clothing, the eating of European food, the taking up of employment. But he was convinced that such signs were superficial. The Aborigines lightly abandoned European clothing, left employment when it suited them, turned their backs on European food, seeking their 'natural subsistence', took no interest in cultivating the soil to produce food or in building better shelters. He had come to the conclusion that there was:

one main error . . . in all the schemes devised at a distance . . . namely, that of taking for granted . . . that the Aboriginal Natives will submit, in a greater or lesser degree to your guidance.[14]

The Aborigines in 1848 still lived in a more or less traditional manner. La Trobe listed the ways they had not changed. But what he was assessing was the ineffectiveness of the Protectorate officials and the missionaries in bringing about the changes they wanted. All round there was evidence of change—of the Aborigines having been forced to change their way of life because of altered circumstances.

Aboriginal food and the method of obtaining it had changed. The murnong still available when Robinson travelled across the District had become increasingly unavailable as sheep ate off the tops and the Aborigines were prevented from burning off which they used to encourage its growth. The animals of the District had changed. By July 1845 there were already 2680 horses, 64 727 cattle and 1 058 366 sheep in the District.[15] At least one species of native animal hunted by the Aborigines rapidly became extinct. The European-introduced animals could not be hunted and taken in the same manner and using the same skills as previously used.

The exclusion from the waterholes and the springs had led to the abandonment of permanent winter housing and the enormous oven mounds seen by Robinson and others. Change was to be seen in the movement of Aborigines close to European home stations and outstation huts. Temporary housing only, windbreaks, were used to make do. Possum skin cloaks became rarer as the possums declined in number. Now relationships with Europeans were virtually unavoidable. New tastes had to be satisfied. Sheep and cattle needed to be bartered for or worked for and the same was true of spirits, tobacco, trousers, and shirts if Aborigines wanted them.

Tribal and clan boundaries had been weakened as Europeans brought 'strangers' from other places to work for them and accompany them in their journeys across the District. Many of the interlopers suffered in the traditional way for their lack of respect for the old ways but the appearance of these outsiders throughout the District was a sign of change in the thinking of the Aborigines who had trusted to a European way of viewing the land and employment.

Smoke signals still called Aborigines to tribal business and not to respond meant death. But it was impossible to keep to the old ways as they had been. The decline in the Aboriginal population, especially the imbalance between the sexes, meant that marriage rules could no longer have been properly observed, and in many places children were noticeably absent.[16] Even the old divisions of labour could no longer have been unchanged, especially as relationships with Europeans now decided in many cases what would be eaten and how one would live. The old custom of fighting over women still existed as in the incident involving Koort Kirrup described below, but now possible European intervention had to be taken into account. Two Europeans passing by heard the struggling woman as she was being taken from her people and rescued her from her captors. Other customs, still strong, such as the reaction to a stranger, persisted though in the new circumstance and the shortage of women it would have been far better had it been less powerful and persuasive. In 1848 Alaverin, tried for the killing of an Aboriginal woman, justified it on the grounds that she was a stranger.

Aborigines had learnt to use guns, not to kill Europeans so much as part of their employment on stations and in their relationships with fellow Aborigines.[17] At Dunmore Campbell reported change in the materials used to make spears: iron spears were now being made. The initial reaction to settlement, the rapid mastering of at least everyday English and the learning of new skills by those who sought employment on European stations all demonstrated an openness to change and an ability to react positively to it.

La Trobe had noticed one significant change. 'Instances of violent collision on either side, are now rarely heard of', he wrote. But murder still occurred and without charges being laid. In 1849, with the Port Phillip District on the verge of life as an independent colony, Koort Kirrup and his men killed two Aborigines and fatally wounded a third in a revenge raid aimed at kidnapping a woman belonging to another group. The incident occurred at a camp near Hector MacDonald's Inn on the Crawford River with Europeans close enough to almost witness events. MacDonald was woken by a 'gin' at his 'window' with news that 'Koort Kirrup was killing the blacks'. Minutes later, he and two of his men were viewing the results of 'the savage attack' and dealing with the wounded. But the incident led to no arrests.[18] Only slightly earlier John Cox J.P. had given permission for a punitive expedition after a shepherd was killed by Aborigines on a Glenelg River run. Two Aborigines were killed but no legal action followed.[19] La Trobe was right: life, at least European life, could no longer 'be sacrificed with impunity'—about Aboriginal life one is far less certain. And attacks on European property had ceased.

At the most basic level European settlement was concerned with the occupation of the land and forcing the Aborigines to accept all that this meant. The District was an extended Convincing Ground with the emphasis being not so much on civilizing and Christianizing the Aborigines as making them realize that they had to accept the new order. By 1848 the Aborigines had been convinced of this.

Epilogue

SOME OF THE Aborigines born before European settlement lived well into the second half of the nineteenth century. They observed the rush to the goldfields and benefited at that time by gaining regular employment on pastoral properties. Most of them were forced on to the Lake Condah and Framlingham Aboriginal stations in the years after 1865. There men like Kaawirn Kuunawarn grumbled about the lack of freedom but were grateful that some land had been set aside for them. Others refused to move to the stations, living their last years on pastoral properties in their own 'country'.

In 1871 Weeratt Kuyuut, a great warrior and chief of the Aborigines inhabiting Spring Creek and parts of the Mt Rouse district, according to James Dawson, was seventy years old. Still with a zest for life, he was intending to take 'a young woman to himself as wife'. Whether he did so or not is not known but Kaawirn Kuunawarn (Hissing Swan/King David) married Queen Mary late in life. She was one of two wives of King Billy of Ballarat and became the wife of Kaawirn Kuunawarn about 1882, after King Billy died.

In 1883 Wombeetch Puyuun, Camperdown George, died and was buried in a boggy swamp to be rescued later by James Dawson and reburied below a towering obelisk which proclaimed the extinction ('extirpation would be a more appropriate word', Dawson wrote) of the Aborigines whose country was around Camperdown. King Tom of Meningoort, who had been persuaded to wear European clothes only in

191

the last years of his life (but never shoes), died in September 1881. His last few months were spoilt by nightmares that originated, one imagines, in the increased vulnerability of Aborigines of one clan to those of another which followed European settlement. He would rush from his mia-mia to the house at Meningoort, begging 'Massr shoot-em wild blackfellow on the hill, kill Tom'.

Life with their own people brought some comfort to the Aborigines, but they like the Europeans were to feel the devastating effects of the economic depression of the late nineteenth century. As the need to conserve resources grew, the Government debated ways of reducing costs. They introduced the Half Caste Act which meant that all able-bodied half-castes under thirty-four had to leave the stations and support themselves. With fewer people to support, the Government considered closing stations and Framlingham was the one selected first. Kaawirn Kuunawarn died in 1890 as his people were being dispossessed for a second time. The news was sent by telegram from the Manager of the Aboriginal station to James Dawson, 'Old Davie (Hissing Swan) dead. Idea of leaving home killed him; buried Thursday'.

One hundred years later Aborigines have gained some recompense. Freehold title to the land once temporarily reserved for their use at Lake Condah and Framlingham has been given to local communities. Cultural centres are being opened as Aborigines, responding to Govern-ment initiatives, take upon themselves the task of sharing their knowl-edge with the wider community. Skills such as basket-making have been revived. Local artefacts are being sought for display, oral history is being recorded and photographs collected. Tourists and locals alike will soon have the opportunity to gain a deeper understanding of the shared past and an appreciation of the Aboriginal mastery of the environment.

In the old Portland Bay District the men and women of two races competed for the use of the land and its resources. One won, but the other has left a legacy still to be seen, the signs of a rich human heritage stretching into the far distant past.

Appendix 1

Western District Aboriginal Tribes 1841 and Census Details

The list of tribes which follows is taken from Appendix F of Robinson's October 1842 'Report of an expedition to the Aboriginal Tribes of the Western Interior during the Months of March, April, May, June, July and August 1841'.[1] Below the name of each tribe is a similar name in brackets. This is the name given to the same tribe in a later but shorter official list—Appendix J of Robinson's Annual report for 1845.[2] Today such groups would be called clans but the word 'tribe' which Robinson used has been kept, as the aim of this Appendix is to make available the information Robinson collected about the Aboriginal groups of the 'Western Interior'. Under each tribal name I have collected together the various references made to it in the various documents left by Robinson. Each entry is therefore an item of information collected by Robinson unless I clearly indicate by square brackets that I am making a comment.

Robinson's recorded information is to be found in various places. As these sources are referred to constantly the reader needs to be aware of them. Two versions of Robinson's official report on the 1841 trip have been used. Firstly, there is the October 1842 report to La Trobe mentioned above.[3] Kenyon's widely known copy of the report in the *Victorian Historical Magazine* is an edited version.[4] Secondly, there are Robinson's Journals, in which he made his notes day by day in the field. Some references are to the Journals but many are also made to the much more easily available copy of the Journals edited by Gary Presland.

In some cases where information has been omitted from Presland's edited version of the Journals reference is made to the Journal only. Third, Robinson also kept Vocabulary books and these are often referred to.

Three other sources are mentioned occasionally. As Robinson on his 1841 journey travelled into the mountainous area to the north and into territory for which Assistant Protector Parker was responsible, I have sometimes drawn attention to Parker's census of 1842. Robinson returned to the Western District in early 1842 and information has been included from his Journal for this period. An edited version by Ian Clark is referred to as it is more easily available than Robinson's Journal. Reference is made to Robinson's letter to La Trobe dated 30 June 1845 which provided a census of Aborigines in the Glenelg River area. It is a restatement of information obtained in 1841.[5]

Robinson made two summaries of tribes as he travelled through the District. The first, a short list, is on the back cover of Robinson's Vocabulary Book, Robinson Papers, vol. 65, part 2, pp. 133-4; the second, headed 'Names of tribes, with their chief men and numerical strength', is to be found in Robinson's Vocabulary Book, vol. 65, part 2, pp. 203-4, 210-12. These two lists are important as he was building up a summary as he travelled. I have referred to them as the first 'List of Tribes' and second 'List of Tribes'.

To make sense of this Appendix one needs to be aware that Robinson was a person with no knowledge of linguistics and he travelled through the area before there were signposts on which he could see how to spell place names. Even when he met settlers, I suspect he did not ask how to spell their names, those of their properties or even of nearby landmarks. He did what we would do travelling in a country where a different language was spoken; he wrote down the sounds he heard, using our alphabet to convey as best he could the sounds he heard. His method of recording words varied, sometimes from day to day. It is frustrating for a researcher but I suspect that any of us placed in a similar position would do much the same. If confused, sound the word, vary the way of sounding a little and I think you will be able to follow the information given.

One further point, under the heading 'Number' the first figure is the total. It is followed by a statement of how many were men (M), women (W), or children (C)—if this information was available. Unfortunately such information was not found for all groups. Again when the total number given for the groups does not agree with a total arrived at by adding the number of men, women and children this is because the information on some members of the group was not given in the documentary sources.

Tribe Name/Locality/Reference	Number

1. *Galgal*

Country N.E. and E. of Irwin's station.

Country north of the Pellerwin bulluc, Robinson's Vocab. Book, vol. 65, part 2, section 287–330, p. 295; along a creek running from Synott's to Francis's station and further north. Mentioned Kenyon, p. 159. 6 Gal Gal bulluc are included with the Beeripmo, tribe 24.

2. *Pellerwin*   2—2M

A high hill range of the Pyrenees bearing N.N.E. from Beerip burbery and 10 miles from Irwin's home station, north-east of Borrumbeep.

Robinson's Vocab. Book, vol. 65, part 2, section 243–286, pp. 276, 286. In the same source, page 243 the locality is given as 10 miles N. by E. of Mt Cole. North of Francis's station, vol. 65, part 2, section 287–330, p. 295. Two individuals named, vol. 65, part 2, section 243–286, p. 253. Mentioned Kenyon, pp. 159–60.

3. *Borrum*

Country at To.lo gun, a hill situated to the N. by W. of Synott's, to the north of Francis's station.

Robinson's Vocab. Book, vol. 65, part 2, section 287–330, pp. 292, 295. Same source provides a list, pages 308–9. Mentioned Kenyon, p. 159. Borrum bulluc also called the To.did.jer.er bulluc, Robinson's Journal, vol. 18, part 2, p. 45 (Presland, 1980, p. 186). Tone.did.jerer is listed No. 31.

4. *Moorngoodeet*

North of Francis's station.

Kenyon, p. 161.

5. *Barconedeet*
(Bart Konedeet)

8—3M 3W 2C

Country from Synott's along the creek NW, 15 to 20 miles, from Synott's below Francis.

The Bar conedeet is bounded by the sandstone range, 1½ miles west from Francis's home station, Robinson's Journal, vol. 18, part 2, p. 156 (Presland, 1980, p. 191). Both Bart conedeet and Bar conedeet are used in the above source. Further information is given in Robinson's Vocab. Book, vol. 65, part 2, section 243–286, p. 244, and section 287–330, pp. 295–6.

Individuals can be counted, Robinson's Journal, vol. 18, part 2, pp. 116–18 and 155–7 (Presland, 1980, pp. 190–1). Bar conedeet mentioned by Kenyon, pp. 159–60. [Parker in his census of 1842, Appendix I to his Annual Report for 1842 calls the Aborigines of the area around Francis's station the Tuan Bulluck and indicates that the section now only numbers six persons.]

6. *Wonerergarerer*

Country north of the Pyrenees.

Plenty sulky with Aborigines on the south side of the Pyrenees, Robinson's Vocab. Book, vol. 65, part 2, section 243–286, pp. 282–3. To the north of Francis's station, vol. 65, part 2, section 287–330, p. 294. Also Kenyon, p. 160.

7. *Pobiberite*

On part of the Bar River. On the creek running north from Synott's station towards Francis's station.

Robinson's Vocab. Book, vol. 65, part 2, section 287–330, pp. 294–5. Mentioned Kenyon, p. 159.

8. Currac   4—1M 2W 1C
(Kurne Bulluk)

A locality in the centre of the Pyrenees, at
Irwin's station.

Kuruc bulluk, vol. 65, part 6, p. 123.
Locality given Robinson's Vocab. Book, vol.
65, part 2, section 243-86, p. 282, and
names of 4 individuals given on p. 284.
Locality given as centre of Pyrenees,
Kenyon, p. 160.

9. Koneneger

On part of the Bar River. North of Synott's
along a creek bearing N.W. towards Francis's station.

Possibly the Kone ne get bulluc, south of
Francis's station, next to the Pobiberite.
Robinson's Vocab. Book, vol. 65, part 2, section 287-330, p. 295. Poneger is mentioned in Kenyon, p. 159.

10. Pubbarden   10—4M 2W 4C
(Parpardeen Bulluk)

On part of the Bar River. Near Captain
Bing's (Briggs) and beyond to the north, 20
miles to the north of Mt William.

No. 23 in list of names of tribes of area of
Mt William and Mt Cole, Robinson's Vocab.
Book, vol. 65, part 2, section 243-286, p.
255. List of names is also given. The name
is given as Capt. Briggs, Robinson's Journal,
vol. 18, part 2, p. 50 (Presland, 1980,
p. 100).

11. Torn

Near the Bar conedeet, south of Francis's
station.

Robinson's Vocab. Book, vol. 65, part 2, section 287-303, p. 295. Kenyon, p. 159.

12. Poit

Area of Francis's station. Sandstone ridge 1½ miles west of Francis's station divides the Bar conedeet from the Poit bulluc country.

Robinson's Vocab. Book, vol. 65, part 2, section 287–303, p. 295. Kenyon, p. 159. North of Mt Cole, Vocab. Book, vol. 65, part 2, section 243–286, p. 249.

13. Larniringoendeet

North of Francis's station.

Robinson's Vocab. Book, vol. 65, part 2, section 287–330, p. 295.

14. Bullengort

North of Francis's station.

Robinson's Vocab. Book, vol. 65, part 2, section 287–330, p. 295.

15. Europin　　　　　　　　　1—1M
(Europine Konedeet)

On the way back to Geelong from the source of the Woode-yallock, a short distance south of Mt Lange station [Could be Mr. Lange's station].

Kenyon, p. 166, and Robinson's Vocab. Book, vol. 65, part 2, section 287–330, p. 300. Also Presland, 1980, Appendix 32 (Bone ne wor rer wor rer a U.ro.pine conedeet at U.ro.pine Yalloke met at Black and Steele's station).

16. Beerequart　　　　　　　　4—3M 1W
(Bierequart Bulluk)

Mt Emu.

Beer.re.quart bulluc, country at Tare.cur.-rum.beet (Mt Emu). Only 4 persons left, Robinson's Journal, vol. 18, part 2, p. 190 (Presland, 1980, p. 195). Robinson's Vocab.

Book, vol. 65, part 2, section 287–330, p. 302.

17. Moijerre   9—2M 4W 3C
(Moygerre Bulluk)

East of Mr Hoyle's home station and the area of Wright and Montgomery's station, three miles below Baillie's station.

Moi.jer.re.bulluc met at Kay.jap (Linton's station). Some came from the east of Mr Hoyle's home station and others from the station of Wright and Montgomery, Robinson's Journal, vol. 18, part 3, pp. 36–40 (Presland, 1980, p. 201). Also Robinson's Vocab. Book, vol. 65, section 287–330, p. 310.

18. Yare rin borin   3—2M 1?
Urquhart's Creek

Yar.run borrin conedeet in Mt Emu area, Robinson's Vocab. Book, vol. 65, part 2, section 287–330, p. 302. Also Robinson's Journal, vol. 18, part 2, pp. 190–1 (Presland, 1980, p. 195).

19. Mone   5—1M 1W 2C
(Mome Bulluck)

Few miles north of Mt Emu at Jacky Jacky, on the creek five miles above Urquhart's station, at McReady's station.

Mone bulluc garroke, country a few miles north of Mt Emu at Jacky Jacky, Robinson's Journal, vol. 18, part 2, pp. 190–4 (Presland, 1980, p. 195). In Robinson's Vocab. Book, vol. 65, part 2, section 287–330, p. 302, states that of the Mone bulluc only one family of five left (1M 1W and 2C). Is mentioned vol. 65, part 2, pp. 312–13. Is listed as Morne bulluk in vol. 65, part 6, p. 123. Is referred to as Morn bulluc in Kenyon, p. 164.

20. *Caringum*   1—1M
(Karingum Bulluk)   included with the Colijon

Car-ren-gum, name of the country round Baylie's station.

Car.rin.gum bulluc. Only one male left and he has joined the Colijon. His country is now occupied by other tribes such as the Beeripmo bulluc, the Utoul bulluc and the Gal gal bulluc, Robinson's Vocab. Book, vol. 65, part 2, section 287–330, p. 306. Also Kenyon, p. 165.

21. *Corerpongerlite*   Extinct
(Korerpongerlite Konedeet)

Near Pellerwin, a hill 10 miles N. by E. of Mt Cole.

Pellerwin is the name of an isolated hill, on the eastern side of the Pyrenees. A section of the Jarjowerong nation. Robinson's Vocab. Book, vol. 65, part 2, section 243–286, p. 245; names of tribes Mt William and Lar.ner jeering (Mt Cole). Also mentioned by Kenyon, pp. 160, 162.

22. *Wong.er rer*   2—2M
(Wongerer Bulluk)

Source of the Worde alloke.

Wong.rer bulluc, source of the Worde alloke, Mr Smyth and Mr Prentice have their station at this place. Only two male adults left. Robinson's Vocab Book, vol. 65, part 2, section 287–303, p. 307.

23. *Tuerite*   Almost extinct
(Tucrite Bulluk)

A hill near Mr Cogles (Coghills).

[For Coghill's see Cannon, 1982, p. 670.] Is listed as Tuerite in Robinson's Vocab. Book, vol. 65, part 6, p. 123 and the locality given vol. 65, part 2, section 287–330, p. 311. Also states nearly all dead.

24. *Beeripmo*
(Beripmo Bulluk)

48—17M 19W 12C

A hill at the south-eastern extremity of the Pyrenees, near Mr Campbell's home station. From Beerip, a hill at the south eastern extremity of the Pyrenees, Kenyon, p. 160. The Aborigines at Mr Baillie's, Robinson's Journal, vol. 18, part 2, p. 171 (Presland, 1980, p. 193). Their country near Mr Campbell's home station, Robinson's Vocab. Book, vol. 65, part 2, section 243-286, p. 264. Names and number given in the same source. Six Gal gal bulluc (1M 2W 3C) are included. Another 22 names are given in the same source, page 285. Two men are repeated and have been counted only once.

25. *Bare re Bare re*
(Barre Barre Bulluk)

1—1M

A locality, 2 miles south-east of Hoil's home station.

Robinson's Vocab. Book, vol. 65, part 2, section 287-330, p. 320. Bare.re.bare.re bulluc, country on the way from Mt Emu to a branch of the Woode-yallock, Kenyon, p. 165. Also mentioned Robinson's Journal, 9 and 10 August 1841. Met Aborigines of this group at Mr Linton's station, Robinson's Journal, vol. 18, part 3, p. 36 (Presland, 1980, p. 201).

26. *Carninger*
(Karinger Bulluk)

1—1M

At Mr Linton's. At the out-station west of Hoil's station.

Carnin.jer bulluc, Robinson's Vocab. Book, vol. 65, part 2, section 287-330, pp. 320-1. Carninje bulluc, Kenyon, p. 166. A Cur.nin.je bulluc mentioned at Mr Linton's station, Robinson's Journal, vol. 18, part 3, p. 39 (Presland, p. 201).

27. *Beeric in moon*
(Bericeninoon Bulluk)

At Mount Misery—Learmonth's station.

Beer.ric.in.moom bulluc, Robinson's Vocab.
Book, vol. 65, part 2, section 287–330, p. 321.

28. *Currac*   4—1M 2W 1C
(Kurne Bulluk)   (Already counted)

A locality in the centre of the Pyrenees, at
Irwin's station.

Kuruc bulluk, Robinson's Vocab. Book, vol.
65, part 6, p. 123. Locality given vol. 65,
part 2, section 243–286, p. 282, and names
of 4 individuals given p. 284. Locality
given as centre of Pyrenees, Kenyon, p.
160. Identical to No. 8.

29. *Wall inne ber*
(Wooleneber Bulluk)

Wotteneber, Robinson's Vocab. Book, vol.
65, part 6, p. 123.

30. *Neet.she*   13—6M 4W 3C
(Nishea Bulluk)

East side of Mt William.

Nee.tcheerer bulluc, tribe at the Grampians inhabiting country on the east side of
Mt William. Robinson's Vocab. Book, vol.
65, part 2, section 243–286, p. 245, number 7 in list of tribes in area of Mt William
and Mt Cole. Also mentioned as Neet.she,
Kenyon, p. 159. [Parker lists 10 people
(census, 1842).] Robinson lists 13 individuals, Journal, vol. 18, part 2, p. 48
(Presland, 1980, pp. 186–7).

31. *Tone.did.jerer*   30—9M 11W 10C
(Tonedidjerer Bulluk)

At Borumbeep, on the Hopkins, 9 miles
WSW of Mt Cole where Kirk's home
station is.

Robinson's Journal, vol. 18, part 2, p. 45
(Presland, 1980, p. 186) and Robinson's
Vocab. Book, vol. 65, part 2, section 243–
286, No. 4 in list of tribes in area of Mt
Cole and Mt William. Also mentioned in
No. 27 of the same list as the Tone.did.jere
bulluc at Mr Bayles, at Jacky Jacky station.
Members listed Robinson's Journal, vol. 18,
part 2, p. 48 (Presland, 1980, p. 187). The
To.did.jer.er bul.luc sometimes called the
Borum bul.luc, Robinson's Journal vol. 18,
part 2, p. 45 (Presland, 1980, p. 186). Some
names given Robinson's Vocab. Book, vol.
65, section 243–286, pp. 265–6. Have
added these 9 and omitted 1 who appeared
in both lists. [This is Parker's Borumbulluk
which has 31 members in his census, 1842.
Note that there is both a Borum bulluk and
Borumbeet bulluc.]

32. Parn   20—7M 7W 6C
(Parn Bulluk)

North of a hill, 3 miles north of
Borrumbeep, a large hill 5 miles south-
west of Blow's station.

Robinson's Journal 1 Aug. 1841 (Presland,
1980, p. 130). Also mentioned as Parin
bulluc and Parn bulluc, Kenyon, pp.
162–3. An old man, 3 wives, 1 child all that
is left of the tribe, Robinson's Vocab. Book,
vol. 65, part 2, section 243–286, p. 251, is
entry No. 18 in list of tribes of Mt William
and Mt Cole area. Location and names of
individuals given in same source, page 271.
[Parker in his census of 1842 lists 6 members of this group.]

33. Bone.ne   13—4M 3W 6C
(Bonene Bulluk)

Victoria Range or north-east of Mt
William.

Bone.ner bulluc, tribe of the Victoria
Range, Robinson's Vocab. Book, vol. 65,

part 2, section 243–286, p. 247, No. 10 in list of tribes of the Mt William and Mt Cole area. Names given p. 250. These include 11 Neetshe bulluc. Bon.ne.bulluc country is to the north-east of Mt William, Kenyon, pp. 156–7. Names of 5 individuals given in Robinson's Journal, 15 July 1841 and 2 Aug. 1841 (Presland, 1980, pp. 186, 192–3) but the list used has been taken from Robinson's Vocab. Book, vol. 65, part 2, section 243–286, p. 250, and includes the Neetshe.

34. Eutoul   27—7M 10W 10C
(Entroal Bulluk)

The swampy river running south from Mt Cole.

Robinson's Vocab. Book, vol. 65, part 2, section 243–286, p. 243, No. 3 in list of tribes in area of Mt William and Mt Cole. The U.toul bulluc at Campbell's, Robinson's Journal, vol. 18, part 2, p. 171 (Presland, 1980, p. 193). About 19 names scattered through the lists (Presland, 1980, p. 190 onwards). Identical list of names is given in Robinson's Vocab. Book, vol. 65, part 2, section 243–286, p. 266, and in vol. 65, part 6, p. 97. [This is Parker's Utowol bulluk for which he lists 41 in his 1842 census.]

35. Teerel   2—1M 1W
(Teril Bulluk)

The area round a small hill 5 miles north of Mt Cole.

Robinson's Journal, vol. 18, part 2, p. 25 (Presland, 1980, p. 185). Also Robinson's Vocab. Book, vol. 65, part 2, section 243–286, p. 243. No. 2 in list of tribes of the Mt William and Mt Cole area. Mentioned Kenyon, p. 159. Is mentioned as Terel bulluk in vol. 65, part 6, p. 123. [Parker's Terilbulluk had 18 members in his 1842 census.] Only 2 names mentioned by

Robinson, Journal, vol. 18, part 2, pp. 45–7
(Presland 1980, p. 186).

36. *Toolerer*
(Tolerer Bulluk)

Near Bacchus Marsh.

Toolerer bulluk, a section of the Waddouro
near Bacchus Marsh, Robinson's Vocab.
Book, vol. 65, part 6, p. 117. Also Tullorer
Bulluk, section of the Wotowerong, vol. 65,
part 3, p. 132.

37. *Talle.willum*

At Bacchus Marsh next to Malcolm.

Wotowerong. Robinson's Vocab. Book, vol.
65, part 3, p. 133.

38. *Mar pre ang bulluk*

Malcolm's tribe. Bacchus Marsh area?

Marpeang bulluc, Robinson's Vocab. Book,
vol. 65, part 3, p. 132.

39. *Yowong geek*
Wotowerong?

Borogowodeet, at Lee river? Robinson's
Vocab. Book, vol. 65, part 3, p. 132.

40. *Cruc er bulluc*
Wotowerong, next to Toolerer bulluk.

Kurer Kurn bulluc, Robinson's Vocab.
Book, vol. 65, part 3, p. 132.

41. *Neerer bulluc*
Wotowerong.

Near to Yowong, Robinson's Vocab. Book,
vol. 65, part 3, p. 132.

42. *Teerinyillum*   1—1C
(Terimpelum Konedeet)   Near extinct

Mt Elephant, the river above Mr Black's.

Teeringillum conedeet, Robinson's Journal, vol. 18, part 3, pp. 48, 60 (Presland, 1980, pp. 149–50). Teer.in.yel.lem section extinct, killed by Europeans, Mr Taylor and others, Robinson's Vocab. Book, vol. 65, part 2, section 25-60, p. 40.

43. *Tarn-berre*   Extinct
(Tarnbere Konedeet)

Area of Black's station.

Killed by Taylor, Robinson's Vocab. Book, vol. 65, part 2, section 287–330, p. 327.

44. *Larnaget*   7—1M 2W 4C

W.S.W. of Borumbeep.

Tribe No. 13 in list of tribes in area of Mt William and Mt Cole. Robinson's Vocab. Book, vol. 65, part 2, section 243–286, p. 249. Is also tribe no. 28, same source, p. 265. Only one family left, same source, p. 266. Mentioned Kenyon, p. 157.

45. *Jackalet*   35—6M 13W 16C

Mr Hall's station.

Tribe No. 17 in list of tribes in the area of Mt William and Mt Cole, Robinson's Vocab. Book, vol. 65, part 2, section 243–286, p. 251. Same source provides names and number in group which includes one Rockburrer and family. Mentioned Kenyon, p. 157.

46. *Boolucburrer*   87—24M 32W 31C
(Bolokeburer Konedeet)

Lake Boloke

Also called the Bulerburers Robinson's Journal, vol. 17, part 3, p. 95 (Presland, 1977, p. 25) and the Boolucburrers. Number less than 80, Kenyon, p. 146. List given in Robinson's Vocab. Book, vol. 65, part 2, section 243–286, pp. 268-9.

47. Morrer.Morrer.berap   23—8M 9W 6C

Dundas or Victoria Range.

Robinson's Vocab. Book, vol. 65, part 2, section 243–286, p. 254. In list of tribes in area of Mt William and Mt Cole. Names and number are given. [Has been included with Tribe No. 106 in the 1845 list.]

48. Alloke Burrer Bulloke   36—13M 10W 13C
(Aloke Burrer Boloke)

Between Boo-uc [Booruc] Mt Shadwell and Lake Boloke—midway.

Listed as No. 31 in tribes of Mt William and Mt Cole area, Robinson's Vocab. Book, vol. 65, part 2, section 243–286, pp. 269–70, where names are given.

49. Bunyap   78—25M 21W 32C
(Bunyap)

Near Bird's home station extending to Colorer. Bird was 6 miles from Whitehead and in 1841 his station belonged to Captain Swanston with Gibbs the younger in charge (Presland, 1977, pp. 73–4). [Bird was licensed to have land on the Hopkins River, 25 miles distant from Whitehead (Whitehead family history, 1986, p. 40).]

Robinson's Vocab. Book, vol. 65, part 2, section 215–242, p. 217. Mentioned in first 'List of Tribes', and a number of 34 given. Names and make-up of family groups given in vol. 65, part 2, section 135–166, p. 156. A further number of 48 is given in Robinson's second 'List of Tribes'. [Robinson made a mistake in counting members. Instead of 48 he has the names of 78 individuals, vol. 65, part 2, section 215–242, p. 217.]

50. Kone.yilwer.in   32—11M 11W 10C
(Koneyilwerin Konedeet)

A short distance south-east of the marsh in a north-east direction from Dr Martin's heiffer station, about 3½ miles up east side of Serra or Grampians.

Also—10 miles north of Boloke, on Hopkins above Officer's station.

Robinson's Journal, vol. 18, part 2, pp. 4–7 (Presland, 1980, pp. 88–9). Would be south-east of the Wattenne.a.bulluc, Kenyon, 156. Robinson's Vocab. Book gives the second description of location, names and a number of 32, vol. 65, part 2, section 217–242, pp. 220–1.

51. Jarcoort   68—30M 21W 17C
(Jarcote Bulluk)

Lake Corangamite and Lake Purrumbete and Manifold's. A native inhabiting the country from Black's River to the Colijon to the east and Lake Kilambete to the south.

The Jarcoort are divided into 2 sections; the Conenegulluc (19 persons) inhabiting the country at Lake Corangamite and the Burrumbeet conedeet inhabiting the country at Lake Burrumbeet [Purrumbete] (39 persons) Kenyon, p. 144. A whole section of the Jarcoort was annihilated by Europeans. Names and numbers in each section given in Robinson's Journal, vol. 17, part 4, pp. 182, 187–8 (Presland, 1980, p. 167). Names given for only 53 individuals. Another list of 68 individuals is given in Robinson's Vocab. Book, vol. 65, part 2, at end of section 167–214.

52. Kone.ne.cut   1—1W
(Konekut Bulluk)

Long way north-east of Mt Emu on the plains.

Robinson's Journal, vol. 18, part 3, p. 26 (Presland, 1980, p. 199). Only one name recorded. May be the Kone ne get bulluc mentioned Robinson's Vocab. Book, vol. 65, part 2, section 287–330 p. 295, as south of Francis in the area of the Bar conedeet.

53. *Colijon*   60
(Koligon Bulluk)

Lake Colac and Mr Murry's.

Number of 60 provided by Tuckfield, Robinson's Journal, 25 March 1841 (Presland, 1977, p. 5). A number of 40 is given in Kenyon, pp. 138, 144. The names of some met at Murray's, Colac, are given vol. 65, part 2, pp. 25–60.

54. *Nillambeer*   82—26M* 20W 36C
(Nillan Konedeet)

Mt Eels? South of the camp, at the great swamp, south of Forlonge's dairy station (formerly Wedge's).

Aborigines at Mt Eels [Eccles]. In Robinson's Journal, vol. 18, part 4, 21 March 1842, he mentions Jupiter, chief, Nillan conedeet, also the entry for 18 May 1842 lists both Jupiter and Cocknose as Nillan conedeet. Robinson doesn't visit them but the names are given to him. Names given in his Journal, vol. 17, part 4, pp. 134–5. Another list is given in Robinson's Vocab. Book, vol. 65, part 2, section 167–214, pp. 170–2. Eighty-two individuals are indicated. The same number is given in the second 'List of Tribes'.

*3 of the men were youths

55. *Tarn.yon.ne.beer*   5—5M
(Tarngonewurer Konedeet)

Fitzroy River area, country to the south-west between the road and the Glenelg.

Robinson's Journal, vol. 17, part 5, p. 70 (Presland, 1980, p. 26). Also Robinson's Vocab. Book, vol. 65, part 2, section 136–166, p. 146. Some names given.

56.   *Yare.her.beer*
(Yarre Beer)

Port Fairy.

This is used in Robinson's Journal, 22 March 1842, for one entry. [It appears to be another name for Yar.rer.conedeet, tribe No 61.]

57.   *Cargin*
(Karging Konedeet)

At Hunter's near the Eumeralla River.

Carng.ging conedeet, Robinson's Journal, 21 March 1842. From Robinson's 1842 trip to Western District.

58.   *Yale.her.rote*
(Yalererote Konedeet)

Country 3 miles east of Hunter's on the Eu.mer.ral.ler River.

Robinson's Journal, 21 March 1842. [Can find no mention of this group on the 1841 trip.]

59.   *Yallobeer.er*
(Yaloberer)

An individual of this group is mentioned as being at Port Fairy in Robinson's Journal, 22 March 1842. Others are named as Yallo conedeet. [I think this is the same group dealt with as either Tribe No. 100 or 121.]

60.   *Pi.ye.kil.beer*
(Piyekill Beer)

Campbell's, Port Fairy.

South wester is chief of the Py ip. gil conedeet. At another place in the same entry, Robinson mentions South wester is a Yarrer conedeet, Robinson's Journal, 22 March 1842. [This group is the same as No. 61 Yarrer which is the name Robinson used on his 1841 trip.]

61. Yarrer   167—38M* 53W 76C
(Yarer Konedeet)

At Campbell's, Port Fairy.

Robinson's Vocab. Book, vol. 65, part 2, section 105-134, pp. 130-2, list of names and
the number of 167 given. This includes 12
individuals marked as Merri conedeet. Is in
first 'List of Tribes' and second 'List of
Tribes' with a number of 167 given each
time.

*includes 3 youths

62. Pyipgil
Same as No. 60.

63. Nartitbeer   40—13M 18W 9C
(Nartit Beer)

Port Fairy area.

Nar it beer conedeet is mentioned in
Robinson's Journal, 22 March 1842, vol. 18,
part 4, 2 Dec. 1841—20 June 1842. This
could easily be Artit conedeet, country at
Mr Campbell's, Robinson's Journal, vol. 17,
part 4, p. 119, where names are given.
[Have three groups whose locality given as
at Mr Campbell's, Yare.rer, Artit and
Pyipkil.]

64. Worrembeet beer   1
(Worembeet Beer)

One individual of the Wor.rem.beet beer
conedeet is mentioned at Port Fairy in
Robinson's Journal, 22 March 1842, vol. 18,
part 4, Journal for 2 Dec. 1841—20 June
1842.

65. How.weet
(Howit Beer)

Swamp or marsh three miles north of Dr
Kilgour's, Tarrone.

Robinson's Vocab. Book, vol. 65, part 5, p. 14. Ow.weet conedeet; country to which Purt.ke.un belongs, Robinson's Journal, 22 March 1842. Also mentioned Robinson's Journal, vol. 17, part 4, p. 96. Is also mentioned in the same source, page 71. [Presland, 1977, p. 102, mistakenly has Or.rope.merite shown as You. en.cor.re.-deet. whereas in the original it is How Weet conedeet. Yow.en.conedeet is shown as at Dr Kilgour's at Tarrone with the chief called Part.kee.an, also being called Wor.-rup.more.rite, vol. 17, part 4, p. 34. Thus this group seems to be closely identified with the Yowen conedeet.]

66. *Corroit*
(Kourt Beer or Koroit Beer)

Cor.roit, valley of the Wannon where Perbrick and White had stations.

Robinson's Vocab. Book, vol. 65, part 2, section 217–242, p. 224. [The spelling Koroit Beer is listed in the copy of the tribes to be found in ML A1240, CY REEL 683, NSW Governor's despatches to the Secretary of State for the Colonies, vol. 51, April—June 1846.]

67. *Mendeet*
(Mendeet Beer)

Murdeet is the river at Campbell's, Port Fairy. Robinson's Journal, 22 March 1842?

68. *Aller conedeet*   64—20M 22W 22C
(Yal Konedeet)

[Goose Lagoon, west of Port Fairy?]

Only mention I can find—'We weet' is a Yal conedeet, Robinson's Journal, 23 March 1842. It is not mentioned in the second 'List of Tribes' and other references in the 23 March 1842 entry are to Yallo conedeet which has been dealt with previously. How-

ever, Robinson lists a section called the Al.-
le.conedeet burn in his Journal, 7 May
1841, with 64 members including Cart.-
car.rer who is listed as chief man of the
Ware.rang.un.conedeet, Robinson's Journal,
vol. 17, part 4, p. 36. Ware rang.er.rang.er is
Mr Ritchie's place, according to Robinson's
Journal, 23 March 1842. [According to
Dawson, p. lxxxiv, 'Yall' was the name for
scrub on the west side of Tower Hill flat.]

69. *Killeyare*
(Killeyarre Konedeet)

[No mention found.]

70. *Merri*
(Merri Konedeet)

98—29M 31W 38C

Bolden's lower station, 18 miles from Port
Fairy.

Country at Ween.cone.deet burn, Bolden's
lower station, 18 miles from Port Fairy.
Robinson's Journal, vol. 17, part 4, p. 32.
There is some confusion for We Weet who
accompanied Robinson to Port Fairy and is
mentioned as being very helpful is listed as
Merri conedeet (Robinson's Vocab. Book,
vol. 65, part 2, section 167–214, pp. 182–3)
and also Wane conedeet burn (Robinson's
Vocab. Book, vol. 65, part 2, section 105–
134, p. 125). There is additional evidence
in that Pal.ly.ling belongs to the plain at
Bolden's lower station called Been.nyturt-
burn (Presland, 1977, p. 53) and he is listed
as Merri conedeet in a list of Yare.rer
conedeet (Robinson's Vocab. Book, vol. 65,
part 2, section 105–134, pp. 130–2). Number (99) given in second 'List of Tribes'.
Names given in Robinson's Vocab. Book,
vol. 65, part 2, section 167–214, pp. 182,
183. [Please note, to add to the confusion,
on his 1842 trip to the Western District,
Robinson states that We Weet is Yal
conedeet (Journal entry for 23 March

1842) and We Weet is listed in the names for Al.le.conedeet.burn taken down 7 May 1841, Robinson's Journal vol. 17, part 4, pp. 116–17.] Robinson's Journal, pp. 117–18, provides a list of the Merri conedeet.

71.   *Tarerer*
(Tarer Konedeet)

Minbum's tribe in the Glenelg River area also called the Cobut Cobut Burrer conedeet (see No. 76).

[The name Tarer bung conedeet is in the second 'List of Tribes' and is given in Robinson to La Trobe, 30 July 1845, yet it is not in the 1845 list of tribes. I think Tarer bung has been shortened to Tarerer.]

72.   *Pat.at.gil*
(Patlatgil Beer or Palatgil Konedeet Beer)

On the Hopkins River just east of where the later town of Warrnambool was established.

The Aborigines at Mr Allan's property Tooram (just to the east of Warrnambool), Robinson's Journal, 24 March 1842, vol. 18, part 4, Journal for 2 Dec 1841– 20 June 1842).

73.   *Artcone.de.yoc*   1—1M
(Art Koneydeyoc Beer)

North-west from Tarrone at Dr Kilgour's.

Art.cone.de.yeer.roc, Robinson's Journal, vol. 17, part 4, p. 41. Only one name given, same source, p. 73. The same person is listed as Art.conedeet on p. 97. [I believe this is the full name for the Art conedeet, No. 126.]

74.   *Meencone.deet*
(Meen Konedeet)

In vicinity of Mt Rouse. Additional sections

of Manmeet nation, Robinson's Journal, vol. 17, part 4, p. 96. No mention in either 'List of Tribes'.

75. *Ome.be.garereger*   Extinct
(Ombegareger)

Loughnan's station on the Merri.

Ome.be.gor.re.ge, the original inhabitants of Loughnan's station on the Merri, Kenyon, p. 147. Kenyon has added the station name, Green Hills. Also given as a section of the Manemeet, country near Lufton's, south of Whitehead's, Robinson's Journal, vol. 17, part 4, p. 38.

76. *Cobut Cobut burer*   32—10M 12M 10C
(Kobut Kobut Burrer Konedeet)

On the old road at Smoky Creek.

Robinson's Journal, vol. 17, part 5, p. 91 (Presland, 1980, p. 30). Cobut Cobut burrer conedeet is No. 52 in Robinson's second 'List of Tribes', but no number is given. However, under it is written Minburn's tribe. Some confusion exists as to whether Minburn's group was called the Tarerbung conedeet or the Co-but-Co-but-burrer conedeet. Robinson seems to have decided the latter is Minburn's tribe while the Tarer bung conedeet is the group in the valley of the Co-nong woo tong. In Robinson's Vocab. Book, vol. 65, part 2, pp. 189–90, the heading Tarer wung has been crossed out and Co-but-Co-but-burer written in above. This is the list which can be seen as Appendix 15, Presland, 1980 p. 178. In Appendix 15 Presland has omitted seven children of Minburn shown in the original copy of the Vocab. Book, as above, p. 189. Also stated to be at the Crawford River, Robinson's Vocab. Book, vol. 65, part 2, section 217–242, p. 233. [I believe this is simply another language name for the Tarer bung conedeet, the name which

Robinson is still using for Minbum's tribe, Robinson to La Trobe, 30 July 1845. In this he gives a slightly different number of 28 (10M 10W 8C).]

77. *Caponet*
(Kaponet Konedeet)

Cup.pone.net conedeet, extra section of Manmeet listed in Robinson's Journal, vol. 17, part 4, p. 94.

78. *Muttechoke*
(Muterchoke Konedeet)

Mt Abrupt

Mut.te.tchoke, Robinson's Vocab. Book, vol. 65, part 2, section 217–242, p. 223. Mautterchoke conedeet listed as section of Manmeet, Robinson's Journal, vol. 17, part 4, p. 94.

79. *Kilcare.rer*   6
(Kilkarer Konedeet)

Of the country between Portland and the Surrey River.

There are only 2 survivors of this group and they have joined the Cart conedeet at Mt Clay, Kenyon, p. 150. Names of 6 individuals are given in Robinson's Vocab. Book, vol. 65, part 2, section 135–166, p. 165. No information on age or sex.

80. *Bung Bung.gel*   37—4M 17W 16C
(Bung Bunggel Konedeet)

Tulloch's station—on the Wannon at the falls.

The place where Tulloch is, is Bung Bungle. This is a marsh called by settlers, Big Marsh of the Wannon, Robinson's Journal, vol. 17, part 5, p. 175 (Presland, 1980, p. 49). Listed No. 25 in Robinson's second 'List of Tribes'. Members of tribe listed vol. 17, part 5, pp. 152–3 (Presland,

1980 pp. 172-3). One more family listed in Presland, 1980, Appendix 18, p. 181. See also Robinson's Vocab. Book, vol. 65, part 2, section 217-242, p. 224. Another family of 5 listed in vol. 18, part 1, pp. 112-13 (Presland, 1980, p. 177).

81. Pone.dul   18—9M 6W 3C
(Ponedal Konedeet)

The valley at John Henty's.

Robinson's Journal, vol. 18, part 1, p. 152 (Presland, 1980, p. 182). They take their name from the Ponedol Hills at McCray's station, Robinson's Vocab. Book, vol. 65, part 2, section 215-242, p. 231. Numbers given Presland, 1980, p. 182.

82. Cobut.Cobut.burer

Has already been dealt with. See above No. 76.

83. Eural   1—1W
(Eural Bulluk)

Country on the plains south-east by south, 7 miles from Kirk's home station.

Robinson's Vocab. Book, vol. 65, part 2, section 243-286, p. 245. Also U.rol bulluc, Robinson's Journal, vol. 18, part 2, p. 45 (Presland, 1980, p. 186). Only one name listed.

84. Tucalut
(Tuckalut Bulluk)

At Victoria Range.

Tuc.al.lut at Towerdeet at Victoria Range, Robinson's Vocab. Book, vol. 65, part 2, section 243-286, p. 249, No. 14 in list of tribes in the area of Mt William and Mt Cole.

85. Yamneborer   29
(Yamneborer Bulluk)

Dundas at Victoria Range.

Yam.ne.bor.rer bulluc, towards Mt Arapiles,
No. 15 in list of tribes in area of Mt
William and Mt Cole, Robinson's Vocab.
Book, vol. 65, part 2, section 243–286, p.
249. Robinson's Journal, vol. 18, part 2, p.
59, states Yam. ne.bor.rer.bulluc at Victoria
Range, probably Dundas group (Presland,
1980, p. 188). For Dundas group, Robinson
gives a number of 29, vol. 18, part 2, p. 71,
which is omitted by Presland—this would
fit in at end of list of Mur.rer.mur.rer.
bulluc (Presland, 1980, p. 189) which
Robinson also names as a Dundas group,
Journal, vol. 18, part 2, p. 99 (Presland,
1980, p. 110). Have only the number, not
sex and age.

86. *Morna*
(Morna Bulluk)

In the area of Mt William and Mt Cole.

Robinson lists Mor.na bulluc as a tribe in
the area of Mt William and Mt Cole,
Robinson's Vocab. Book, vol. 65, part 2, section 243–286, p. 250. Also mentioned in
vol. 65, part 6, p. 99.

87. *Weer.ip.cut*   19—4M 7W 8C
(Weripkut Bulluk)

Dundas, where Mr Thomson's station was.

No. 16 in list of groups in area of Mt
William and Mt Cole, Robinson's Vocab.
Book, vol. 65, part 2, section 243–286, p.
250, where a number of 19 is given.
Weer.rip.cort is suggested as a Dundas
group, Robinson's Vocab. Book, vol. 65,
part 2, section 217–242, p. 233. Different
site suggested in Robinson's Journal, 13
April 1843—Weer.ip.cut, a mountain at the
back of Mt William (Clark, 1988, p. 102).

88. *Tolelemit*   40—13M 14W 13C
(Tolemit Koroke Konedeet)

Mt Sturgeon.

Tolemit, the southern most point of the Grampians, Kenyon, p. 154. No. 19 in names of tribes of Mt William and Mt Cole area is Tol.len.nt corroke at Sturgeon, Robinson's Vocab. Book, vol. 65, part 2, section 243–286, pp. 251–3. Names are given in this source.

89. *Whitecone de yoke*   9—3M 3W 3C
(White Konedeyoke Konedeet)

The Wimmera near Mt Arapiles.

White conde yoke is No. 22 in the list of names of tribes in the Mt William and Mt Cole area, Robinson's Vocab. Book, vol. 65, part 2, section 243–286, pp. 254–5. Number of nine is given.

90. *White.burer*   2
(Whiteburer Konedeet)

To the westward at Victoria Range.

Wite burrer is No. 21 in the list of names of tribes in the Mt William and Mt Cole area. Robinson's Vocab. Book, vol. 65, part 2, section 243–286, p. 253. Two names are given.

91. *Parparden*

Already dealt with. See above, No. 10.

92. *Conicum*   9—2M 2W 5C
(Konikum Bulluk)

North of Captain Briggs.

Is No. 24 in list of tribes of area of Mt William and Mt Cole, Robinson's Vocab. Book, vol. 65, part 2, section 243–286, p. 255, where a list is given. [Parker lists the Konukinbulluk as inhabiting tributaries of the Wimmera. He names 12 individuals in the 1842 census.]

93. *Corac*   22—7M 6W 9C
(Korac Bulluk)

To the east of Mt Cole.

Cor.rac.bulluc is No. 26 in list of tribes of the area of Mt William and Mt Cole. Robinson's Vocab. Book, vol. 65, part 2, section 243–286, p. 265, with the location given. Robinson's Vocab. Book, section 287–330, p. 319, states 'the Woode alloke from Linton's north and country about' and on p. 326 he states 'Those inhabiting a branch of the Woode alloke called Cor.rac, a river a few miles East of the Woode alloke on the Mt William road, where Mr Macmillan has a station. Tribe extinct a long time ago'. Similar information on p. 327. However, names are given, vol. 65, part 2, section 243–286, p. 265.

94. *Rockburer* 2—2M
(Rockburrer Bulluk)

[Wannon—Glenelg area?]

Is included in second 'List of Tribes'. Members were present at Winter's station on the Wannon River. Only 2 individuals named. Robinson's Journal, vol. 17, part 5, pp. 144–6 (Presland, 1980, p. 172).

95. *Buckarer* 40—7M 15W 18C
(Buckarer Konedeet)

Glenelg River.

Bo.ker.re, the Glenelg (Presland, 1980, p. 174). Robinson refers to the Aborigines of the Glenelg as Wol.lore.rer. natives, Robinson's Journal, vol. 17, part 5, p. 104 (Presland, 1980, p. 171). A list is given in Robinson to La Trobe, 30 July 1845.

96. *Wanedeet* 23—5M 11W 7C
(Wanedeet Konedeet)

At Winter's on the Wannon.

Robinson's Journal, vol. 17, part 5, pp. 144–6, 151 (Presland, 1980, p. 172). There were about 50 Aborigines at Winter's according to Robinson, but many were from other groups.

97. *Tapper conedeet*
(Taper Konedeet)

59—17M 21W 21C

Mt Tapoc (or Napier).

The Aborigines were living beside the swamp into which a creek flowed which ran south from Furlonge's dairy station. They were not living at the swamp near to Mt Napier.

Kenyon, p. 149, and Robinson's Journal, vol. 17, part 4, pp. 125-57 (Presland, 1977, pp. 85-92). List of names is not given in Presland. The tribe is in both the first and second 'Lists of Tribes'. However, no number is given. Three lists of names given in Robinson's Journal, vol. 17, part 4, pp. 133-6, 150-2. List (I) gives 8 names, List (II) 5 names, List (III) 20 names, List (1V) 26 names. There may be another 13 mentioned by Robinson (Presland, 1977, p. 93).

98. *Colorer*
(Kolorer Konedeet)

Kolor (Mt Rouse).

Kenyon, p. 148. Is not mentioned in first 'List of Tribes' but is in second 'List of Tribes' but no number is given. However, there is evidence that Robinson may have confused the Col.lor.rer and the Buller buller cote conedeet, for in his Vocab. Book, vol. 65, part 2, section 25-60, p. 54, he puts the two names under each other as alternatives and states country NW of the Hopkins. He also states that the Bul.ler.-bul.le cort are extinct, Robinson's Journal, vol. 17, part 3, p. 187 (Presland, 1977, p. 48) but there are 2 lists of names while there are no names for the Col.lor.rer who we know existed even though their numbers had been reduced, Kenyon, p. 148.

[The most logical conclusion would be that there are no numbers for the Colorer conedeet. Robinson may have meant 2 groups NW on the Hopkins. Evidence that there were definitely two groups is that one of his guides, Ben.ne.mo.long is listed as Buller buller cote conedeet consistently (Presland, 1980, p. 38).]

99. *Yiyar*
(Giyar Konedeet)

21—8M* 9W 4C

Boorn Boorn (Mt Eckersley).

Kenyon, p. 151. List of names, Robinson's Journal, vol. 18, part 1, p. 132 (Presland, 1980, p. 181). Also mentioned Journal, vol. 18, part 1, p. 85 (Presland, 1980, p. 70). Robinson's Vocab. Book, vol. 65, part 2, section 135–166, p. 144, states Yi Yar Conedeet, country on the Fitzroy at the crossing place. At the Fitzroy on the country to the west of the road, Robinson's Journal, vol. 17, part 5, pp. 69–70 (Presland, 1980, p. 26). List is given in Robinson's Vocab. Book, vol. 65, part 2, section 167–214, p. 197. (The Bung Bunggel family have not been counted.) A list is also given in Robinson to La Trobe, 30 July 1845.

*includes 2 boys

100. *Yallone*
(Yalone Konedeet)

Country at Bolden's lower station.

Sections of Manemeet nation, Robinson's Journal, vol. 17, part 4, p. 34. Minmalk named as chief. Yallone conedeet is in the second 'List of Tribes'. In this source the place is given as Tulloch's on the Grange. No list of names is given. Minmalk is given as Wane conedeet burn, Robinson's Vocab. Book, vol. 65, part 2, section 107–134, p. 125.

101. *Nillan*

Already dealt with, see No. 54.

102.   Baller.Baller cote
(Buller Buller Kote Konedeet)

129—34M* 39W 56C

Country at small river, east of the woolshed at the Hopkins River.

Robinson's Vocab. Book, vol. 65, part 2, section 107–134, p. 113. Is in Robinson's first 'List of Tribes' with number of 129. Is in Robinson's second 'List of Tribes' with the number 192. Bennemolong belonged to this group and Robinson met him after crossing the Merri (Kenyon, p. 145). List is given in Robinson's Vocab. Book, vol. 65, part 2, section 135–166, pp. 160–2. Chief is father to Benne.mo.long. Robinson stated this group was extinct, Journal, vol. 17, part 3, p. 187 (Presland, 1977, p. 48). [As the tribe is mentioned in both lists this appears to be a mistake.]

*includes 5 youths

103.   Cart
(Kart Konedeet)

159—47M* 60W 52C

Mt Clay.

Robinson's Journal, vol. 17, part 5, p. 3 (Presland, 1980, p. 7). The Borne, Kil.car.-rer, Eurite sections combined with the Cart conedeet when the first white men came to their country, Kenyon, p. 150. In the second 'List of Tribes' the number of 157 is given. There is a mistake in the addition. Names are given in Robinson's Vocab. Book, vol. 65, part 2, section 167–214, pp. 173–6. Those Robinson met are listed in his Journal, vol. 17, part 4, pp. 206–8, and part 5, pp. 11–12, 80–1 (Appendices 3, 4 & 5 Presland, 1980).

*of these 11 were youths

104.   Bart
(Bart Konedeet)

Tribe belonging to the country of Portland Town.

Robinson, in his Vocab. Book, vol. 65, part 2, section 105–134, p. 109, states that an old man whose native place was at Portland is an En.re.conedeet now a Bar conedeet. In the Kenyon account, Robinson states 'The Eurite occupied the locality of the township of Portland' and that the only survivors have joined the Cart conedeet. In the second 'List of Tribes', the Cart conedeet, the Eue.re conedeet, the Bart conedeet and the Kil.care.rer conedeet are all listed but only the Cart conedeet has a number given. [I believe this group has been counted in the Cart conedeet.]

105. *Wornabul*
(Wornambul Konedeet)

Around a hill north-west of Kilambete, called Wor.ner.bul.

Robinson's Language Book, vol. 65, part 2, section 25–60, p. 55. In the second 'List of Tribes' but no number given.

106. *Kone ne.warer*
(Konewurer Konedeet)

W.S.W. from Kilambete.

Kone wurt conedeet at a river called Winburren at Con.ne.wurt, Robinson's Vocab. Book, vol. 65, part 2, section 25–60, p. 54. A second reference in the same source states Kone.wurt, west by north from Kilambete 9 or 10 miles—section of the Manemeet, p. 55. Also mentioned Kenyon, p. 143.

107. *Ellengermot*
(Elingermot Konedeet)

Round Lake Elingamite, south-east of Kilambete.

Robinson's Vocab.Book, vol. 65, part 2, section 25–60, p. 40. In the second 'List of Tribes', this tribe is not mentioned but two associated with it are, No. 65 Wane Conedeet Colac near Ellingermot and No. 66 Horong Conedeet east of Ellingermot. No numbers are given. [Chief of the Elingermat is mentioned, Presland, 1977, p. 40.]

108. *Weenyap*
(Weenyap Konedeet)

No. 17 in the second 'List of Tribes' but no number is given. [Believe it may be in the area of the Upper Glenelg or the Grange.]

109. *Pone.un.deet*
(Pornndeet Konedeet)

176—25M 72W 79C

Junction of Emu Creek and the Glenelg.

Ponung deet conedeet, Robinson's Journal, vol. 18, part 1, pp. 129-31 (Presland, 1980, p. 180). Also mentioned, Journal, vol. 18, part 1, p. 85 (Presland, 1980, p. 70). List also given Robinson's Vocab. Book, vol. 65, part 2, section 167-214, pp. 195-6 and the locality given. Number of 175 is given in the second 'List of Tribes'. In the original copy (pp. 195-6) there were 176 names. Pone.un.deet is mentioned as a long way north of the Woollorer, vol. 65, part 2, p. 138. But the Pornungdeet is named as a group on the Glenelg River area in Robinson to La Trobe, 30 July 1845, in which a number of 167 is given (25M 71W 71C).

110. *Bite.poren*
(Boitporen Konedeet)

Merri River below Bolden's.

Bite.bor.ron conedeet, Merri River below Bolden's, Robinson's Journal, vol. 18, part 1, p. 232 (Presland, 1980, p. 184). Also in second 'List of Tribes' with place given as above.

111. *Tarngonne wurrer*
(Tarngonewurer Konedeet)

Fitzroy River area, country to the south-west between the road and the Glenelg.

Robinson's Journal, vol. 17, part 5, p. 70 (Presland, 1980, p. 26). Also Robinson's Vocab. Book, vol. 65, part 2, section 136–166, p. 146. Some names given. Have treated as the same as Tribe No. 55. Numbers already listed.

112. *Wallowerer*
(Woolowerong)

Glenelg: at or near Winter's station. Maybe at the Grange.

Robinson's Vocab. Book, vol. 65, part 5, p. 8. Wool.ler.ware.rong, Robinson's Journal, vol. 17, part 5, pp. 144–6 (Presland, 1980, p. 172). Wal.lo.er.rer. or Glenelg tribe, Robinson's Journal, vol. 17, part 5, p. 73 (Presland, 1980, p. 27). It appears that this was the name of a larger group than a clan as Robinson gives a census of some of the sections of the Woolomero inhabiting the country . . . by the Glenelg in his letter to La Trobe, 30 July 1845. However, he also states Wol.lor.rer, original inhabitants at the Grange, Kenyon, p. 151.

113. *Yowen*
(Yowen Konedeet)

43—10M 14W 15C

At Tarrone, station of Dr Bernard and Dr Kilgour, Moyne swamp area.

Kenyon, p. 147. Mentioned also in first 'List of Tribes' and second 'List of Tribes', each time with a number of 43 being given. Names are given in Robinson's Vocab. Book, vol. 65, part 2, section 135–166, p. 164.

114. *Colac*
(Kolac Konedeet)

122—30M 44W 48C

Glenelg River area? At Farie's?

In both first 'List of Tribes' as having 36 members and second 'List of Tribes' as having 118 members. Names and number of 36 given in Robinson's Vocab. Book, vol. 65, part 2, section 135–166, p. 158. Names and number of 122 given in Robinson's Vocab. Book, part 2, section 167–214, pp. 186–7. The Colac Konedeet are listed following on from the Pal.lap.nue conedeet and may therefore be a Glenelg River group. However, they are named as at Farie's on the Hopkins in Robinson Papers, vol. 18, part 9, p. 35.

115. *Meen*
(Meen Konedeet)

In vicinity of Mt Rouse.

Additional sections of Manmeet nation, Robinson's Journal, vol. 17, part 4, p. 96. No mention in either 'List of Tribes'.

116. *Eure*
(Euri Konedeet)

2—Already counted in the Cart conedeet

Locality of the township of Portland.

Kenyon, p. 151. U.re.conedeet, belonging to the township of Portland, Robinson's Journal, vol. 17, part 5, p. 11 (Presland, 1980, p. 11). Only 2 survivors who have joined the Cart conedeet at Mt Clay.

117. *Mane*
(Mane Konedeet)

92—21M 39W 32C

Mentioned in both first and second 'List of Tribes' with a number of 92 being given in both cases. List of members given in Robinson's Vocab. Book, vol. 65, part 2, section 105–134, pp. 118–19.

118. *Moperer*
(Moperer Konedeet)

109—24M 36W 49C

Spring Creek, north of Dr Kilgour's. [Dawson, 1981, p. 2.]

Mentioned in both first and second 'List of Tribes' with a number of 109 given in both places. Robinson was given two lists of the Moper.rer conedeet, Robinson's Vocab. Book, vol. 65, part 2, section 105–134, pp. 121–4. Though the names are different he states they may be the same people.

119. *Teerer* (Terer Konedeet)

257—41M 100W 116C

Country short distance to the south-east of Whitehead's.

Mentioned in both first and second 'List of Tribes' with 257 members. Names listed in Robinson's Vocab. Book, vol. 65, part 2, section 105–134, pp. 127–9. Names given to him on 23 May 1841.

120. *Wane.cone.deet* (Wane Konedeet Burn)

31—11M 11W 9C

Mr Bolden's Upper Station.

In both first and second 'List of Tribes' with the number of 33 given. Individuals are listed, Robinson's Vocab. Book, vol. 65, part 2, section 105–134, p. 125. Ben.ne.-wonghome is son to the chief and Robinson met the chief between Mr Bolden's upper and lower stations (same source). Benne-wonham's country is said to be at Mr Bolden's upper station, vol. 65, part 2, section 105–134, p. 113.

121. *Yallo* (Yalo Konedeet)

94—29M* 37W 28C

Junction of the Crawford and Glenelg.

Not in first 'List of Tribes'. In the second 'List of Tribes' as Yal.lo conedeet at junction of Crawford and Glenelg rivers with a number of 94 members given. Names and numbers given in Robinson's Journal, 24 June 1841, vol. 18, part 1, pp. 126–9 (Presland, 1980, p. 179). In the original the place is given as the junction of the Crawford River down water of Snakey River. Names and number also given in vol. 65, part 2, section 167–214, pp. 192–3. Another list totalling 100 (31M 36W 33C) is given in Robinson to La Trobe, 30 July 1845.

*includes a boy

122. Narcurer
(Narkerer Konedeet)

54—11M 18W 25C

Part of the Glenelg.

Kenyon, p. 153. Robinson's Vocab. Book, vol. 65, part 2, section 167–214, p. 199, states SW from Mingburn's camp. Is mentioned in second 'List of Tribes' as Nar.cur.rer conedeet with 54 members. Names are given in Robinson's Journal, vol. 18, part 1, p. 109 (Presland, 1980, p. 176) and also in the Vocab. Book, vol. 65, part 2, section 167–214, p. 199. Is included in Robinson to La Trobe, 30 July 1845, with 154 members (35M 55W 64C), however this list consists of both Narcurer and Netnetyune.

123. Net netyune
(Netnetyoon Konedeet)

110—25M 41W 44C

Lake Condah, Darlot Creek area?

Not in first 'List of Tribes' but in second, with a total of 110. Members are listed under Bor.rup.bur.re.min in Robinson's Journal, vol. 18, part 1, pp. 110–12 (Presland, 1980, Appendix 12). Robinson's Journal, page 110, also states 'Net net yune conedeet, SE from Mingburn's camp— plenty big tribe'. The same list is given in the Vocab. Book, vol. 65, part 2, 167–214, p. 205. In the Vocab. Book, which was probably the original source, the phrase read 'Plenty big Duck there'. [See also Vanda Savill, 1976, p. 15.]

124. *Wercarer*
(Workarer Konedeet)

65—17M 27W 21C

Head of Emu Creek, NE of Mingburn's camp.

Robinson's Journal, vol. 18, part 1, pp. 112–13 (Presland, 1980, p. 177). In second 'List of Tribes' with the number of 60. List is given in Robinson's Vocab. Book, vol. 65, part 2, section 167–214, pp. 207–8. Robinson incorrectly added the list. It includes 5 Bung bunggel which have been counted as Bung bunggel. Is also listed in Robinson to La Trobe, 30 July 1845, having 59 members (14M 24W 21C).

125. *Tolite*
(Bolite Konedeet)

To lite conedeet is mentioned in the second 'List of Tribes' but no number is given. Can find no other mention.

126. *Art conedeet*
(Art Konedeet)

1—1M

North-west from Tarrone.

In second 'List of Tribes'. Also named as section of Manmeet, Robinson's Journal, vol. 17, part 4, p. 97, country north-west of Cor.lor.rer. Name of member of this group met, Robinson's Journal, vol. 17, part 4, p. 69 (Presland, 1977, p. 69). [I believe this is the same group as No. 73. Yere.roc means weir and Robinson visited a weir while at Tarrone. In the additional sections of the Manmeet he lists Art.cone.de.yeer.roc. as NW from Tarrone (misspelt Tallone in the original) at Dr Kilgowers, vol. 17, part 4, p. 41. Same source, Robinson lists Wore.rer.-mor.ar.ong as belonging to the Art cone-deet, p. 97. However, on p. 73 Robinson states that Wor.rer.mor.or.ong is an Art cone de yoc, which is the area NW from Tarrone at Dr Kilgour's.] Has been counted before.

127. Moonwer
(Moonwer Konedeet)

Area of the Grange?

Named in second 'List of Tribes' but no number given. One individual met at the Grange near Tully's, Robinson's Vocab. Book, vol. 65, part 2, section 167–214, p. 177.

128. Cone.cone
(Kone Konedeet Burn)

Between Mt Warnnambul and Tarong [Terang].

Cone conedeet burn, Robinson's Journal, vol. 18, part 1, p. 233 (Presland, 1980, p. 184, has left out the burn which is in the original). In second 'List of Tribes'.

129. Kiblet
(Kilitmurer Konedeet)

On Hopkins west of Tarong [Terang].

Robinson's Journal, vol. 18, part 1, p. 232 (Presland, 1980, p. 184). Named in second 'List of Tribes'.

130. Tonebeer
(Zone Beer)

Country north-east of Port Fairy near the Hopkins.

Mentioned in Robinson's Journal, 22 March 1842. Also in the list of Manmeet sections, Robinson's Journal, vol. 17, part 4, p. 18, with the area given as country east-south-east from Col.lor.rer.

131. Carng.be.gang
(Karnghegang Konedeet)

South-west of Tarong [Terang].

Carng.he.young conedeet, south-west of Tarong, Robinson's Journal, vol. 18, part 1,

1—1M

p. 233 (Presland, 1980, p. 184). Also named in the second 'List of Tribes'.

132. *Mumdorong*
(Mumdorong Konedeet)

West of Mt Warnnambul.

Mentioned in second 'List of Tribes' and in list of places given in Robinson's Journal, vol. 18, part 1, p. 232 (Presland, 1980, p. 184) as Mum.der.rong conedeet.

133. *Carerer*
(Karerer Konedeet)

North of Mt Warnnambul.

Care.rer conedeet, Robinson's Journal, vol. 18, part 1, p. 233 (Presland, 1980, p. 184). Also in second 'List of Tribes'.

134. *Worn*
(Worn Konedeet)

West of Mt Warnnambul.

Mentioned in second 'List of Tribes' and in Robinson's Journal, vol. 18, part 1, p. 232 (Presland, 1980, p. 184).

135. *Allo conedeet*

Between the second river on coast— between the Merri and the Hopkins?

Robinson's Journal, vol. 18, part 1, p. 232 (Presland, 1980, p. 184) and second 'List of Tribes'. [As this name is given in a list of groups in the vicinity of Mt Warrnambool this may be on the coast between the Merri and the Hopkins. It may also be the Fitzroy River which was known as the Second River.]

136. *Waneconedeet*
(Wane Konedeet Kolac)

No. 120 and No. 136 are identical. This

may be Wane conedeet colac. Near Lake Elingarmot.

Mentioned in second 'List of Tribes' and in Robinson's Journal, vol. 18, part 1, p. 232 (Presland, 1980, p. 184).

137. Orrong
(Horong Konedeet)

East of Ellengermot.

Mentioned in second 'List of Tribes'; no number is given.

138. Lay.conedeet.mallo   2—1M 1?
(Lay Konedeet Mallo)

In area of Wannon and Glenelg Rivers.

A couple of individuals of this group were at Winters' station on the Wannon River, Robinson's Journal, vol. 17, part 5, pp. 144–6 (Presland, 1980, p. 172).

139. Carnbul   1
(Karnbul Konedeet)

South-west from Winters' station.

Mentioned in second 'List of Tribes'. No number is given. One individual named, Robinson's Journal, vol. 17, part 5, p. 153 (Presland, 1980, p. 173).

140. Ballumin
(Balumin Konedeet)

Bal.lum.in conedeet in second 'List of Tribes'. Have found no other mention.

141. Tolelineut
(Tolunit Konedeet)

South-east of Tappoc [Mt Napier].

Mentioned in second 'List of Tribes' as Tole.line.ut conedeet, south-east of Tappoc. [I think this is Tol.len.nt corroke at Sturgeon. Same as tribe No. 88.]

142. *Canel*
(Kanel Konedeet)

6—3M 3W

At Norris's on the Chetwynd.

Canel or Ca.nel conedeet mentioned in second 'List of Tribes' and also in Robinson's Journal, vol. 18, part 1, p. 37 (Presland, 1980, p. 174) where individuals are listed.

143. *Care.re.bil*
(Karebit Konedeet)

Pidgeon Ponds.

Care.re.bil conedeet mentioned in second 'List of Tribes' and also in Robinson's Journal, vol. 18, part 1, p. 37 (Presland, 1980, p. 174). Presland has not accurately copied the information. In the original it clearly states Car.re bill conedeet—the tribe at Pidgeon Ponds.

144. *Bate*
(Bate Konedeet)

Between junction of Crawford and Wannon rivers.

Mentioned in second 'List of Tribes' with the locality given as above and in Robinson's Journal, 23 June 1841, vol. 18, part 1, p. 85 (Presland, 1980, p. 70). There is also a mention in vol. 18, part 1, p. 114. In this the area is given as junction of Emu Creek. The name Ponung Bate is given as a section from the Glenelg, Kenyon, p. 153, however the Po.nung deet conedeet is given as a separate entry in the second 'List of Tribes'. Same as U.roc.u.roc.burer, Robinson's Journal, vol. 18, part 1, p. 114. Also see the second 'List of Tribes'.

145. *Darkogang*
(Darkogang Konedeet)

4—1M 1W 2C

At Frank Henty's and the head of the Wando.

Dar.ko.gang conedeet, Robinson's Journal, 20 June 1841, vol. 18, part 1, pp. 61–4 (Presland, 1980, pp. 65–6) where names of members of one family are given. Mentioned in the second 'List of Tribes'.

146. *Polapune*   34—12M 12W 10C
(Palapnoo Konedeet)

Emu Creek, on the old road.

Pal.lap.nue conedeet mentioned in second 'List of Tribes'. Names are given in Robinson's Journal, vol. 18, part 1, pp. 133–4 (Presland, 1980, p. 181). Also mentioned in Robinson's Journal, vol. 18, part 1, p. 85 (Presland, 1980, p. 70). A different number of 46 (15M 17W 14C) is given in Robinson to La Trobe, 30 July 1845.

147. *Carubul*

Think this must be Carnbul. Already dealt with above as No. 139.

148. *Mal.lun*   2—1W 1C
(Malone Konedeet)

Griffiths Island.

Two individuals at Winters' on the Wannon. The island at Port Fairy called Mal.lin, Presland, 1977, p. 60. See also Robinson's Journal, 22 March 1842.

149. *Euroc.eure.burer*
(Eurokeurokburer Konedeet)

Between junction of Crawford and Wannon rivers.

U.rok.u.re.bur.rer conedeet is in the second 'List of Tribes' with the information that the area is the same as that of the Bate conedeet. They are Aborigines of the Glenelg, Kenyon, p. 153. Their area is at the junction of Emu Creek (Robinson's Journal, vol. 18, part 1, p. 118) though this is also given as the place of the Po.nung deet conedeet, Robinson's Journal, vol. 18, part 1, pp. 129–31 (Presland, 1980, p. 180).

150. *Bone.Bone.dul*
(Bonebonedul Konedeet)

South of Winters'.

Bone.bone.del conedeet is mentioned in the second 'List of Tribes' with the locality given.

151. *Cobut cobut burer*

Identical to No. 76 and No. 82.

TOTAL 2949

759M, 1011W, 1074C
105 unknown

Appendix 2

Whites killed by Aborigines

Name	Where	Date	Source
2 employees from a farm on the Werribee River	Indented Head	Feb. or May 1836	Cannon, 1982, pp. 40–1; Bride, pp. 39–42.
Mr Franks and his shepherd Flinders	Werribee River	Early July 1836	Cannon, 1982, pp. 41–3.
Mr Cadden	The Grange	*c.* 8 July 1836	Trangmar, p. 11.
Gellibrand and Hesse (Aborigines suspected of their murder)	In country towards Colac	Feb. 1837	Cannon, 1982, pp. 271–84.
Terence McMannis	Thomas Learmonth's station near Buninyong	Apr. 1838	Cannon, 1982, pp. 288–9.

William Heath	Employee of John Henty	Oct. 1838	Cannon, 1983, pp.632–3; Presland, 1980, p. 67.
Patrick Codd	John Cox's station near Mt Rouse	19 May 1840	Aborigines (Australian Colonies), *BPP*, 1844, pp. 123–4.
Thomas Hayes, John Thomson's shepherd	Keilambete	16 June 1840	Aborigines (Australian Colonies), *BPP*, 1844, p. 89; Robinson Papers, vol. 57, p. 55.
Williams, Gibson's shepherd	Glenelg River area	1841	Presland, 1980, p. 27.
John Collicot	Wills's shepherd	Early 1841	Presland, 1980, p. 110.
Oliphant's man	Pyrenees	Mar. 1841	Presland, 1980, pp. 110, 129; Bride, p. 334.
Francis Morton and William Lawrence	Glenelg River area	May 1841	Presland, 1980, pp. 13–14; Fyans to La Trobe, Return of Outrages, VPRS 19, 41/2046.
One of the Border Police	Wounded at Hunter's—died months later	1842	Brown, 1986, p. 246.
Hutcheson's shepherd	Hopkins River	Early 1842	Fyans's Itinerary for Mar, Apr, May, June 1842, VPRS 19, 42/178 enclosure in 42/2364.

Mr Purchus' shepherd (possibly Ritchie copied incorrectly — counted below)	Shot dead at Port Fairy	Early 1842	Fyans's Itinerary for Mar., Apr., May, June 1842, VPRS 19, 42/178 enclosure in 42/2364.
James Robertson	Died accidentally as a result of fighting with an Aborigine, Kilgour's station	Early 1842	Fyans's Itinerary for Mar., Apr., May, June 1842, VPRS 19, 42/178 enclosure in 42/2364.
Mr Ritchie's shepherd, Thomas Bird	Near Port Fairy	6 Feb. 1842	Aborigines (Australian Colonies), *BPP*, 1844, p. 208.
John Cox's shepherd	Near Mt Napier	4 Mar. 1842	Fyans's Itinerary for Mar., Apr., May, June 1842, VPRS 19, 42/178 enclosure in 42/2364.
Donald McKenzie and Frederick Edinge	At Emu Creek near the Glenelg River	15 Mar. 1842	French to Crown Prosecuter, 22 May 1842, MS 10053.
Mr Ricketts's shepherd, Foreman (or maybe Freeman)	The Glenelg	Early July 1842	Aborigines (Australian Colonies), *BPP*, 1844, p. 233.
Woolley's hutkeeper	Victoria Valley		Fyans to La Trobe, VPRS 19, 42/333.

Mr De Soilly's shepherd	The Glenelg, neighbour of Ricketts	Aug. 1842	Aborigines (Australian Colonies), *BPP*, 1844, p. 236.
Shepherd	Near Port Fairy (Possibly Ritchie's shepherd killed in 1842)	1843	Bride, p. 190. Mistake in year by Foster Fyans.
Child of Abraham Ward	Near Portland		*Portland Guardian*, 16 Sept. 1843.
Christopher Bassett	At the head of the Crawford River	31 Aug. 1843	French to La Trobe, 10 Sept. 1843, MS 10053.
Ricketts's shepherd. (Same case dealt with in July 1842?)	Glenelg	Apr. 1844	Official list of Whites killed 1836–44, NSWLC *V & P*, 1844, vol. 1, pp. 718–19.
Thomas Casey	Shepherd on Dunrobin, station of Addison and Murray	Apr. 1844	Cannon, 1990, p. 145.
William Higgins	Shepherd, Dowling Forest run of W. H. Pettett and W. J. T. Clarke	May 1844	Cannon, 1990, pp. 143-4.
James Saunders	South of Geelong, near Torquay	28 Sept. 1844	Cannon, 1990, p. 148.

Kiernan's servant, neighbour of Allen	Moonlight Head	Feb. 1845	Blair to La Trobe, 1 Mar. 1845, VPRS 19, both in file 45/1721.
William Brown	In the 'New Country' over the South Australian border	1 July 1845	Blair to La Trobe, 31 July 1845, with enclosures, VPRS 19, 45/1391 in file 45/1721.
James Conroy	Cape Otway District	July 1846	Fels, 1988, p. 280, footnote 64; Osburne, p. 194; Cannon, 1990, p. 147.
Lang and Elms' shepherd	Near Mt Napier	Before 7 Oct. 1947	Watton to Robinson, 7 Oct. 1847, VPRS 11, Unit 9.

Appendix 3

Aborigines killed by Europeans

Number	Sex	Names	By Whom/Where	Date	Source
Unknown			Convincing Ground near Portland	Before 27 Oct. 1835	Presland, 1980, pp. 2–3.
10			In retaliation for the murder of Franks and his servant	Before 16 Aug. 1836	John Montague to Col Sec. reporting a rumour, Cannon, 1982, pp. 41–2.
2			George Russell's on the Leigh	c. Nov. 1837	Bride, p. 148.
1			Hugh Murray's station	1837 or 1838	Bride, p. 104.
1	M		Edward Henty's outstation	June 1838	Deposition of Henty taken by Fyans, Cannon, 1983, pp. 631–2.

1	M	Thomas Learmonth's station (died from own action trying to escape capture)	June 1838	Cannon, 1982, p. 290.
1	M	Caught at Learmonth's drowns in a waterhole because of the weight of chains on his body.	July 1838	Cannon, 1982, p. 309.
1	M	John Henty's station	c. Oct. 1838	Deposition of Smead, Cannon, 1983, p. 633.
2	M	Winters' station	c. Oct. 1838	Deposition taken by Fyans, Cannon, 1983, pp. 635–7.
1	boy	Charles Corrigan at Winters'	Nov. 1838	Depositions taken by Fyans, Cannon, 1983, pp. 635–7; Fyans to La Trobe, VPRS 19, 41/2046.
2 (maybe up to 6-8)		Allan's station on the Geelong Road	Early 1839	Sievwright to Robinson, 2 Apr. 1839, Add 86, DL.
2 (maybe same case as above)		Bowerman's station N.N.W. of Geelong	Apr. 1839	Cannon, 1983, pp. 641–3

			Date	Source
5		Winters'	Oct. 1839	La Trobe to Col Sec., 7 Oct. 1840, Aborigines (Australian Colonies), *BPP*, 1844, pp. 136–7.
1	M	by Slyod Jun. near Lake Colac	Nov. 1839	Sievwright to La Trobe, 13 Nov. 1839, VPRS 11, Unit 6, Item 280 (see enclosure).
1	M	Synnot at Corio	Dec. 1839	Robinson to La Trobe, 21 Dec. 1839, enclosing letter from Sievwright, VPRS 10, Unit 2.
35–40		Frederick Taylor's station		Black, Journal, p. 54. Sievwright to La Trobe, 13 Nov. 1839, VPRS 11, Unit 6; Rev. Orton's Journal, vol. 2, p. 144.
1	Wool.an.wang	Shot by Blood, servant of J. Henty	Early 1840	Deposition taken by Sievwright, 21 Mar. 1840, VPRS 21.
2		F. Henty's station	*c.* Mar. 1840	Sievwright to Robinson, 14 Apr. 1840, VPRS 21.

Number	Sex	Name	Details	Date	Source
1	M	Lanky Bill	Shot by George MacNamara, hutkeeper to F. Henty	Mar. 1840	Deposition of Frank Henty, 13 Apr. 1840, VPRS 21.
Number varies: Robertson 51 men; Aborigines claimed 41; James Whyte, not less than 30			Whyte brothers	8 or 9 Mar. 1840	Croke's opinion, 17 June 1840, VPRS 21; Robinson Papers, vol. 57, p. 55.
1	M	Boljo Jaik	Near Mr Hamilton's station, Colac area		Croke to Robinson, 23 Mar. 1841, VPRS 21.
Likely that some were killed			Whyte's second collision	1 Apr. 1840	Croke's opinion, 18 June 1840, VPRS 21; Robinson Papers, vol. 57, p. 55
3 or 4			In retaliation for death of Codd	c. 19 May 1840	J. H. Wedge, Aborigines (Australian Colonies), BPP, 1844, p. 125.

Place/Event	Date	Casualties		Authority
Aylward and two other settlers	June 1840	Several and a great many wounded 5		Sievwright to Croke, 21 Oct. 1840, VPRS 21. Number of five given in official list of Aborigines killed in the Port Phillip District, 1836–44, NSWLC *V & P*, 1844, vol. 1, pp. 718–19; Robinson Papers, vol. 57, p. 55.
Wedge's station at the Grange—3 different collisions	Aug, Sept. 1840	10	1W 9M	Sievwright to Croke, 17 Oct. 1840, VPRS 21. Figure of 10 given in official list of Aborigines killed 1836–1844, NSWLC *V & P*, 1844, vol. 1, pp. 718–19; Robinson Papers, vol. 57, pp. 55–6.
Glenelg River area— after Gibson's shepherd murdered	1841	At least 2		Bride, pp. 163–4. McCulloch says the Aboriginal taken escaped, Aborigines (Australian Colonies), *BPP*, 1844, p. 190.

'Fearful loss of life'			On Dergholm and Roseneath in the Glenelg River area after Gibson and Bell left leaving overseers in charge		Bride, p. 164.
3	2W 1M	Mary, Kitty, Picaninny Jemmy	Men at an outstation in the valley of Cor.roit at W. J. Pubrick's station	June 1841	Presland, 1980, pp. 42, 43, 48.
8	3M 4W 1 child	Tolort Bokar.car.reep Marn.der.re.min Loo.he.chur.ning Joeing.joeing.burmin Cor.roit.leek Yango.larri	Allegedly by Thomas Connell at one of Henty's stations. Seven names given to Winter, eight to Sievwright	Before 3 June 1841	Presland, 1980, pp. 44–5; Sievwright to Robinson, 15 Jan. 1842, enclosed in VPRS 19, 42/2330. Claimed as alleged deaths of 15 or 17 Aborigines in Robinson Papers, vol. 57, p. 56.
1	W	Nar.rer.burnin (an old woman belonging to Cartcarip)	By Tom at J. Henty's outstation	Before 26 June 1841	Presland, 1980, p. 74.
2	M		Savage and Dance at Nangeela on the Glenelg River.	June/July 1841	Statement of R. Savage, 14 Jan. 1842, Aborigines (Australian Colonies), *BPP*, 1844, p. 191.

2	2W	Yang.ar.re.min or Crip.be.ar.rer.min Mip.bur.nin	Bill, Hall's cook		Presland, 1980, pp. 112–13.
3	2M 1W	Wob.bur.rer.min Wot.te.co.er.rer.min In.bo.ter	Horatio Wills	Before 23 July 1841	Presland, 1980, p. 109.
7 (Francis admitted 5)		Kome.bone.ar.re.min Poit.chun.dar.rer.min Jare.jow.wel Nar.toeng.ar.ra.min Cow.quin.in.ur.nin Croeng.en.oke Wet.tone.ar.ra.min	Shot by John Francis	Before 25 July 1841	Presland, 1980, pp. 112, 125–7; Robinson Papers, vol. 57, p. 57.
2	1W 1M		John Collicott, a shepherd, at Wills's station.	Before 25 July 1841	Presland, 1980, pp. 110, 113.
3	1W 1M	Good Morning Bill, a woman, and one girl (Por.ring.ur.nin Cow.ar.re.min Win.now.are.rer.min)	Tarenbe or Tanabe, a shepherd at Kirk's	Before 25 July 1841	Presland, 1980, pp. 109, 113, 123, 132.
2		Car.der.neen Pul.let.puc.coren.	Shot by Gibb Junior	Before 25 July 1841	Presland, 1980, pp. 113.

2	2W	Wills, Kirk and Rutter	Before 29 July 1841	Presland, 1980, p. 123.
1	1M	Sandford George Bolden, settler on the Hopkins, tried for murder but aquitted	27 Oct. 1841	Croke, 28 Nov. 1847, VPRS 10, Unit 8; Queen v. Bolden, VPRS 30, box 185, Criminal Trial Briefs 1841, 1842.
1	Boy	Jimmy	Desailly's station on the Glenelg—accidentally shot	Jan. 1842	Blair to La Trobe, 22 Feb. 1842, VPRS 19, 42/438.
2	M	Shot by John Williams	Before Mar. 1842	Quarterly report of Parker, Mar. to May 31, 1842, Archival estray, Add 90, DL.
5	4W 1M (child)	Wooi-gouing Neal Sowchee Canayer Wonigoniber, wounded woman who later died Male child, no name	At station of Osbrey and Smith, Caramut	23 Feb. 1842	*Portland Mercury and Normanby Advertiser*, 7 Sept. 1842; Aborigines (Australian Colonies) *BPP*, 1844, pp. 218–19.
1	M	Jackey	Foster Fyans at Eumeralla station, Jupiter captured	Mar. 1842	Fyans to La Trobe, 26 Dec. 1842, Aborigines (Australian Colonies), *BPP*, 1844, p. 259.

1	M	Doctor	Foster Fyans at Eumeralla station, captured Cocknose	Mar. 1842	Fyans to La Trobe, 26 Dec. 1842, Aborigines (Australian Colonies), *BPP*, 1844, p. 259; Fyans to La Trobe, VPRS 19, 42/929.
9	5M 4W		Settlers after murder of McKenzie and his man	Mar. 1842	Robinson Papers, vol. 57, p. 46.
3 shot several wounded			Hunter's men at Eumeralla station	*c.* 18 July 1842	Hunter to La Trobe, 1 Sept. 1842, Aborigines (Australian Colonies), *BPP*, 1844, p. 234
1	M		Winter's station	Aug. 1842	Blair to La Trobe, 5 Sept. 1842, Aborigines (Australian Colonies), *BPP*, 1844, p. 235.
1	M		Webster and Farie	*c.* 16 Sept. 1842	French to La Trobe, 13 Oct. 1842, MS10053.

No.		Name	Location	Date	Reference
9	3M 3W 3 children		Dr Kilgour's station Port Fairy area—poisoned	End 1842	Watton to Robinson, 10 Dec. 1842, Aborigines (Australian Colonies), *BPP*, 1844, p. 296.
1	M	Babngarnin	At Robert Whitehead's by his shepherd	8 Feb. 1843	Return of Aborigines at Kolore for Feb. 1843, VPRS 12, Unit 4, Item 17; Clark, 1988, p. 83.
1	M	Big Fred	Near 'Picanini Water Holes'	Apr. 1843	*Portland Mercury and Normanby Advertiser*, 19 Apr. 1843.
1	boy		Ritchie's station near Port Fairy	Aug. 1843	Watton to Robinson, 11 Aug. 1843. VPRS 11, Unit 9.
Some			Area of Grange		French to La Trobe, 10 Sept. 1843, MS 10053.

17–20 (8?)	Native Police following Aborigines who had attacked Purbrick's 'Koroite' station	Aug. 1843	*Port Phillip Gazette*, 26 Aug. 1843; Daybook Native Police 16 Nov. 1846; Thomas, Report 1 Sept.–1 Dec. 1843. All quoted in Christie, 1979, p. 75. Dana provides a different story. The incident concerned Dwyer's sheep. He doesn't say how many were killed but implies that no more than twelve was possible, Dana to La Trobe, 12 Jan. 1844, enclosed in La Trobe to Col Sec., 24 Jan. 1844, 44/882, LA 32. His report stated four were killed and one (possibly more) wounded, Fels, 1988, p. 145.
9 or 10	Native police and Mr Edgar—Fitzroy River area	Early Sept. 1843	Dana to La Trobe, 6 Sept. 1843, Archival Estray, Add 86, DL.

Description	Date	Source	Number
Native police—near Mt Eckersley	mid-Sept. 1843	La Trobe to Col Sec., 18 June 1846, Governor's Despatches, vol. 52, July-December 1846, A1241 ML.	2 and 1 wounded
Collision with Mr Ricketts and others	Nov. 1843	Official list of Aborigines killed 1836–1844, NSWLC V & P, 1844, vol. 1, pp. 718–19; Cannon, 1990, p. 122.	6
Dana and Native Police at Dowling Forest run of Pettett and Clarke	Jan. 1844	Cannon, 1990, p. 143.	1
Native and Border Police at north of Pyrenees	May 1844	Cannon, 1990, pp. 149-50.	1
George Fairburn		French to the Crown Prosecutor, 7 Sept. 1945, MS 10053.	Some

Number		Date	Event	Source
Some		2 July 1845	John Oliver and neighbours after William Brown murdered by Aborigines in the 'New County' over the South Australian border	Blair to La Trobe, 31 July 1845, with enclosures including statement by Oliver, VPRS 19, 45/1391 in file 45/1721.
At least 3 killed and many others wounded		July 1845	Dana and the Native Police hunting Aborigines who had attacked the station of Baillie and Hamilton near Mt Arapiles	Dana to La Trobe, July 1845, VPRS 19, 45/1379 in file 46/89.
9	M, W, C	July 1846	Cape Otway area by William Roadknight and others looking for the murderers of James Conroy	Cannon, 1990, p. 147.
1	child	12 Sept. 1846	Mr Cunningham near Yambuk	Annie Maria Dawbin, Diary, 12 Sept. 1846.
2			Mt Napier	Report for 1846, VPRS 4399, Unit 1.

2		Party seeking retaliation for the murder of Lang and Elms shepherd		Watton to Robinson, 7 Oct. 1847 enclosing a deposition, VPRS 11, Unit 9.
1	M	John Stokel near Horsham	Oct. 1847	Thomas to Robinson, 16 Dec. 1847, VPRS 11, Unit 9; VPRS 30, Box 6, 1-43-19.
1	W	Mr Ralston's (accidental)	Sept. 1849	Watton to Robinson, 5 Sept. 1849, VPRS 11, Unit 9.

Abbreviations

AH	*Aboriginal History*
AIAS	Australian Institute of Aboriginal Studies
AJCP	Australian Joint Copying Project
BPP	*British Parliamentary Papers*
Col Sec.	Colonial Secretary
CSIL	Colonial Secretary In Letters
DL	Dixson Library, Sydney
LA35	New South Wales Legislative Council Records, Parliamentary Archives, Sydney
LaT SLV	La Trobe Collection, State Library of Victoria
ML	Mitchell Library, Sydney
MUP	Melbourne University Press
NSWLC *V&P*	New South Wales Legislative Council *Votes and Proceedings*
NSWA	Archives Authority of New South Wales
SUP	Sydney University Press
VHM	*Victorian Historical Magazine*
VPRS	Victorian Public Records Series

Notes

Introduction

[1] In using the word 'chief' I have relied on the evidence of either James Dawson or George Augustus Robinson. The word has generally been placed in inverted commas to indicate this and my awareness that there has been debate on whether there were chiefs in Aboriginal society. In recent times the existence of tribal chiefs and clan-heads has been supported by Diane Barwick, well known for her research and deep knowledge of the anthropology and history of Aboriginal societies in south-eastern Australia. See 'Mapping the Past', *Aboriginal History*, vol. 8, part 2, 1984, pp. 107-8.

1: 'and the shout was given that the black fellows were coming'

[1] M. Cannon (ed.), *Aborigines and Protectors 1838–1839*, pp. 453-4.

[2] La Trobe to Col Sec., 21 Nov. 1840, Aborigines (Australian Colonies), *BPP*, 1844, p. 139.

[3] G. A. Robinson, Annual Report for 1845, Robinson Papers, vol. 61, part 2, pp. 29-30.

[4] G. Presland (ed.), *Journals of G. A. Robinson March-May 1841*, 1977, p. 43.

[5] Ibid., p. 85.

[6] Ibid., p. 94.

[7] N. J. B. Plomley (ed.), *Friendly Mission*, p. 202.

[8] Presland, 1977, p. 44; G. Presland (ed.), *Journals of G. A. Robinson May to August 1841*, 1980, p. 110.

[9] Presland, 1980, p. 98.

[10] Ibid., p. 95.

[11] J. Dawson, *Australian Aborigines*, p. 74.

[12] Presland, 1980, p. 10.

[13] Ibid., p. 13.

[14] Ibid., p. 17.

[15] Ibid., p. 19.

[16] Ibid., p. 15.

[17] Ibid., p. 32.

[18] Ibid., pp. 20-1.

[19] Presland, 1977, pp. 91-2.

[20] Robinson, Journals, Robinson Papers, vol. 17, part 4, pp. 26-32.

[21] Presland, 1980, p. 19.

[22] Ibid., p. 134.

[23] Robinson to La Trobe, 7 Oct. 1842, Appendix C, Robinson Papers, vol. 65, part 6, p. 57.

[24] Presland, 1977, p. 93.

[25] Ibid., pp. 57, 70.

[26] Ibid., p. 88.

[27] Robinson to his wife, undated, Robinson Papers, vol. 63, part 2, pp. 177-8.

[28] A. S. Kenyon, 'Aboriginal Protectorate of Port Phillip', pp. 138-71.

[29] La Trobe to Col Sec., 15 Nov. 1842, 42/1579 enclosed in 4/7153 file 41/8829, Col Sec. Special Bundles.

[30] Ibid., summary attached.

[31] Cannon, p. 725.

[32] I. McBryde, 'Ethnohistory in an Australian context', p. 144.

[33] Ibid., p. 144.

[34] V. Rae-Ellis, *Black Robinson*, p. xvii.

[35] Ibid., p. xix.

2: 'the savage tribes are ... intermingled with us'

[1] J. Dawson, *Australian Aborigines*, p. 105.

[2] Ibid., pp. 105-6.

[3] G. Presland (ed.), *Journals of G. A. Robinson March-May 1841*, 1977, p. 88.

[4] G. Presland (ed.), *Journals of G. A. Robinson May to August 1841*, 1980, p. 19.

[5] Presland, 1977, p. 61.

[6] J. Morgan, *The Life and Adventures of William Buckley*, p. 21.

[7] Presland, 1980, p. 73.

[8] H. Anderson, *The Flowers of the Field: a history of Ripon Shire*, p. 199.

[9] Morgan, p. 21.

[10] Presland, 1980, p. 71.

[11] C. Gray, *Western Victoria in the Forties*, p. 10. Other cases are mentioned in Anderson, p. 183, Presland, 1980, p. 73, and Rev. Joseph Orton, Letters 1826-1841, p. 91.

[12] Presland, 1980, p. 138.

[13] G. T. Lloyd, *Thirty-three years in Tasmania and Victoria*, p. 457.

[14] J. R. Carroll, *Harpoons to Harvest*, p. 66.

[15] La Trobe to Col Sec., 7 Oct. 1840, Aborigines (Australian Colonies), *BPP*, 1844, p. 138.

[16] J. M. Powell, 'Squatting expansion in Victoria, 1834-1860', foreword in R. Spreadborough and H. Anderson (eds.), *Victorian Squatters*, p. x.

[17] Ibid., p. xxii.

[18] T. F. Bride (ed.), *Letters from Victorian Pioneers*, pp. 120, 125.

[19] Ibid., p. 124.

[20] Ibid., p. 94.

[21] Powell, p. xxvii.

[22] N. F. Learmonth, *The Portland Bay Settlement*, p. 223.

[23] G. A. Robinson to La Trobe, 30 December 1843, Report with abstract of journey, Aborigines (Australian Colonies), *BPP*, 1844, p. 282.

[24] La Trobe, 26 March 1842, to the Gentlemen signing a Representation without date ..., Aborigines (Australian Colonies), *BPP*, 1844, p. 214.

[25] Presland, 1977, p. 61.

[26] Presland, 1980, p. 134.

27 Bride, p. 289.

28 Robinson to La Trobe, 10 Sept. 1841, VPRS 19, 41/1369 enclosed in 41/1374.

29 P. L. Brown (ed.), *Memoirs recorded at Geelong, Victoria, Australia by Captain Foster Fyans*, 1986, p. 238.

30 Bride, p. 42.

31 M. Kiddle, *Men of Yesterday*, p. 44.

32 Bride, pp. 138, 335.

33 P. L. Brown (ed.), *The Clyde Company Papers*, vol. II, 1836-40, 1952, p. 193.

34 Gray, p. 6; P. L. Brown (ed.), *The Narrative of George Russell of Golf Hill with Russellania and Selected Papers*, 1935, p. 186.

35 Gisborne to La Trobe, 29 Dec. 1839, VPRS 25, vol. 1.

36 Gisborne to La Trobe, 29 Dec. 1839 enclosed in La Trobe to Col Sec., 4 Jan. 1840, CSIL 1840, 4/2510.

37 Brown, 1986, p. 241.

38 Ibid., p. 242.

39 J. Hawdon, *Joseph Hawdon's tandem journal 1839*, unpaged.

40 M. Cannon (ed.), *Aborigines and Protectors 1838-1839*, 1983, pp. 635-6.

41 Memorandum of Robert Hamilton, Appendix II in Anderson, p. 221.

42 Ibid., p. 217; M. Cannon (ed.), *Beginnings of Permanent Government*, p. 250; Bride, p. 177.

43 Hawdon, 23 July 1839.

44 Bride, p. 42.

45 Dawson, p. 3.

46 Sievwright to Robinson, Report of Proceedings 1 Dec. 1841 to 28 Feb. 1842, Archival estrays, CSIL/11, DL.

47 Sievwright to Robinson, Proceedings from 1 Dec. 1840 to 28 Feb. 1841, Archival estrays, CSIL/11, DL.

48 Bride, pp. 94-5, 98.

49 Quoted in Kiddle, p. 122.

50 Bride, p. 167.

51 Presland, 1977, p. 66.

52 Ibid., p. 73.

53 Kiddle, p. 89.

54 Anderson, p. 200.

55 Bride, pp. 161-2, and Presland, 1980, p. 37, for example.

56 A. M. Dawbin née Baxter, Diary, 21 May 1846.

57 Ibid., 14 June 1846.

58 Ibid., 27 June 1845.

59 Ibid., 28 March 1847.

60 Ibid., 13 May 1849.

61 Ibid., 6 April 1847.

62 Ibid., 16 May 1847.

63 Quoted in Kiddle, p. 52.

64 N. Black, Journal of the first few months spent in Australia—30 Sept. 1839 to 8 May 1840, p. 33.

65 Kiddle, p. 51.

66 Ibid., p. 52.

67 NSWLC *V & P*, 1844, vol. 1, pp. 718-19.

68 Presland, 1977, p. 100.

69 Robinson to La Trobe, 30 Aug. 1841, Aborigines (Australian Colonies), *BPP*, 1844, p. 132.

70 Presland, 1977, pp. 65, 68.

71 J. Kirby, *Old Times in the Bush of Australia*, p. 119.

72 Cannon, 1983, pp. 652-3; Presland, 1977, p. 100; Presland, 1980, p. 101.

73 Presland, 1980, pp. 77, 142, and Presland, 1977, p. 100.

[74] Bride, p. 124.

[75] Presland, 1977, p. 99.

[76] *Portland Guardian*, 17 Feb. 1844.

[77] P. Selby to her sister, Mary, 1 Mar. 1845.

[78] A. S. Kenyon, 'Aboriginal Protectorate of Port Phillip', p. 149; also Presland, 1977, p. 83.

[79] Gisborne to La Trobe, 29 Dec. 1839, VPRS 25, vol. 1.

[80] S. P. Winter to Editor, *Hamilton Spectator*, 25 June 1873.

[81] Presland, 1980, pp. 28, 73.

[82] Presland, 1980, pp. 62, 39 (Presland's word 'sent' has been corrected to 'send'), 129-30, 145.

[83] R. Boldrewood, *Old Melbourne Memories*, p. 63.

[84] Robinson, Vocabulary Book, 1841, Robinson Papers, vol. 65, part 2, pp. 118-19, 123-4, and pp. 125-32.

[85] Report of the Select Committee of the Legislative Council on the Aborigines, *Votes and Proceedings of the Legislative Council of Victoria*, Session 1858-59, Appendices, Replies to a Circular Letter, pp. 27-8.

[86] Presland, 1980, p. 108.

[87] Robinson to La Trobe, 7 Oct. 1842, pp. 107, 109, Museum of Victoria.

3: 'that's my country belonging to me'

[1] Edward Stone Parker, Quarterly Journal from 1 Dec. 1841 to 28 Feb. 1842, Archival estrays, CSIL/11, DL.

[2] Parker, Quarterly Journal from March to 31 May 1841, Archival estrays, Add 89, DL.

[3] Charles Wightman Sievwright, Report of Proceedings 1 June to 31 Aug. 1841, Archival estrays, Add 86, DL.

[4] Gary Presland (ed.), *Journals of G. A. Robinson May to August 1841*, 1980, pp. 12-13.

[5] Thomas to Robinson, 11 March 1842, transmitting report for the three months to March and summary of the last six months, Archival estrays, CSIL/11, DL.

[6] Sievwight, Proceedings from 1 Dec. 1840 to 28 Feb. 1841, Archival estrays, Add 86; Proceedings from 1 Dec. 1841 to 28 Feb. 1842, Archival estrays, CSIL/11, both DL.

[7] Sievwright, Precis of Quarterly Reports dated 1 Dec. 1841 and 1 March 1842, Archival estrays, CSIL/11, DL.

[8] Lourandos has called them bands, pointing out that in doing so he is using the term strictly to describe the land-using unit because Robinson 'did not distinguish between the economic (land-using) and the ritual (land- owning) aspects of these groups'. In calling the same local groups clans, I am following Diane Barwick who in 'Mapping the Past', *Aboriginal History*, vol. 8, part 2, 1984, p. 106, states clan names for Central Victoria 'were distinguished by the suffixes *-balluk* or *-bulluk* meaning a number of people and *-(w)illam* (in northern dialects *-yellam*) meaning dwelling place; *-bulluk* or *-goondeet* and *-lar* were the Jajowrong equivalents'. Robinson on his 1841 expedition through the Western District found the suffix used of groups in the Mt William and Mt Cole area to be *-bulluk* which agrees with Barwick's statement. Throughout most of the District, however, the term used was *conedeet* not *bulluk* (see Appendix I: List of Tribes). This term was still used by Dawson's Aboriginal informants some thirty years later and was spelt by him *kurndit*. Another word used by the Aborigines of the Port Fairy area instead of conedeet was *beer*. Thus they described the Yarrer conedeet as Yarrer beer and the Nillan conedeet as the Nillan beer (see Robinson's Journal, 22 March 1842). The point is that the different words are used for the same kind of group for which Barwick has used the word clan. See also Ian Clark, 'The Spatial Organisation of the Chap Wurring—a Preliminary Analysis', in *Australia Felix: The Chap Wurrung and Major Mitchell*, p. 18.

[9] Barwick, p. 106.

[10] R. M. Berndt (ed.), *Aboriginal Sites, Rights and Resource Development*, p. 4.

[11] Barwick, p. 106.

[12] James Dawson, *Australian Aborigines*, p.lxxix.

13 Ibid., p. viii.

14 E. S. Parker, *The Aborigines of Australia A Lecture delivered in the Mechanics' Hall, Melbourne, before the John Knox Young Men's Association, on Wednesday, May 10th, 1854,* 1854, p. 12.

15 Gary Presland (ed.), *Journals of G. A. Robinson March to May 1841,* 1977, p. 23; Presland, 1980, p. 102.

16 Dawson, p. 7.

17 Ibid., pp. 41, 44.

18 Jacky White to Mr Winters, 7 Jan. 1877, Winter Cooke Papers, Item 2.3.19.

19 Parker, 1854, p. 13.

20 Presland, 1980, pp. 65-6, and A. S. Kenyon, 'Aboriginal Protectorate of Port Phillip: Report of an Expedition to the Aboriginal Tribes of the Western Interior by the Chief Protector, George Augustus Robinson', *VHM,* 1928, p. 152.

21 For example, while at Lake Keilambete listing the names of the Aborigines, he was given the terms in.do.cer.deen and un.do.cer.deen and putting them after each name he wrote down, he noted 'In oc er deer Bullerburer and the native to the north—Unocerdeen the natives to the north of Kilambeet'. A little later he made a note 'in do cer deen is Jarcoort [,] means wild blackfellow'. But he was still confused. On 15 April he wrote, 'Kone ne wurt a tribe S.W. of Kilambete, in oc er deen—a term for a wild black or a term of reproach I don't know which'. Later at the Grange (now Hamilton) he was still trying to make sense of these terms. He wrote, 'Wondeline—all those natives to the North of Mt Shadwell. All south are inocerdeen or undocerdeen'. All one can be sure of is that Robinson was confused and that Mt Shadwell was possibly a boundary line. Robinson, Vocabulary Books, Robinson Papers, vol. 65, part 2, pp. 25-6; part 2, p. 108; part 2, section 77-104; part 2, p. 185.

22 For discussion of the criteria for recognizing a tribe see R. M. W. Dixon, *The Languages of Australia,* pp. 30-1; N. B. Tindale, *Aboriginal Tribes of Australia,* pp. 30-8.

23 Sievwright, Precis of Quarterly Report dated 1 June and 1 Sep. 1841, Archival estrays, Add 86, DL.

24 Dawson, pp. 1-2.

25 Dixon, pp. 33-8, 241, 259-60; Dawson p. 2.

26 Lorimer Fison and A. W. Howitt, *Kamilaroi and Kurnai,* p. 275; Stähle to Howitt, 6 May 1880, Howitt Papers, Box 5, Folder 2, Museum of Victoria; A. W. Howitt, *The Native Tribes of South-East Australia,* p. 69 and map facing p. 72; N. B. Tindale, *Aboriginal Tribes of Australia.*

27 Dawson, pp. lxxxii, 3.

28 Ibid., p. 75.

29 Ibid., p. 78.

30 R. Brough Smyth, *The Aborigines of Victoria,* vol. 2, p. 186. For confirmation of the meaning of Warrnambool, see J. Critchett (ed.), *Richard Bennett's Early Days of Port Fairy,* p. 43.

31 Quoted by Manning Clark, 'Child of his Age—Mitchell in Perspective', in *Australia Felix: The Chap Wurrung and Major Mitchell,* p. 91.

32 M. Cannon (ed.), *The Aborigines of Port Phillip 1835-1839,* p. 279.

33 T. F. Bride (ed.), *Letters from Victorian Pioneers,* p. 103.

34 Cannon, p. 283.

35 Incident related by Tuckfield to William Thomas, 9 Sept. 1843, Notebook in R. B. Smyth Papers, Box 1176/6, Folder B, MS 8781, LaT SLV.

36 Rev. Joseph Orton, Journal, 14 May 1839, MSS 942, ML.

37 VPRS 11, Unit 11, Item 708.

4: *'when the white people come the water goes away'*

1 Diary of J. Ritchie for Nov. and Dec. 1841, 'Tour of the West', pp. 21-3.

2 M. Kiddle, *Men of Yesterday,* p. 3.

[3] H. Anderson, *The Flowers of the Field*, pp. 182-3.

[4] W. B. Withers, *The History of Ballarat*, p. 12.

[5] Ritchie, p. 20.

[6] T. F. Bride (ed.), *Letters from Victorian Pioneers*, pp. 329, 336.

[7] Ritchie, p. 40.

[8] P. L. Brown (ed.), *The Clyde Company Papers*, vol. II, 1836-40, 1952, p. 249.

[9] G. Presland (ed.), *Journals of G. A. Robinson March-May 1841*, 1977, pp. 57-61.

[10] Presland, 1977, pp. 86-92; J. Dawson, *Australian Aborigines*, p. 20; B. Gott, 'Grampians and District Aboriginal Plants' in *Australia Felix: The Chap Wurrung and Major Mitchell*, 1987, p. 41.

[11] G. Presland (ed.), *Journals of G. A. Robinson May to August*, 1841, 1980, pp. 98-100.

[12] Ritchie, pp. 5-7.

[13] P. L. Brown (ed.), *Memoirs recorded at Geelong, Victoria, Australia by Captain Foster Fyans*, 1986, p. 227.

[14] Bride, p. 96.

[15] Ibid., p. 271.

[16] Presland, 1977, pp. 49, 53, 62, 65.

[17] Presland, 1980, pp. 91-2.

[18] H. Lourandos, 'Swamp Managers of Southwestern Victoria', in D. J. Mulvaney and J. P. White (eds), *Australians to 1788*, pp. 306-7.

[19] P. J. F. Coutts, R. K. Frank and P. J. Hughes, 'Aboriginal Engineers of the Western District', *Records of the Victoria Archaeological Survey*, No. 7.

[20] E. Williams, Wet Underfoot? Earth Mound Sites and the Recent Prehistory of Southwestern Victoria, 1985, pp. 293-5, and 'Complex hunter-gatherers: A view from Australia', 1987, p. 314. Mound sites are clearly marked on the Archaeological Sites map in J. S. Duncan's *Atlas of Victoria*, pp. 68-9.

[21] Dawson, p. 103.

[22] P. J. F. Coutts, 'An Archaeological perspective of the Western District, Victoria', in J. Sherwood, J. Critchett and K. O'Toole (eds), *Settlement of the Western District. From Prehistoric Times to the Present*, 1985, p. 31.

[23] Presland, 1977, pp. 48-9.

[24] Presland, 1980, p. 92.

[25] Coutts, 1985, pp. 32, 38; Williams, 1987, pp. 317-19.

[26] Gisborne to La Trobe, 29 Dec. 1839, enclosed in La Trobe to Col Sec., 4 Jan. 1840, CSIL 1840, 4/2510, 40/543, NSWA.

[27] Presland, 1977, pp. 86, 87.

[28] Aborigines (Australian Colonies), *BPP*, 1844, p. 240.

[29] E. R. Trangmar, *The Aborigines of Far Western Victoria*, p. 87.

[30] Presland, 1977, pp. 91, 117; Presland, 1980, p. 87, and Fig. 34; Presland, 1977, pp. 32, 36.

[31] Robinson to La Trobe, 9 Apr. 1842, Archival estrays, Add 77, DL.

[32] M. H. Douglas and L. O'Brien (eds), *The Natural History of Western Victoria*, p. 93.

[33] C. Griffith, *The Present State and Prospects of the Port Phillip District of New South Wales*, pp. 152-3. See also Rev. Joseph Orton, Journal, vol. 1, pp. 262-3.

[34] Dawson, p. 10.

[35] Francis to Dawson, 14 Apr. 1868, Dawson Scrapbook, p. 35a.

[36] Dawson, p. 11.

[37] Quoted by Williams, 1987, pp. 310-11.

[38] Report of the Select Committee of the Legislative Council on the Aborigines, *Votes and Proceedings of the Legislative Council of Victoria*, Session 1858-59, p. 61.

[39] R. B. Smyth, *The Aborigines of Victoria*, vol. 1, pp. 123-6.

[40] Ibid., p. 127; N. J. B. Plomley (ed.), *Friendly Mission*, p. 144.

[41] Presland, 1977, p. 73; Dawson, 1981, pp. 10-11, 20; Gott, p. 41.

[42] Smyth, vol. 1, p. 128.

[43] Bride, p. 84; M. Kiddle, 'Vandiemonian Colonists in Port Phillip, 1834-50', p. 40.

44 Bride, p. 182.
45 Ritchie, pp. 2-7, 8.
46 P. McCann, Reminiscences, unpublished manuscript, pp. 19-23.
47 Presland, 1977, pp. 71-3.
48 Ritchie, p. 14.
49 R. B. Smyth, *The Aborigines of Victoria*, p. 186.
50 Papers of William Thomas, 1832-1902, MSS 214, Box/vol. 22, p. 537. See also notebook of William Thomas, Papers of R. Brough Smyth, MS 8781, Box 1176/7, Folder (c).
51 Aborigines Superior Race, Papers of William Thomas, MSS 214, Box 24, Item 11.
52 1858-59 Select Committee Report, p. 86.
53 Presland, 1977, p. 64.
54 Ibid., p. 85.
55 Ibid., p. 63.
56 Niel Black, Journal of the first few months spent in Australia—30 Sept. 1839 to 8 May 1840, p. 65.
57 S. P. Winter to Editor, *Hamilton Spectator*, 25 June 1873.
58 Dawson, p. 11; Griffith, pp. 152-3; 1858-59 Select Committee Report, p. 86.

5: *'and yet it is singular so few are met'*

1 D. J. Mulvaney and J. P. White (eds), *Australians to 1788*, p. 115.
2 J. Dawson, *Australian Aborigines*, pp. 3-4.
3 Select Committee on the Condition of the Aborigines, NSWLC *V&P*, 1845, p. 43.
4 Ibid., p. 45.
5 Harry Lourandos, Forces of Change: Aboriginal Technology and Population in South Western Victoria, 1980, p. 20.
6 Mulvaney and White (eds), p. 116.
7 N. J. Butlin, *Our Original Aggression*, pp. xi, 11-16.
8 Mulvaney and White, p. 117.
9 Butlin, p. xi.
10 G. A. Robinson, Vocabulary Book, Robinson Papers, vol. 65, part 2, p. 122.
11 Ibid., p. 124.
12 G. Presland (ed.), *Journals of G. A. Robinson May to August 1841*, 1980, p. 116.
13 E. Williams, Wet Underfoot? Earth Mound Sites and the Recent Prehistory of Southwestern Victoria, p. 88.
14 Robinson to La Trobe, 7 Oct. 1842, p. 254, Museum of Victoria.
15 Robinson, Annual Report for 1845, Robinson Papers, vol. 61, part 2, p. 32.
16 Lourandos, 1980, Table 4.1, pp. 52a, 52b.
17 Ibid., pp. 80-93.
18 E. S. Parker, Appendix 1 of Special Report, 5 Jan. 1843, Aborigines (Australian Colonies), *BPP*, 1844, pp. 312-16.
19 Aborigines (Australian Colonies), *BPP*, 1844, p. 182.
20 Robinson, Journal, 22 March 1842, Robinson Papers, vol. 18, part 4.
21 J. Bonwick, *Western Victoria: Its Geography, Geology and Social Condition*, p. 85.
22 A. S. Kenyon, 'Aboriginal Protectorate of Port Phillip', p. 143.
23 Lourandos, p. 93.
24 Robinson, Annual Report for 1845.
25 Lourandos, p. 93.
26 I counted the number of individuals in 'tribes' west of the Hopkins as shown in Appendix 1. The area was calculated using a map of the Portland Bay District.
27 Butlin, pp. 126-7; Williams, p. 88.
28 Butlin, p. 25.
29 J. Campbell, 'Smallpox in Aboriginal Australia, the early 1830s', pp. 351, 347.
30 C. W. Sievwright, Report for Mar. to Sept. 1839, Archival estrays, Add 86, DL.

[31] Dawson, pp. 60-1.

[32] Ibid., p. 61.

[33] Dawson Scrapbook, MS 11514, LaT SLV.

[34] J. C. Hamilton, *Pioneering Days in Western Victoria*, p. 100.

[35] Ibid., p. 102.

[36] E. R. Trangmar, *The Aborigines of Far Western Victoria*, p. 8.

[37] W. B. Withers, *The History of Ballarat*, p. 10.

[38] Campbell, p. 349.

[39] Robinson, Vocabulary Book, vol. 65, part 2, p. 40.

[40] Campbell, p. 351.

[41] Robinson, vol. 65, part 2, p. 109; Kenyon, p. 150.

[42] Ibid., p. 150; Robinson, vol. 65, part 2, p. 165.

[43] Kenyon, p. 150.

[44] Robinson to La Trobe, 7 Oct. 1842, pp. 76-7; see also Presland, 1980, pp. 2-3, 6.

[45] Campbell, p. 351.

[46] Robinson, vol. 65, part 2, pp. 118-19, 164.

[47] Robinson, Journal, 11 May 1841, vol. 17, part 4; G. Presland (ed.), *Journals of G. A. Robinson March-May 1841*, 1977, p. 92.

[48] Robinson, Journal, vol. 17, part 4, pp. 133-52.

[49] D. Barwick, 'Changes in the Aboriginal Population of Victoria 1863-1966', p. 302.

[50] Campbell, p. 356.

[51] Robinson, Journal, vol. 17, part 4, pp. 71-4. More easily accessible in Presland, 1977, p. 102 though some words have been incorrectly copied.

[52] Robinson, Journal, vol. 17, part 4, pp. 133-52.

[53] Presland, 1977, p. 48.

[54] Robinson, Vocabulary Book, vol. 65, part 2, pp. 160-2.

[55] Campbell, p. 349; J. Morgan, *The Life and Adventures of Wiliam Buckley*, pp. x, 68.

[56] Butlin, pp. 25, 64, 27, 36, 84.

[57] Ibid., pp. 138-9.

[58] Ibid., pp. 140-1.

[59] Robinson, Journal, vol. 17, part 4, pp. 26-32.

[60] Robinson, Vocabulary Book, vol. 65, part 2, pp. 105-83. The two exceptions are the Bunyap conedeet (11 males, 10 females) and the Nillan conedeet (26 males, 20 females).

[61] Morgan, p. 111.

[62] Hamilton, pp. 15, 100.

[63] Presland, 1980, pp. 194, 169, 201, 199, 70, 65, 66.

[64] Robinson, Vocabulary Book, vol. 65, part 2, pp. 25-60, 127-9, 121-2, 118-19.

[65] Robinson, Vocabulary Book, vol. 65, part 2, pp. 105-83. The eight clans are the Yarrer conedeet, Teer-rar conedeet, Wane conedeet burn, Moper er conedeet, Mane conedeet, Yowen conedeet, Buller Buller cote conedeet, Nillan conedeet.

[66] Kenyon, pp. 143, 145.

[67] E. S. Parker, *The Aborigines of Australia*, 1854, p. 18.

[68] J. Kirby, *Old Times in the Bush of Australia*, p. 78.

[69] Parker, 1854, p. 18.

[70] Parker, Appendix 1 of Special Report, 5 Jan. 1843, Aborigines (Australian Colonies), *BPP*, 1844, pp. 312-16.

[71] Parker, Aborigines (Australian Colonies), *BPP*, 1844, p. 174.

[72] Butlin, p. 138.

[73] D. Barwick, 'Mapping the past: an atlas of Victorian clans 1835-1904', p. 109.

[74] Butlin, p. 40.

[75] H. Lourandos, 'Aboriginal Spatial Organisation and Population: South Western Victoria Reconsidered', pp. 216, 219; H. Lourandos, Forces of Change: Aboriginal Technology and Population in South Western Victoria, p. 91.

[76] Kenyon, p. 149.

[77] Robinson to his wife, Robinson Papers, vol. 63, part 2, pp. 177-8.

6: 'every gentleman's establishment . . . has been molested by the natives'

[1] M. Cannon (ed.), *The Aborigines of Port Phillip 1835-1839*, 1982 p. 306.

[2] M. Cannon (ed.), *Beginnings of Permanent Government*, 1981, p. 220.

[3] Aborigines (Australian Colonies), *BPP*, 1844, p. 51.

[4] Ibid., p. 89.

[5] *Portland Mercury*, 2 Nov. 1842, mentioned an attack on Mt Shadwell station just east of the Hopkins. Farie and Webster had both been attacked; A. French to La Trobe, 13 Oct. 1842, MS 10053, LaT SLV.

[6] W. L. Warner, *A Black Civilisation*, pp. 18-19.

[7] R. M. and C. H. Berndt, *The World of the First Australians*, pp. 334, 356.

[8] J. Dawson, *Australian Aborigines*, pp. 68-9.

[9] R. M. and C. H. Berndt, p. 358.

[10] Warner, pp. 155, 162, 166-7.

[11] P. Corris, *Aborigines and Europeans in Western Victoria*, p. 68.

[12] Aborigines (Australian Colonies), *BPP*, 1844, p. 127.

[13] M. Cannon (ed.), *Aborigines and Protectors 1838-1839*, 1983, p. 633.

[14] T. F. Bride (ed.), *Letters from Victorian Pioneers*, p. 88, footnote 2.

[15] Aborigines (Australian Colonies), *BPP*, 1844, p. 142; M. F. Christie, *Aborigines in Colonial Victoria 1835-86*, p. 69, quoting *Port Phillip Herald*, 6 Sept. 1842.

[16] Bride, p. 165; J. G. Robertson to La Trobe, 26 Sept. 1853, MS 10749 LaT SLV; G. Presland (ed.), *Journals of G. A. Robinson May to August 1841*, 1980, p. 28.

[17] Presland, 1980, p. 28; Cannon, 1982, p. 290.

[18] Cannon, 1982, pp. 40-1, 279-80; Cannon, 1983, p. 633; Presland, 1980, pp. 28, 113; Cannon, 1982, pp. 48, 50.

[19] *Portland Guardian*, 16 Sept. 1843, p. 3.

[20] Aborigines (Australian Colonies), *BPP*, 1844, pp. 187-8.

[21] H. Anderson, *The Flowers of the Field*, p. 191.

[22] Bride, p. 148.

[23] H. E. P. Dana to La Trobe, 6 Sept. 1843, Archival estrays, Add 86, DL.

[24] Joseph Wheatley, evidence sworn before Blair, 6 Nov. 1844, VPRS 19, 45/2106 in 46/892.

[25] W. Thomas to Robinson, 29 July 1845, Robinson Papers, vol. 57, p. 46.

[26] Presland, 1980, p. 139.

[27] Aborigines (Australian Colonies), *BPP*, 1844, pp. 181, 184, 189; Presland, 1980, p. 64; Blair to La Trobe, 19 July 1842, VPRS 19, 42/1451 enclosed in 42/1892.

[28] S. Winter to the Editor, *Hamilton Spectator*, 25 June 1873.

[29] G. Presland (ed.), *Journals of G. A. Robinson March-May 1841*, 1977, p. 46.

[30] Ibid., pp. 58, 20-1; Presland, 1980, pp. 75, 140.

[31] Presland, 1977, p. 22.

[32] P. L. Brown, *The Clyde Company Papers*, vol. II, 1952, pp. 89-90.

[33] F. Henty, Diary, 29, 30 Dec. 1837.

[34] Presland, 1980, p. 55.

[35] Ibid., p. 78.

[36] Ibid., p. 94.

[37] Presland, 1977, p. 59; I. D. Clark, *The Port Phillip Journals of George Augustus Robinson: 8 March-7 April 1842 and 18 March-29 April 1843*, p. 22.

[38] C. W. Sievwright to Robinson, 25 Apr. 1842, enclosed in Robinson to La Trobe, VPRS 19, 42/1104; Clark, p. 83.

[39] Bride, p. 94.

[40] Brown, 1952, p. 250.

[41] Bride, p. 163.

[42] N. Black to Gladstone, 5 Aug. 1840, Letterbook; T. Learmonth's shepherd, deposition

dated 27 July 1838, VPRS 109, p. 14; A. French to La Trobe, 25 Sept. 1842, MS 10053.

43 Aborigines (Australian Colonies), *BPP*, 1844, p. 142.

44 Presland, 1980, p. 44.

45 M. Bassett, *The Hentys*, p. 405.

46 Brown, 1952, p. 306.

47 Presland, 1977, p. 28.

48 Presland, 1980, pp. 113, 126-7.

49 Presland, 1980, pp. 141, 143, 150; Presland, 1977, p. 63.

50 Presland, 1980, p. 74.

51 Ibid., p. 42.

52 S. Winter to Editor, *Hamilton Spectator*, 25 June 1873; Bride, pp. 334-5; Aborigines (Australian Colonies), *BPP*, 1844, p. 282.

53 Robinson to La Trobe, 7 October 1842, Report, Appendix C.

54 *Portland Mercury*, 31 Aug. 1842, p. 3.

55 Blair to La Trobe, 29 Jan. 1842, VPRS 19.

56 Sievwright, Report for period 1 Mar. to 31 May 1842, Archival estrays, CSIL/11, DL.

57 R. Broome, *Aboriginal Australians*, p. 44.

58 Robinson, Journal, 18 May 1842, Robinson Papers, vol. 18, part 4; McGregor to French, 8 Aug. 1842, VPRS 19, enclosed in 42/1822.

59 *Portland Mercury*, 9 Nov. 1842; C. P. Cooke to the Editor, *Portland Mercury*, 16 Nov. 1842, W. Learmonth to Blair, 16 May 1845, enclosed in Blair to La Trobe, 19 May 1845, VPRS 19, 45/875 in file 45/1721.

60 Dr Bernard to Fyans, 16 Feb. 1842, VPRS 19, 42/333, enclosure in 42/2364.

61 Robinson, Journal, 1842, Robinson Papers, vol. 18, part 4, p. 73.

62 Aborigines (Australian Colonies), *BPP*, 1844, pp. 213-14; names added from the *Geelong Advertiser*, 4 April 1842.

63 F. Fyans, Itinerary for Mar., Apr., May, June 1842, VPRS 19, 42/178, enclosed in 42/2364.

64 Aborigines (Australian Colonies), *BPP*, 1844, p. 210; Robinson to La Trobe, 10 Aug. 1842, VPRS 19, 42/1492; Robinson, 1842 Journal, Robinson Papers, vol. 18, part 4, p. 100; Robinson 1841 Journal, vol. 17, part 4, pp. 34, 71, 96; Robinson, 1842 Journal, vol. 18, 22 Mar. 1842; Presland, 1980, p. 171, Robinson, Vocab. Book, vol. 65, part 2, pp. 132-4; Blair to La Trobe, 13 May 1842, VPRS 19, 42/917.

65 Fyans to Gipps, 1 July 1842, VPRS 19, enclosure in 42/1492.

66 Blair to La Trobe, 29 Jan. 1842, VPRS 19; 23 Mar. 1842, VPRS 19, 42/751.

67 Blair to La Trobe, 17 May 1842, VPRS 19, 42/924; 16 May 1842, VPRS 19, 42/926.

68 *Portland Guardian*, 23 Sept. 1843; Jacky Jacky is mentioned in deposition of Joseph Ellis, NCR 42, The Queen v. Cold Morning for Highway Robbery, Portland, July 1842, VPRS 30, Box 185, Criminal Trial Briefs 1841, 1842.

69 Aborigines (Australian Colonies), *BPP*, 1844, pp. 233-4.

70 Fyans, Itineraries Sept. to Dec. 1842, NSWA; French to La Trobe, 28 July 1842, MS 10053.

71 Blair to La Trobe, 5 Sept. 1842, VPRS 19, 42/1886.

72 H. Wills to La Trobe, Mar. 1842, VPRS 19, 42/626; Blair to La Trobe, 29 Jan. 1842, VPRS 19; 7 Mar. 1842, VPRS 19, 42/753; Bride, p. 279.

73 *Portland Mercury*, 31 August 1842.

74 Aborigines (Australian Colonies), *BPP*, 1844, p. 234.

75 Blair to La Trobe, 10 Dec. 1842, VPRS 19, 42/2329.

76 *Portland Mercury*, 7 Dec. 1842, p. 3.

77 Aborigines (Australian Colonies), *BPP*, 1844, pp. 259-60; *Portland Mercury*, 1 Feb. 1843.

78 Blair to La Trobe, 1 Oct. 1845, VPRS 19, 45/1721; 15 Sept. 1845, VPRS 19, 45/1627 in 45/1721.

79 R. Boldrewood, *Old Melbourne Memories*, pp. 45, 50, 55-7.

80 N. F. Learmonth, *The Portland Bay Settlement*, p. 244.

81 M. Cannon, *Who Killed the Koories?*, p. 191.

82 M. Clarke, *'Big' Clarke*, p. 91.
83 *Portland Mercury*, 7 Sept. 1842.
84 *Portland Mercury*, 31 Aug. 1842, 7 Sept. 1842; Fyans to Gipps, 1 July 1842, enclosed in VPRS 19, 42/1492; Fyans to La Trobe, 14 Apr. 1840, VPRS 19, 42/931; Dana to La Trobe, 26 May 1845, VPRS 19, 45/919, enclosed in 46/892.
85 Hunter to La Trobe, 1 Sept. 1842, Aborigines (Australian Colonies), *BPP*, 1844, p. 234; Blair to La Trobe, 10 Dec. 1842, VPRS 19, 42/2329.
86 French to La Trobe, 8 Aug. 1842, MS 10053; Hunter to La Trobe, 1 Sept. 1842, Aborigines (Australian Colonies), *BPP*, 1844, p. 234.
87 French to La Trobe, 9 Aug. 1842, MS 10053.
88 Aborigines (Australian Colonies), *BPP*, 1844, p. 233.
89 *Portland Mercury*, 3 Aug. 1842, p. 2.
90 French to La Trobe, 28 July 1842, MS 10053; Blair to La Trobe, 5 Sept. 1842, VPRS 19, 42/1886; Ricketts to the Editor, *Portland Mercury*, 19 Oct. 1842.
91 Dana to La Trobe, July 1845, VPRS 19, 45/1379 in 46/89; Bride, p. 279; Whitehead, deposition dated 15 Sept. 1840, in La Trobe to Col Sec. 22 Oct. 1840, CSIL 1840, Port Phillip, 4/2511; Aborigines (Australian Colonies), *BPP*, 1844, p. 187; A. M. Dawbin, Diary, 25 Apr. 1846, MS Q181, DL.
92 Statement by Campbell, 22 July 1845, enclosed in Campbell to La Trobe, 22 July 1845, VPRS 19, 45/1370.
93 Robinson to La Trobe, 5 Jan. 1850, forwarding Thomas's half-yearly report for the year ending Dec. 1849, VPRS 10, p. 11, 1850/55.

7:   'more than thirty are said to have been thus laid low'

1 J. Power to Lord John Russell, 30 Nov. 1840, Aborigines (Australian Colonies), *BPP*, 1844, p. 123.
2 La Trobe to Col Sec., 7 Oct. 1840, Aborigines, (Australian Colonies), *BPP*, 1844, p. 138.
3 P. L. Brown (ed.), *The Clyde Company Papers*, vol. II, 1952, pp. 318-19.
4 *Port Phillip Gazette*, 25 July 1840.
5 La Trobe to Col Sec., 7 Oct. 1840, and 21 Nov. 1840, Aborigines (Australian Colonies), *BPP*, 1844, p. 139.
6 La Trobe to Col Sec., 21 Nov, 1840, Aborigines (Australian Colonies), *BPP*, 1844, pp. 139-40.
7 La Trobe to Col Sec., 24 July 1840, Aborigines (Australian Colonies), *BPP*, 1844, p. 133.
8 Port Fairy Settlers to La Trobe, 23 Apr. 1842, CSIL Port Phillip 1843, Part 1, 4/2626, in accumulated file 42/2847, NSWA.
9 W. Campbell to La Trobe, 22 July 1845, VPRS 19, 45/1370.
10 La Trobe to Bench of Magistrates, 8 July 1845, 45/857, VPRS 16, vol. 5, p. 189.
11 Campbell to La Trobe, 22 July 1845.
12 *Portland Mercury*, 1 Feb. 1843.
13 M. Cannon (ed.), *Aborigines and Protectors 1838-1839*, 1983, pp. 628-37.
14 J. Blair to La Trobe, 15 Jan. 1842, Aborigines (Australian Colonies), *BPP*, 1844, p. 184.
15 La Trobe to Col Sec., 1 Feb. 1842, Aborigines (Australian Colonies), *BPP*, 1844, p. 183.
16 La Trobe to Blair, 12 Feb. 1842, Aborigines (Australian Colonies), *BPP*, 1844, p. 204.
17 La Trobe to the Gentlemen signing a Representation without date ..., 26 Mar. 1842, Aborigines (Australian Colonies), *BPP*, 1844, pp. 214-15.
18 Settlers to La Trobe, 23 Apr. 1842, CSIL Port Phillip 1842, Part 1, 4/2626, in accumulated file 42/2847, NSWA.
19 La Trobe to the Gentlemen signing a communication dated the 23 Apr. entrusted to the care of Messrs. Claud Farie and Niel Black, 15 July 1842, Archival estrays, Add 87, DL.
20 Col Sec. to La Trobe, 17 June 1842, CSIL Port Phillip 1843, Part 1, 4/2626, in accumulated file 42/2847.

[21] N. Black and others to La Trobe, 1 Aug. 1842, VPRS 19, 42/1418; copy enclosed in CSIL Port Phillip 1843, Part 1, 4/2626, in accumulated file 42/2847.

[22] *Portland Mercury*, 7 Sept. 1842.

[23] M. Kiddle, *Men of Yesterday*, pp. 3-13, 120-31; P. Corris, *Aborigines and Europeans in Western Victoria*, p. 157; R. H. W. Reece, *Aborigines and Colonists*, p. 23; M. Christie, *Aborigines in Colonial Victoria 1835-86*, pp. 61-3; R. Broome, *Aboriginal Australians*, pp. 36-45.

[24] M. Cannon (ed.), *Beginnings of Permanent Government*, 1981, p. 252.

[25] N. J. B. Plomley (ed.), *Friendly Mission*, p. 279.

[26] Cannon, 1981, pp. 34-5.

[27] Blair to La Trobe, 8 Dec. 1840, VPRS 19, 40/1275.

[28] E. Henty, Portland Journal, 2 Dec. 1834, 24 Jan. 1835.

[29] Ibid., 29 Mar. 1835.

[30] B. Barrett, 'What the 150th Anniversary is all about', pp. 3-9.

[31] G. Presland (ed.), *Journals of G. A. Robinson May to August 1841*, 1980, pp. 2-3.

[32] Barrett, p. 6.

[33] I. D. Clark (ed.), *The Port Phillip Journals of George Augustus Robinson*, p. 22.

[34] See p. 78.

[35] F. Fyans to La Trobe, 20 Sept. 1840, Aborigines (Australian Colonies), *BPP*, 1844, p. 89.

[36] La Trobe to Col Sec., 24 July 1840, Aborigines (Australian Colonies), *BPP*, 1844, p. 134.

[37] Memorial of Proprietors of Land and Stock in the County of Grant to Governor Gipps, 18 Apr. 1840, Aborigines (Australian Colonies), *BPP*, 1844, p. 52.

[38] T. F. Bride (ed.), *Letters from Victorian Pioneers*, p. 167.

[39] A. M. Dawbin, Diaries, MSQ 181, DL.

[40] J. Cox and W. Campbell to La Trobe, 18 June 1845, VPRS 19, 45/1061.

[41] S. Carter, *Reminiscences of the Early Days in the Wimmera*, p. 15.

[42] R. Boldrewood, *Old Melbourne Memories*, p. 57.

[43] La Trobe to Col Sec., 5 November 1840, including the depositions of P. C. Aylward, Mr. Knolles and R. W. Tulloh, CSIL 40/11 571, Port Phillip 1840, 4/2511, NSWA.

[44] A. French to La Trobe, 1 Jan. 1842 and 23 May 1842. Also William Campbell to La Trobe, 22 July 1845, second letter of this date, VPRS 19, 45/1370.

[45] C. W. Sievwright, Proceedings from 1 Dec. 1840 to 28 Feb. 1841, Archival estrays, Add 86, DL.

[46] N. Black to Gladstone, 4 August 1840, Letterbook.

[47] J. Bonwick, *Western Victoria*, pp. 170-1.

[48] For example, Dana to La Trobe, 6 Sept. 1843, Archival estray, Add 86, DL.

[49] Dana, 30 August 1843, included in La Trobe to Col Sec., 24 Jan. 1844, 44/882, LA 35.

[50] M. Cannon (ed.), *The Aborigines of Port Phillip 1835-1839*, 1982, p. 279.

[51] Presland, 1980, p. 55.

[52] Ibid., p. 27.

[53] Cannon, 1982, pp. 41-2, 46-50.

[54] J. H. Wedge to Lord John Russell, 8 Feb. 1841, Aborigines (Australian Colonies), *BPP*, 1844, p. 125.

[55] G. Presland (ed.), *Journals of G. A. Robinson March-May 1841*, 1977, p. 63.

[56] Presland, 1980, p. 27; Bride, pp. 163-4.

[57] A. French to La Trobe, 1 Jan. 1842, MS 10053.

[58] Presland, 1980, p. 123.

[59] Col Sec. to La Trobe, 16 Jan. 1841, VPRS 10, Unit 3, 1841/164; Presland, 1977, p. 21.

[60] W. Thomas to Robinson, 29 July 1845, Robinson Papers, vol. 57, p. 46, ML.

[61] Brown, 1952, p. 90.

[62] N. Black, Journal. p. 56.

[63] Carter, pp. 14-17.

[64] Ibid., p. 15.

[65] Brown, 1952, p. 417.

[66] Black, Journal, p. 41; Black to Gladstone, 31 July 1841, Letterbook.

67 Presland, 1980, p. 60.
68 Brown, 1952, p. 245.
69 Bride, p. 76.
70 Presland, 1980, pp. 44. 49, 55; Presland, 1977, p. 20.
71 J. Ritchie, Diary, p. 35, University of Melbourne Archives.
72 Black, Journal, p. 69.
73 Bride, p. 164.
74 Presland, 1980, pp. 88, 125.
75 Black, Journal, p. 69.
76 La Trobe to Col Sec., 3 Apr. 1840, Aborigines (Australian Colonies), *BPP,* 1844, pp. 136-7; Cannon, 1983, p. 631.
77 C. Wedge to J. H. Wedge, 13 Nov. 1839, Aborigines (Australian Colonies), *BPP,* 1844, pp. 121-2; Bride, p. 88.
78 G. Presland (ed.), *Journals of G. A. Robinson January 1840-March 1840,* 1977, p. 18; Rev. J. Orton, Journal, vol. 2, pp. 143-4, A1715, ML.
79 Black, Journal, p. 54.
80 J. Dawson, *Australian Aborigines,* p. lxxxiii.
81 C. Gray, *Western Victoria in the Forties,* p. 7.
82 Black, Journal. p. 29.
83 Brown, 1952, p. 204.
84 Robinson to La Trobe, 5 Jan. 1850 forwarding Thomas's report for the half year ending December 1849, Appendix B, VPRS 10, Unit 11, 1850/55.
85 Deposition of Officer Jnr, 7 Nov. 1847, VPRS 30, Box 6, Case of John Stokel 1-43-19; M. Cannon, *Who Killed the Koories?,* pp. 192-3.
86 Corris, p. 157.
87 Christie, p. 78.
88 E. Rutledge to M. Hamilton, 31 Jan. 1885, in possession of David Hamilton, Geelong.
89 Quoted in Christie, p. 78.
90 W. Westgarth, *A Report on the Condition, Capabilities and Prospects of the Australian Aborigines,* p. 8.
91 Robinson to La Trobe, 7 October 1842, p. 252, Museum of Victoria.
92 Select Committee on the condition of the Aborigines, NSWLC *V&P,* 1845, p. 45.
93 Fourth Report of the Central Board, p. 13.
94 Robinson to La Trobe, 5 Jan. 1850, forwarding Thomas's half-yearly report ending December 1849, VPRS 10, Unit 11.

8: *'it's too bad to shoot the unfortunates like dogs'*

1 M. Cannon (ed.), *The Aborigines of Port Phillip 1835-1839,* pp. 309-10.
2 Deposition of J. Wheatley, 6 Nov. 1844, VPRS 19, 45/2106 enclosed in 46/892.
3 Ibid.
4 G. Presland (ed), *Journals of G. A. Robinson May to August 1841,* 1980, p. 69.
5 Ibid., pp. 42, 45.
6 *Portland Mercury and Normanby Advertiser,* 7 Dec. 1842.
7 Ibid., 31 Aug. 1842.
8 Ibid., 9 Nov. 1842.
9 Presland, 1980, p. 109.
10 Ibid., pp. 117, 122.
11 H. Reynolds, *Frontier,* p. 14.
12 Presland, 1980, p. 101.
13 Ibid., p. 68.
14 Ibid., p. 74.
15 Ibid., pp. 60-1, 70.
16 Ibid., p. 43.

17 Ibid., p. 48.
18 Ibid., pp. 40-1.
19 Ibid., p. 56.
20 Robinson, Vocabulary Book, Robinson Papers, vol. 65, part 2, p. 227.
21 Presland, 1980, pp. 60, 62.
22 Ibid., p. 74.
23 Ibid., p. 39.
24 M. Cannon (ed.), *Aborigines and Protectors 1838-1839*, p. 633.
25 Presland, 1980, pp. 73, 28.
26 Ibid., p. 43.
27 Ibid., pp. 44, 45.
28 Ibid., p. 74.
29 G. A. Robinson, Journey into the Western Interior, 1845, MS Q648, DL.
30 E. S. Parker, Quarterly report from Mar. to 31 May 1842, Archival estrays, Add 90, DL.
31 Presland, 1980, pp. 108-9.
32 Parker, Quarterly report from March to 31 May 1842, Archival estrays, Add 90, DL.
33 G. Presland (ed.), *Journals of G. A. Robinson March-May 1841*, 1977, p. 27; Presland, 1980, p. 71.
34 Presland, 1980, pp. 105-6, 108.
35 Ibid., pp. 109, 162.
36 J. G. Robertson to La Trobe, 26 Sept. 1853, MS 10749, LaT SLV.
37 T. McCulloch to La Trobe, 21 July 1840, enclosed in La Trobe to Col Sec., 22 Oct. 1840, CSIL 40/11 108, Port Phillip 1840, 4/2511, NSWA.
38 Robertson to La Trobe, 26 Sept. 1853, MS 10749.
39 Presland, 1980, p. 44.
40 N. F. Learmonth, *The Portland Bay Settlement*, p. 230.
41 A. G. L. Shaw and C. M. H. Clark (eds.), *Australian Dictionary of Biography 1788-1850*, vol. 1, p. 297.
42 A. M. Dawbin, Item 7, p. 41; Item 11, p. 158, MS Q181, DL.
43 Ibid., Item 11, p. 171.
44 Ibid., Item 4, p. 10.
45 Ibid., 20 Sept. 1846.
46 W. Hamilton to La Trobe, 5 Aug. 1847, VPRS 19, 47/1503.
47 W. Adeney, Diary, 7 Feb. 1843, MS 8520A, LaT SLV.
48 Ibid., 18 Mar. 1843.
49 W. Adeney, Letters, 26 Feb. 1844, MS 9111, LaT SLV.
50 H. Adeney, Diary, 21-22 Aug. 1855, MS 9110, LaT SLV.

9:   'the Governor would give them plenty flour, tea, sugar and Bulgarrer'

1 M. Cannon, (ed.), *The Aborigines of Port Phillip 1835-1839*, 1982, p. 6.
2 Ibid., p. 8.
3 M. Cannon (ed.), *Aborigines and Protectors 1838-1839*, 1983, p. 378.
4 Cannon, 1983, pp. 385-7.
5 La Trobe to Col Sec., 18 Nov. 1848, Report of the Select Committee on the Aborigines and Protectorate, NSWLC *V & P*, 1849, Appendix, pp. 7-8.
6 Aborigines (Australian Colonies), *BPP*, 1844, p. 87.
7 C. W. Sievwright, Proceedings from 1 Dec. 1840 to 28 Feb. 1841, Archival estrays, Add 86, DL.
8 Ibid.
9 Robinson to La Trobe, 7 Oct. 1842, Museum of Victoria.
10 G. Presland (ed.), *Journals of G. A. Robinson March-May 1841*, 1977, p. 25.

11 Sievwright, Proceedings from 1 Dec. 1841 to 28 Feb. 1842, 42/5708, Archival estrays, CSIL/11, DL.

12 Sievwright, Proceedings from 1 Mar. to 31 May 1842, 42/5708, Archival estrays, CSIL/11, DL.

13 H. E. P. Dana to La Trobe, 22 Nov. 1842, VPRS 19, 42/2153; T. O'Callaghan, Police and other people, pp. 409-20, MS 11682, LaT SLV.

14 Sievwright, Proceedings from 1 Mar. to 31 May 1842, Archival estrays, CSIL/11, DL; Sievwright to Robinson, 11 July 1842, VPRS 11, Unit 6, Item 287.

15 For more detail see J. Critchett, A 'distant field of murder': Portland Bay District Frontiers, 1988, pp. 395-6.

16 Sievwright, Proceedings from 1 Mar. to 31 May 1842, Archival estrays, CSIL/11, DL.

17 Sievwright, Precis of Quarterly Reports dated 1 June and 1 Sept. 1841, Archival estrays, Add 86, DL; Sievwright, Returns of Numbers, VPRS 12, Unit 2, Item 7.

18 Sievwright, Report of Proceedings from 1 June to 31 Aug. 1841, Archival estrays, Add 86, DL.

19 Sievwright to Robinson, 11 July 1842, VPRS 11, Unit 6, Item 287.

20 I. MacFarlane, 1842 The Public Executions at Melbourne, p. 48, quoting a letter from La Trobe, VPRS 16, vol. 3, pp. 60-1.

21 Robinson to La Trobe, Nov. 1847, VPRS 4397, Unit 1, Item 11.

22 P. Corris, Aborigines and Europeans in Western Victoria, p. 97.

23 La Trobe to Col Sec., 18 Nov. 1848, Appendix to the Report of the Select Committee on the Aborigines and the Protectorate, NSWLC V&P, 1849, p. 8.

24 La Trobe to Robinson, 28 Feb. 1842, VPRS 11, Unit 3, Item 104.

25 Watton to Robinson, 5 June 1843, VPRS 11, Unit 9, Item 476.

26 Annual Report for 1846, VPRS 10, Unit 8, 1847/716.

27 Watton to Robinson, 12 June 1846, VPRS 11, Unit 9, Item 515.

28 Sievwright to Robinson, 11 July 1842, VPRS 11, Unit 6, Item 287.

29 Watton to Robinson, 12 June 1846, VPRS 11, Unit 9, Item 515.

30 Watton to Robinson, 4 Oct. 1847, VPRS 11, Unit 9, Item 538.

31 Annual report for Mt Rouse station for 1848, VPRS 4410, Unit 4, Item 123.

32 Watton, Medical reports for Jan., Feb., Mar., Apr. 1843, VPRS 4410, Unit 4, Items 116, 117, 118, 119.

33 Watton, Medical reports, 1 Jan. to 31 June 1844, VPRS 4410, Unit 4, Items 120, 121.

34 Watton, Returns, VPRS 12, Unit 6, Item 26.

35 Report for Mt Rouse station for 1848, VPRS 4410, Unit 4, Item 123.

36 J. Croke to La Trobe, 28 Nov. 1847, VPRS 10, Unit 8, 1847/2379; Sievwright to Col Sec., 8 May 1847, enclosed in Col Sec. to La Trobe, 5 Oct. 1847, VPRS 10, Unit 8, 1847/1864.

37 R. V. Billis and A. S. Kenyon, Pastoral Pioneers of Port Phillip, p. 29.

38 Depositions of S. G. Bolden, S. Bolden, P. Carney, W. Kiernan and Sievwright to Robinson reporting the incident, VPRS 30, Box 185, Criminal Sessions: Port Phillip, Criminal Trial Briefs 1841, 1842, pp. 1-49.

39 MacFarlane, pp. 19-20; Law Intelligence, notes on the case held in the Aboriginal Cultural Heritage Unit, Museum of Victoria; Rev. J. Orton, Journal, vol. 2, p. 180, A1715, ML.

40 Rev. F. Tuckfield to Rev. B. Hurst, 17 Jan. 1840, copied into Tuckfield's Journal, pp. 113-16, MS 11341, LaT SLV.

41 Portland Mercury, 31 Aug. 1842, p. 2.

42 R. Boldrewood, Old Melbourne Memories, p. 121.

43 Presland, 1977, p. 41.

44 Sievwright to the Sec. of State, 8 May 1847, enclosed in Col Sec. to La Trobe, 5 Oct. 1847, VPRS 10, Unit 8, 1847/1864.

45 Portland Mercury, 7 Sept. 1842.

46 Robinson to La Trobe, 1 Mar. 1848, VPRS 10, Unit 9, 1848/553.

47 Presland, 1977, p. 32.

[48] G. Presland (ed.), *Journals of G. A. Robinson May to August 1841*, 1980, pp. 134-5.

[49] In fact during 1843 a decision was made in Sydney to leave much of the Protectorate correspondence unopened. See 1858-59 Select Committee Report, Minutes of Evidence, p. 23.

[50] Dr Watton, Daily returns 1842-3, VPRS 12, Unit 3, Item 12; Unit 4, Item 17.

[51] Watton, Return of Medical and Surgical Cases at Mt Rouse 1843, VPRS 4410, Unit 4, Items 116, 117, 118, 119.

[52] J. Dawson, *Australian Aborigines*, Introductory Note.

[53] For details see Critchett, 1988, Appendix 5.

[54] Dawson, p. 2.

[55] J. Critchett, *Our Land Till We Die*, Appendix III.

[56] Presland, 1980, p. 184.

10: *'making them feel that they shall not murder and plunder with impunity'*

[1] W. Thomas, 29 Apr. 1845, statement sworn in the Supreme Court during the trial of Koort Kirrup, VPRS 19, in accumulated file 46/892.

[2] La Trobe to Col Sec., 22 Aug. 1842, Aborigines (Australian Colonies), *BPP*, 1844, p. 231.

[3] *Portland Mercury*, 14 Sept. 1842, p. 3.

[4] La Trobe to Col Sec., 29 Mar. 1842, Aborigines (Australian Colonies), *BPP*, 1844, p. 213.

[5] P. L. Brown (ed.), *Memoirs recorded at Geelong, Victoria, Australia by Captain Foster Fyans*, p. 260.

[6] Ibid., p. 248.

[7] J. Blair, 22 Mar. to La Trobe, VPRS 19, 42/751.

[8] Robinson, Journal, 18 May 1842, Robinson Papers, vol. 18, part 4.

[9] J. Croke to La Trobe, 14 Mar. 1842, VPRS 19, 45/527.

[10] Croke to Plunkett, the Attorney-General, 29 Sept. 1840, VPRS 21.

[11] Notes following Croke to La Trobe, 11 July 1842, in which Croke notifies La Trobe that the Aborigines have been discharged from custody, VPRS 21.

[12] Ibid.

[13] F. Fyans to Gipps, 1 July 1842, VPRS 19, enclosure in 42/1492.

[14] I. MacFarlane (comp.), *1842 The Public Executions at Melbourne*, Documents 32 and 33.

[15] C. W. Sievwright to Croke, 1 Aug. 1842, VPRS 21.

[16] MacFarlane, p. 51.

[17] Ibid., p. 52.

[18] Ibid., p. 53.

[19] Judge Willis to La Trobe, 19 July 1842, VPRS 19, 42/1388 included in 42/1545.

[20] Sievwright to Robinson, enclosed with Robinson to La Trobe, 6 June 1842, VPRS 19, 42/1091.

[21] La Trobe to Gipps, 26 July 1842, MS 7662, LaT SLV.

[22] MacFarlane, p. 54.

[23] Ibid., p. 56.

[24] Thomas to Robinson, 8 Dec. 1842, Journal of Proceedings for Sept., Oct., Nov., LA 35.

[25] Thomas to Robinson, Sept. 1845, Quarterly Report; *Portland Mercury*, 23 Nov. 1842.

[26] Thomas to Robinson, 8 Dec. 1842, Journal of Proceedings for Sept., Oct., Nov., LA 35; Sievwright to Robinson, 25 Apr. 1842, enclosed in Robinson to La Trobe, VPRS 19, 42/1104.

[27] La Trobe to Col Sec., 13 Sept. 1842, Aborigines (Australian Colonies), *BPP*, 1844, p. 233.

[28] Fyans to La Trobe, 9 Oct., 1842, Aborigines (Australian Colonies), *BPP*, 1844, p. 235.

[29] H. E. P. Dana to La Trobe, 16 June 1843, VPRS 19, 43/1038.

[30] T. O'Callaghan, Police and other People, Dana's diary, entry for 4 Oct. 1842, MS 11682, LaT SLV.

31 Dana to La Trobe, 22 Nov. 1842, VPRS 19, 42/2153.
32 O'Callaghan, pp. 409-20, MS 11682.
33 Dana to La Trobe, 16 June 1843, VPRS 19, 43/1038; Dana to La Trobe, 24 July 1843, VPRS 19, 43/200.
34 La Trobe to Col Sec., 14 Sept. 1843, 43/1339, Archival estrays, List 30, CSIL/11, DL; Fyans to La Trobe, 13 Mar. 1843, VPRS 19, 43/472.
35 M. H. Fels, *Good Men and True*, p. 138.
36 Ibid., p. 145.
37 *Port Phillip Gazette*, 26 Aug. 1843; Dana to La Trobe, 20 Aug. 1843, enclosed in La Trobe to Col Sec., 14 Sept. 1843, 43/1339, Archival estrays, CSIL/11, DL; *Portland Guardian*, 26 Aug. 1843.
38 Fels, p. 148.
39 *Portland Guardian*, 28 Oct. 1843.
40 Fels, p. 143.
41 *Portland Guardian*, 30 Sept. 1843; 4 Nov. 1843.
42 Fels, p. 140.
43 Ibid., pp. 150-1.
44 Dana to La Trobe, 16 Sept. 1844, VPRS 19, 44/1706, paraphrased in Fels, p. 150.
45 Dana to La Trobe, 26 May 1845, VPRS 19, 45/919 enclosed in 46/892.
46 La Trobe to Col Sec., 4 July 1846, 4/7153, file 42/8829, Col Sec. Special Bundles, NSWA.
47 Dana to La Trobe, 25 Aug. 1845, VPRS 19, 45/1489.
48 S. McGregor to Dana, 23 May 1847, enclosed in Dana to La Trobe, 5 June 1847, VPRS 19, 46/1040.
49 Dunmore Journal, 28 Mar. 1843, 24 Aug. 1843, 4 Jan. 1844; R. Boldrewood, *Old Melbourne Memories*, p. 58.
50 W. Campbell to La Trobe, 22 July 1845, VPRS 19, 45/1370.
51 W. Rutledge to Dana, 25 May 1847, enclosed in Dana to La Trobe, 5 June 1847, VPRS 19, 47/1040; McGregor to Dana, 23 May 1847, enclosed in Dana to La Trobe, 5 June 1847, VPRS 19, 47/1040.
52 McGregor to Dana, 23 May 1847, enclosed in Dana to La Trobe, 5 June 1847, VPRS 19, 47/1040.
53 Thomas Papers, Criminal Depositions, Box 23, Item 6, Set 214, ML.
54 Ibid.
55 Thomas to Robinson, 11 Nov. 1848, VPRS 11, Unit 11, Item 708; Thomas, Half-yearly report to 30 June 1849, 4/2872, NSWA.
56 Boldrewood, pp. 67-71.
57 A. M. Dawbin, Diary, 20 Sept. 1846, MS Q181, DL.
58 Quoted in P. Corris, *Aborigines and Europeans in Western Victoria*, p. 115.
59 Rutledge to Dana, 25 May 1847, enclosed in Dana to La Trobe, 5 June 1847, VPRS 19, 47/1040.
60 Fels, p. 151.
61 P. Chauncy, Diary, 27-28 Feb. 1848, MS Q11, DL.

11: 'if ever anything is done with the natives, it will be by their good example'

1 C. J. La Trobe to Col Sec., 18 Nov. 1848, Report of the Select Committee on the Aborigines and Protectorate, NSWLC *V&P*, 1849, Appendix p. 5.
2 Ibid., p. 4.
3 M. Cannon (ed)., *The Aborigines of Port Phillip 1835-1839*, pp. 78-9.
4 Rev. J. Orton, Journal, vol. 1, p. 171, A1714, ML.
5 Ibid., p. 222.
6 Cannon; p. 123, Orton, vol. 1, p. 165.

7 Orton, pp. 260-1.
8 Ibid., pp. 120-1.
9 Ibid.
10 Ibid., pp. 278-87.
11 Cannon, pp. 98, 137.
12 Ibid., p. 136.
13 Ibid., p. 137.
14 Ibid., p. 112.
15 Tuckfield's Journal, pp. 319-22, MS 11341, LaT SLV.
16 E. S. Parker, Report for the year 1844, Col Sec. Special Bundles, 42/8829, NSWA.
17 Cannon, pp. 121-2, 139, 149.
18 Ibid., p. 149.
19 Tuckfield's Journal, pp. 319-22.
20 Cannon, pp. 148-9, 141-2, 144.
21 Cannon, p. 149; Tuckfield's Journal, 24 May 1841.
22 Tuckfield's Journal, 10 May 1841.
23 Ibid., 29 May 1841.
24 Ibid., 13 June 1841, 16 Sept. 1841, 30 May 1842.
25 Tuckfield to La Trobe, 17 Mar. 1843, enclosed in La Trobe to Col Sec., 28 Apr. 1843, CSIL 42/3434, LA35.
26 Tuckfield to La Trobe, VPRS 19, 46/1217; P. Corris, *Aborigines and Europeans in Western Victoria*, pp. 76-7.
27 J. Dawson, *Australian Aborigines*, p. 22.
28 Cannon, p. 142.
29 Tuckfield's Journal, 11 Jan. 1840.
30 Hurst to La Trobe, 21 Oct. 1842, Aborigines (Australian Colonies), *BPP*, 1844, p. 243; Corris, p. 75; Tuckfield's Journal, 12 Jan. 1840.
31 Cannon, p. 146.
32 Tuckfield's Journal, 11 May, 22 June 1841.
33 Ibid., 16 Jan., 18 Feb. 1840.
34 Ibid., 18 Dec. 1839.
35 Ibid., pp. 113-16.
36 Ibid., 12 Dec. 1840.
37 La Trobe to Col Sec., 13 Aug. 1846, CSIL, 46/6070 in 47/9943, Port Phillip, 1847, 4/2784, NSWA.
38 Tuckfield to La Trobe, Report for year ending 30 June 1846, enclosed with La Trobe to Col Sec., 13 Aug. 1846, CSIL, Port Phillip, 1847, 4/2784.
39 Tuckfield to La Trobe, Report for the year ending 30 June 1845, enclosed in La Trobe to Col Sec., 1 Oct. 1845, CSIL, 45/7288 enclosed in 47/9943, Port Phillip, 1847, 4/2748; Tuckfield to La Trobe, Report for the year ending 30 June 1846, enclosed in La Trobe to Col Sec., 13 Aug. 1846, NSWA.
40 Orton's Journal, vol. 2, pp. 123-4.
41 Ibid., vol. 2, p. 159.
42 Ibid., p. 196.
43 Cannon, p. 113.

12: 'instances of violent collision . . . are now rarely heard of'

1 E. Willmot, *Pemulwuy: The Rainbow Warrior*, p. 14.
2 N. F. Learmonth, *The Portland Bay Settlement*, pp. 232-3.
3 T. F. Bride (ed.), *Letters from Victorian Pioneers*, p. 88.
4 Ibid., pp. 148, 329, 334; J. Ritchie, Diary, 28 Dec. 1841; H. Anderson, *The Flowers of the Field*, p. 217; M. Cannon (ed.), *Aborigines and Protectors 1838-1839*, pp. 631-2;

G. Presland (ed.), *Journals of G. A. Robinson March-May 1841*, 1977, p. 19; N. Black to Gladstone, 5 Aug. 1840, Letterbook; La Trobe to Col Sec., 2 Mar. 1842, Aborigines (Australian Colonies), *BPP*, 1844, p. 208; *Portland Mercury*, 31 Aug. 1842, p. 2; Ibid., 24 Apr. 1844, quoted in P. Corris, *Aborigines and Europeans in Western Victoria*, p. 101.

[5] Bride, p. 290.

[6] Ibid., pp. 290, 297.

[7] *Portland Mercury*, 31 Aug. 1842, p. 2.

[8] Bride, p. 178.

[9] M. Cannon, *Who Killed the Koories?*, 1990, p. 145.

[10] Bride, p. 279.

[11] *Portland Mercury*, 31 Aug. 1842, p. 2.

[12] C. J. Griffiths, Diary, pp. 165, 234, MS 9393, LaT SLV.

[13] Bride, p. 334.

[14] La Trobe to Col Sec., 18 Nov. 1848, Appendix to the Report of the Select Committee on the Aborigines and the Protectorate, NSWLC *V & P*, 1849.

[15] Fyans, July 1845 census of stations and stock, Microfilm No. 2748, NSWA.

[16] Dr Watton, Annual Report for the year 1846, VPRS 4410, Unit 4, Item 122.

[17] Rev. Tuckfield to La Trobe, 13 Jan. 1844, enclosed in La Trobe to Col Sec., 15 Feb. 1844, 44/1469, CSIL, Port Phillip 1844, 4/2665 NSWA; C. W. Sievwright, Proceedings from 1 June to 31 Aug. 1841, Archival estrays, Add 86, DL; Tuckfield, Journal, pp. 113-16, MS 11341, LaT SLV.

[18] Documents regarding outrages on the blacks by Koort Kirrup, Portland Bay, 1849, MS 3194, LaT SLV.

[19] Cannon, 1990, p. 192.

Appendix 1

[1] La Trobe to Col Sec., 15 Nov, 1842, enclosing Robinson to La Trobe, 7 Oct. 1842, Col Sec. Special Bundles 4/7153, file 42/8829, NSWA. A copy of the Appendix is also to be found in the Robinson Papers, vol. 65, part 6, pp. 51-4, A7086 ML.

[2] Two copies of the source were referred to—(i) NSW Governor's Despatches to the Secretary of State for the Colonies, vol. 51, April-June 1846, ML 1240, CY reel, p. 683; (ii) Robinson's Annual Report for 1845, Governor's Despatches, Despatch No. 75, AJCP Microfilm No. 371.

[3] The copy that went to Sydney is so faded that it is illegible. The missing Public Records copy has been located in the Museum of Victoria but with the Appendices missing.

[4] A. S. Kenyon, 'Aboriginal Protectorate of Port Phillip: Report of an Expedition to the Aboriginal Tribes of the Western Interior by the Chief Protector, George Augustus Robinson', *VHM* 12, 1928, pp. 138-71.

[5] Robinson to La Trobe, 30 July 1845, VPRS 19, 45/1328 enclosed in 46/892.

Bibliography

OFFICIAL PRINTED SOURCES

New South Wales

Legislative Council, Votes and Proceedings

1844   New South Wales. (Aborigines.) Return to 'an address made by Sir Thomas Mitchell . . . for numbers of Whites and Aborigines killed in conflicts in the Southern District since settlement of that part of the Colony'. Vol. 1, pp. 717-19.

1845   Report from the Select Committee on the Conditions of the Aborigines, with Appendix, Minutes of Evidence and Replies to a Circular Letter. Vol. 2, pp. 117-358.

1846   Replies to a Circular Letter addressed to the clergy of all denominations by order of the Select Committee on the condition of the Aborigines.

1849   Report from the Select Committee on the Aborigines and Protectorate, with Appendix, Minutes of Evidence and Replies to a Circular Letter. Vol. 2, pp. 417-75.

Victoria

Legislative Council, Votes and Proceedings

1858-59 Report of the Select Committee of the Legislative Council on the Aborigines, together with the Proceedings of Committee, Minutes of Evidence and Appendices. D8.

Parliamentary Papers
1861-69   First to the Sixth Annual Reports of the Central Board
          appointed ... to watch over the Interests of the Aborigines,
          presented to both Houses of Parliament.
1871-90   Seventh to the Twenty-sixth Annual Reports of the Board for
          the Protection of Aborigines, presented to both Houses of
          Parliament.

Britain

House of Commons, Sessional Paper
1844   Aborigines (Australian Colonies). Return to an Address ...
          Copies or Extracts from the Despatches of the Governors of
          the Australian Colonies, with the Reports of the Protectors of
          Aborigines, and any other Correspondence to illustrate the
          Condition of the Aboriginal Population of the said Colonies
          ... vol. 34, no. 627.

OFFICIAL MANUSCRIPT SOURCES

Public Record Office of Victoria

Aboriginal Protectorate Records
VPRS 10   Registered Inward Correspondence to the Superintendent
            Port Phillip District relating to Aboriginal Affairs.
VPRS 11   Unregistered Inward Correspondence to the Chief
            Protector of Aborigines.
VPRS 12   Aboriginal Protectorate Returns.
VPRS 2893   Registered Inwards Correspondence to the Superin-
            tendent Port Phillip District from W. Thomas and E. S.
            Parker.
VPRS 2895   Chief Protector of Aborigines Outward Letter Book.
VPRS 2896   Registered Inward Correspondence to the Surveyor-
            General, Board of Land and Works.
VPRS 2897   Registered Inward Correspondence to the Land Branch,
            Superintendent of Port Phillip District relating to Abor-
            iginal Stations.
VPRS 4397   Unregistered Correspondence relating to the suspension
            of Charles Sievwright from the Office of Assistant
            Protector of Aborigines, Western District.
VPRS 4399   Duplicate Annual Reports of the Chief Protector of
            Aborigines.
VPRS 4410   Aboriginal Protectorate Weekly, Monthly, Quarterly and
            Annual Reports and Journals.

VPRS 4414   Copy (abridged) of the Chief Protector's journal of an expedition to the Eastern Interior.

Other Series
VPRS 4   Police Magistrate Port Phillip District Inward Registered Correspondence, 1836-39.
VPRS 19   Superintendent Port Phillip District Registered Inwards Correspondence, 1839-51.
VPRS 21   Crown Law Office—Inward Unregistered Correspondence.
VPRS 30   Crown Solicitor's Criminal Trial Briefs.
VPRS 34   Police Magistrate Portland Letter Books.
VPRS 109   Geelong Police Office—Deposition Book.

Archives Office of New South Wales

Colonial Secretary's Correspondence, In Letters
Col Sec. Special Bundles
4/7153, file 42/8829
Port Phillip Papers
1840   4/2510, 4/2511, 4/2512-1
1841   4/2547
1843   4/2626
1844   4/2665
1846   4/2741, 4/2742, 4/2743, 4/2744, 4/2745-1
1847   4/2748
Colonial Secretary, Commissioners of Crown Lands—Itineraries, Microfilm roll no. 2748 (positive).

OTHER MANUSCRIPT SOURCES

La Trobe Library

Adeney, Henry. Diary 24 April-27 September 1855, MS 9110.
Adeney, William. Diary 19 August-17 March 1843, MS 8520A.
Adeney, William. Letters 22 June 1843 to 13 November 1854, MS 9111.
Black, Niel. Journal of the first few months spent in Australia— 30 September 1839 to 8 May 1840, MS 11519.
Black, Niel. Outward Letterbook January 1840 to October 1841, MS 8996.
Brown, Margaret Emily. Memoirs, MS 11619.
Dawson, James. Scrapbook, MS 11514.
French, Acheson Jeremiah. Letterbook 1 October 1841 to 10 October 1862, MS 10053.
Griffith, Charles James. Diary 1840-41, MS 9393.

Henty, Edward. Daily Journal Portland Bay 19 November 1834 to 5 July 1839, 118A.

Henty, Francis. Diary December 1834 to February 1838, H15592.

Howitt, Alfred William. Papers. Box 1053/1 (a)(b)(c)(d), Box 1053/5(a), Box 1054/3(b), MS 9356.

Kirrup, Koort. Documents regarding outrages on the blacks by Koort Kirrup, Portland Bay District 1849, MS 3194.

La Trobe, Charles Joseph. Letters, La Trobe to Gipps, 4 April 1840 (H6959) and 26 July 1842 (H6956), Gipps–La Trobe Private Correspondence.

Macknight, Charles Hamilton. Journals (known as the Dunmore Journals), MS 8999.

O'Callaghan, Thomas. Police and other people: A history of the New South Wales and Victorian Police, 1921, MS 11682.

Robertson, John G. Letter to Charles Joseph La Trobe 26 September 1853, MS 10749.

Selby, Penelope. Letters, MS 9494.

Smyth, H. Letter, H. Smyth to Mrs. Allan 12 November 1841, Miscellaneous Letters from the Office of Edward Doyle, Solicitor, MS 11642.

Smyth, R. Brough. R. Brough Smyth Papers, MS 8781.

Tuckfield, Francis. The journal of Francis Tuckfield, missionary to Port Phillip, Southern Australia, 1839-42, MS 11341.

Winter Cooke family. Papers, MS 10840.

Museum of Victoria

Howitt, A. W. Papers, boxes 1-10.

Robinson, George Augustus. Robinson to La Trobe, 7 Oct. 1842, Report of an expedition to the Aboriginal Tribes of the Western Interior during the months of March, April, May, June, July and August 1841, 42/1870.

University of Melbourne Archives

Ritchie, James. Diary for November and December 1841, 'Tour of the West', collection of R. B. Ritchie and Son.

Mitchell Library

Robinson, George Augustus. Papers.
Vol. 17   Journals, Port Phillip Protectorate, 4 Feb.-14 June 1841, parts 1-5, A7038.

Vol. 18   Journals, Port Phillip Protectorate, 8 June 1841-3 Nov. 1842, parts 1-5, A7039. Field Journals, 3 Nov.-2 Dec. 1842, Mar.-April 1843, Oct.-Nov. 1843, parts 7-9, A7039.

Vols 57, 57A   Correspondence and other papers, Mar. 1839-49, A7078-A7078-2.

Vol. 59   Official reports, 1841, 1845-47, A7080.

Vol. 61   Annual reports, 1844-49, A7082.

Vols 62-3   Port Phillip Protectorate, Miscellanea, includes sketches and aboriginal vocabularies, A7083-4.

Vol. 65   Aboriginal vocabularies, South-east Australia, A7086.

Vol. 66   Miscellanea, A7087.

Vol. 67   Aboriginal vocabularies, South-east Australia, part 1, A7088.

Thomas, William. Papers, Uncatalogued MSS, Set 214, Items 1-24.

Orton, J. Journal 1832-39 (vol. 1) A1714; Journal 1840-1 (vol. 2) A1715; Letterbook 1836-42 (vol. 4) A1719; Letters 1826-41, MSS 942.

New South Wales Parliamentary Archives

New South Wales Legislative Council manuscript records. Copies of many documents concerning the Aborigines of the Port Phillip District, LA 35.

Dixson Library

Archival estrays. Official papers of New South Wales with individual items organized in lists: List 11, Protector and Assistant Protectors of Aborigines; List 20, Aborigines; List 30, Port Phillip District and Victoria.

Chauncy, Philip La Mothe Snell. Diary. Feb. 1841, MS Q11.

Dawbin, Annie Maria. Diaries, 1844-49, MS Q181.

Others

Lindsay, James. Notebook, Aboriginal Language and Legends, Lake Condah Feb. 1892, in possession of John Lindsay, Warrnambool.

McCann Papers. Port Fairy Historical Society.

Rutledge, Eliza. Letter to Martha Hamilton 31 January 1885, in possession of David Hamilton, Geelong.

NEWSPAPERS

Camperdown Chronicle
Geelong Advertiser
Hamilton Spectator

Port Phillip Gazette
Port Phillip Herald
Portland Guardian and Normanby General Advertiser
Portland Mercury and Normanby Advertiser
Portland Mercury and Port Fairy Register
Terang Express.

THESES

Barwick, Diane. 1963. A Little More Than Kin: Regional Affiliations and Group Identity among Aboriginal Migrants in Melbourne. Ph.D., Australian National University.

Blaskett, Beverley A. 1979. The Aboriginal Reponse to White Settlement in the Port Phillip District 1835-50. M.A., University of Melbourne.

Fels, Marie Hansen. 1986. Good Men and True: The Aboriginal Police of the Port Phillip District 1837-53. Ph.D., University of Melbourne.

Kerley, William D. 1981. In My Country: Race Relations in the Portland-Warrnambool District 1834-1886. M.A., La Trobe University.

Lourandos, Harry. 1980. Forces of Change: Aboriginal Technology and Population in South Western Victoria. Ph.D., University of Sydney.

Williams, Elizabeth. 1985. Wet Underfoot? Earth Mound Sites and the Recent Prehistory of Southwestern Victoria. Ph.D., Australian National University.

PUBLISHED SOURCES

Anderson, Hugh. 1969. *The Flowers of the Field: a history of Ripon Shire. Together with Mrs. Kirkland's Life in the Bush from Chamber's Miscellany, 1845.* Hill of Content, Melbourne.

Andrews, Alan E. J. (ed.). 1986. *Stapylton With Major Mitchell's Australia Felix Expedition, 1836 largely from the journal of Granville William Chetwynd Stapylton.* Blubber Head Press, Hobart.

Arden, George. 1977. *Latest information with regard to Australia Felix, the finest province of the great territory of New South Wales including the history, geography, natural resources, government, commerce, and finances of Port Phillip; sketches of the Aboriginal population and advice to immigrants.* Queensberry Hill Press, Victoria. First published in 1840.

Baillieu, Darren. 1982. *Australia Felix: A miscellany from the Geelong Advertiser 1840-1850.* The Craftsman Press, Hawthorn, Victoria.

Barrett, Bernard. 1984. 'What the 150th Anniversary is all about'. Royal Historical Society of Victoria *Journal*, vol. 55, part 3, pp. 3-9.

Barwick, Diane. 1971. 'Changes in the Aboriginal Population of Victoria 1863-1966'. D. J. Mulvaney and J. Golson (eds), *Aboriginal Man and Environment in Australia*. ANU Press, Canberra.

Barwick, Diane. 1984. 'Mapping the past: an atlas of Victorian clans 1835-1904'. *Aboriginal History*, vol. 8, part 2, pp. 100-31.

Bassett, Marnie. 1962. *The Hentys: An Australian Colonial Tapestry.* Melbourne University Press, Melbourne.

Berndt, Ronald M. (ed.). 1982. *Aboriginal Sites, Rights and Resource Development.* Academy of the Social Sciences in Australia, Perth.

Berndt, R. M. and C. H. 1977. *The World of the First Australians.* Second edition, Ure Smith, Sydney.

Billis, R. V. and Kenyon, A. S. (eds). 1974. *Pastoral Pioneers of Port Phillip.* Second edition, Stockland Press, Melbourne.

Boldrewood, Rolf. 1969. *Old Melbourne Memories.* William Heinemann, Melbourne. First published in 1884.

Bonwick, James. 1970. *Western Victoria: Its Geography, Geology and Social Condition: The Narrative of an Educational Tour in 1857.* William Heinemann, Melbourne. First published in 1858.

Bourke, Erle. 1985. *Victorian Year Book.* Australian Bureau of Statistics, Melbourne.

Bride, Thomas Francis (ed.). 1983. *Letters from Victorian Pioneers.* Lloyd O'Neil, South Yarra. First published in 1898.

Broome, Richard. 1982. *Aboriginal Australians: Black Response to White Dominance 1788-1980.* George Allen and Unwin, Sydney.

Broome, Richard. 1984. *The Victorians: Arriving.* Fairfax, Syme and Weldon Associates, Sydney.

Brown, P. L. (ed.). 1935. *The Narrative of George Russell of Golf Hill with Russellania and Selected Papers.* Oxford University Press, London.

Brown, P. L. (ed.). 1952. *The Clyde Company Papers*, Volume 2, 1836-40. Oxford University Press, London.

Brown, P. L. (ed.). 1986. *Memoirs recorded at Geelong, Victoria, Australia by Captain Foster Fyans.* Geelong Advertiser Pty Ltd, Geelong.

Brownhill, Walter Randolph. 1955. *The History of Geelong and Corio Bay.* Wilke and Co. Ltd, Melbourne.

Butlin, Noel. 1983. *Our Original Aggression: Aboriginal Populations of Southeastern Australia 1788-1850.* George Allen and Unwin, Sydney.

Campbell, Judy. 1985. 'Smallpox in Aboriginal Australia, the early 1830s'. *Historical Studies*, vol. 21, no. 84, pp. 336-58.

Cannon, Michael (ed.). 1981. *Beginnings of Permanent Government.* (Historical Records of Victoria. Foundation Series, Volume 1.) Victorian Government Printing Office, Melbourne.

Cannon, Michael (ed.). 1982. *The Aborigines of Port Phillip 1835-1839.* (Historical Records of Victoria. Foundation Series, Volume 2A). Victorian Printing Office, Melbourne.

Cannon, Michael (ed.). 1983. *Aborigines and Protectors 1838-1839.* (Historical Records of Victoria. Foundation Series, Volume 2B.) Victorian Government Printing Office, Melbourne.

Cannon, Michael. 1990. *Who Killed the Koories?* Heinemann, Melbourne.

Carroll, J. R. 1989. *Harpoons to Harvest: The story of Charles and John Mills, Pioneers of Port Fairy.* Warrnambool Institute Press.

Carter, Samuel. 1911. *Reminiscences of the Early Days of the Wimmera.* No details of publication.

Christie, M. F. 1979. *Aborigines in Colonial Victoria 1835-86.* Sydney University Press, Parramatta.

Clark, Ian. 1987. 'The Spatial Organisation of the Chap Wurrung—a Preliminary Analysis'. *Australia Felix: The Chap Wurrung and Major Mitchell,* pp. 1-36. Dunkeld and District Historical Museum, Dunkeld.

Clark, Ian D. (ed.). 1988. *The Port Phillip Journals of George Augustus Robinson: 8 March-7 April 1842 and 18 March-29 April 1843.* Department of Geography, Monash University, Melbourne.

Clark, Manning. 1987. 'Child of His Age—Major Mitchell in Perspective'. *Australia Felix: The Chap Wurrong and Major Mitchell,* pp. 91-100. Dunkeld and District Historical Museum, Dunkeld.

Clark, Michael. 1980. *'Big' Clarke.* Queensberry Hill Press, Melbourne.

Corris, Peter. 1968. *Aborigines and Europeans in Western Victoria.* Occasional Papers in Aboriginal Studies, no. 12, Ethnohistory Series 1, Australian Institute of Aboriginal Studies, Canberra.

Coutts, P. J. F. *et al.* 1976. 'The Mound People of Western Victoria: A Preliminary Statement'. *Records of the Victoria Archaeological Survey,* no. 1, Ministry for Conservation, Victoria.

Coutts, P. J. F., Frank, R. K., and Hughes, P. J. 1978. 'Aboriginal Engineers of the Western District'. *Records of the Victoria Archaeological Survey,* no. 7, Ministry for Conservation, Victoria.

Coutts, P. J. F., Witter, D. C. Parsons, D. M. 1977. 'Impact of European Settlement on Aboriginal Society in Western Victoria'. *Records of the Victoria Archaeological Survey,* no. 4, pp. 17-58.

Coutts, P. J. F. 1981. *Readings in Victorian Prehistory Volume 2: The Victorian Aboriginals 1800 to 1860.* Ministry for Conservation, Victoria.

Coutts, Peter J. F. 1985. 'An archaeological perspective of the Western District, Victoria'. J. Sherwood, J. Critchett, and K. O'Toole (eds). *Settlement of the Western District: From Prehistoric Times to the Present,* pp. 21-67. Warrnambool Institute Press, Warrnambool.

Critchett, Jan. 1980. *Our Land Till We Die: A History of the Framlingham Aborigines.* Warrnambool Institute Press, Warrnambool.

Critchett, Jan. 1984. 'A closer look at cultural contact: some evidence from "Yambuck", Western Victoria'. *Aboriginal History*, vol. 8, part 1, pp. 12-20.

Critchett, Jan. (ed.). 1984. *Richard Bennett's Early Days of Port Fairy*. Warrnambool Institute Press, Warrnambool.

Davies, Suzanne. 1987. 'Aborigines, Murder and the Criminal Law in Early Port Phillip, 1841-1851'. *Historical Studies*, vol. 22, no. 88, pp. 313-32.

Dawson, James. 1981. *Australian Aborigines: The Languages and Customs of Several Tribes of Aborigines in the Western District of Victoria, Australia*. Australian Institute of Aboriginal Studies, Canberra. First published in 1881.

Dixon, R. M. W. 1980. *The Languages of Australia*. Cambridge University Press, Cambridge.

Donaldson, Ian and Tamsin. 1985. *Seeing the First Australians*. George Allen and Unwin. Sydney.

Douglas, M. H. and O'Brien, L. (eds). 1971. *The Natural History of Western Victoria*. Australian Institute of Agricultural Science, Horsham.

Duncan, J. S. (ed.). 1982. *Atlas of Victoria*. Victorian Government, Melbourne.

Durus, Rosamund. 1980. *The Curdies of Tandarook*. PAP Book Company, Warrnambool.

Elkin, A. P. 1951. 'Reaction and Interaction: A Food Gathering People and European Settlement in Australia'. *American Anthropologist*, vol. 53, pp. 164-86.

Fels, Marie Hansen. 1988. *Good Men and True: The Aboriginal Police of the Port Phillip District 1837-1853*. Melbourne University Press, Melbourne.

Fison, L. and Howitt, A. W. 1880. *Kamilaroi and Kurnai*. George Robertson, Melbourne.

Foxcroft, E. J. B. 1941. *Australian Native Policy: Its History especially in Victoria*, Melbourne.

Godfrey, Michael C. S. 1983. 'Historical Sources as Aids to Archaeological Interpretation—Examples from Discovery Bay, Victoria'. *The Artefact*, vol. 8, parts 1-2, pp. 55-60.

Godfrey, Michael C. S. 1988. 'Oxygen isotope analysis: a means for determining the seasonal gathering of the pipi (*Donax deltoides*) by Aborigines in prehistoric Australia'. *Archaeology in Oceania*, vol. 23, pp. 17-21.

Gott, Beth. 1985. 'Plants Mentioned in Dawson's *Australian Aborigines*'. *The Artefact*, vol. 10, pp. 3-14.

Gott, Beth. 1987. 'Grampians and District Aboriginal Plants'. *Australia Felix: The Chap Wurrung and Major Mitchell*, pp. 37-51. Dunkeld and District Historical Museum, Dunkeld.

Gray, Charles M. 1932. *Western Victoria in the Forties: Reminiscences of a Pioneer*. Reprinted from the *Hamilton Spectator*.

Griffith, Charles. 1845. *The Present State and Prospects of the Port Phillip District of New South Wales*. William Curry, Junior and Company, Dublin.

Hamilton, J. C. 1981. *Pioneering Days in Western Victoria*. Facsimile edition, Warrnambool Institute Press, Warrnambool. First published in 1914.

Hawdon, Joseph. 1984. *Joseph Hawdon's journal of his overland journey by tandem from Port Phillip to Adelaide, with Alfred Mundy, in 1839: With accounts of the earlier journeys of Charles Bonney (1839) and Foley, Stone and Stanley (1837)*. Facsimile edition, Sullivan's Cove, Adelaide.

Head, L. and Stuart, I. M. F. 1980. *Change in the Aire: Palaeoecology and Prehistory in the Aire Basin, Southwestern Victoria*. Department of Geography, Monash University, Melbourne.

Howitt, A. W. 1904. *The Native Tribes of South East Australia*. Macmillan, London, 1904.

Kenyon, A. S. 1928. 'Aboriginal Protectorate of Port Phillip: Report of an Expedition to the Aboriginal Tribes of the Western Interior by the Chief Protector, George Augustus Robinson'. *Victoria Historical Magazine*, vol. 12, no. 3, pp. 138-71.

Kerr, William. 1978. *Kerr's Melbourne almanac and Port Phillip directory for 1841: a compendium of useful and accurate information connected with Port Phillip*. Facsimile edition, Landsdown Slattery, Mona Vale, New South Wales.

Kiddle, Margaret. 1954(9). 'Vandiemonian Colonists in Port Phillip, 1834-50'. *Tasmanian Historical Research Association Papers and Proceedings*, vol. 3, pp. 37-45.

Kiddle, Margaret. 1962. *Men of Yesterday: A Social History of the Western District of Victoria*. Melbourne University Press, Melbourne.

Kirby, James. Undated. *Old Times in the Bush of Australia: Trials and Experiences of Early Bush Life During the Forties*. Geo. Robertson and Co., Melbourne.

Learmonth, Noel F. 1983. *The Portland Bay Settlement*. Baulch Publications, Hawkesdale. First published in 1934.

Lloyd, George T. 1862. *Thirty-three years in Tasmania and Victoria*. London.

Lourandos, Harry. 1976. 'Aboriginal Settlement and Land Use in South Western Victoria: A Report on Current Field Work'. *The Artefact*, vol. 1, no. 4, pp. 174-93.

Lourandos, Harry. 1977. 'Aboriginal Spatial Organisation and Population: South Western Victoria Reconsidered'. *Archaeology and Physical Anthropology in Oceania*, vol. 12, no. 3, pp. 202-25.

Lourandos, Harry. 1980. 'Change or stability?: hydraulics, hunter–gatherers and population in temperate Australia'. *World Archaeology*, vol. 11, no. 3, pp. 245-64.

Lourandos, Harry. 1987. 'Swamp Managers of Southwestern Victoria'. D. J. Mulvaney and J. Peter White (eds), *Australians to 1788*, pp. 292-307. Fairfax, Syme and Weldon Associates, Sydney.

McBryde, Isabel. 1979. 'Ethnohistory in an Australian Context: Independent Discipline or Convenient Data Quarry?'. *Aboriginal History*, vol. 3, part 2, pp. 128-51.

MacFarlane, Ian (compiler). 1984. *1842 The Public Executions at Melbourne*. Public Record Office of Victoria, Melbourne.

Markus, Andrew. 1977. 'Through a glass darkly: aspects of contact history'. *Aboriginal History*, vol. 1, part·2, pp. 170-80.

Massola, Aldo. 1969. *Journey to Aboriginal Victoria*. Rigby, Adelaide.

Massola, Aldo. 1971. *The Aborigines of South-Eastern Australia As They Were*. Heinemann, Melbourne.

Morgan, John. 1967. *The Life and Adventures of William Buckley: Thirty-two years a wanderer amongst the Aborigines of the then unexplored country around Port Phillip now the Province of Victoria*. William Heinemann, Adelaide. First published in 1852.

Mulvaney, D. J. 1962. 'Archaeological excavations on the Aire River'. *Proceedings of the Royal Society of Victoria*, vol. 75, pp. 1-15.

Mulvaney, D. J. 1964. 'Prehistory of the Basalt Plains'. *Proceedings of the Royal Society of Victoria*, vol. 77, no. 2, pp. 427-832. Issued separately, 12 June 1964.

Mulvaney, D. J. and White, J. Peter (eds). 1987. *Australians to 1788*. Fairfax, Syme and Weldon Associates, Sydney.

Osburne, Richard. 1887. *The History of Warrnambool from 1847 up to the end of 1886*. Chronicle Printing and Publishing Company Ltd, Prahran.

Parker, Edward Stone. 1854. *The Aborigines of Australia, A lecture delivered in the Mechanics' Hall, Melbourne, before the John Knox Young Men's Association, on Wednesday, May 10th, 1854*. Hugh McColl, Melbourne.

Plomley, N. J. B. (ed.). 1966. *Friendly Mission: The Tasmanian Journals and Papers of George Augustus Robinson 1829–1834*. Tasmanian Historical Research Association, Kingsgrove, New South Wales.

Powell, J. M. 1983. 'Squatting expansion in Victoria, 1834–1860'. Foreword in R. Spreadborough and H. Anderson (eds), *Victorian Squatters*, Red Rooster Press, Victoria.

Poynter, John. 1987. 'Child of His Age—Major Mitchell in Perspective'. *Australia Felix: The Chap Wurrung and Major Mitchell*, pp. 76-90. Dunkeld and District Historical Museum, Dunkeld.

Presland, Gary (ed.). 1977. 'Journals of G. A. Robinson January 1840-March 1840'. *Records of the Victoria Archaeological Survey*, no. 5,

Ministry for Conservation, Victoria.

Presland, Gary (ed.). 1977. 'Journals of G. A. Robinson March-May 1841'. *Records of the Victoria Archaeological Survey,* no. 6, Ministry for Conservation, Melbourne.

Presland, Gary (ed.). 1980. 'Journals of G. A. Robinson May to August 1841'. *Records of the Victoria Archaeological Survey,* no. 11, Ministry for Conservation, Melbourne.

Rae-Ellis, Vivienne. 1988. *Black Robinson: Protector of Aborigines.* Melbourne University Press, Melbourne.

Reece, R. H. W. 1974. *Aborigines and Colonists: Aborigines and Colonial Society in New South Wales in the 1830s and 1840s.* Sydney University Press, Sydney.

Reynolds, Henry. 1982. *The Other Side of the Frontier: Aboriginal resistance to the European invasion of Australia.* Penguin, Melbourne.

Reynolds, Henry. 1987. *Frontier: Aborigines, Settlers and Land.* Allen and Unwin, Sydney.

Roberts, Jan. 1986. *Jack of Cape Grim.* Greenhouse Publications, Melbourne.

Savill, Vanda. 1976. *Dear Friends, Lake Condah Mission, etc.* Kalprint Graphics, Hamilton.

Scarlett, N. H. 1977. 'The Aborigines of the Otway Region', *Proceedings of the Royal Society of Victoria,* vol. 89, no. 1, pp. 1-6.

Shaw, A. G. L. and Clark, C. M. H. (eds). 1968. *Australian Dictionary of Biography 1788-1850.* Melbourne University Press, Melbourne.

Smyth, R. Brough. 1878. *The Aborigines of Victoria with Notes Relating to the Habits of the Natives of other parts of Australia and Tasmania.* 2 volumes, George Robertson, Melbourne.

Spreadborough, R. and Anderson, H. (eds). 1983. *Victorian Squatters.* Red Rooster Press, Ascot Vale.

Stanner, W. E. H. 1969. *After the Dreaming: Black and White Australians—An Anthropologist's View.* The Boyer Lectures 1968, Australian Broadcasting Commission, Sydney.

Stuart, I. M. F. 1981. 'Ethnohistory in the Otway Ranges', *The Artefact,* vol. 6, pp. 79-88.

Tindale, N. B. 1974. *Aboriginal Tribes of Australia: their terrain, environmental controls, distribution, limits and proper names.* ANU Press, Canberra.

Trangmar, E. R. [1960.] *The Aborigines of Far Western Victoria.* No details of publication.

Tyers, C. J. 1976. *Report of an Expedition to ascertain the position of the 141st degree of east longitude being the boundary line between New South Wales and South Australia.* Queensberry Hill Press, Victoria. First published in 1840.

Warner, W. Lloyd. 1958. *A Black Civilisation: A Social Study of an Australian Tribe.* Revised edition, Harper and Brothers, New York.

Westgarth, William. 1846. *A Report on the Condition, Capabilities and Prospects of the Australian Aborigines.* Printed by William Clarke, at the Herald Office, Melbourne.

Whitehead, Diana and Wendy. 1986. *The Whitehead Family on Spring Creek.* F.R.P. Printing, Wendouree.

Williams, Elizabeth. 1984. 'Documentation and Archaeological Investigation of an Aboriginal "Village" Site in South Western Victoria'. *Aboriginal History,* vol. 8, part 2, pp. 173-88.

Williams, Elizabeth. 1985. 'Estimation of prehistoric populations of archaeological sites in southwestern Victoria: some problems'. *Archaeology in Oceania,* vol. 20, pp. 73-80.

Williams, Elizabeth. 1987. 'Complex hunter-gatherers: A view from Australia'. *Antiquity,* vol. 61, no. 232, pp. 310-21.

Willmott, Eric. 1987. *Pemulwuy: The Rainbow Warrior.* Weldon, Sydney.

Withers, William Bramwell. 1980. *The History of Ballarat from the First Pastoral Settlement to the Present Time.* Facsimile edition, Queensberry Hill Press, Melbourne. First published in 1870.

Index